MW00813340

PROGRAMMING & RESEARCH
Skills and Techniques for Interior Designers

PROGRAMMING & RESEARCH

Skills and Techniques for Interior Designers

Second Edition

Rose Mary Botti-Salitsky PhD, ASID, IIDA

MOUNT IDA COLLEGE

Fairchild Books
An imprint of Bloomsbury Publishing Inc

BLOOMSBURY

NEW YORK · LONDON · OXFORD · NEW DELHI · SYDNEY

Fairchild Books
An Imprint of Bloomsbury Publishing

1385 Broadway   50 Bedford Square
New York   London
NY 10018   WC1B 3DP
USA   UK

www.bloomsbury.com

FAIRCHILD BOOKS, BLOOMSBURY and the Diana logo are trademarks of Bloomsbury Publishing Plc

First Edition published 2009

This edition published 2017

© Bloomsbury Publishing Inc, 2017

All rights reserved. No part of this publication may be reproduced or transmitted in any form or by any means, electronic or mechanical, including photocopying, recording, or any information storage or retrieval system, without prior permission in writing from the publishers.

No responsibility for loss caused to any individual or organization acting on or refraining from action as a result of the material in this publication can be accepted by Bloomsbury Publishing Inc or the author.

Library of Congress Cataloging-in-Publication Data
Names: Botti-Salitsky, Rose Mary, author.
Title: Programming & research : skills and techniques for interior designers
/ Rose Mary Botti-salitsky, Mount Ida College.
Other titles: Programming and research
Description: Second edition. | New York, NY, USA : Fairchild Books, an imprint of
Bloomsbury Publishing Inc., 2017. | Includes bibliographical references and index.
Identifiers: LCCN 2016042720| ISBN 9781628929546 (pbk.) | ISBN 9781628929560 (ePDF)
Subjects: LCSH: Interior decoration--Textbooks.
Classification: LCC NK2116 .B68 2017 | DDC 747--dc23
LC record available at https://lccn.loc.gov/2016042720

ISBN: PB: 9781628929546
ISBN: ePDF: 9781628929560

Typeset by Lachina
Printed and bound in the United States of America

Dedication

This book is dedicated to all the inquisitive students of design who embrace programming and research as a way to improve environments for all to occupy.

Contents

Extended Contents

Preface to the Second Edition

The first edition of *Programming and Research Skills and Techniques for Interior Designers*, was inspired by years of professional practice, teaching programming and research skills. Throughout that experience, I found that most of the programming textbooks fell in the realm of architecture, a parallel profession to interior design. With work, much in these texts could be adapted for the interior design profession, but I became increasingly motivated to create a textbook that focused specifically on interior design and the unique programming and research skills needed for the profession.

Having taught programming as an independent course, part of studio classes, and as a precursor to thesis, I have learned a great deal over the years about the benefits of programming and the skills needed to do it well. The end results are considerably stronger when the appropriate amount of time is committed on the front end of the design process. Clients are keenly aware of the benefits of programming and research skills; the knowledge that these skills bring to their businesses increases their capacities for strategic planning and decision making.

The industry and expectations have expanded since the first edition. Now interior designers are expected to implement programming and employ research techniques as part of their design decision making. The specialty training that interior designers bring to the table benefits a multitude of spaces that all sectors of our society occupy. Think, for instance, of the health care worker in a hospital setting, the student in a classroom, or the elderly couple adapting their residence in order to age in place.

The second edition expands the inclusion of case studies and examples from design firms. Their approaches to programming and research are included, as well as steps that are incorporated in the design process and decision making.

The second edition also includes many more examples from colleges and universities that have adopted the textbook. Faculty, undergraduate, and graduate examples have been included. The student examples are a direct outcome of implementing the textbook in a studio setting or as a step-by-step model to create a program as the precursor to thesis development.

The chapters and delivery of content remain, but many updates have been included. CIDA & NCIDQ standards that fall in the realm of programming and research have been updated and included. The design process has been redefined since the last edition with the advancement of technology and more focuses on building information management, integrated project delivery, LEED, WELL, resiliency strategies, and universal design are all factored into decision making during the programming of a space. All of these have been addressed in the new edition.

Interior designers, in my opinion, are the most potent type of artist, we envelope and encompass our occupants in what we have designed. Think of the ramifications of our decision making. The information gleaned from the research and programming phase should aid both the designer and client in creating a successful environment. People occupy what has been created, and in some cases they have no choice in the matter. It might be their work location, school, hospital, or a public building, but in any case it is where they will spend their time. This power is not to be taken lightly. You must be keenly sensitive to these end users' needs. This book will help you create the best environments for all who occupy them.

Acknowledgments

The author would like to express sincere appreciation to all the designers that took the time to share with her their unique approaches and diverse expertise with programming. Specifically to the following design professionals and educators: Anne Brockelman, AIA, LEED AP BD+C, Associate & Director of Sustainable Design, Perry Dean Rogers, Partners Architects; Blake Jackson, AIA, LEED Faculty, WELL AP, Associate & Sustainability Practice Leader, Tsoi/Kobus & Associates; Christine Shanahan NCIDQ Managing Director of Design, HVS Design Group; Colleen Lowe NCIDQ, Interior Designer for the U.S. Department of Veterans Affairs; Courtenay Dean Wallace, Principal, e-Volutions Designs; David D. Stone, IIDA, LEED AP, NCIDQ, Design Director – Boston, NELSON; Dianne A. Dunnell, IIDA, NCIDQ, LEED AP Interior Design Director & Associate Partner MPA, Margulies Perruzzi Architects; Gable Clarke, NCIDQ IIDA, LEED AP, Associate and Director of Interior Design, SGA, Spagnolo Gisness & Associates; Jeanne Kopacz, IIDA, ASID, LEED AP, NCIDQ Managing partner, Allegro Interior Architecture; Joan Riggs, ASID, IIDA, IDEC, NCIDQ, CAPS, Associate Professor and the Director of the Environmental + Interior Design program at Chaminade University of Honolulu; Kate Wendt NCIDQ, IIDA, Tsoi/Kobus & Associates; Laurie DaForno, AIA, LEED AP BD+C, Architect Tsoi/Kobus & Associates; Lisa C. Bonneville, NCIDQ, FASID, Founding Owner/Principal, Bonneville Design; Marlo Ransdell, PhD, NCIDQ Associate Professor, Director of Graduate Studies, Florida State University; Michael Fior, NCIDQ, LEED ID+C, IDEC, ASID Visiting Professor Endicott College; Michael Schroeder, Director of Virtual Design and Construction, SGA, Spagnolo Gisness & Associates; Monica Mattingly NCIDQ, LEED AP Interior Designer, CBT Architects; S. Christine Cavataio, NCIDQ, Associate Professor Newbury College; Shirin Karanfiloglu, AIA, Director of Programming Services at DCAMM Office of Planning, Design and Construction Division of Capital Asset Management Commonwealth of Massachusetts; Stephanie McGoldrick, IDEC, NCIDQ, LEED AP BD+C Assistant Professor, Interior Architecture + Design Mount Ida College.

A special thanks to all the design

undergraduate and graduate students who allowed their work to be included in this book: Aprilyn Arca; Ashley Benander; Ashley Johnson; Bella Lei; Caitlin J. Davis; Cassidy Dickeson; Catherine Shibles; Christina Gedick; Domeny Anderson; Erin Anthony; Gavin Steinhoff; Jeanna Richard; Jen Cilano; Jessica Breton; Kasandra Westgate; Katie Timmerman; Katrina Rutledge; Kelsey Creamer; Kelsey Jones; Kerri LaBerge; Kristen Patten; Liz Carter; Lucrecia Ela Ebang; Marcia Gouveia; Mary Kate Reidy; Monica Johnson; Nicole Handzel; Nicole Heerdt; Nicole Stewart; Nicolette Gordon; Priscilla Ong; Samantha Roblee; Stephanie Scheivert; Taylor Birse. And to design firms, colleges and universities: Allegro Interior Architecture; Bonneville Design; Chaminade University of Honolulu; Corcoran College of Art + Design; DCAMM Massachusetts state agency—Division of Capital Asset Management and Maintenance; e-Volutions Designs; Endicott College; Florida State University; Greg Premru Photography; HVS Design Group; Mount Ida College; MPA | Margulies Perruzzi Architects; NELSON-Boston; Newbury College; Perry Dean Rogers | Partners Architects; Robert Benson Photography; Spagnolo Gisness & Associates; Tsoi/Kobus & Associates; The Architects Collaborative (TAC)

I am very grateful to the reviewers for their critique of the second edition: Reza Ahmadi, Ball State University; Nancy Hackett, Suffolk University; Catherine Anderson, George Washington University; Chip Dupont, Florida Atlantic University; Johnnie Stark, University of North Texas.

Their comments became the basis for many of the improvements that we made.

Heartfelt thanks to my husband Joe and our two beautiful daughters Ava and Madisyn—I am forever grateful for our life journey together. I'm also extremely fortunate for the past twenty-five years to have such fabulous colleagues at Mount Ida College, and I am appreciative for their ongoing support of my endeavors. Special thanks to Grace Herron and Ani Moushigian for their ongoing help and ability to always make me laugh!

Sincere thanks to the Fairchild Books' team: Noah Schwartzberg, Joseph Miranda, and Edie Weinberg for their unwavering support and encouragement. Special thanks to Margaret Manos and her editorial magic. The Fairchild team made this book a reality, with the first edition and then their continued support to commit to a second edition. I am extremely grateful for their guidance and persistence throughout this endeavor.

Bloomsbury Publishing wishes to gratefully acknowledge and thank the editorial team involved in the publication of this book:

Acquisitions Editor: Noah Schwartzberg
Development Manager: Joseph Miranda
Assistant Editor: Kiley Kudrna
Art Development Editor: Edie Weinberg
In-House Designer: Eleanor Rose
Production Manager: Claire Cooper
Project Manager: TK

CHAPTER 1

What Is Programming?

After reading this chapter, you should be able to:

- Define programming.
- Explain how and why programming is used in the profession.
- Describe how research skills and techniques enhance programming.
- Recognize how programming is implemented in an academic setting.

WHAT IS PROGRAMMING?

Programming, the preliminary research and analysis of all facets of a design project, is critical to the entire process of interior design. Interior designers must gather and analyze information, identify problems, and solve them to meet their clients' needs. Professionals in architecture, facilities management, and engineering all use programming as an essential tool. This textbook focuses on how the study of programming prepares students for work in the field of professional interior design.

Students are sometimes inclined to jump right into a project, trying to solve the problem and generate the best design solution immediately. This is not the most advantageous approach. The preliminary programming phase at the front end of a project allows students to become more knowledgeable on their topics, engage in more thorough research, and gain a greater insight into their design options. It can help both the designer and the client make informed and intelligent decisions. The resulting road map will be a clear and shared vision of common goals that will lead smoothly toward the final design.

Often, interior designers are pulled in to help evaluate a proposed site's demographics, location and the efficiency of the proposed space. Interior designers are trained to evaluate space occupancy and anticipate projected growth or shrinkage. They are trained to look at **energy efficiency, life cycle cost,** and **space-planning adjacencies** to evaluate individual, group, and **location productivity.**

HOW AND WHY PROGRAMMING IS USED IN THE PROFESSION

The **National Council for Interior Design Qualification** (NCIDQ) defines interior design as "a multi-faceted profession in which creative and technical solutions are

BOX 1.1 NCIDQ SCOPE-OF-SERVICE DEFINITIONS

NCIDQ lists the following definition of interior design on their website:

Interior design includes a scope of services performed by a **professional design practitioner**, qualified by means of education, experience and examination, to protect and enhance the health, life safety and welfare of the public. These services may include any or all of the following tasks:

- Research and analysis of the client's goals and requirements; and development of documents, drawings and diagrams that outline those needs.
- Formulation of preliminary space plans and two and three dimensional design concept studies and sketches that integrate the client's program needs and are based on knowledge of the principles of interior design and theories of human behavior.
- Confirmation that preliminary space plans and design concepts are safe, functional, aesthetically appropriate, and meet all public health, safety and welfare requirements, including code, accessibility, environmental, and sustainability guidelines.
- Selection of colors, materials and finishes to appropriately convey the design concept and to meet socio-psychological, functional, maintenance, lifecycle performance, environmental, and safety requirements.
- Selection and specification of furniture, fixtures, equipment and millwork, including layout drawings and detailed product description; and provision of contract documentation to facilitate pricing, procurement and installation of furniture.

- Provision of project management services, including preparation of project budgets and schedules.
- Preparation of construction documents, consisting of plans, elevations, details and specifications, to illustrate non-structural and/or non-seismic partition layouts; power and communications locations; reflected ceiling plans and lighting designs; materials and finishes; and furniture layouts.
- Preparation of construction documents to adhere to regional building and fire codes, municipal codes, and any other jurisdictional statutes, regulations and guidelines applicable to the interior space.
- Coordination and collaboration with other allied design professionals who may be retained to provide consulting services, including but not limited to architects; structural, mechanical and electrical engineers, and various specialty consultants.
- Confirmation that construction documents for non-structural and/or non-seismic construction are signed and sealed by the responsible interior designer, as applicable to jurisdictional requirements for filing with code enforcement officials.
- Administration of **contract documents**, bids and negotiations as the client's agent.
- Observation and reporting on the implementation of projects while in progress and upon completion, as a representative of and on behalf of the client; and conducting post-occupancy evaluation reports.

(NCIDQ, 2015)

applied within a structure to achieve a built interior environment" (NCIDQ, 2015, Section Definitions; see Box 1.1).

Note that the first two points in NCIDQ's scope of services in Box 1.1 have to do with programming: analyzing the client's goals and formulating plans and drawings based upon those goals and the theories of interior design. Both points will be covered in detail throughout this textbook.

According to NCIDQ, "Programming" means the scope of work, which includes, but is not limited to, conducting research; identifying and analyzing the needs and goals of the client and/or occupant(s) of the

space; evaluating existing documentation and conditions; assessing project resources and limitations; identifying life, safety, and code requirements; and developing **project schedules** and budgets (NCIDQ, 2015). Understanding programming is essential not only for preparing to enter the field of design but also for taking the NCIDQ exam, which many states require interior designers to pass. Appendix A outlines the NCIDQ exam content distribution that falls in the scope of programming.

The interior design field is vast: designers work in the residential, corporate, institutional, healthcare, retail, and hospitality fields. Each type of design comes with its own set of requirements and unique features. Because it is virtually impossible to become an expert in all areas, many designers choose to work within a specific application, which becomes their specialty. Some designers take a multidisciplinary approach and choose to work in more than one area. However, all of the design firms discussed in this text begin with programming. Interviews with some of these firms throughout the book provide a broader perspective on how professionals implement programming.

FIGURE 1.1
Jeanne Kopacz of Allegro Interior Architecture.

FIRMS THAT PRACTICE SUCCESSFUL PROGRAMMING

Allegro Interior Architecture and Spagnolo Gisness & Associates implement similar programming techniques, but they have different styles.

Professional Example: Allegro Interior Architecture

Allegro Interior Architecture specializes in **interior architecture** and design for corporate, hospitality, and academic clients. Workspace projects developed by the team include offices for consultants in the fields of law, accounting, and technology, as well as headquarters space for pharmaceutical, retail, healthcare, venture capital, **asset management** companies and innovation centers. Allegro's team effort shows in its attention to programming.

Allegro's Approach to Programming

Jeanne Kopacz, IIDA, ASID, is a NCIDQ-certified interior designer who serves as managing partner at Allegro Interior Architecture (see Figure 1.1). Her expertise includes **strategic planning**, alternative workspace analysis, and color/form integration. She frequently speaks at industry events on topics related to **color theory** and practice. Her book, *Color in Three-Dimensional Design*, is well-known in the field of interior design.

For the Allegro team, programming is the key to getting diverse results. Each project begins with a series of interviews with key people on the client side. Questionnaires are issued in advance, to stimulate thought for the discussions, but they are usually completed during the interview. Through conversation, the designers often find the answer to one question generates another—something that a questionnaire may not address. Through direct probing, the individual nature of the client's activities are uncovered. **Adjacency requirements**—such as who needs to be near whom—are documented. **Diagrams** are often sketched during the interview to more precisely ascertain what is being shared.

Questions usually include those about the client's professional vision, specific space needs, such as the quantity and size of the workstations, and inquiries as to what works and what doesn't work within the space currently occupied. Ms. Kopacz finds the interview is best done in the client's space so designers can observe what the users are comparing their requests to.

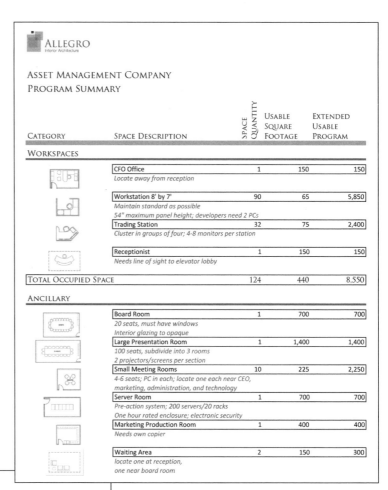

FIGURE 1.2 A and B
Program summary for Asset Management Company project.

CATEGORY	SPACE DESCRIPTION	SPACE QUANTITY	USABLE SQUARE FOOTAGE	EXTENDED USABLE PROGRAM
ANCILLARY (CONTINUED)				
	Lunch Room	1	350	350
	2 full refrigerator, 2 microwave, 2 coffee maker			
	sink, 2 trash, recycle bin, cabinets, beverage cooler			
	Kitchenette	1	100	100
	1/2 refrigerator, sink, microwave			
	Quality Control/Quality Assurance	1	400	400
	Include 2 racks for test equipment			
	Seat 5 people for training			
	Records Storage Room	1	300	300
	Rolling file system; locking			
	Operations File Room	1	120	120
	Lateral files; locking			
	Pre-action Room	1	100	100
	Adjacent to Server Room			
	Service Area	2	13	26
	Include copier, printers, supplies			
	AV Equipment/PC Closet	2	13	26
	Locate adjacent to Presentation Room			
	Shower Room	1	100	100
	Locate away from Reception			
	Client Powder Room	1	75	75
	Locate near Reception Area			
	Meditation Room	1	75	75
	Locate near Reception Area			
	Coat Closets	2	35	70
	One adjacent to Server Room, one opposite end of floor			
	IDF Room	2	13	26
	One adjacent to Server Room, one opposite end of floor			
	Storage Cabinets	6	13	78
	Compliance binders, locate near marketing			
	Files, Lateral	10	13	130
	Locate in common area			
TOTAL ANCILLARY SPACE				7,726
TOTAL PROGRAMMABLE SPACE (OCCUPIED + ANCILLARY)				16,276
	Circulation factor at 35% of total usable			8,789
TOTAL USABLE SQUARE FOOTAGE				25,065
	Average Rentable Factor of 18%			4,512
TOTAL RENTABLE SQUARE FOOTAGE				29,577

When the users describe something they envision, the Allegro team asks if they have seen anything similar. For example, for the desired atmosphere in their medical suite, one client referenced a Starbuck's retail space. Word descriptions are relative to one's individual experience, so what is sophisticated to one may be staid to another. Visual examples are better communicators. Realizing this, the Allegro team often follows interviews with an initial concept meeting, at which time images of spaces or products are shown for confirmation of the client's vision.

According to Kopacz, there is often a key program element or two that drive the clients' business. It may take some conversation for designers to get at the essence of this. When they do, they are empowered to develop something beyond what clients could ever envision for themselves. For some clients, visual access to a media board, each other, or the leadership can expedite communications, which means the designer needs to understand the appropriate limits and their associated implications. For others, document management is critical, in which case it may be worth spending thirty minutes just to follow an original record through its logical process in the current facility. Some companies need specific sensations, such as the presence of earthy materials, irregular forms, a structured environment, or the stimulation of surprise. Others need to position critical cogs-in-the-wheel such that everyone has an immediate access to use, in the case of tools, or the person, in the case of individuals.

It is the designer's job, through programming, to uncover the things that give the client entity its advantage over its competitors so that the new space may help the client increase that advantage. At the same time, the designer tries to establish the unique character of the client organization so that its individuality may be fully expressed in the new environment.

At the end of the interview process, the designer produces a **program summary** that includes space needs calculated as a sum of the parts, plus appropriate mark-ups for circulation, rentable factors, and so on (see Figure 1.2). If the space is already selected, an Allegro designer uses the program summary to confirm a match. In the absence of one, she will determine what adjustments might be needed to manage expectations. For example, if a workspace program has a wish list that calculates out to 20,000 usable square feet, but the space available is only 19,000 square feet, designer and client would need to discuss program compromises. Could fewer workspaces meet the business goals? Might some items, such as a very large and infrequently used presentation room, or stored records, be moved off-site?

For more complex projects, Allegro uses diagrams to articulate conclusions about new work processes. Like the program summary, diagrammatic information becomes a baseline for evaluating design recommendations. (See Figure 1.4, work flow diagram.) The workflow diagram is helpful when physical materials must move through departments, such as original documents in banking or small scale products in light manufacturing. Sketches are also prepared to communicate the key solutions that will make the project more effective. These need to be loose and apparently incomplete so that clients will feel comfortable participating in their resolution. If the sketches are too polished, the idea may be accepted as final prematurely or rejected because it was assumed to be a finished solution. The example in Figure 1.3 is a quick three-dimensional view generated using Revit.

Allegro prepared two different diagrams prior to space planning the Asset Management Company, to be located on three floors of a high-rise building in Boston. This company is culturally more collaborative and

FIGURE 1.3 Revit model of design by Allegro Interior Architecture.

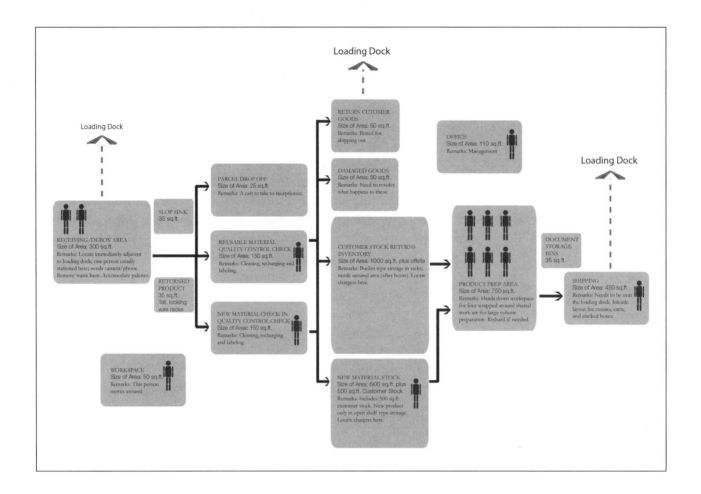

FIGURE 1.4
**Workflow diagram
for PHT Corporation
project flowchart.**

less hierarchical than some of its competitors. During programming, the design team worked to reinforce the organization of the business without restricting team members to conventional rows of workspace.

The bubble diagram and the concept diagrams are two tools used in programming. The **bubble diagram** indicates what functions go where relative to each other and gives the client an overall idea of where each space is designated (see Figure 1.5). The bubble diagram responds directly to program conclusions about the relative size of spaces and their adjacency requirements. This is very different from a **concept diagram** (see Figure 1.6). A designer uses the concept diagram to begin organizing the physical form of the space so that it makes sense as a whole and addresses the program

conclusions about image and functional style through the architecture.

The concept diagram in Figure 1.6 is a simple illustration of how the designers at Allegro organized the form within a rectilinear building to be anything but rectilinear. The circles show how Allegro's designers intended to impose radial forms onto the space. The concept illustrates the designers' intention to drop the ceiling and change materials and color of horizontal planes to emphasize their vision of the space. The black dashed lines show major circulation, that is, movement inside the office space. By imposing the circles, the designers were able to shift the viewers' perspective so that nothing along the main path of circulation appears long and straight. At the ends of the floor, the circulation was fanned out in

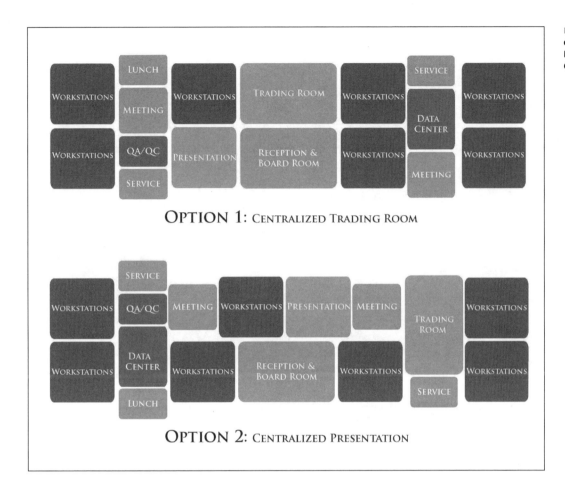

FIGURE 1.5 **Bubble diagram for Asset Management Company project.**

OPTION 1: CENTRALIZED TRADING ROOM

OPTION 2: CENTRALIZED PRESENTATION

a radial movement rather than in parallel rows. According to Kopacz, this planning diagram was an in-house study done in response to the client's request for "no rows of Dilbert cubes."

Figure 1.7 shows the final layout for the Asset Management Company project, showing workstations and freestanding furniture. The result is a conscious effort to ensure that every workspace has a direct line of sight out through the full-height glass windows to the dramatic views of the city. The curves break up what could be long corridors, and the workstations fan out at each end of the floor. Note that the large meeting room is split into three analysis rooms for the company's global teams to compare data during non-meeting days. Figure 1.8 shows the view from one entry

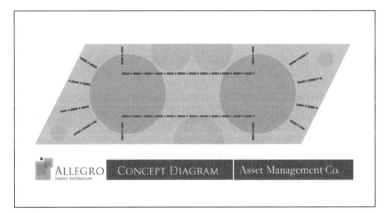

FIGURE 1.6 **Concept diagram for Asset Management Company project.**

point toward the new internal stair, which was developed as the company expanded.

Figure 1.9 shows the final design of the main reception area. The entrance to the boardroom is on the right. Notice the curved elements winding through the lobby and drawing the eye to the view. Curved

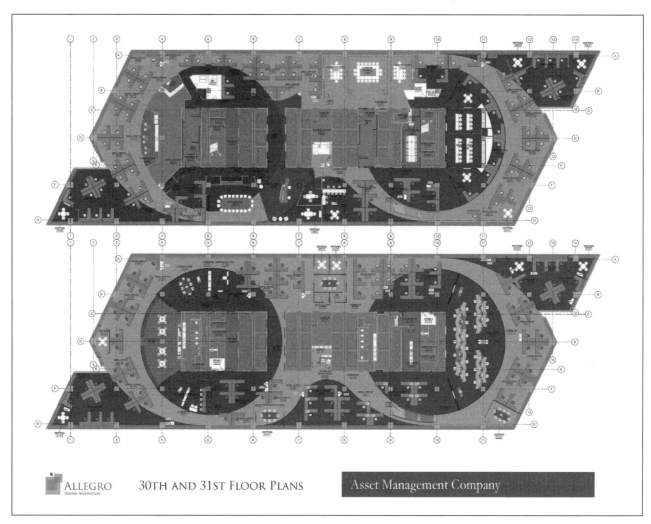

FIGURE 1.7 Furniture plans for Asset Management Company project.

FIGURE 1.8
Rendered view of
new internal stair at
Asset Management
Company project.

FIGURE 1.9 **Reception area designed by Allegro Interior Architecture.** *Photo © Greg Premru Photography.*

sections of ceilings and built-ins have LED lights along the face. Where workstations occur rectilinear with the building, they do not appear so because the eye follows the radial form.

Figure 1.10 is the walkway around the lunchroom where the client sets up catered lunches on trading days. On nontrading days, this space doubles as an eat-in kitchen. Stools and tables are high enough to offer views through the curved glass panels toward Boston harbor. This gathering area has been so popular in the company that it is being replicated and tripled in size on another floor at the time of this writing.

Kopacz and her team listened closely to their clients' needs, requirements, and desires at the beginning—the programming phase of design. This early effort is reflected in their final design, which dovetails programmatic needs with a beautifully designed work environment.

FIGURE 1.10 **Lunch area designed by Allegro Interior Architecture.** *Photo © Greg Premru Photography.*

Professional Example: Spagnolo Gisness & Associates

Spagnolo Gisness & Associates, Inc. (SGA) is a full-service architecture, planning, interior design, branded environments, and virtual design + construction firm built around a strong, client-inclusive design culture. Headquartered in Boston with an office in New York, SGA offers comprehensive design services for office buildings, mixed-use buildings, corporate interiors and higher-education projects throughout the northeast and beyond.

SGA's Approach to Programming

SGA's Associate and Director of Interior Design Gable Clarke, IIDA, **LEED AP**, has worked in a variety of market sectors and currently focuses on corporate interiors and higher education (see Figure 1.11). Along with her work at SGA, she is heavily involved in the New England chapter of the **International Interior Design Association (IIDA)** and formerly taught at the Boston Architectural College. Here, Clarke provides an overview of the firm's programming work.

"We spend a significant amount of time at the beginning of the process listening and learning, as it's critical to understand an organization's evolution and goals for the future," Clarke says. "The program sets the stage for all the decisions to come, so it's important to get it right. Initially, the program helps confirm a client's square footage needs to ensure they're making a prudent real estate decision. We bring our expertise to the table with regard to trends, metrics, etc. to help clients understand how similar corporations are organized spatially and how they may gain some efficiency by perhaps rethinking antiquated metrics (i.e. workstation size). It's important to note that it's never a one-size-fits-all solution, however; each client is unique. But oftentimes they haven't re-thought their space in years, so exposing them to how the workplace has evolved provides them with information to make informed choices for their own design."

The program, which includes metrics, adjacency requests, and information regarding a company's culture and brand, serves as the baseline for the design process. However, Clarke notes that it is a living document. Flexibility is not uncommon as the design evolves.

For SGA it's important to include the personal element in programmatic research: the designer gets the specifics and actual feel of the space instead of just collecting an "inventory" of formal data (e.g., number of conference rooms and cubicles). During the interview, a knowledgeable programmer can make note of workflow and understand how the existing space is being utilized. Then, the programmer creates an applicable programming strategy for the client to consider. According to Clarke, "Programming is the process of understanding and documenting the client's project requirements, which include quantitative as well as qualitative data."

During the programming phase, SGA designers have a kickoff meeting with the client's leadership to define the goals and programming strategy, followed by an extensive interview process and concluding

FIGURE 1.11 Gable Clarke, IIDA, LEED AP, SGA Associate and Director of Interior Design.

with another meeting with the leadership team to summarize their findings.

At SGA the information gathered is considered in the development of a "test fit" for the proposed space. This helps address issues that might surface very early in the process and lays the foundation for schematic design.

During the interview process, the programmer is a **mediator**, working with all client members involved, as well as the countless industry standards and further analytical research and requirements. Tangible and nontangible issues are addressed and documented. An example of a nontangible issue might be the need to promote collaboration, while a tangible issue would be more specific, such as the need for a fifty-person training room.

A walk-through of the existing space helps the programmer understand and plan for feasible design options. Getting to know the client company is vital to understanding what is truly required; otherwise, the information gathered is just numbers and data.

According to Clarke, often the hardest thing for clients to project is growth. To help plan for headcount changes, a conference room that is designed to be equivalent to the space of two offices can be reconfigured if the firm grows and requires more office space (see Figure 1.12).

For SGA, Clarke says, "the programming document is now a roadmap for design" test-fitting the interpreted data and designing with imagination to fit the needs.

Education is the key to all programming. The client will often dictate the specific details and requirements. It is then the programmer's job to design and teach. While acknowledging the client's wants and needs, the programmer must, demonstrate all applicable codes. This may be seen as a push-and-pull function in areas such as **net-to-gross ratios,** for example. It is essential for the client to understand the functional usage of any space.

Clarke notes that a successful program relies on the ability to "listen … truly listen." By hearing what the client says, the programmer can understand what is truly needed. Comprehending the client's "philosophy and culture" not only moves the process along and keeps it up-to-date, but it also provides the data the designer needs to program and plan out the space. The technical process essentially depends on the ease of programming, but many designers find interviews and spreadsheets convenient programming tools.

The idea is to work "**macro-to-micro,**" that is, to start on the large scale, initially noting all the key concepts and necessities, before moving to a smaller scale. It is easier

FIGURE 1.12
Schematic drawings for a conference room that demonstrates potential growth options.

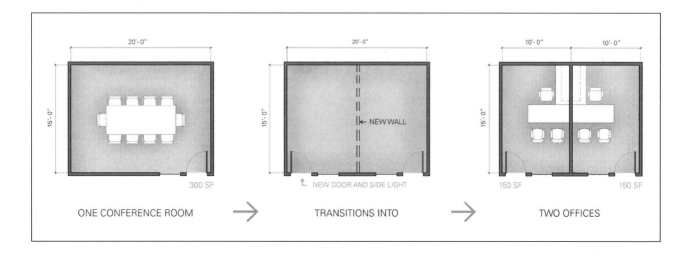

ONE CONFERENCE ROOM → TRANSITIONS INTO → TWO OFFICES

to move large groupings during the exploratory phase than it is to revisit the space at a later point. Once all that information has been gathered, the programmer analyzes the facts and sorts the responses, creating the fundamental information for the **Schematic Design** phase of the design process.

Clarke offers the example of Monotype, one of the world's best known providers of type-related products, technologies, and expertise headquartered in Woburn, MA. After interviewing this client, SGA created a test fit plan (Figure 1.13) that explored department placement within the building and was used to help the client understand how the offices and workstations could be oriented. This plan allows the client to visualize traffic flow, adjacencies, and access to natural light.

While meeting the programmatic needs for layout and floor plan, designers are also gathering information about the client. Sketches or renderings of the space can lead to new ideas and concepts that then become part of the three-dimensional design. Figure 1.14 show the progression of a concept from rendering to the final photographed space.

Clients have become increasingly aware of the importance of their brand, Clarke says, and realize that their workplace is an extension of that brand. Not only does a client's space speak to visitors, but it becomes a vital tool for attracting and retaining employees. Culture and brand play an important role in workspace design.

To fold that study and evaluation in with more traditional programming, SGA encourages clients to start with surveys and an "envisioning session," Clarke says. This session is made up of a group of people who aren't necessarily decision makers, but who

FIGURE 1.13
Monotype department plan.

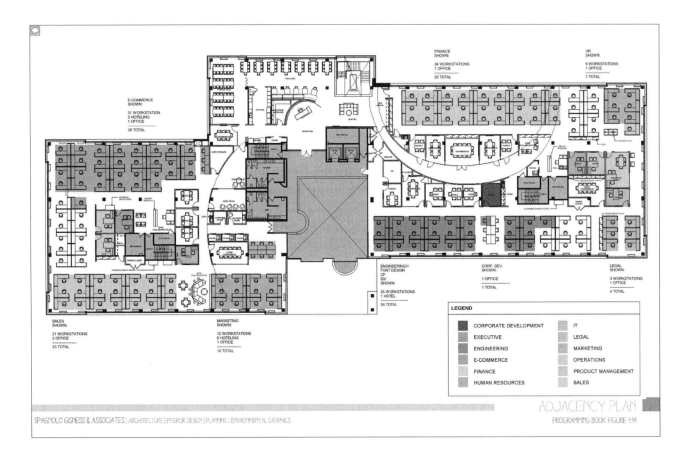

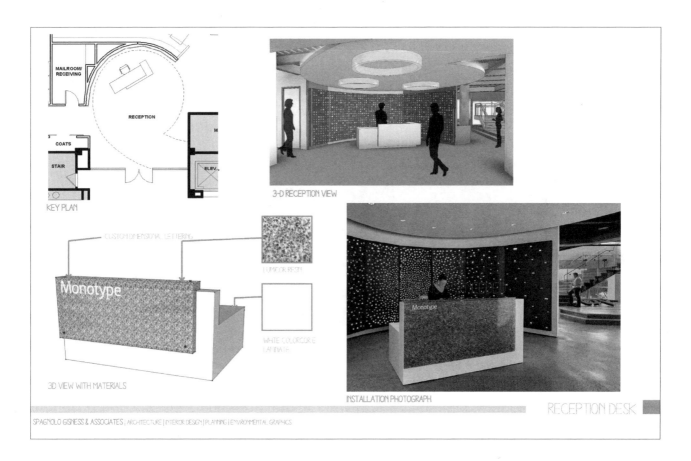

MAILROOM/RECEIVING

RECEPTION

COATS

STAIR

ELEV.

KEY PLAN

3-D RECEPTION VIEW

CUSTOM DIMENSIONAL LETTERING

Monotype

LUMICOR RESIN

WHITE COLORCORE LAMINATE

3D VIEW WITH MATERIALS

Monotype

INSTALLATION PHOTOGRAPH

RECEPTION DESK

SPAGNOLO GISNESS & ASSOCIATES | ARCHITECTURE | INTERIOR DESIGN | PLANNING | ENVIRONMENTAL GRAPHICS

represent a cross section of the company's employees (according to tenure, departments, and generations). This group participates in the design process at key intervals, offering insights and then sharing among their peers in order to generate excitement and gain buy-in from all employees.

The envisioning session is preceded by the circulation of a thought-starter questionnaire, seen in Figure 1.15, and the session itself may include group and break-out sessions, image sharing, and a roundtable discussion. SGA finds that envisioning helps "complete the picture" and is the art to the science of traditional program metrics. It also is a critical component to change management, how it will impact their employees, the importance of which clients increasingly take to heart.

"The survey, envisioning and programming sessions culminate in a document that memorializes the project metrics as well as each company's unique business, brand and culture" as seen in Figure 1.16.

PROGRAMMING IN AN ACADEMIC SETTING

This book will guide you as you practice your research, programming, and design skills, tightly weaving these skills into a single set that is critical to employing great design. The model in Figure 1.17 will help you visualize the path we will follow in this book. Note that the research and programming process are integrated. By the end of the course, you will have become a holistic thinker with analytical skills that help in programming and design decision making. In many ways, the process of programming parallels standard research methods. This text aims to bridge the research process

FIGURE 1.14
Monotype reception visuals. *Photo © Robert Benson Photography.*

FIGURE 1.15 Online envisioning survey.

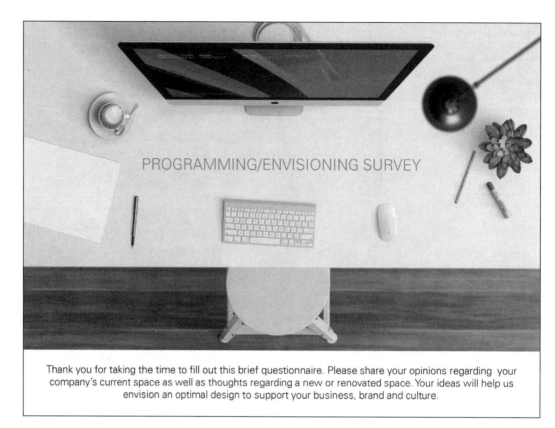

Thank you for taking the time to fill out this brief questionnaire. Please share your opinions regarding your company's current space as well as thoughts regarding a new or renovated space. Your ideas will help us envision an optimal design to support your business, brand and culture.

FIGURE 1.16 Monotype envisioning image collage.

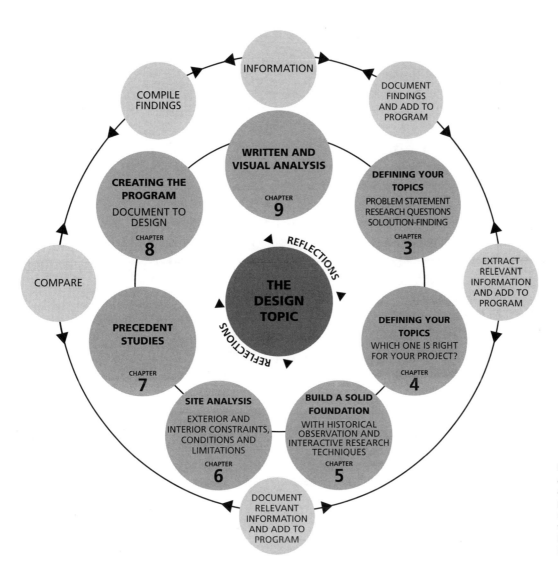

FIGURE 1.17
A diagram depicting
a circular model of
programming and
research. This model
was developed
by Dr. Rose Mary
Botti-Salitsky.

with the programming process that an interior designer employs. It will guide you through a step-by-step process to create strong programming documents and research proposals.

Chapter 2, "The Process of Design," provides an overview of the design process. It represents a holistic interpretation of the process and varied approaches and addresses special considerations during the design process. It will also help you place programming in the context of the design process. In Chapter 3, "Defining a Topic and Structuring Your Program Document," we begin to identify the selected design project

and generate a problem statement with questions. Chapter 4, "Research Methods," outlines selected research methods that are most applicable to the design fields. Chapter 5, "Historical, Observational, and Interactive Research," discusses research as it applies to selected design topics. Chapter 6, "Exterior, Interior, and Site Analysis," outlines how to document and analyze the site location of the design project—specifically with regard to interiors and how decision making can affect location and site. Chapter 7, "Precedent Studies," covers precedent studies and how to analyze the data collected in order to make informed decisions about the design and programmatic requirements within the space. Chapter 8, "Generating the Program," identifies how to document the programming requirements and space adjacencies. Chapter 9, "Written and Visual Analysis," is an analysis of the solutions presented and addresses the visual language used in programming. Chapter 10, "Challenging Your Thinking," draws together all that is covered in the previous chapters, emphasizing the advantages to programming as well as careers in programming.

KEY TERMS

- Adjacency requirements
- Asset management
- Bubble diagram
- Color theory
- Concept diagram
- Contract documents
- Diagrams
- Energy efficiency
- Interior architecture
- International Interior Design Association (IIDA; www.iida.org)
- LEED AP (www.usgbc.org)
- Life cycle cost
- Location productivity
- Macro-to-micro
- Mediator
- National Council for Interior Design Qualification (NCIDQ; www.ncidq.org)
- Net-to-gross ratios
- Precedent studies
- Professional design practitioner
- Program summary
- Programming
- Project schedule
- Schematic design
- Space-planning adjacencies
- Strategic planning

CHAPTER 2

The Process of Design

After reading this chapter, you should be able to:

- Discuss the process of design.
- Recognize how the process of design in academia differs from that in the professional setting.
- Define what is expected in each step in the process of design.
- Distinguish between the different models in the profession.
- Describe the special considerations during the design process.
- Identify where programming fits into the process of design.

Descriptions of the design process have evolved over the years as researchers have struggled to capture the essence of what people do when they invent ways of doing things (Duerk, 1993). A project involves many steps from inception to completion.

THE PROCESS OF DESIGN: STEPS

According to Duerk, the design process involves three activities: analysis, synthesis, and evaluation (1993). The process is complex and collaborative. It has five phases:

1. Programming
2. Schematic design
3. Design development
4. Construction documentation
5. Final critique

The process can be cyclical, with designers adding information as they glean greater insight. It should be inclusive. In recent years, the profession's traditional linear step-by-step approach (seen in Figure 2.1) has changed significantly, reflecting both advancements in technology and clients that have become very active in the process. In many ways, what happens in the classroom is very similar to what goes on out in the field. Figure 2.2 depicts the steps in an interior design studio class, where specific tasks are completed while critique and analysis take place simultaneously. Note that the client is a participant throughout the professional process; in the studio setting, the educator (while making the critique) often assumes the role of the client.

Some aspects of the two models, however, differ. Note, for example, how the last phase of design, in the professional model in Figure 2.1, is construction administration. This phase can, of course, only be studied in theory and through limited observation within an academic setting. In Figure 2.2's academic model, the last phase focuses on the final presentation and critique. Both Figures 2.1 and 2.2 share ongoing analysis, but critique and review are performed by different parties. Another important distinction is that in the profession, the client controls the passage from one phase to the next. In academia, the professor and external critics typically give students the approval to move on to the next phase of design. In academia, the course calendar also limits the number of revisions that can be made, whereas other influences, such as time and money, can restrict professional revisions.

EXPECTED OUTCOMES FOR EACH PHASE OF DESIGN

Within each phase of design during a studio course, students are expected to perform the following tasks.

Phase 1: Programming

In the programming phase, students research the topic and space under investigation. Typically, the instructor outlines a fictitious client or provides a realistic scenario with a list of requirements. The instructor might have a client for students to interview and interact with. Often, students will be expected to examine and document research findings and precedent studies.

In this phase, students generate a problem statement that describes the basic concept and nature of the project (Neilson & Taylor, 2002; Tate, 1987). Interviews, adjacency space studies, and space requirements are also included in this preliminary phase. Often, images of the site and building orientation on the site are included to help students understand how the interior would be affected by exterior conditions and site placement (Duerk, 1993; Pena, 1987).

At the completion of the programming phase, students are expected to have a solid understanding of the project and the documented research. The program is specific, including **square footage** requirements, space needs, and the preliminary development of a concept. Typically, students have an ongoing dialogue and critique with the instructor, a peer review, and a self-evaluation. Some instructors hold mini-group critiques at the end of each phase of design, designating benchmarks for the transition to the next phase. Within the profession, common practice is to have client approval, signature, and payment upon completion of each phase of design.

Phase 2: Schematic Design

In the schematic phase, students will be expected to begin the allocation of space by generating bubble or blocking diagrams through which to explore potential options. Pile (1995) refers to this phase as preliminary steps, stating: "This is the most crucial point in the design process, creativity comes into play in the effort to find approaches that will be original, aesthetically satisfying, and valid solutions to the problems defined through programming" (p. 133).

In developing the idea, the **concept** or theme of the project begins to infuse itself into the design. Once a concept is developed, it begins to influence every decision you make, from sculpting the interior surfaces, to selecting fabric and furnishings, to impacting the physiological human interaction within the environment. Tate (1987) believes that a concept or theme "in interiors therefore, means some dominant characteristic; and this characteristic may be thought of as a theme; in every complex work of art, there is a dominating characteristic" (p. 98).

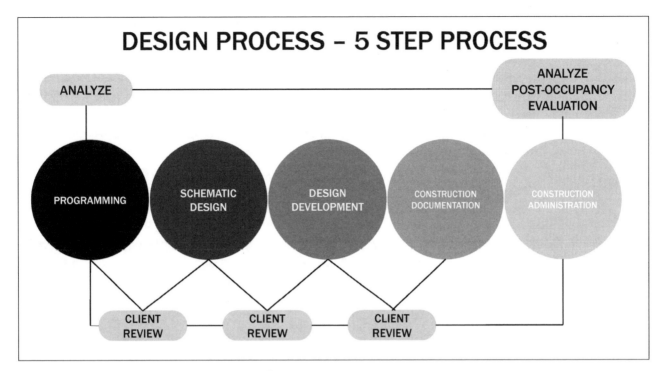

FIGURE 2.1 **Process of design within the interior design profession**

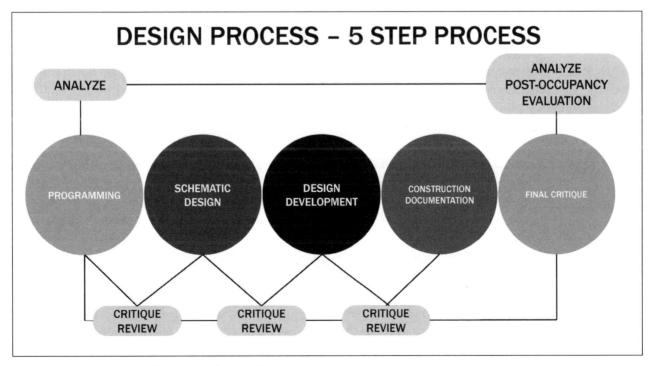

FIGURE 2.2 **Process of design within an interior design studio class.**

While developing a concept, you are also expected to begin to visualize the space not only two-dimensionally but also three-dimensionally. Freehand sketches and schematic models will help you visually articulate your ideas, as will working on the computer to generate some quick models, layouts, and massing studies.

Often a professional interior designer in the schematic phase of design will implement the information gleaned during the programming phase, using schematic drawings, elevations, sketches, and possibly some animated walk through. Sometime, for larger projects, mock-ups are developed to give the client the opportunity to see sample spaces or product before fully committing.

Phase 3: Design Development

In the design development phase, the design is in transition from sketches to more defined drawings, using dimensions, color, fabric, and finishes (Pile, 1995). Students begin to generate hard-line perspectives, elevations, sections, and details in order to explore the development of the space. This is also the point in the process when you begin to select the color schemes, materials, equipment, accessories, and lighting that will be integrated within the space. Hard-line documentation of the design can be done by hand or by using CAD software.

According to the NCIDQ, a professional interior designer actually completes both design development and construction documentation (phase 4 in an academic setting; see below) in one step (see Figure 2.2). In an academic setting, however, this is a two-step process. To mark the completion of design development, it is common in the class setting to have a group, an individual, or even a guest critic evaluate the design up to this point.

Phase 4: Construction Documentation

In the **construction documentation** phase of design, students are expected to generate a complete set of working drawings, specifications, and schedules of interior construction. The **working drawings** consist of a title sheet, index, site plans, demolition plans, floor plans, electrical plans, reflected ceiling plans, elevations, details, and schedules. Specifications are also generated for furnishings, equipment, materials, accessories, and lighting. These can be separate from the working drawings, or they can be included within the packet. Often you will also be asked to generate a projected estimated cost or a budget based on the specifications. Available drafting software can easily generate specifications and schedules.

While you work on the execution of your designs, you produce a set of working drawings, specifications, and a presentation. Presentations can vary. Traditional presentations, mounted on boards, and including fabrics and finishes, are visually pleasing. But many presentations today are digitally created.

Students will often include a model to accompany their presentation. A virtual walk through or animation might be included as well. Typically, boards document all phases of the design.

Phase 5: Final Critique

The last phase of design in an academic setting is the final **critique**. "A critique is unique in the dominant position it holds within the framework of studio design education; it is the central experience of design schools" (Dozois, 2001, p. 1). The design studio critique, or "crit," is a unique educational event with strong historical patterns (Anthony, 1991; Eisner, 1985, 2002). These traditional architectural design experiences continue to be embedded in the design studio practice as well as in general applied arts education.

The critique experience brings together undergraduate students and their faculty in a review process. Peers are encouraged to participate and critique each other. Many programs include upper-level and graduate students as critics in introductory studios. This is wonderful preparation for working in the design office where teamwork and ongoing collaboration is expected.

It is not uncommon for programs in the applied arts to host or even pay guest critics. The goal is to entice prestigious design professionals to participate and critique the students' final work (Anthony, 1991; Tate, 1987). Many programs post a brief biography of the critic, along with the dates he or she will be visiting the school, for all to see.

Both **Council for Interior Design Accreditation (CIDA)** and the **National Architectural Accrediting Board (NAAB)** include in their accreditation standards and guidelines a section in which all visiting critics are to be listed.

The critique is an essential tool in the evaluation and assessment process of your work within the art and design curriculums. You spend long hours in the studio classroom to complete the bulk of your design work, and you depend highly on your professors' critiques throughout the process of design (Anthony, 1991; Tate, 1987). The critique is an ongoing process in the studio community, shared between classmates and the professor. It also helps prepare you for a formal final design critique or jury.

Instructors determine readiness for criticism in several ways. Some instructors may invite students to sign up for a private critique (Tate, 1987, p. 74). In some cases, the instructor might float from student to student, critiquing each one and committing varying amounts of time to each depending on the level of work completed. And in some instances, instructors will draw while they give their critique, unable to explain with words alone (Tate, p. 74).

The History of the Critique

The critique originates far back in the seventeenth century. The **École des Beaux Arts** was founded in France in 1648 for the purpose of having artists available to decorate the palaces and paint the royal portraits. Students studied architecture, drawing, painting, sculpture, engraving, modeling, and gem cutting. Now nearly 370 years old, today it is a destination for people studying studio arts.

During the early years of the École des Beaux Arts, final critiques were held behind closed doors, and students received their work back with only a letter grade and perhaps a few comments (Anthony, 1991; Bosworth & Jones, 1932). In 1919, the German architect Walter Gropius founded the **Bauhaus School,** which promoted individual creative expression and collaboration among the art and design disciplines. Since then, the critique has become an inclusive experience. Often, the critique is treated like an event, with invitations sent out to students of design as well as the faculty and the local design community. This philosophy of inclusion is still alive in design firms today. Many firms will display process work and development drawings and invite their colleagues to stop by and "critique" the work to date, seeking all viewpoints in order to help improve the final design.

In both the École des Beaux Arts and the Bauhaus School, "it was common for faculty to compete informally with each other to see who could invite the most prestigious practitioners to serve as a critic—a practice that remains to this day" (Anthony, p. 11).

DIFFERENT MODELS IN THE PROFESSION

The prior section outlined what you may experience within the classroom setting. Here, we will review what is actively happening in the profession. Significant advancements in technology have changed how programming and design are occurring. In many cases, the models outlined below are the result of integrating **Building Information Modeling (BIM)** technology with more cost-efficient best practices. BIM refers to interactive, model-based software. It allows all stake holders to work on the same model concurrently, which helps prevent errors and makes collaboration easier.

The Integrated Project Delivery Model

The **integrated project delivery (IPD)** model is designed to promote collaboration from the very beginning. Many firms offer this inclusive approach, which places the client at the center of the process. According to the AIA National/AIA California Council (American Institute of Architects, 2007), IPD "integrates people, systems, business structures and practices into a process that collaboratively harnesses the talents and insights of all participants" (AIA, 2007).

In the IPD model, all key players come to the table at the beginning of the project. Therefore more time is spent in the programming and predesign phase, in this model, than is spent in the traditional linear model seen in Figure 2.1. Figure 2.4a & 2.4b, from the AIA, compares the traditional project delivery model to an IPD model.

Figure 2.5 demonstrates the impact of the IPD model in the **MacLeamy curve.** In 2004 HOK Chairman and Chief Executive Officer Patrick MacLeamy, FAIA, drew the set of curves based on his observations that design projects becomes more complex and difficult to change the more developed they are. The ability to change can happen easily in the beginning of the project. MacLeamy recognizes that the traditional process is broken and there needs to be a new process. He refers to this as building smart design, which focuses more effort in the beginning of the process and using smart technology such as BIM, which has resulted in a paradigm shift to the design process with more resources focused in the early stages.

The IPD model is further demonstrated in Figure 2.5. According to the AIA, "In addition to shifting design decision making forward, redefinition of phases is driven by two key concepts: the integration of early input from constructors, installers, fabricators and suppliers as well as from designers; and the ability to model and simulate the project accurately using BIM tools. These two concepts enable the design to be brought to a much higher level of completion before the documentation phase is started" (p. 22).

Jeanne Kopacz of Allegro Interior Architecture (see Chapter 1) noted that the speed of project delivery is increasing. The average timeline for programming through

FIGURE 2.3
Integrated project delivery (IPD).

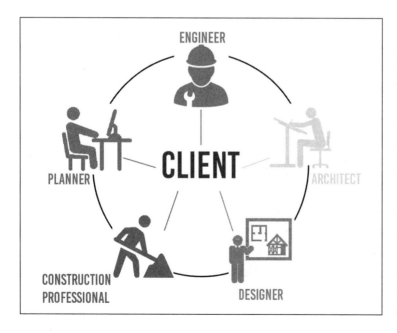

Traditional Project Delivery		Integrated Project Delivery
Fragmented, assembled on "just-as-needed" or "minimum-necessary" basis, strongly hierarchical, controlled	teams	An integrated team entity composed of key project stakeholders, assembled early in the process, open, collaborative
Linear, distinct, segregated; knowledge gathered "just-as-needed"; information hoarded; silos of knowledge and expertise	process	Concurrent and multi-level; early contributions of knowledge and expertise; information openly shared; stakeholder trust and respect
Individually managed, transferred to the greatest extent possible	risk	Collectively managed, appropriately shared
Individually pursued; minimum effort for maximum return; (usually) rst-cost based	compensation/reward	Team success tied to project success; value-based
Paper-based, 2 dimensional; analog	communications/technology	Digitally based, virtual; Building Information Modeling (3, 4, and 5 dimensional)
Encourage unilateral effort; allocate and transfer risk; no sharing	agreements	Encourage, foster, promote and support multi-lateral open sharing and collaboration; risk sharing

FIGURE 2.4A **IPD AIA model table.**

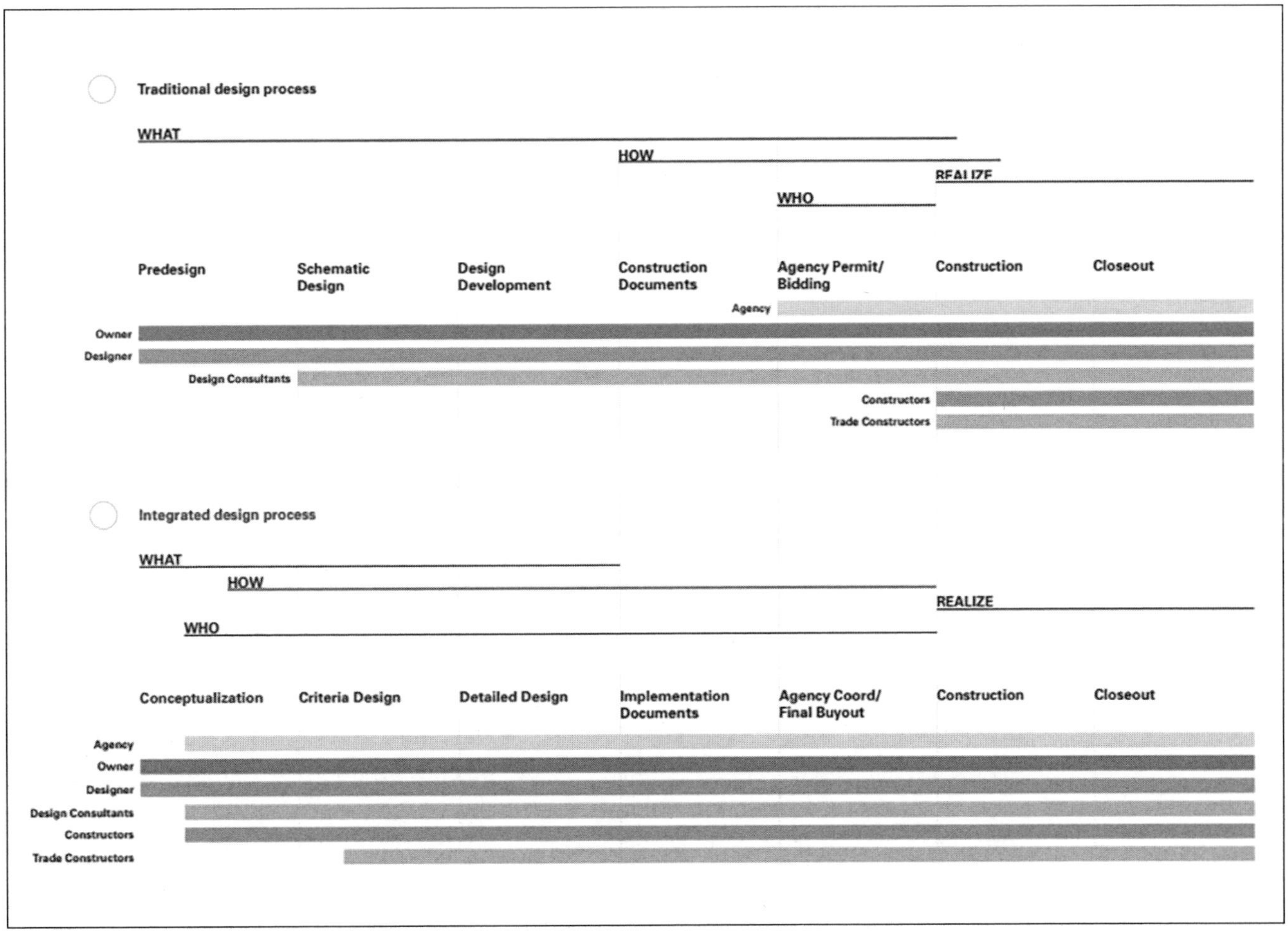

FIGURE 2.4B **AIA traditional and new model comparison.**

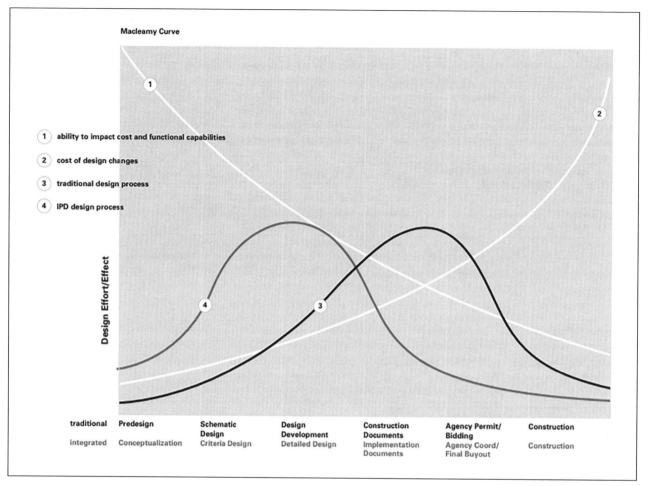

Macleamy Curve

① ability to impact cost and functional capabilities

② cost of design changes

③ traditional design process

④ IPD design process

Design Effort/Effect

| traditional | Predesign | Schematic Design | Design Development | Construction Documents | Agency Permit/ Bidding | Construction |
| integrated | Conceptualization | Criteria Design | Detailed Design | Implementation Documents | Agency Coord/ Final Buyout | Construction |

FIGURE 2.5 **Impact of the IPD model in the MacLeamy curve.**

move-in gets shorter every year, a pattern that shows no signs of stopping. Statistical needs, branding intentions, known building restrictions, and/or the bottom-line budget can change midstream due to a change in leadership, movement in the client's market, or a shift in the economy. Consequently, the program that has been designed to is often revised while the project is still in process. The idea of a finite program that is adhered to religiously during design has given way to the need to stay flexible. As a designer, you will succeed by establishing your process in a way that will accommodate changes in the program during the later stages. BIM tools such as Revit help designers manage programs that have evolved into moving targets. Increased use of BIM tools in design has impacted design, and the program, significantly.

In their Interior Design 2014 Outlook and state-of-the-industry research report, the American Society of Interior Designers (ASID) identified "IPD and BIM as two of the fastest-growing trends in the field. 'Faster, better, cheaper' is the mantra in today's construction industry, forcing architecture and design firms to change their business models to a more collaborative, shared responsibility approach. BIM technology makes it easier for the various members of a team to share designs, plans, and information—both in the office and, via mobile technology, on site" (p. 39).

Project Start	Requirements	Design Development		Implement Documentation		Commissioning	CofO

ESP session | Co-location | | Tracking Preformance Metrics

Architecture BIM Development

CM Engagement | GMP Development | GMP

Assist Partner Interviews | Awards Assist Partners | BIM FM Integration

De-scoping | Construction

Design Consultations Design BIM Development | Desin Assisnt Fabrication BIM Development

FIGURE 2.6A Spagnolo Gisness & Associates (SGA); virtual design construction (VDC).

Virtual Design and Construction

Spagnolo Gisness & Associates, Inc. (SGA; see Chapter 1) offers dedicated virtual design construction (VDC) services. With VDC, project teams can construct buildings virtually, fostering collaboration among project stakeholders and eliminating mistakes before a project is built. Michael Schroeder is the director of BIM/VDC services. The VDC model developed by SGA (shown in Figure 2.6a) is eliminating a lot of the wasted time and energy that has dragged down the construction experience for decades. Marrying project success factors with the actual team member's goals and applying the best of lean thinking has proven very successful. Schroeder explains "Not only do we measure success from a cost and schedule standpoint, but also from a social and emotional level as well. True collaboration is based on trust and we do everything possible to build trust early in the process," a shift in focus to the early stages of programming in the project similar to the MacLeamy. Autodesk BUILD is a recent project completed by SGA that implemented the VDA approach. Figure 2.6b is one of many images that were rendered during the development phase to show the executive team the space. The results are realistic and help both the client and design team visualize the space during all the phases of design. Changes in the virtual world cost almost nothing compared to changes to bricks and mortar.

FIGURE 2.6B
Rendering created by SGA for the Autodesk BUILD project.

SPECIAL CONSIDERATIONS DURING THE DESIGN PROCESS

Designers in both school and the professional world need to be mindful of some special considerations during the programming phase. Is the project going to be LEED certified? Will BIM software be used? Is the project located in a high-risk area based on the resiliency index?

Planning for Sustainability

Sustainability should always be part of the initial conversations with a client. **Leadership in Energy & Environmental Design (LEED)** certification and how to meet the criteria should be discussed with the whole team during the programming phase of design. Five rating systems apply to multiple types of project types (Figure 2.7).

There are four levels of certification, and each level has specific criteria that the project needs to fulfill in order to receive the possible points. Many of these decisions are made during the initial programming phase. Therefore, it is critical that all project participants be committed to this goal at the outset. More information can be found at the U.S. Green Building Council (USGBC) website *http://www.usgbc.org/*.

Blake Jackson, AIA, LEED faculty, and WELL faculty, is an associate and the sustainability practice leader at Tsoi/Kobus & Associates. According to Jackson, "Sustainability permeates every aspect of our firm culture and is constantly evolving. We believe in supporting a healthy ecosystem through design, outreach, service and mentorship to inspire our work as well as those we serve."

The WELL Building Standard® (WELL)

According to its website, "The WELL Building Standard is the world's first building standard focused exclusively on human health and wellness. It marries best practices in design and construction with evidence-based medical and scientific research—harnessing the built environment as a vehicle to support human health and wellbeing." Founded by Paul Scialla, the WELL standard is helping designers rethink what should be included in the built environment, especially considering that most individuals spend 90 percent of their time inside.

Jackson, Tsoi/Kobus & Associates sustainability practice leader, is part of the first class of WELL accredited professionals. The new certification, from the International WELL Building Institute, recognizes extensive knowledge of health and well-being in the built environment. Blake states "that the real innovation with WELL is that it encompasses and seals loopholes in three key areas: 1) design + construction, 2) operations, and 3) behavior (policy of the owner/operator)." This scope is far beyond what is normally considered on a typical project, and he believes it is the tool that can help designers have a more integrated life cycle in a building.

The WELL Building Standard considers sustainable features that improve the environment and takes a holistic approach to the wellness of a building's occupants. Figure 2.8 shows the seven key concepts relevant to "occupant health": air, water, nourishment, light, fitness, comfort, and mind.

FIGURE 2.7 Types of LEED ratings.

Building Design and Construction   Interior Design and Construction   Building Operations and Maintenance   Neighborhood Development   Homes

BOX 2.1 **BLAKE JACKSON, SUSTAINABILITY PRACTICE LEADER AT TSOI/KOBUS & ASSOCIATES**

I have found the greatest success at integrating sustainability into a project comes when we come right out of the gate, so to speak, with a strong design proposal that emphasizes sustainability as a major driver. Often, clients solicit several firms via **request for qualifications (RFQ)** to narrow the field of potential firms/candidates. Once you get through this phase, firms submit a **request for proposal (RFP)**, which can be used to entice a client. Often, their briefs leave a lot to the imagination and are an open-ended means of solving their particular problem. What I like to do is to exploit the open-endedness to discuss not just the solving of their unique design challenge but also the open-endedness where sustainability can serve to differentiate and inspire them to reach for more. I like proposing the building that should be rather than the one they are saying will be built, and this subtle approach has helped us land work where a client becomes excited about the sustainable design potential. I am typically involved in key interviews, helping to show teams and clients the sustainable design potential through climate analysis, energy and water benchmarking, LEED analysis and building performance simulations for daylighting and energy modeling. These tools can help develop and compare design ideas early before they are set into place, as well as helping create a dialogue with consultants, particularly engineers whose systems will greatly impact performance and comfort. I am one of

the few team players involved with a project from RFP through construction. After many decisions are made throughout the schematic design to construction documentation phases of the project, I work with contractors and lease with third-party certification bodies to maintain the integrity of design intent, particularly for LEED projects. This entails verifying integrity of specification of green materials, construction practices and even future marketing efforts well beyond substantial completion of the project.

BOX FIGURE 2.1A **Blake Jackson.**

Many hospitals, offices, and hotels have been integrating the WELL Building Standard, which takes as its premise the life and health of the occupant. At the MGM Grand Hotel & Casino in Las Vegas, Delos's wellness-themed hotel rooms include air purification systems, energizing lights, and blackout shades.

The concept of looking at not just the design and location but also the occupant was the premise of Delos founder Paul Scialla. Critics point out that there is still a need to evaluate the effectiveness of these strategies once implemented.

Whole Systems Design Process

Another example from the profession is Tsoi/Kobus and Associates, who have developed their own model for project delivery:

The Seven Concepts of The Well Building Standard

AIR
WATER
NOURISHMENT
LIGHT
FITNESS
COMFORT
MIND

FIGURE 2.8 The seven concepts of the WELL Building Standard.

a Whole Systems Design process (WSD). Although it aligns with many features of the IPD model, WSD is tailored to facilitate project delivery by aligning key stakeholders and benchmarks along a project timeline. WSD is inclusive and mindful of the many factors that need to be considered

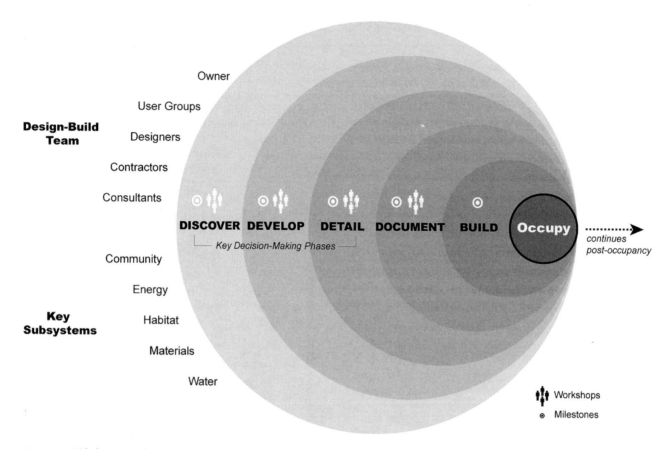

Design-Build Team

Owner
User Groups
Designers
Contractors
Consultants
Community
Energy
Habitat
Materials
Water

Key Subsystems

DISCOVER   DEVELOP   DETAIL   DOCUMENT   BUILD   Occupy
Key Decision-Making Phases
continues post-occupancy

Workshops
Milestones

FIGURE 2.9 **Whole systems design process, a model for project delivery by Tsoi/Kobus & Associates.**

on the front end of design, including resiliency and sustainability. The WSD process establishes a simple framework of critical milestones at each step of the design and construction process (Figure 2.9). These keep a project on target and moving forward while leaving processes of revision and review open.

Planning for Resiliency

In recent years, repeated natural disasters have forced the design profession to rethink how we approach design. Designers now need to plan for resiliency at the very beginning of the design process, hoping to be proactive instead of reactive during unforeseeable situations. According to Gensler's 2015 Design Forecast, "Wellness and resilience are getting widespread attention, not least because of the global threats posed by epidemics and climate change. Urbanization is leading to new city forms, denser yet more livable" (p. 1). In cities, for example, natural areas that once absorbed rainfall have been built upon, and in this time of climate change, flooding now occurs in areas where it has never been seen before. Resiliency conversations and strategies must be included at the forefront of design. Programming will need to be inclusive of resilient strategies, and in the long run it will save time and money on the back end of the project. Planning for resiliency is not a perfect science, but it is possible. In some cases we have the knowledge to plan ahead; we have water tables, climate and weather indicators, and general geographic elements. We can look at data we have collected and make some smart assumptions about the future.

Such planning, which might seem like commonsense, is often overlooked by designers—but not by insurance companies, whose goal is to keep losses to a minimum. They are on the forefront of planning for resiliency. Box 2.3 shows a Tsoi/Kobus & Associates focus on resiliency for The Cuisinart Center for Culinary Excellence at Johnson & Wales University and Box 2.4 is a student example focused on resiliency & design.

The R!SE Initiative is an ambitious global response to a daunting global challenge. "It is a new way of collaborating, on a global scale, to unlock the potential for public and private sector actors who are ready and willing to make a step forward and take leadership on disaster risk reduction" (R!SE program report UNISDR, 2015). This United Nations initiative has the overall goal of generating collaboration across private and public business sectors to identify and create effective disaster risk management strategies and share knowledge; the hope is to build a global alliance by the year 2020.

According to ASID, "Concerns about climate change and the rise in catastrophic natural disasters have focused attention on designing buildings to withstand extraordinary conditions, such as hurricanes, tornadoes and floods" (2014).

The Insurance Institute for Business & Home Safety lists the key weather events that require resiliency planning: earthquake, flood, freezing weather, hail, high wind, hurricane, lightning, tornado, and wildfire. Some of their recommendations fall into the realm of interior design:

- If the facility is located in an earthquake-prone area, all suspended ceilings and the fluorescent light fixtures associated with them should be properly braced. Ceilings and light fixtures must be properly attached to avoid damage.

BOX 2.2 QUOTE FROM R!SE PROGRAM

"From response to prevention,
from competing to collaborating,
from suffering and losses to
resiliency and shared value, the
time to act is now, one step at a
time, working together to reduce
disaster risks and build more
resilient communities and a more sustainable global economy"

(R!SE program report, UNISDR, 2015)

- Older buildings may not have the additional reinforcement that is needed to prevent a suspended ceiling and lights from collapsing.
- Be mindful where to install electrical and heating systems controls; install them above the flood zone, which may preclude a typical basement location.
- Secure bookcases, art work, and large screen TVs.
- Install or design ledge barriers.
- Secure and add extra strapping to wall-attached cabinets and drawers.
- Choose wood-based products over paper-backed products for walls.
- Choose area rugs, which can be rolled up if a flood threatens or removed to dry out after a flood, instead of wall-to-wall carpeting.
- Place electrical outlets higher up on walls to avoid contact with water should flooding occur.
- Always place electronics on higher shelves or keep them up off the floor.
- Choose plastic storage options for important records or papers or store them on a higher floor.

Emergency planning is often not included in designs for commercial spaces. Of course codes, life safety, and emergency exits are always included in design plans,

BOX 2.3 **THE CUISINART CENTER FOR CULINARY EXCELLENCE AT JOHNSON & WALES UNIVERSITY**

Resiliency is a design concept that considers sustainability in the context of environmental volatility, future-proofing, disaster preparedness and mitigation. Today's projects will be tomorrow's buildings and time is a critical parameter in their evaluation. We must consider the relevance of a building over time with special regard to climate change and the ability of the project to passively cope with disaster, to preserve life and property. Blake Jackson explains "The Cuisinart Center for Culinary Excellence at Johnson & Wales University is situated on reclaimed land, which was once a fully paved, low-lying former industrial area within view of the Narragansett Bay in Providence, RI. Here, the asphalt was recycled on site to build up a protective plinth that placed all critical elements of the building (levels 2 and up) 14 feet above sea level, safe from projected storm surge lines based on FEMA maps. FEMA, is the Federal Emergency Management Agency. The FEMA Flood Map Service Center (MSC) is the official public source for flood hazard information produced in support of the National Flood Insurance Program (NFIP). Use the MSC to find your official flood map, access a range of other flood hazard products, and take advantage of tools for better understanding flood risk. (FEMA, 2015) The building now hovers safely above newly planted green spaces, offering better views of the bay and beautification with greater site porosity. In the event of a storm surge, considered an inevitability, the building is designed to act as a pier. The first floor features breakaway walls that under high pressure during a surge event, break off to minimize the building up of wave action forces on the overall structure of the building. Less critical infrastructure and program (lobby, storage and parking) were placed at grade as a 'sacrificial layer' and dictated the placement of other critical elements safely above the FEMA datum. This 'fail fast, fail cheap' methodology ensures the maintenance of overall structural integrity while safeguarding expensive equipment and providing an area of refuge for occupants. By building in passive resilience, the project and environment both benefit, and the architecture becomes an expression not of fear but of celebration of its unique location."

BOX FIGURE 2.3 The Cuisinart Center for Culinary Excellence at Johnson & Wales University, designed by Tsoi/Kobus & Associates.

BOX 2.4 STUDENT RESILIENCY EXAMPLE: MONICA JOHNSON, MOUNT IDA COLLEGE, 2013

MODULE ANALYSIS AND RECOMMENDATIONS

This housing unit was created by Monica Johnson; information below outlines how it is structured and how it works. She analyzed this structure with the five factors of resilience: to adapt, challenge, maintain, communicate, and remain optimistic. These five factors were also used to analyze the precedent studies.

The module itself is created from a standard 30' x 8' steel shipping container with two fiberglass inserts that allow for easy travel and delivery by truck, train and ship but also an expansion from 185.5 square feet to 525 square feet. Opening the module will be the responsibility of the truck driver. The expanding side of the module is held closed by the steel side that was removed to install the inserts. After all inserts have expanded and dropped to the same level, that steel piece now flips up and creates an awning while allowing for the porch/ramp to fall and separate. Supports and stairs, stored underneath the unit, are then placed appropriately.

The gaps between each of the inserts wil be closed usinging a rubber piece that is cut to shape and attached to the wall and ceiling. Solar panels flip over to expose and angle them to the sunlight, gathering energy to run the module with help from small generators, if needed.

This module provides a home for a family to continue living as a family, along with the following:

- Kitchen unit with height adjustable sink, microwave, mini fridge, counter space, and storage.
- Bathroom equipped with a waterless toilet, shower, and a small sink inset in the wall. The bathroom is mounted on top of a black box (a container meant to hold waste) that gets lifted up into the module when it closes. This is better seen in the animation of the module opening.
- Three modular furniture pieces:
  - Two of the pieces contain a loveseat, desk, shelf, and full-sized bed.
  - The third piece contains a desk, additional storage, and a twin-sized bed.
- Two adjustable tables, which adjust in height from 10.5' to 30.75'. Closed, the table is 48' × 30', but it is expandable up to 78' × 30'. In their smaller forms, they can be used as a coffee or side table. Their maximum size works great as a dinner table.
- Wall-mounted television.

The images below show the module in its closed and compact form, along with the module while open with day and night furniture plans.

BOX FIGURE 2.4A **30' × 8' portable steel shipping container.**

BOX FIGURE 2.4B **30' × 8' converted container.**

BOX FIGURE 2.4C **30' × 8' fully extended container.** Image created by researcher in SketchUp.

(continued on next page)

BOX 2.4 STUDENT RESILIENCY EXAMPLE: MONICA JOHNSON, MOUNT IDA COLLEGE, 2013 *(cont.)*

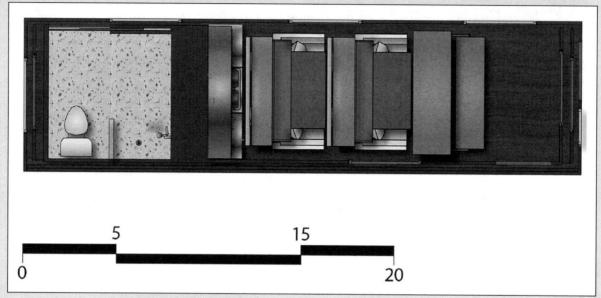

BOX FIGURE 2.4D **30' × 8' floor plan closed module.**

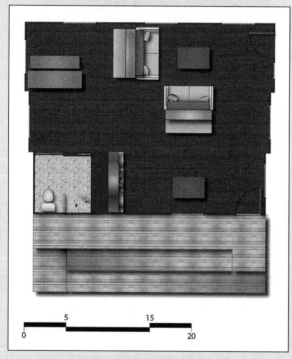

BOX FIGURE 2.4E **30' x 8' open module day floor plan.**

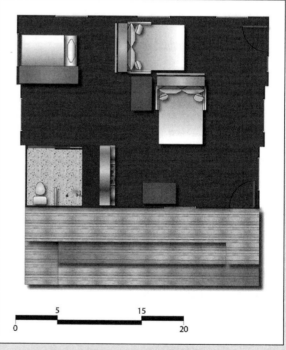

BOX FIGURE 2.4F **30' x 8' open module night floor plan.**

BOX 2.4 STUDENT RESILIENCY EXAMPLE: MONICA JOHNSON, MOUNT IDA COLLEGE, 2013 *(cont.)*

ANALYSIS

The chart below outlines five factors of resilience; they are used to analyze the portable housing module.

BOX FIGURE 2.4G **Five factors of resilience chart.**

	Module
To Adapt	Yes
To Challenge	Yes
To Maintain	Yes
To Communicate	Yes
To Remain Optimistic	Yes
Total	100%

To Adapt: By providing families a place to live that is their own with all necessities, it allows for each individual and the family as a whole to start to reground themselves with something that feels familiar. For example, living in their own space as a family is familiar, whereas living in a shelter with many families and no privacy is not familiar, comfortable, or an appropriate place for regrounding. Giving families a space allows for one less worry. The most important aspects (shelter, food, and water) are taken care of. Without that weight on their shoulders, they can begin to rebuild and restructure both buildings and homes, and their lives.

To Challenge: Allowing the families to adapt is the prerequisite for being able to face and handle stressful and tough situations. While it may not fix everything

immediately, the modules let families start getting back to living their lives and looking toward the future.

To Maintain: The modules are meant for single families only, meaning only one family per unit. This allows families to have a private space to grieve and express themselves in a comfortable and supportive environment.

To Communicate: Each module holds a single family; however, the modules can be arranged in such a way that allows for communal activity and interaction. Being able to problem solve, not only individually but as a group, is an important aspect in growing community resiliency.

To Remain Optimistic: Without having the stress of where to live, where to stay, and how long they will be allowed to stay, families and communities can look toward how to live in the future rather than how to survive in the present.

CONCLUSION AND RECOMMENDATIONS

All five factors are clearly presented in the module, making this an excellent candidate for rebuilding resilience in communities after a natural disaster.

The next step would be to create working drawings, specifications, and pricing in order to build a full scale prototype of the module. After a functional evaluation of the module, six to ten additional modules will be created. This amount will allow for a communal arrangement of the modules. Further studies can be done through observations and interviews given to individuals, families, and the community as a whole by a psychologist who specializes in resiliency. (Refer to Appendix B for full layout of presentation boards.)

but interior designers should start to think deeper. Think about and plan for the unexpected disaster, small or large. This is where interior designers can certainly bring their expertise to the table. For example, consider the convenient storage of supplies for assisted living facilities or schools. These institutions have an emergency plan they implement if a percentage of the residents or students get a stomach virus, for example. In response to the outbreak of such an infectious disease, the kitchen will stop serving in the dining hall and switch to plastic/disposable materials until the percentage of residents or students goes below the number mandated by the state. Typically, these institutions do not have a space allocated for emergency storage, one conveniently located and that people have access to. This becomes problematic. Additional resiliency strategies can be implemented for extra food storage, for example, especially in schools. Schools are often converted to temporary shelters during natural disasters, and yet there is no—or very little—preplanning for this when these structures are designed. This is where interior designers can work together with the community to help plan for the unexpected—to be resilient. One example of resiliency planning is a school constructed with a finished floor elevation two feet over the 500-foot flood level, ensuring that the school will remain dry in the case of a widespread flood event.

Employing Resilient Strategies

The Cuisinart Center for Culinary Excellence at Johnson & Wales University, designed by Tsoi/Kobus & Associates, employed resilient strategies from the very beginning of the project.

Another example of employing resilient strategies is from Monica Johnson, Mount Ida College Class of 2013, who wrote her senior thesis on developing portable living structures. (See Appendix C.) Identifying a need for post-disaster housing solutions that could help rebuild communities, Johnson designed temporary housing using recycled shipping containers. Her temporary housing module will be successful in rebuilding community resilience quickly once a disaster occurs.

WHERE DOES PROGRAMMING FIT INTO THE PROCESS OF DESIGN?

In an academic setting, students are able to experience most of the phases of design as a hands-on experience, which helps build their skills and knowledge as designers. This text is focused on strengthening student skills in programming and research, the first phase of design. Your goal as reader is to grasp the full realm of programming. Once you've achieved that, the attributes of programming will become a natural part of your approach as you design projects in academia and in your future professions.

KEY TERMS

- Bauhaus School
- Building Information Modeling (BIM)
- Concept
- Construction documentation
- Council for Interior Design Accreditation (CIDA; www.accredit-id.org)
- Critique
- École des Beaux Arts
- Integrated Project Delivery (IPD)
- Leadership in Energy & Environmental Design (LEED)
- MacLeamy curve
- National Architectural Accrediting Board (NAAB)
- Request for proposal (RFP)
- Request for qualifications (RFQ)
- Resiliency
- Square footage
- Working drawings

CHAPTER 3

Defining a Topic and Structuring Your Program Document

After reading this chapter, you should be able to:

- Select a topic.
- Appreciate the usefulness of a program document template.
- Generate a problem statement and concept statement.
- Describe the differences between concept, idea, and parti.
- Create the first chapter of your program.

Typically, within the academic setting the instructor assigns a design topic to the student. Many students within their senior year or graduate studies, however, may select a topic of their own. Selecting your own topic is a wonderful opportunity to focus on an area of design that you feel passionate about. Your choice may represent cumulative knowledge from your academic experience. Nevertheless, defining the parameters of your programming topic can feel overwhelming. This chapter outlines steps to follow and shares some examples to help you achieve that task.

The selection of your topic should not be taken lightly. Your topic can build on existing research within the field of interior design and explore original ideas that will add to the body of knowledge within this profession. Best results often come when you pursue an area of design that you find both enjoyable and challenging. Thus, topics tend to vary from student to student.

WHAT IS A PROGRAMMING TOPIC?

When talking about a "topic" for the programming phase of design, we mean a type of subject, study, or theme that you are planning to research. It can encompass commercial or residential design applications or another subject that you find interesting. The term **topic** in the programming phase of design is not unlike a topic of a research paper. It is the subject area that you will be exploring and researching.

Selecting Your Topic

Many students find it hard to select and then commit to a topic. In most situations, your professor assigns you one. In professional practice the selection of a topic arises directly from the needs of the clients you work for and their requirements for a particular job. This could be a new restaurant for a local chef or examination rooms for a healthcare client. It is imperative for you to take time to investigate your topic as it relates to the practice of design. Begin by selecting a topic that you find particularly interesting. Choose something that you discovered through previous studies and that you'd like to study further. Programming a topic can take a semester, a year, or even multiple years of study. This will be time well spent, if you choose well, because you will gain greater insight into a topic that truly matters to you. Moreover, your efforts will contribute to the advancement of the greater body of knowledge and research within interior design.

Topics that would contribute to this advancement of the profession include the following:

- **Aging in place**
- **Anthropometry/anthropometrics**
- Barrier-free design
- Biomimicry
- Business of design
- Corporate design
- **Environmental behavior**
- **Ergonomics**
- **Facilities planning**
- **Green/sustainable design**
- **Healthcare design**
- **Historic preservation and restoration**
- Hospitality design
- **Human factors**
- Institutional design
- **Lighting design**
- **Museum and exhibit design**
- Residential design
- Resiliency
- Retail design
- Set design
- **Universal design**
- **Way-finding methods**

The programming topic could also be a social issue or a special interest you have. Or you could focus on an area of design that you might be interested in pursuing as a career upon graduation. As you begin, spend some time familiarizing yourself with current and emerging trends within the realm of interior design.

Gensler, one of the leading design firms in the country, generates a top trends report. This is an excellent resource for students and designers alike to gain insight into the profession and current developments. The Interior Design Outlook and State of the Industry Report, published yearly by the American Society of Interior Designers (ASID), is also a great resource.

FIGURE 3.1 Word cloud identifying current industry trends.

When conducting your preliminary research on a topic that you think you would like to pursue, you should always include a few examples from around the world. Today the world of design operates in a global context, and significant issues surface when you use an international perspective that includes diverse global cultures. Sometimes as you conduct a preliminary search of your topic, too much information surfaces, indicating you may need to consider refining or narrowing your topic. On the other hand, if too little information emerges, you might consider expanding your topic to include related issues.

The interior design profession truly embraces all facets of our society. The profession touches all aspects of design, encompassing the health, safety, and welfare of the spaces where individuals live, work, learn, heal, worship, and play.

STRUCTURING YOUR PROGRAM DOCUMENT

After you've arrived at your topic, you need to begin structuring your program through the creation of a **programming document**. A programming document is a comprehensive report detailing the programmatic requirements for the design. This document addresses an abundance of issues to identify and outlines the needs of the potential users of the space.

Following is a versatile general template for creating a comprehensive programming document. You can follow this template each time you begin working on a design problem. Sections of the template will vary based on the study problem, the scope of the project, and the time constraints. In some cases you may only need to employ portions of this template as it relates to your studio project. But if you are creating

a comprehensive programming document for your thesis, you will probably utilize the entire template.

We will follow this template throughout this book, with each of the template parts being discussed in the ensuing chapters.

Your Programming Document Template

Each document should contain but not be limited to the following:

Title page:
- Student's name and the date
- Course name; in addition, faculty advisors sometimes have a sign-off sheet that might appear on the title page.
- Note at the bottom of your title page: This document has been prepared for educational purpose only. Limited edition: [the number you plan on making] printed. No further copies shall be made.

Table of contents, including page numbers
Acknowledgments
List of tables
List of figures and illustrations

Chapter 1: Introduction
- Introduction to the study
- Statement of the problem
- User client needs
- Rationale for the study
- Constraints and limitations
- Organization of the project

Chapter 2: Historical, Observational, Interactive Research
- Introduction: Research topic
- Part 1: Historical documentation—Type of research completed and documented

- Part 2: Observational research—Type of research completed and documented
- Part 3: Interactive research—Type of research completed and documented
- Conclusions—Synthesize the data documented in the research
    What observations can be gleaned from this data?

Chapter 3: Building Interior, Exterior, and Site Study
- Introduction
- Part 1: Overview of state
    Introduction (text)
    Maps (images)
    Major forms of transportation (air, train, highway)
- Part 2: Overview of town
    Introduction (text)
    About the community (text and images)
    Places of particular interest (text and images)
    Demographics
- Part 3: Overview of building interior and exterior
    Introduction to the structure
    Location and street (text and images)
    Surrounding structures
    The exterior of the building
    Interior of the building
- Part 4: Conclusions
    Synthesize the data documented in the chapter that validate the appropriate application of design usage.

Chapter 4: Precedent Study
- Part 1: Introduction to the sample selected sites that will be studied
    General guidelines: Pick five to eight examples to study.

Select and illustrate examples that represent a global perspective of your topic (e.g., photos that you have taken or from a book or the Internet, assuming you have permission to use, of course).
- Part 2: Study the same information from each one
    Employ qualitative and quantitative research techniques.
- Part 3: Analyze the information
    Introductory statement: What have you discovered?
    Matrix or chart outlining the information in a visual format.
- Conclusions
    Reflect on the five to eight you selected to study and the findings of your matrix. Summarize your findings.
    Predict what you will include for your programmatic requirements based on the findings of the precedent study.

Chapter 5: The Program
- Introduction addressing significant findings
- Part 1: Existing space conditions
    Existing square footages
    Space utilization
    Space adjacencies
    Issues related to building permits/activities
- Part 2: Proposed program
    The program exterior
        Space requirements
        Space square footages
        Space adjacencies
    The program interior
        Space requirements
        Space square footages
        Space adjacencies bubble/blocking plans
        Space diagrams
- Part 3: Conclusion

Chapter 6: Analysis of the Solution
- Include analysis of the best solution and proposal for the problem stated in Chapter 1.
- Discuss limitations and recommendations.
- Include visuals with your written text.
- Conclusion

References
Appendix

Programming Document Tips
When you are preparing a comprehensive programming document, it is hard not to try and solve the problems. Within the last section of the document, you can begin to address and position some ideas about how the problems and sub-problems will be addressed.

You should start the first chapter of your programmatic research with a clear and concise statement, often referred to as a **problem statement**. Along with the problem statement, the first chapter should include the following, each of which is further discussed below:

- Problem statement, including research questions/sub-problems
- Mission statement
- Concept statement
- Introduction to the project

GENERATING YOUR PROBLEM STATEMENT

When generating a problem statement, you need to provide a background for the research study and typically identify questions that the research hopes to answer. It is important to create a few problem statements during the beginning exploratory phases of your topic. You need to take the time to think about the issues surrounding the problem. Try to envision all scenarios when looking at the proposed problem. The problem should have some questions within it. These questions would then become focus areas and be defined by a research question. Examples of problem statements and questions are included in Boxes 3.1, 3.2, and 3.3.

What, How, Where, When, Why, and Who?
It is important to ask yourself the following about the problem: what, how, where, when, why, and who? Specifically, address the following:

- What is the problem?
  Why is it worth pursuing?
  Are there many areas of opportunity within the problem?
  Are there sub-problems to the problem?
  Have others tried to solve the problem or a similar one?
- What are the scope and limitations of the problem?

Finding the answers to these questions can be a tad tricky. As you are exploring your proposed problem, you also need to remember to keep it very focused when writing the final problem statement. It must be focused and concise, not only for you to keep on track but also for the scope to be defined and achievable in the given time frame. Throughout the process, successful researchers and practitioners pause to ask themselves, "What am I doing and for what purpose am I doing it?" (Leedy, 1989).

Composing Your Mission Statement
Often within the profession, the designer will interview the client and ask if he or she has a "specific goal to be accomplished." The designer then transcribes this into the mission statement for the project. Many clients already have a very specific mission

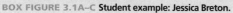

BOX 3.1 SELECTING A TOPIC

STUDENT EXAMPLE: JESSICA BRETON

A recent student of mine selected her programming topic to focus on healthcare, specifically an assisted living Alzheimer's unit.

"I selected this area of design for a few reasons. (1) My grandmother recently passed away from Alzheimer's. (2) The exposure to the various types of facilities when my parents and I were looking for the right location for her to live in. (3) During this experience I realized this is an area of design that not only could benefit from interior design but one that I'm passionate about. I gained such insight during my programmatic research phase; one example was the use of color and lighting to help Alzheimer's patients recall the time of day and recall various locations."

Jessica's first job out of school as an interior designer was with a multidiscipline firm known for their outstanding commitment to healthcare design.

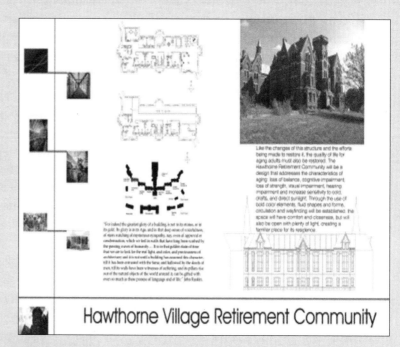

BOX FIGURE 3.1A–C **Student example: Jessica Breton.**

statement with accompanying goals (Duerk, 1993; Pena, 1987). Clients might defer to their mission statement, to assist in the programming process.

Composing mission statements is slightly different than creating problem statements. Mission statements are very specific to the company's image or goals and may have nothing to do with space and how the employees interact. A mission statement is often posted for all internal and external components of the company to see. Some firms have an internal mission statement regarding corporate goals, but others may use an external motto or brand identity, such as Nike's "Just do it." Problem statements are somewhat different; they describe the problem to be solved. Ideally, problem statements should be one sentence followed by supportive sentences that describe the problem and identify a range of sub-problems. It is in these supportive sentences where you include the client's mission statement. Your client's mission statement and goals are extremely valuable in backing up your stated problem.

Keeping Your Statements Straight

Students often confuse the terms **problem statement, thesis statement,** and **mission statement.** Most students are familiar with generating thesis statements for writing assignments. Such thesis statements usually summarize the main point of a paper in a nutshell, expressing the clear position of the research or essay. Often a thesis statement is expressed in a sentence or two. It is sometimes limited and does not encompass solving a problem but merely addresses issues and ideas of a problem.

Each academic institution and practitioner's office will employ standardized terminology. For the purpose of this text and its focus on programming, the term that will be used is problem statement. That said, you should be aware that some academic institutions and practitioner's offices might use these terms interchangeably.

Creating Your Concept Statement

Typically students are asked to create a **concept statement** in all of their studio courses. A concept statement is often confused with a problem statement, but the two terms are not synonymous. When you are creating a concept statement at the beginning of a project, much is unknown because most of the ideas are yet to be explored; therefore, a concept statement usually describes the anticipated outcome of the design. The exploration of these ideas lies in the preliminary phases of thinking. Hence, it is vital to revisit the original concept statement at the end of the design project. This allows the designer the opportunity to reflect on the design, the process, and the element of discovery, which can then be documented. The transformation of the design can then be articulated in greater detail.

The process of moving forward and then revisiting your work is important throughout your work here. In generating your problem statement, for example, your first attempt is simply to state the facts of the problem. Then, after you've completed all of the introductory elements of the program, revisit that first attempt at the problem statement and see if it could be better stated. And then, after all of the precedent studies have been identified and researched, do this again. (Precedent studies will be covered in Chapter 7.) At each point, as you develop your research, you'll find that you have a greater understanding of what exists relative to your topic and you can revisit your problem statement and reevaluate your design ideas and solutions. In Chapter 2, the process of design was laid out in a linear fashion; programming, however, is a cyclical process (refer back to Figure 1.17). As you complete each step of research on your topic, turn back, revisit, and reevaluate your initial statements with a new perspective and sharpened insight.

Concept – Idea – Parti: What's the difference?

Many students often confuse the terms *concept, idea,* and *parti.* In fact each one has a standalone role in the process of creating the program and developing a design. Courtenay Dean Wallace is a practicing architect and educator in the Washington, D.C., area. In Box 3.2 he shares a bit about his process and terminology.

BOX 3.2 DEVELOPING YOUR IDEA: PROFESSIONAL EXAMPLE

Design begins with an idea. Great design solutions are not only visually stimulating but are also driven by fundamental ideas. Underlying ideas become specific mental maps by which we organize, comprehend, and give symbolism to spatial experiences and information. Without contextual ideas informing design, arbitrary characteristics begin to consume the project, which results in a watered down design solution and changes being made in the later stages of the project. To combat against this, the implementation of a "design process" allows designers to resolve programmatic design problems with a dynamic and effective solution. Figure 3.2b is a graphic representation of the process that I follow to solve a design problem. It outlines the entire design process.

BOX FIGURE 3.2A
Courtenay Dean Wallace.

Identifying the design problem

Problem Definition: This is critical to the success of the design project. There must be a clear understanding of the problem to be solved, scope of the project, and the goal(s) of the project. Through critical thinking, organization, and following the programming process, a designer can successfully create and execute good design. Remember it is critical to comprehend a design problem before pursuing solutions.

During the programming phase, a key factor that is always on the forefront of my design process is the client. When meeting with clients, try to pick up words they use to convey their business to clients. Try to speak their language when it comes to their business. The key words and catch phrases don't always come as directly as you would like, so the following skillset are inherent to develop in order to cultivate a true comprehension of a client's needs and wants.

- *"Parler leur langue" (speak their language)*: Veer from using design terminology and use the context (wording and phrases) your clients use.
- *Listen/scan proactively*: Reading between the lines is sometimes necessary to cultivate design signifiers that will be in alignment with your clients design objective.
- *Ask ancillary questions*: Clients will often disclose things about themselves and their businesses when speaking candidly about other topics.

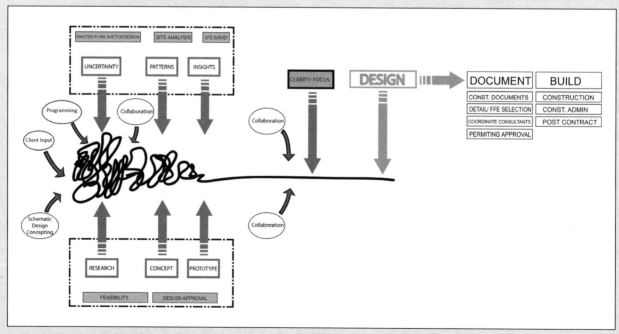

BOX FIGURE 3.2B Design process.

- *Understand your clients on a personable level*: The more you know them outside their business, the better you'll know their business. (Example: How does a residential client live in their particular space?)
- *Search for contextual words*: Words like luxe, economical, universal, and green are ideological words that express context about the client's brand. Take note of these words and process them to structure parti sketches. These words help me form the verbal concept for the design as well as prompting me in the direction of creating a parti.

What Is a Parti?

Parti (par·ti) [pahr-tee] is the basic or most true/primary foundation of a design solution. It is a scheme or variation of schemes that strengthens the foundation of a design idea. A foundation in which your thoughts go from pencil to paper or glue to foam-core/ chipboard. It could be a collage, a drawing, or a physical model, which helps a designer grasp what form a design [problem] wants to

take. Parti is a must have tool that designers need to master and possess in order to realize concise designs.

Figure 3.2c is a sketch exploring the parti for the retail client 344. Creating a strong base of design idea and theory through parti will allow your design to take shape and have a clear directive so it can be relayed to the project team. An idea of parti will fortify ideas, spatial guidelines, context, and conceptual elements. It offers variables and rules that take the project from concept to a complete design product solution.

Concept Visualization

At the completion of the parti phase, the design concept takes shape. It's the hypothesis of your design philosophy, thinking, and reasoning of how you solve the initial design problem. By developing a thoughtful concept (derived from parti), the decisions of color, shape, experience, and so on will take shape. This in turn will generate the design aesthetic and determine the overall direction of the project. For a successful resolution of the design

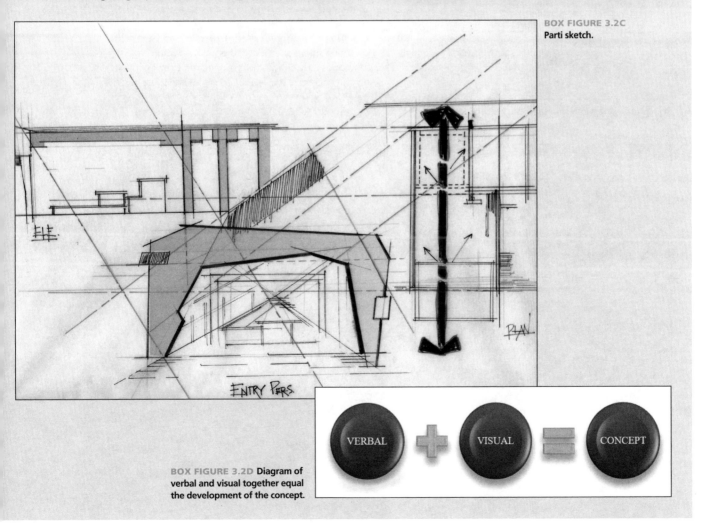

BOX FIGURE 3.2C
Parti sketch.

BOX FIGURE 3.2D Diagram of verbal and visual together equal the development of the concept.

(continued on next page)

BOX 3.2 DEVELOPING YOUR IDEA: PROFESSIONAL EXAMPLE *(cont.)*

problem, each decision made should relate back to the design concept. Creating a strong concept can be done in a combination of two ways: verbally and visually.

Verbal and concept statements are meant to concisely and quickly communicate the designers' method and style for a space to any variety of audience. The narrative should convey the designer's intent to develop a spatial experience within the space.

Concept Visualization & Typology

The visual components of a concept could be a particular image or color strategy. It could be a decision to utilize geometric patterns distinctly. Visual imagery concepts are usually more definite and are focused more on the method of communicating the design intent. Imagery should derive from the verbal statement of a concept.

BOX FIGURE 3.2E **Inspiration develops into a concept.**

Visual concepts are concentrated further on how to convey the design intent. Concept statements are developed prior to visual imagery because the images are developed to convey the concept.

Options and possible solutions for the problems are distilled from information and research gathered in the problem definition phase. This is the phase where a design proposal for the client is developed and structured. This is a critical stage for selling your ideas and thoughts as a design solution. If you are not in love with the ideas or can't explain/convey the design, there is a great risk of losing the client's support.

Typology is defined as the practice of representing things by symbols, or of investing things with a symbolic meaning or character. In terms of design, we begin to give shape to our conceptual ideas from the basis of our concept visions and statements. In a typology study, start creating a model or models that represent each word or feeling that was developed from the brainstorming process in parti. From the primary ideas, whether it's a color, shape or spatial feeling/experience, try to make a physical or digital model which represents the parti. This brings the concept into the realm of realization. The result can be an array of numerous versions of typology. The outcome of the typology study allows the designer to begin to distill (take certain characteristics from each type) each version and have a concentrated version of the typology models as seen in the image above 3.2g Typology drawing.

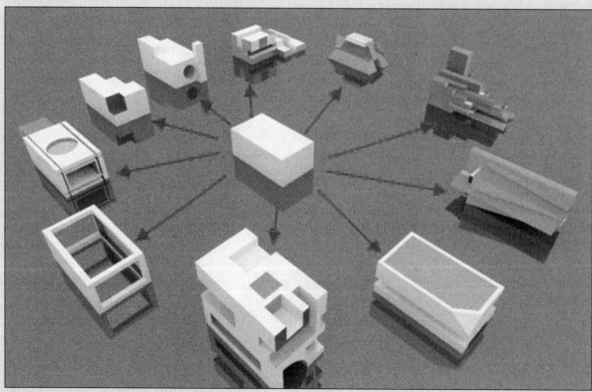

BOX FIGURE 3.2F **Typology: model & prototyping.**

Create or Make the Solution

Once the theoretical processes of parti, concepting, and typology have been completed, the step of actually creating something visual and tangible that a client/audience can comprehend is next. Try to take mental snap shots of all of the work that has been compiled and create a digital spatial model that incorporates each of the designs. Using 3D software (3DMax, SketchUp, AutoCAD, and Lumion) allows the designer to dissect the space and experience the spatial restraints, opportunities and values by visually experiencing the boundaries of the project. Not only will it help to understand the design problem but the end results of this investigative resolution produces visual material to even further market the design to the client. The process of taking parti and typology to construction document form is essential. The question to persistently ask while creating a floor plan, elevation, or section is, "Is it keeping true to the integrity and distilled 'pure' form of the parti and typology?" It can be very easy to stray away and lose initial design concepts to real world construction methods and practices. As a designer it is imperative to stay current with building/construction methods. Knowing how certain materials react when placed adjacent to each other, how to correctly detail attaching connections, and how to use standard construction practices allows

designers to "dream up" designs with fewer limitations. Sometimes clients don't know exactly what they want until a designer gives them a visual bench mark. Output from digital modeling, FFE mock boards, and several schematic options will all help narrow the focus and lead to design solutions. This phase can be time consuming if the client is indecisive, but it's easier to make changes in the virtual world. Presenting your design solutions with passion and vigor will help strengthen your proposal as well as give your client confidence in your design. Visual images help guide the client to understand the ideas and concepts.

Implementation

Ideas become reality! The problem has been identified, sketched, and modeled; the concept design and statement has been formalized; several design prototypes have been drawn, the design has been refined and a design resolution has been provided. Now all of these steps are implemented into a cohesive realized design package. During the production phase the key factor is SCHEDULE, SCHEDULE, SCHEDULE. This is applied to the acquisition of the production team and due date for deliverables (construction documents).

Below in Figure 3.2i is the completed 344 commercial retail store, at the North Shore Mall, Peabody, MA.

BOX FIGURE 3.2G **Rendering of 344 commercial retail store, North Shore Mall, Peabody, MA.**

BOX FIGURE 3.2H **Rendering of 344 commercial retail store, North Shore Mall, Peabody, MA.**

BOX FIGURE 3.2I **A photograph of the completed 344 commercial retail store, North Shore Mall, Peabody, MA.**

INTRODUCING YOUR PROGRAM

Once you have embarked on the topic of your choice, embrace it. Engross yourself in the subject. Discuss it with your professor, other faculty members, and classmates. Seek input from everyone, everywhere. Take the opportunity to conduct preliminary investigative research to evaluate the viability of your topic. This will provide vital information to help you outline your problem statement and its sub-problems. Remember to keep documenting the client and the user's preliminary needs of the space as you identify each one over the course of your research.

The student example in Box 3.3 documents the facts about the site and why they are important. The student then begins to tell us about the design problem as well as some of the design ideas.

When generating your own problem statement, consider the following:

- What am I aiming to accomplish?
- What is the location of the site?
- Who will be its users?
- What are my anticipated outcomes?

The introduction to your project should include the scope of the project and anticipated users of the space. It should also mention the actual space interior and exterior of its site location as well as the site location's size and conditions. You might also include the fiscal impact of the project and a historical perspective and the current and future impacts of the project.

Joan Riggs, ASID, IIDA, IDEC, CAPS, is an associate professor and the director of the Environmental + Interior Design program at Chaminade University of Honolulu. When teaching studio programming in the E+ID curriculum, Professor Riggs explains that "Programming is introduced in the lower division studio courses by way of its place and importance to the design effort and, largely through precedent study

exercises. Then as students advance to Programming & Space Planning, their first upper division studio course, the focus for the first third of the semester is Programming—information gathering about the client, the project location and the building/space itself. Toward this end, whenever possible, the semester project is a Service Learning project for a non-profit organization where students engage with an actual client with real needs. The resulting work has often been the catalyst for fundraising efforts as well as design inspiration for actual installations. Overall, studying the theory behind Programming, learning to use the tools associated with information gathering on a design project, and implementing the knowledge and skill sets gained, sets the foundation for methodical and creative problem-solving on any design project or in most any life situation. These skills are further employed/practiced in subsequent upper division studio courses."

Box 3.3 illustrates examples from Chaminade University students for a group project, designing the Oncology Play Area & Display Area at Kapiolani Medical Center for Women & Children. They provide clear examples of a client profile, concept statement, inspiration statement, and problem statement. The presentation boards demonstrate how all of the written information can be included as part of the design presentation.

Constraints and Limitations

It's important to also address any constraints or limitations that may exist. It could be as simple as having limited time, or access to the site. Environmental, legal, and economic constraints could also be addressed. It's important to address these upfront and understand the limitations of the proposed project. This will help in the long run and may even improve your creativity and problem-solving skills as you work through the project.

BOX 3.3 KAPIOLANI CHILDREN'S PLAY AREA + DISPLAY AREA

Priscilla Ong - May 2016
Bella Lei - May 2016
Gavin Steinhoff - May 2016
Kelsey Jones - Dec 2016

Chaminade University students, working for a group project, designed the Oncology Play Area & Display Area for Kapiolani Medical Center for Women & Children.

CLIENT PROFILE

In 1890, Queen Kapiolani founded a hospital to care for mothers and infants through their stages of growth and healing. More than a century later, this legacy of care still remains. Kapiolani Medical Center for Women and Children, located in Honolulu, Hawaii, has been dedicated to providing care for women and children in Hawaii and the Pacific Region for over one hundred years. Various services include maternity and newborn care, child life services, and women's services.

In the beginning of 2014, Kapiolani began new construction for the expansion of the Neonatal Intensive Care Unit (NICU) and Pediatric Intensive Care Unit (PICU). With the emergence of new technologies and healthcare models, Kapiolani continuously strives to provide exceptional care for their families. The oncology department, located in the existing building adjacent to the new construction, aims to reflect the same family-focused care for their patients.

Heather Tamaye is the lead child life specialist at the Kapiolani Women's and Children's Hospital. She currently oversees all child life services provided to patients. Coordinating with other specialists, health professionals, and volunteers, they assist children in coping with their treatment and hospital stay through education, special activities, and play.

Although it is located in the oncology department, the playroom is open for all children staying at the hospital. In the new design of the play space, the objective is to create an area designed to serve all end users and better address their needs:

1. provide an area for administrative activities
2. integrate interactive and educational activities
3. improve outdoor conditions to include more group activities
4. receive visitors
5. maximize storage using minimal space

The end users of this space will be:

- Staff, including specialists, physicians and caregivers, and volunteers
- Patients
  - age ranges from infant to twenty-six years old
  - medically cleared patients (noncontagious, no low stimulation, no active seizures, suctioning or oxygen)
- Parents/families
- Therapists, including therapy dogs (i.e., Tucker), musicians, and other special guests (i.e., Mickey and Minnie)

Down the hall between the children's oncology department and the cafeteria is a dedicated display area. Here visitors and staff are able to view children's artwork, their families' artwork, and sometimes donated artwork from the community. The display area is located in the hospital's main circulation hall; therefore, the work displayed will be viewable by all members of the community who pass by. It is important for this area to be designed to reflect the healing spirit behind the staff, patients, and the families who participate in the healing work of this department.

By dedicating spaces for each end user and improving current conditions, Heather and her team are able to provide recreation and respite for children and their families during hospitalization. Volunteers, visitors, and special guests from the community will also be able to utilize the space during their visit.

As designers, we have been given the responsibility of redesigning and renovating these two spaces to meet the needs and requirements of our client. Implementing a more open play space, creative storage solutions, and an efficient office layout are part of the overall vision for this project. The design of an inspirational, fun, and healing space will enhance the lives of the patients, their families, and the medical professionals who care for them.

CONCEPT STATEMENT

The objective of the redesign is to create an inviting environment where kids can be expressive, unrestricted (as much as possible), and curious. The theme of the indoor space to the "outdoor" space is tied together with organic lines, textures, and colors pulled from a kalo patch and nature. By contrasting the ordinary indoor play room to the unconventional outdoor space, users walking through will feel a progression of awe and wonderment.

When the children enter the "outdoor" play space, they will feel as if they were a part of a kalo patch as they walk under giant kalo leaves. Implementation of glass ceilings and the translucent leaves will allow light to penetrate through into the space, simulating the sense of looking up from under the leaves. The oversized proportions of the interior structural element and furnishings encourages the children to interact and explore their environment.

In the main hallway of the hospital is a display area where passersby can view artwork made by Kapiolani's patients. The shape of the display grid mimics the horizontal lines found on the kalo roots. The suspended ceiling design reflects how the kalo root fibers connect the kalo to the ground, bringing nutrients to the plant, just as the hospital is the nourishment to the patients' spirits.

(continued on next page)

BOX 3.3 KAPIOLANI CHILDREN'S PLAY AREA + DISPLAY AREA (cont.)

INSPIRATION STATEMENT

The Kapiolani Medical Center for Women and Children has been caring for families for over a century. The inspiration for the redesign of the Kapiolani children's oncology play area and display space is based on the representational and functional components of the taro patch (lo'i) and the taro plant. As the stream flowing into the taro patch, Kapiolani provides sustenance to its patients through state-of-the-art technology and collaboration of its leaders and medical staff.

In a taro patch, rainwater from the mountains fills the lo'i and provides the optimal conditions needed for the taro plant to thrive. The water in the lo'i symbolizes the redesign of the children's play area and the relating second floor display area near the cafeteria. The lo'i represents the hospital, in that it provides an environment that fosters optimal health for its patients. Taro plants in the lo'i also symbolize the families who are an integral component to the children's recovery and restoration to optimum health.

The kalo (taro plant) is representative of the patients—women and children—at Kapiolani Medical Center. The heart-shaped kalo leaf symbolizes the loving bond between children and their families, staff and their patients. The point where stem and the leaf meet symbolizes the piko (navel), which represents the connection between a mother and the life in her womb. The stem symbolizes ha (breath), which represents the birth of a child. The cluster of shoots symbolizes the keiki (children) of Kapiolani Medical Center, which surround the mother plant creating an ohana (family). The root symbolizes the foundation of the family at large.

The display space, located in the main corridor of the second floor, is a representation of the kalo root. To the native Hawaiians, the kalo root is revered and used during celebratory gatherings and rituals, which, overall, support the relationship of ohana (family). Due to the kalo's sacredness, the natives consume only small amounts at a given time, providing nourishment to the community. The majority of kalo consumption occurs during special gatherings. In a similar manner, the display space is intended to be a small gathering area for passersby to view the artwork made by Kapiolani's patients. The emphasis of nature as the overall theme creates a magical setting that is therapeutic for patients, their families, and staff.

PROBLEM STATEMENT

Function
- Due to the intensity of treatment, the design should incorporate areas of respite that are relaxing and stimulating for the variety of users.
- Because of the use of multiple mobility devices and medical equipment, the circulation of the space is critical to optimum use of the space.

- *Because many patients are confined to the hospital setting, simulation of the outdoor environment will enhance their mood and productivity.*
- Because the well-being of patients and their families are a main concern for the hospital, fixtures, furnishings, and equipment must be easy to maintain for sanitary and hygienic purposes.

Form
- Because the Kapiolani children's oncology playroom is located adjacent to a freeway and ongoing construction, the space must consider barriers against noise and debris exposure, as most patients have compromised immune systems.
- Recognizing budget restrictions and pending future plans for the center, renovations will be limited to the existing structure.
- *Because of Hawaii's warm tropical weather with favorable tradewinds, the building can implement passive and active cooling systems.*
- The space is used by toddlers to teens? therefore the design should reflect the user demographic.

Economy
- As the funding amount and sources are pending ($50,000.00 min. budget), it will be important to make cost-conscious decisions in all areas of the project.
- Because of rising operational costs, efficient design and sustainable features will be considered for implementation.
- Material selection should be durable to maximize the life of the products.

Time
- Because part of the renovation project is state funded, a design proposal should be finalized as soon as possible to have construction completed for occupation by 2016.
- Conceptual design package is due to the client by May 7, 2015.
- Because the playroom will still be operable during and after the new NICU and PICU building, the space is expected to be in use for a minimum of five years.

The italicized statements were developed from the initial project information provided by Heather Tamaye, Kapiolani's lead child life specialist, during the students' first visit with her.

Then as a result of students doing background research, precedent studies, and a couple of site visits to other children's play spaces (e.g., Shriner's Hospital for Children), the students developed additional statements for each of the categories function, form, economy, and time.

The students had a follow up meeting with the staff at Kapiolani to discuss the project and provide better focus and understanding of the problems/challenges.

Professor Riggs, explains that when analyzed, the statements are able to *guide* the design process. There are still no solutions—but good guidance—so the students/designers can be creative in how they solve the identified problems. This then, speaks to the statements regarding the circular nature of programming and revisiting the problem statement as the project progresses, both for refining as information is gained and as a checklist for the design solutions.

BOARD 1
Loʻi

The design for the Kapiolani Medical Center for Women and Children's Oncology play area and display space is based on the representational and functional components of the taro patch (loʻi) and the taro plant. In a taro patch, rainwater from the mountains fills the loʻi and provides the optimal conditions needed for the taro plant to thrive. As the stream flows into the taro patch, it nourishes and provides sustenance to the community.

With the same intention, Puʻuwai Oʻ Kaleʻa ("heart of joy") and Puʻuwai Oʻ Kaʻaina ("heart of the land") foster healing, growth, joy, and community. With the use of natural finish materials; patterns, textures, and motifs inspired by the loʻi; and a color palette inspired by nature, an inviting environment is created where patients or guests can be expressive, unrestricted (as much as possible), and curious. The design of Puʻuwai Oʻ Kaleʻa and Puʻuwai Oʻ Kaʻaina expresses the various attributes of the taro plant in a way that improves the well-being of guests, patients, and staff.

BOX FIGURE 3.3A **Taro leaf (left).**

BOX FIGURE 3.3B **Kapiolani play space floor plan (below).**

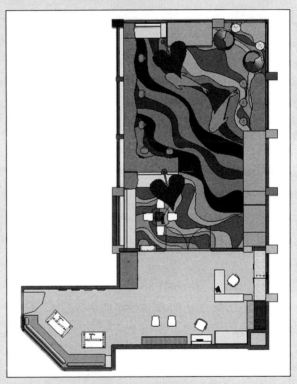

BOX FIGURE 3.3C **Outdoor play space.**

(continued on next page)

BOX 3.3 KAPIOLANI CHILDREN'S PLAY AREA + DISPLAY AREA *(cont.)*

BOX FIGURE 3.3D **Entrance hallway.**

BOX FIGURE 3.3E **Creative space.**

BOX FIGURE 3.3F **Office space.**

Pu'uwai O' Kale'a
Heart of Joy
Pu'uwai O' Kale'a houses a small office area for several staff members who oversee the oncology department's patient rooms and play area. Upon entering the space, guests are greeted by a wall of frames with interchangeable artwork made by the patients in the playroom. This area provides a more comfortable space where patients can be creative and relax indoors. Open sight lines from the office area to the entrance and outdoor play space give staff the ability to supervise children's activities with confidence. Soft earth tones in the finishes mimic the natural landscape of the lo'i, while the light finishes brighten up the overall space.

BOARD 2
Pu'uwai O' Ka'aina
Heart of the Land
Pu'uwai O' Ka'aina is a small gathering area for passersby to view artwork made by Kapiolani's patients. Inspired by the kalo root, the shape of the display grid mimics the horizontal lines on the kalo root. The suspended structure above represent the root's fibers that connect the kalo to the ground. The structure branches from the display soffit and connects to the existing "Wall of Hope." The placement of the mural in the background is intended for children passing by in strollers to feel as if they are passing through a kalo patch.

The oversized kalo evokes a sense of being in a lo'i, while the glass roof and floor-to-ceiling windows open and brighten the space with ample daylight to simulate an outdoor experience. Children are able to interact with the oversized foam fish ottoman, observe the real fish in the aquaponics tank, tend to the plants, and write on the whiteboard cabinet doors. Curvilinear patterns and colors on the floor mimic the water that runs through the lo'i, creating a fun and interactive play space throughout the play area.

BOX FIGURE 3.3G
Kalo root.

BOX FIGURE 3.3H **Display area.**

BOX FIGURE 3.3I **Outdoor play area.**

BOX FIGURE 3.3J **Private seating area.**

Zoned areas within the space allow for specific activities to occur. The reading nook is flanked with a bookshelf and provides private seating area for more intimate conversations. Integrated outlets and data ports are available for more personal alone time and recharging. Bench seating surrounding the aquaponics tank allows for full visibility of the system, and the toddler's table is positioned for convenient supervision.

A variety of customized storage solutions ensure that all toys are kept organized and within safe and manageable reach range for both children and adults.

Refer to Appendix D to view the presentation boards 1 & 2 in their original presentation format incorporating the "statement" information in the context of the presentation—Kapiolani Chaminade University students for a group project, designing the Oncology Play Area & Display Area for Kapiolani Medical Center for Women & Children.

BOX FIGURE 3.3K **Exterior play area—day.**

BOX FIGURE 3.3L **Exterior play area—night.**

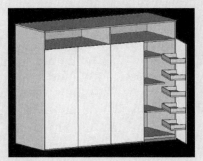

BOX FIGURE 3.3M **Custom cabinet detail.**

Organizing the Project

The last section of chapter should introduce the organization of the overall project. A simple outline of what will be included in each chapter is extremely advantageous to add. This is helpful to the reader and is a good time management tool, preventing overlap and creating a clear path to the completion of the programming document.

KEY TERMS

- Aging in place
- Anthropometry/anthropometrics
- Barrier-free design
- Concept statement
- Environmental behavior
- Ergonomics
- Facilities planning
- Green/sustainable design
- Healthcare design
- Historic preservation and restoration
- Human factors
- Lighting design
- Museum and exhibit design
- Parti
- Problem statement
- Programming document
- Thesis statement
- Topic
- Universal design
- Way-finding methods

CHAPTER 4

Research Methods

After reading this chapter, you should be able to:

- Describe different research methods.
- Explain the varying degrees of reliability and validity of different research methods and how different methods are more appropriate for different projects.
- Recognize which method would work best for your design project.

As designers, most of us are visual thinkers. How we analyze data is personal, reflecting our level of interest in what we see and how and where we intend to apply our observations. There are at least as many different approaches to a project as there are designers; however, a few basic modes of research can serve every designer equally.

This chapter provides an overview of research methods, encompassing both quantitative and qualitative methods as well as the two combined, which is referred to as a **mixed method approach**. As a researcher, you may choose to employ any of these modes. The intent of this chapter is to show how you can easily apply them in your own

work. While these research methodologies may sound daunting at first, most of these practices become easy with experience. Then, in Chapter 5, "Historical, Observational, and Interactive Research," we will see how the research methods directly apply to interior design.

As you read this chapter, you need to think as a student, as a designer, as a researcher, and as a programmer—all at the same time. As a professional designer, you will be applying the same multipurpose approach. This chapter shows how all of these roles fit neatly—and, with practice, easily—into the job requirements of one person.

There is a fine line where researcher becomes programmer, and then programmer becomes designer. As a student, you need to engage in each activity mindful that you are also going to facilitate the program and design. Taking on all these roles will be expected of you when you enter the profession. As a designer/researcher/programmer you will be engaging in Evidence-based design (EBD)—looking at the evidence, analyzing it, and basing your design decisions on your findings. Mastering research skills and techniques is extremely valuable for a designer.

INTRODUCTION TO RESEARCH

The intent of this chapter is to provide you with a foundation in research methodology, as it relates to collecting data, and to analyzing and documenting your findings. As you take up these tools and begin to practice using them, choose the method or methods that meet your own level of comfort or are best suited for the information available. In this way, you'll build expertise and eventually find yourself engaging the methodology that best suits any given project naturally.

Qualitative? Quantitative? Mixed Method?

How do you choose the one that's right for you? How do you even begin to understand what they mean and how to apply them to interior design? The term "research methods" alone may certainly make you nervous. But the truth is that the research methods described below run parallel to normal practices that you are accustomed to using in your everyday life and are well familiar to you; here, you will be introduced to the formal terminology for research skills you use informally all the time.

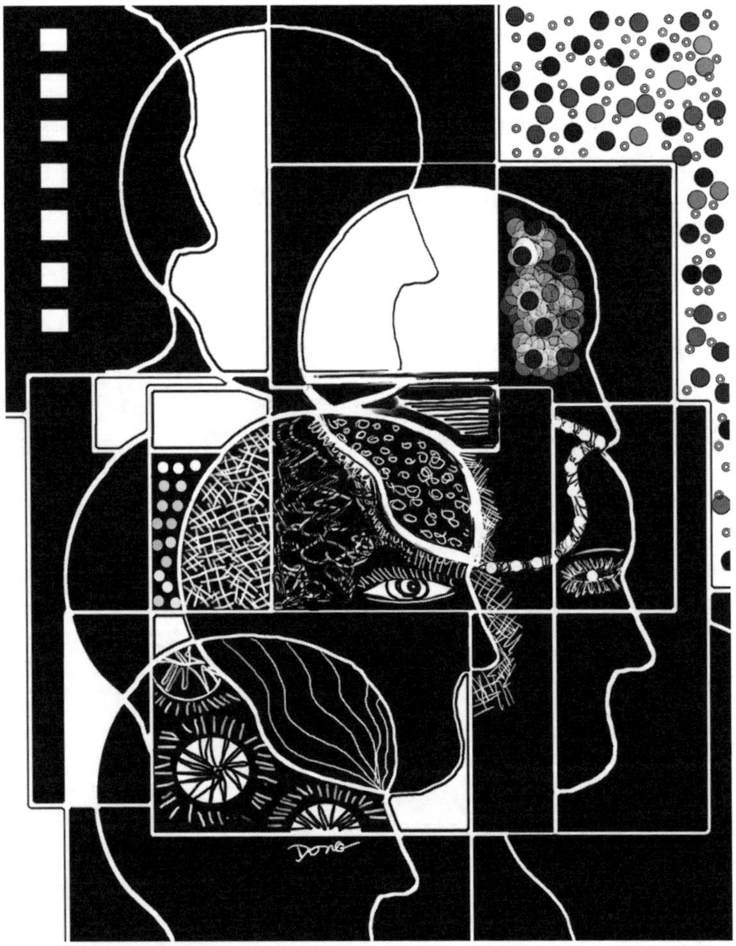

For this chapter (and the book as a whole), numerous sources supplied insight into the research methods discussed. You might consider adding them to your personal reference list. One book you might consider purchasing, for example, is *An Introduction to Educational Research*, by Meredith D. Gall, Walter R. Borg, and Joyce P. Gall. Also, there are numerous texts written by John W. Creswell, Ph.D., who is the Clifton Institute Professor of Educational Psychology at the University of Nebraska-Lincoln. Creswell specializes in research methods, and he writes, teaches, and conducts research about mixed method research, qualitative research, and research designs. At Nebraska, he co-directs the Office of Qualitative and Mixed Methods Research, a service/research unit providing methodological support for proposal development and funded projects. Included in the references for this chapter are not only text citations but also some very helpful websites. Be sure to also browse through the Resources appendix and Appendix J at the back of this book.

Qualitative Research

Qualitative research methods were developed in the social sciences for researchers to study social and cultural experiences. Gall, Borg, and Gall offer the following definition:

> Qualitative research or post-positivist research [is] the inquiry that is grounded in the assumption that

FIGURE 4.1 Researcher, programmer, designer—all three roles fit neatly into your job as interior designer.

individuals construct social reality in the form of meaning and interpretations, and that these constructs tend to be transitory and situational. The dominant methodology is to discover these meanings and interpretations by studying case intensively in natural settings and by subjecting the resulting data to analytic induction. (p. 767)

Following are some examples of qualitative methods that can be easily applied to the interior design discipline:

- **Action research** is a focused effort to find a solution to improve the quality of an organization or group and its performance in its particular setting. In many cases, educators or practitioners who analyze the data to improve the outcomes carry out action research.
- **Case study research** is an in-depth study of an instance, event, or situation; in short, a case. When you look at more than one instance to document and compare the findings, it's called comparative case study research. When looking at the case studies, you may begin to identify emerging themes.
- **Ethnography** is observation in the field of a group in its natural setting. It is important to record as much as possible in the setting being studied. This can be extremely helpful when researching the layout of classroom and educational facilities to understand, for example, how students and teachers interact.

Sometimes it is hard to read about a type of research method and think of how or when you might apply it. A good example is Christina Gedick, a graduate student at Mount Ida College who had the opportunity to participate in a service learning alternative spring break trip to South Dakota. This experience changed her enormously,

inspiring her choice of thesis project: an ethnographic study entitled "Pallet House: An Adequate Living Solution for the Native America Reservations" seen in Box 4.1. Her ethnographic observations paint a picture of her experience and support her argument for the necessity of new housing solutions.

Qualitative Data

Qualitative data sources include observation and participant observation, interviews and questionnaires, documents and texts, and the researcher's impressions and reactions (Creswell, 1998, p. 15).

Quantitative Research

Quantitative research methods were originally developed in the natural sciences to study natural observable facts. Following are some examples of quantitative methods accepted in the social sciences:

- **Survey methods** are commonly used in business, educational, healthcare, and government settings. Surveys are implemented to retain an abundance of information based on the research topic.
- **Laboratory experiments** can include observation that employs statistical techniques. The selection of a sample group can vary from specific to random.
- **Formal and numerical methods** include the testing of a specific group using statistical methods to analyze the data.

Gall, Borg, and Gall offer the following definition:

Quantitative research or positivist research [is] the inquiry that is grounded in the assumption that features of the social environment constitute an objective reality that is relatively constant across time and settings. The

BOX 4.1 MOUNT IDA COLLEGE STUDENT CHRISTINA GEDICK STUDENT EXAMPLE: ETHNOGRAPHY RESEARCH DURING A SERVICE TRIP TO DUPREE, SOUTH DAKOTA, LAKOTA SIOUX TRIBE

The inspiration behind this design thesis is derived from a recent service trip to South Dakota, which greatly impacted the author's outlook on life. Many previously undiscovered topics that were observed during this service trip to South Dakota led the author to one single conclusion: the Lakota Sioux tribe, along with many others living on Native American reservations, live in less than acceptable conditions.

Ethnographic Observation

Educational Research: An Introduction, Sixth Edition defines a thick description, also known as ethnographic observation: "In qualitative research, a richly detailed report that re-creates a situation and as much of its context as possible, along with the meanings and intentions inherent in that situation" (Gall, Borg, & Gall, 1996). The following is a thick description of the service trip to South Dakota that took place from March 8th to March 16th, 2014:

Although I did not quite know what to expect when traveling to a Native American reservation for the first time, I partially expected to be culture shocked. I had studied Native Americans throughout my entire education, but I believe that a person can truly never understand a community to its full extent without visiting and experiencing it first-hand. I was told before going on this service trip to expect to either be ignored or teased by the Native American children on the Lakota Sioux reservation, and to be treated more coldly by the adults than the average American. This brought a sense of anxiety before traveling to South Dakota from Boston.

BOX FIGURE 4.1B **View of the plains of South Dakota.**

We drove for hundreds of miles across the plains of South Dakota only to realize the scenery would not change. The contrast between flat prairies and hilly mountainous terrain was constant, as was the view of livestock and cows. Signs for far away store locations occasionally passed by, but there was not much else to look at out the car window besides an occasional tree or bush. Miles and hours passed until we finally approached the reservation that we were staying on for the week. We drove off the paved road onto an extremely dusty dirt road.

The very first sight that I saw as we were nearing the entrance of the reservation was a tepee. Although I had previously learned that most of the residents have moved beyond tepees and now currently live in homes or trailers, the reality struck me that tepee used to be their way of life before they were displaced and taken over by the Americans. Immediately I felt a feeling of sympathy for the culture.

As we drove through the reservation to the YMCA building, I noticed a lot of the houses/mobile homes looked run down. Some had trash and junk laying around, some seemed to be falling apart. On the contrary, some were quite nice and petite. I also noticed two very small children standing on the side of the road, wide eyed and without parental supervision. They watched our shiny and relatively new van slowly drive down the road. The cars parked at the houses, which were few, seemed to be older models with rot.

When we arrived at the YMCA, we unpacked our bags and walked inside the nicely painted building. It was a log cabin style that had murals of Native American culture

BOX FIGURE 4.1A **Dupree, South Dakota, "Beware of Rattlesnake" sign.**

BOX FIGURE 4.1C **View of a tepee at the entrance of the Lakota Sioux tribe.**

painted on the sides. On the inside, it smelt slightly musty but had a welcoming sensation to it. There stood three staff members awaiting our arrival. They were not Native Americans, but they worked and lived on the reservation. They informed us that soon the children would be arriving from school, and that we should prepare ourselves to meet them. As soon as the words were out of their mouths, the children ran in the front door and the feeling of anxiety and fear slowly crept across our group.

To all of our surprise, the children came inside and asked us if we wanted to play kickball. As we were walking out to the field, a little girl not more than five years old grabbed my hand and continued to walk with me to the field. A feeling of relief filled my heart and mind. I also felt sympathy for this girl because she felt comfortable enough to grab a stranger's hand. That was an unusual thing to see.

As the week went on and our knowledge grew of the Native American culture, it became more and more apparent that the people we met did not want to be helped; they just want to be understood. They want us to know that despite all that was taken away from them they are still prideful of what they have. One Lakota man showed us how he carves animal bones into jewelry and sells them to make a living. He took the time out of his day to show us how he lives his life, and as wonderful as it was, it was deeply saddening.

I realized that Native Americans do not know the joy of going to the movie theatres. They don't browse Facebook on their cell phones when they're bored. They don't go shopping in a mall or ride roller coasters in an amusement park. Native American tribes go to school if they're lucky, get a job if they're lucky, and survive alcoholism, drug abuse, and suicide if they're lucky. Hearing one man talk about the suicide rates of children under ten years old hit home the most. What is so terrible about reservations that make children less than ten years old believe that there is no possibility of their life getting any better? It all came down to one thing; the living conditions. Native American reservations need better living conditions.

BOX FIGURE 4.1D **YMCA Lakota Sioux tribe.**

BOX 4.2 STUDENT EXAMPLE OF A LABORATORY EXPERIMENT: CAITLIN J. DAVIS HEALING THROUGH HOLISTIC DESIGN

WEDNESDAY, JULY 20, 2011—"HEALING THROUGH HOLISTIC DESIGN ROOM STUDY"

Natural lighting, natural ventilation, and nature-related images have been tied to positive psychological effects on patient healing. The purpose of this study is to prove that people respond around natural light and other healing, holistic elements, assessing that a person's productivity is greater in a more healing environment.

The Location

The participants will be asked to spend approximately seven minutes in two differently designed/staged rooms. The first room will have no windows, no artwork, and no other natural elements. The second room will have big windows, artwork, plants, music, and aromatherapy. In each room the participants will be asked to observe their surroundings, record their observations, and answer five simple questions (recording the time it took to finish the questions). Also, the participants' heart rates will be recorded after four minutes have elapsed in each room. This study will take approximately fifteen minutes in its entirety—seven minutes over two sessions (one session meaning one room) with a one minute break in between.

Risk Factors

The study has minimal risks. First, there is the risk of feeling too constrained or enclosed from spending time in Room One. Second, there is the risk of allergies to certain smells. Both risks are very minimal and unlikely, but the participants did inform the researcher of any aroma-type allergies or any concerns they had regarding Room One beforehand. The benefits of participation are becoming relaxed and stimulated from the healing characteristics of Room Two.

Process

The study was conducted in the order of the steps listed below:

1. Get approval for project from the college internal review board.
2. Select the participants.
3. Select the appropriate rooms for the study (there will be a total of two rooms).
4. Select the most appropriate settings for each room (a room with operable windows and natural lighting, and a room with no windows).
5. Set the controls for each room.

6. Participants will have their blood pressure and pulse taken during their time in each room (approximately four minutes after entering the room).
7. Each participant will start in the room with no windows and artificial light, and then they will move onto the room with operable windows and natural lighting and ventilation.
8. Each participant will spend seven minutes in each room, with a one minute break in between. While in the room, participants will be asked to sit for seven minutes and observe their surroundings while answering simple questions on paper.
9. As described above, the participants will take notes and answer questions during their time in each room, to see how their overall attitude has changed.
10. During each participant's stay in the rooms, their heart rate/pulse and blood pressure will be monitored.

Setting

Room One and Room Two went through mild transitions for this study. Figures 4.2e and figure 4.2f depict Room One before the artwork was taken down—Room One needed to be cleared of all artwork and objects that would add personality or interest to the room. Room One was meant to be plain, sterile, and clean. Room Two was organized but kept the character of the original occupant—the room was already nicely painted and had unique artwork and plant life. Additional artwork and plant life was added, as well as music, and aromatherapy in sandalwood scent.

BOX FIGURE 4.2A **Room Two—Selected for the experiment.**

BOX FIGURE 4.2B **Room Two—Selected for the experiment.**

BOX FIGURE 4.2C **Room Two—Participants in the experiment will sit at the table.**

BOX FIGURE 4.2D **Room Two—Table with art, plants, and aromatherapy features.**

BOX FIGURE 4.2E **Room One—Selected for the experiment, with no natural light, plants.**

Once each room was set up, the participants began the study—recording every observation they had while in the rooms. Examining the after pictures of both rooms, one can see the difference in lighting, color, artwork, plant life, and any other form of stimulation. Room One was sterile; the only light source was the fluorescent bulb on the wall and the recessed fluorescent light in the ceiling. Both rooms were close in size; the participants were asked to sit at the desk depicted in figure 4.2e and sit at the small table shown in figure 4.2d. In Room Two, carefully positioned healing elements, meant to heighten the senses while the patient was in the room, were placed on the table where the participants' sat. Figure 4.2d shows the art pieces that were added for intrigue and stimulation in Room Two.

BOX FIGURE 4.2F **Room One— Modified for the experiment, all artwork removed.** Photos Taken by Caitlin Davis.

(continued on next page)

BOX 4.2 STUDENT EXAMPLE OF A LABORATORY EXPERIMENT: CAITLIN J. DAVIS HEALING THROUGH HOLISTIC DESIGN *(cont.)*

Findings

After the study was complete, the responses recorded in each room were read; the responses and reactions of each room were interesting. First observing only the amount of text on the page, it appears the participants wrote more words on their question sheet while in Room Two compared to Room One. Participant One is quoted with saying that they felt they were able to write more in Room Two, and wanted to take more time to write. From the recorded time, it shows that Participant One took more time to answer the questions in Room Two than they did in Room One. After reading through the questions sheets from each participant, in Room Two the participants answered in more detail; in Room One many of the answers were "one-word" answers. Participant Two stated that they started the study with a mild headache, which stayed while they were in Room One; this participant was quoted with saying that after spending a few minutes in Room Two their headache had completely disappeared.

There were a series of follow-up questions that were asked of the participants, based on the responses that the researcher received from each participant during the study.

1. During each participant's stay in the rooms, their heart rate/pulse and blood pressure will be monitored, the participants in Room One had no change in their heart rate/pulse or blood pressure. Compared to participants in Room Two who experienced an overall 5 percent increase in their rate/pulse signs at the end of the experiment.

2. After compiling the follow-up data, a graph was created that reflected the particular answers from the question, "When you are relaxing or healing from an injury, which of these options would keep your mind off the injury or help you to recover quicker?" Interestingly, the researcher thought that both natural light and views would be the most important or selected options, when in fact that was not the case; as seen in Table 1, natural light was not selected. The participants found that soft and comfortable textures/materials would be more beneficial.

Natural lighting and ventilation can be designed within a patient's room to promote healing, which was mentioned in the Evidence-based design research presented in the prior section. To reiterate the words of evidence-based design professional Patricia Malick, "We know that from evidence-based design research that color, light, access to nature and control over one's environment improves clinical outcomes and promotes a sense of calm." Nature-inspired colors and textures can complement a space quite nicely. The research gathered in the study coincides perfectly with the historical research regarding evidence-based design; people are profoundly attracted to nature, views of nature, and textures.

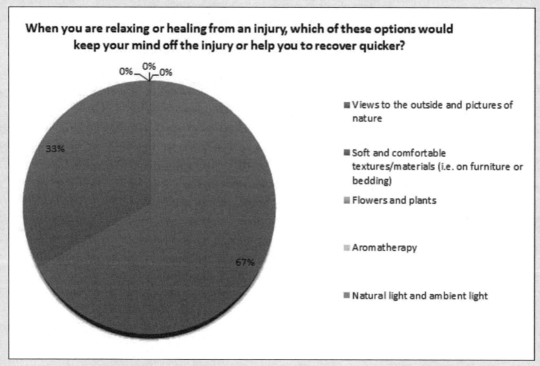

BOX FIGURE 4.2G Response results to question asked of participants/patients.

dominant methodology is to describe and explain features of this reality by collecting numerical data on observational behaviors of samples and by subjecting these data to statistical analysis. (p. 768)

Quantitative Data

While qualitative data is the descriptive, personal data observed and gathered by the researcher of impressions and reactions, quantitative data, on the other hand, is the numerical information that the researcher charts and/or graphs to represent the **statistics** of that research.

Mixed Method Research

Combining qualitative and quantitative techniques within a single research design represents a methodological union between two different research traditions. A mixed method research process is defined by Creswell:

A mixed method approach is one in which the researcher tends to base knowledge claims on pragmatic grounds (e.g., consequence-oriented, problem-centered, and pluralistic). It employs strategies of inquiry that involve collecting data either simultaneously or sequentially to best understand research problems. The data collection also involves gathering numeric information (e.g., on instruments) as well as text information (e.g., on interviews) so that the final database represents both quantitative and qualitative information. (p. 20)

For the mixed method researcher, Creswell suggests that "pragmatism opens the door to multiple methods, different worldviews, and different assumptions, as well as to different forms of data collection and analysis in the mixed methods study" (Creswell, 2003, p. 12). Table 4.1, developed by Creswell, outlines strategies of inquiry.

To help situate and validate findings within a mixed method approach, Gall, Borg, and Gall refer to a **triangulation** process of using multiple data collection methods. They state that it helps to eliminate biases that might result from relying exclusively on any one data collection method, source, analyst, or theory (p. 575). Simply put, you, the student/researcher/designer, should select a professional array of sources from both sides of any argument. This way, you can formulate your own opinion based on and supported by cited information.

TABLE 4.1 ALTERNATIVE STRATEGIES OF INQUIRY

INQUIRY METHOD	APPLICATIONS
Quantitative	• Experimental designs • Nonexperimental designs, such as surveys
Qualitative	• Phenomenologies • Ethnographies • Grounded theory • Case studies
Mixed Methods	• Sequential • Concurrent • Transformative

Adapted from *Research Design Quantitative, Qualitative and Mixed Methods* by J. Creswell, 2003, p. 13.

Promoting Patient Well-Being for Veteran Inpatients
Through the Use of Interior Design Strategies

Project   Problem   History   Research   Recommendation   Contact

Observational Research

Interviews

Questionnaire

Observational Research   Interviews   Questionnaire

FIGURE 4.2
**Mount Ida College
graduate student
outlining her research
that employed a
triangulation process.**

Figure 4.2 is from Aprilyn Arca's graduate work entitled Promoting Patient Well-Being for Veteran Inpatients Through the Use of Interior Design Strategies. She conducted three different data collection methods: observational research, interviews, and a questionnaire. Her varied approach using a multimethod approach is the triangulation process.

RELIABILITY AND VALIDITY: YOUR METHOD-CHOOSING GOAL

Our goal in defining various research methods is to ensure that the methods selected are sound and demonstrate **reliability** and **validity**. Reliability is an important concept that is defined in terms of its application to a wide range of activities. In identifying key methods and creating a project outline, the hope is that the experiments and tests would yield the same result on repeated trials. According to William Trochims (2006) of The

Research Methods Knowledge Base, there are four key types of reliability estimates, each of which estimates reliability in a different way:

- **Inter-Rater or Inter-Observer Reliability**—Used to assess the degree to which different raters/observers give consistent estimates of the same phenomenon
- **Test-Retest Reliability**—Used to assess the consistency of a measure from one time to another
- **Parallel-Forms Reliability**—Used to assess the consistency of the results of two tests constructed in the same way from the same content domain
- **Internal Consistency Reliability**—Used to assess the consistency of results across items within a test

Validity is important because a study needs to be truthful and objective. When research is valid, it accurately reflects and assesses the specific concept being measured. While reliability is concerned with the accuracy of the actual measuring instrument or procedure, validity is concerned with the study's success at measuring what it set out to measure. Suppose, for example, a student designer plans to create an office space. Through extensive research, the student finds various reliable sources supporting the concept that ergonomic considerations are key to a successful office design. It is at this point that the student can personalize the research by citing specific information supporting and validating that concept.

Applying Qualitative Research

There are numerous research methods you might choose to employ a qualitative study. However, we will focus here on **case study** and **observational research** because of their natural application to the field of interior design.

Qualitative Case Study Research

Case studies are a standard form of research, and they include multiple methods and approaches. Case studies typically examine all facets of an experience in order to provide a complete understanding of what is being studied. Often the term "precedent study" will replace "case study" within the design field; however, the two are different. A case study is a qualitative form of research that aims to provide in-depth documentation of a single experience, situation, or condition. These formal studies are often used in the medical profession and business schools. Harvard University is famous for its business case studies. A **precedent study**, on the other hand, focuses on one specific type of design and compares a group of similar previous examples. These examples can be in the form of individual case studies. As it relates to interior design, a precedent study could include similar retail, educational,

or healthcare spaces in different locations. The researcher compiles a list of attributes to compare from each example in order to assess which might best contribute to a successful new design. As a student in the field, you are often asked to analyze precedent studies prior to starting a design project. Chapter 7, "Precedent Studies," discusses these studies further.

Categories of Case Studies

There are many types of case studies. The researcher needs to carefully select the appropriate one depending upon the goals and/or objectives of the project (Clandinin, 1994). The categories of case study include the following:

- **Cumulative case studies** combine information from different locations collected at different times that bring together findings from many case studies. The goal is to answer an evaluation question, whether descriptive, normative, or cause-and-effect.
- **Critical instance case studies** examine one or more sites for either the purpose of examining a situation of unique interest with little to no interest in generalization-ability, or to call into question or challenge a highly generalized or universal assertion. This method is useful for answering cause-and-effect questions.
- **Exploratory case studies** are descriptive and condensed. Sometimes referred to as pilot studies, researchers perform them before implementing large-scale studies.
- **Illustrative case studies** are descriptive in character and intended to add realism and in-depth examples to other information about a program or policy.
- **Program implementation** investigates operations, often at several sites and normatively.

- **Program effects** use the case study to examine causality and usually involve multisite, multimethod assessments.

(CSU Writing Guide, 2002, Reliability and Validity, ¶5)

Thick Description and Thin Description

When writing case studies or observational research, two modes of description are commonly used: **thick description** and **thin description**. Thick description is a process used to give an in-depth account of the study being evaluated (Lincoln & Guba, 1985, p. 363). A thick description details characteristics of the people involved and the nature of the community and/or setting where the case study is being conducted (p. 363). In the field of design, thick description is frequently used within the context of qualitative research and naturalistic inquiry.

Thin descriptions, in contrast, outline the facts with limited storytelling experience of inquiry (Lincoln & Guba, 1985, p.363): the facts are stated with little or no elaboration.

Pilot Studies

Pilot studies, by definition, are condensed case studies performed prior to implementing a large-scale investigation. Many researchers perform pilot studies first in order to fine-tune and focus the scope of their research problem. Valerie J. Janesick points out, "[B]efore devoting oneself to the arduous and significant time commitment of a qualitative study, it is a good idea to do a pilot study ... [T]he pilot study allows the researcher to focus on particular areas that may have been unclear previously" (1994, p. 213).

In fact, before a pilot study is launched, exploratory or field test studies are highly advisable. You might think of these as the *pre-pilot* study. Such smaller exploratory studies allow you to develop relationships to pursue in a pilot study in the same way that the pilot study prepares for the full study. In doing this, researchers can uncover some insight into the shape of the study that was not apparent previously (Janesick, 1994).

Qualitative Observational Research

Qualitative observational research consists of many different approaches that often overlap and possess subtle distinctions. The type of approach used depends on the research question and area of discipline. The observer's role is to record group interactions and behaviors as objectively as possible using various qualitative inquiry tools (e.g., interviews, questionnaires, impressions, and reactions). It is the observer's responsibility to record his or her participation as the observer during the research and identify his or her point of view as the observer. The researcher is in essence "telling the story" (Stake, 1994, p. 239). A qualitative observational research is naturalistic because it studies a group in its natural setting. As Yvonne S. Lincoln and Egon G. Guba suggest in their text, *Naturalistic Inquiry,* the term "naturalism" is hard to pin down; instead, one needs to gain an overall understanding of the concept (1985, p. vi).

Qualitative observational research is often used by designers researching within the built environment. As an example, suppose you were planning to design an educational facility. You could observe existing educational facilities and classroom layouts as they relate to student participation and productivity. You could select four elementary classrooms with different layouts and observe the environment and the students' interaction within the space.

In the design fields, this might be called observational research. You can photograph or even film a specific space over time—almost like a video diary that documents the users in the space. This form of analysis is extremely helpful, as it gives you a tangible picture of the everyday life of the users and how they interact with their space. Also, it can allow you to document long periods of time and look for repeating themes that might begin to emerge.

Key themes often emerge from recurring phrases culled from observational research. Authors Anselm Straus and Juliet Corbin (1998) refer to this step "as axial coding in axial coding, which is to say that categories are related to their subcategories to form more precise and complete explanations about the phenomena" (p. 124). This cross-analysis of identified phrases from the data collected and analyzed can then be categorized into main themes. Straus and Corbin (1998) refer to this process as **selective coding**. This is a useful tool when analyzing thick or thin descriptions of space and interviews. The concept of identifying repeating themes will be explored in detail in Chapter 7, "Precedent Studies," where examples of analyzing such studies are addressed.

Tsoi/Kobus & Associates is a firm that is an expert in healthcare design. Observational research is part of their everyday process, especially during the programming phase of design.

Evidence-Based Design

The concept of EBD was built around the platform of evidence-based medicine, which began in 1972 with the publication of Professor Archie Cochrane's book "Effectiveness and Efficiency: Random Reflections of Health Services." Robert Ulrich became a pioneer in EBD when he published his findings from a study relating views of nature to a patient's recovery. There is an accreditation and certification program for EBD, and they recommend following eight steps to achieve the best possible outcomes:

1. Define evidence-based goals and objectives.
2. Find sources for relevant evidence.
3. Critically interpret relevant evidence.
4. Create and innovate evidence-based design concepts.
5. Develop a hypothesis.
6. Collect baseline performance measures.
7. Monitor implementation of design and construction.
8. Measure post-occupancy performance results.

Taken from: *https://www.healthdesign.org/edac/about*

Even though the above was developed within the healthcare realm of design, the process and steps can certainly be applied to other areas of the built environment.

Shaping Your Study to Reach the Goal

The goal of qualitative observational research is to define and answer a specific research problem or question. The problem or question may or may not be defined at the time when the researcher first begins the study. Some researchers, however, like to enter the field with a specific research problem already in mind (Stake, 1994). This certainly would be the case for observing environments within the space. Either your client has specific goals that he or she would like to accomplish or you, as the designer of a space, can make recommendations based on your observations.

The qualitative observational researcher must determine what underlying theory or model should document the research. This may mean replicating or building on an earlier study, or it may mean formulating a new model or theory by which to conduct the study. Either way, the theory or model chosen will help the researcher determine how to structure the study (e.g., whether exclusively to study participants in the classroom or to study them outside of the classroom as well, and how and when to use interviews) (Denzin, 1994; Lincoln and Guba, 1985).

BOX 4.3 RESOURCES TO HELP INITIATE RESEARCH AND COLLECT INFORMATION

(Also see Appendix J: Helpful Resources)

ORGANIZATIONS

American Academy of Healthcare Interior Designers (AAHID)
AAHID is a nonprofit, organization that board-certifies interior designers in the United States and Canada who specialize in healthcare—including acute care, ambulatory care, and residential care facility design. Led by a volunteer board of directors, they are constantly striving to improve our certification process, study materials, and exam. They depend on the experience and expertise of those in the field to maintain the highest standards of professionalism, integrity, and competence (www.aahid.org).

American Society of Interior Designers (ASID)
ASID is the largest organization of professional interior designers in the world. ASID is a community of people driven by a common love for design and committed to the belief that interior design, as a service to people, is a powerful, multifaceted profession that can positively change people's lives. Through education, knowledge sharing, advocacy, community building, and outreach, the society strives to advance the interior design profession and, in the process, to demonstrate and celebrate the power of design to positively change people's lives. A list of schools with ASID student chapters can be obtained from the national headquarters (www.asid.org).

Building Green
Articles, reviews, and news from Environmental Building News (EBN) are integrated with product listings from the GreenSpec products directory and project case studies from the High-Performance Buildings Database (www.buildinggreen.com).

Council for Interior Design Accreditation
CIDA leads the interior design profession to excellence by setting standards and accrediting academic programs. CIDA sets standards for post-secondary interior design education, evaluates college and university interior design programs, and publishes a list of accredited programs that meet the standard (www.accredit-id.org).

InformeDesign
InformeDesign transforms research into an easy-to-read, easy-to-use format for architects, graphic designers, housing specialists, interior designers, landscape architects, urban designers and planners, and the public. It contains a database of RESEARCH SUMMARIES about design and human behavior research, accessible through either a full-text search or by using the topics listed within the three main categories, "Space," "Issues," or "Occupants." InformeDesign was co-created by Denise Guerin, PhD, and Caren Martin, PhD, at the University of Minnesota, in the Department of Design, Housing, and Apparel (www.informedesign.org).

International Furnishings and Design Association (IFDA)
IFDA is the only all-industry association whose members provide services and products to the furnishings and design industry, and it is the driving force through its programs and services to enhance the professionalism and stature of the industry worldwide (www.ifda.com).

Interior Designers of Canada (IDC). IDC is the national advocacy association for the interior design profession. As the national advocacy body, IDC represents more than 5,500 members, including fully qualified interior designers, Intern members (who have yet to pass their exams), students, educators and retired members. In addition, they have as members over 300 manufacturers and suppliers who provide products and services for interior design projects and firms (www.interiordesigncanada.org).

International Interior Design Association (IIDA)
IIDA is an internationally recognized organization representing design education and professional interior designers practicing in commercial, education and research, facility planning and design, government, healthcare, hospitality, residential, and retail design (www.iida.org).

National Council for Interior Design Qualification (NCIDQ)
This organization serves to identify to the public those interior designers who have met the minimum standards for professional practice by passing the NCIDQ examination. The Council maintains the most advanced examining procedures, and to update continually the examination to reflect expanding professional knowledge and design development techniques (www.ncidq.org).

Network of the Hospitality Industry (NEWH)
NEWH is the premier networking resource for the hospitality industry, providing scholarships, education, leadership development, recognition of excellence, and business development opportunities. It's about scholarship, education, and business networking. Members of NEWH, Inc. are professionals actively engaged in development, management/ operations, architecture, communications, design, distribution, education, manufacturing, production, purchasing, and sales of the hospitality, foodservice, senior living, and related industries. They sponsor scholarships and actively promote the education of eligible students aspiring to enter these industries, as well as encouraging cooperation and exchange of information among those engaged in all aspects of these industries (http://newh.org).

United States Access Board ADA Research Reports
A key mission of the board is developing and maintaining accessibility guidelines and standards under several different laws, including the Americans with Disabilities Act (ADA). This includes design requirements for facilities in the private and public sectors, transportation vehicles, telecommunications equipment, and federal electronic and information technology. Most Board research projects are designed to develop information for its use in writing or updating these design criteria. The board also funds the development of technical assistance and training materials useful to its audience, including designers, specifiers, and consumers. Such materials offer guidance on accessible design, compliance with board guidelines, and best practices (*www.access-board.gov/research/project-list.htm*).

United States Green Building Council (USGBC)

This nonprofit organization is committed to expanding sustainable building practices. USGBC is composed of more than 13,500 organizations from across the building industry that are working to advance structures that are environmentally responsible, profitable, and healthy places to live and work. Members include building owners and end users, real estate developers, facility managers, architects, designers, engineers, general contractors, subcontractors, product and building system manufacturers, government agencies, and nonprofits (www.usgbc.org).

WELL Building Standard®

WELL is a performance-based system for measuring, certifying, and monitoring features of the built environment that impact human health and well-being, through air, water, nourishment, light, fitness, comfort and mind. WELL is grounded in a body of medical research that explores the connection between the buildings where we spend more than 90 percent of our time, and the health and wellness impacts on us as occupants. WELL Certified™ spaces development can help create a built environment that improves the nutrition, fitness, mood, sleep patterns, and performance of its occupants. (www.wellcertified.com/well)

DATABASES

Access to the databases typically is not free. Check with your library, as most have institutional memberships.

Applied Science & Technology Index

This index references articles from 1983 to present in journals, magazines, and trade publications in engineering, technology, and construction management; a good database for searches on construction topics.

Architectural Index

Online coverage indexing articles from major architectural periodicals are available in this database for 1982 to 1988; print versions of the index are available from 1950 to present.

Art Full Text

This bibliographic database indexes and abstracts articles from art periodicals, yearbooks, and museum bulletins published throughout the world.

Avery Index to Architectural Periodicals

This database offers a comprehensive listing of journal articles on architecture and design, including bibliographic descriptions on subjects such as the history and practice of architecture, landscape architecture, city planning, historic preservation, and interior design and decoration.

DAAI

Design and Applied Arts Index is the leading source of abstracts and bibliographic records for articles, news items, and reviews published in design and applied arts periodicals from 1973 to present. An indispensable tool for students, researchers, and practitioners worldwide, DAAI covers both new designers and the development of design and the applied arts since the mid-nineteenth century, surveying disciplines including ceramics, glass, jewelry, wood, metalsmithing, graphic design, fashion and clothing, textiles, furniture, interior design, architecture, computer-aided design, Web design, computer-generated graphics, animation, product design, industrial design, garden design, and landscape architecture. As of November 2007, DAAI contains more than 177,193 records, with around 1,200 new records added in each monthly update.

InformeDesign

Interior designers, architects, graphic designers, and landscape architects—use more than 2,400 research summaries to inform their design solutions—explore new design/human behavior topics in Implications—engage in research-based design—learn from tutorials, white papers, and Web casts (www.informedesign.org/Home).

MADCAD

This database provides building codes, knowledge-based design solutions, and guidelines to meet the codes. It also provides cross-referenced collections of building, electrical, mechanical, plumbing, fire, and maintenance codes from BOCA, SBCCI, ICBO, ICC, and NFPA, as well as access to comprehensive state and local codes (www.madcad.com/index.php).

ProQuest

UMI Dissertation Publishing ProQuest has been publishing dissertations and theses since 1938. In that time, they have published more than 1 million graduate works from graduate schools around the world. ProQuest has more than 700 active university publishing partners and publishes more than 70,000 new graduate works each year (www.proquest.com/products_umi/dissertations/).

PUBLICATIONS
DesignIntelligence

DesignIntelligence is the Design Futures Council's bimonthly report on the future and the repository of timely articles, original research, and industry news. Design leaders rely on DesignIntelligence to deliver insight about emerging trends and management practices, allowing them to make their organization a better-managed, more financially successful enterprise (www.di.net).

The *Journal of Interior Design (JID)*

This is a scholarly, refereed publication dedicated to issues related to the design of the interior environment (*www.journalofinteriordesign.org*).

APPLICATIONS
SimplyMap

An internet mapping application that lets users create professional-quality thematic maps and reports using United States demographic, business, and marketing data. Data sources include the U.S. Census and Census projections.

Selecting *how* and *when* data will be collected is another essential step in designing qualitative observational research studies. It is extremely important to be aware of and sensitive to this. If you make the decision to conduct an observational study of different spaces, proper scheduling and—in most cases—permission and release forms will need to be completed. Questionnaires and student journals can be part of the data-collecting process as well; therefore, it is imperative that the student/researcher be respectful of the participants' time and willingness to help. If questions can be automated online for ease of access and time, this is advantageous. On the other hand, if the researcher would like the participants to fill out information, it should all be organized and completed within a specific time frame.

Internal Review Boards

Many academic institutions will have an **Internal Review Board (IRB)**. When students want to conduct research at these institutions, they must fill out the proper forms and adhere to the guidelines. It is always wise to check with the academic offices at your institution to see if there is an IRB and, if so, what the expectations are. Typically the IRB reviews proposals related to human and animal subjects, and some departments have their own code of ethics with which one must comply. You are not to begin your research until the IRB committee or board has approved your proposal. This committee does not judge or evaluate your research but rather reviews how your data-collecting and documenting methods will protect the participants and their privacy.

Applying Qualitative Research

The final two steps to be taken by the qualitative observational researcher are analyzing the data and writing the research report.

In **analyzing descriptive data**, the researcher reviews what was witnessed and recorded, and synthesizes it with the observations and words of the participants themselves (Alverman et al., 1996; Huberman, 1994). What researchers choose to include or exclude from the final text can have a tremendous effect on how their results are interpreted by others. Alvermann et al. (1996) proposes that conscientious qualitative researchers might pose the following questions when writing up their findings:

- How much information needs to be included in the text about theories that may have guided the research, disciplinary biases, personal hunches that were followed, etc.?
- Should I include my original research and its changing forms as I conducted my research?
- How much description of myself needs to be included to reveal possible biases or perspectives (gender, ethnicity, age, academic/social theories adhered to, etc.?
- How can I ensure that the research is interesting without compromising credibility?
- How can I fairly and accurately report my findings within the length limitations of where it will appear (journal, paper presentation, etc.)?
- Are the representations of myself and the studied group fair? Is it clear that there are mere representations or have I presented them as definite factual evidence? (CSU Writing Guide, 2002, Observation)

They suggest that researchers who take the time to confront these possible problems will produce fairer, clearer reports of their research. Even when the report takes the form of a narrative, researchers must be sure that their "telling of the story" (Denzin, 1994, p. 507) gives readers an accurate and complete picture of the research.

In writing a case study, you're seeking a holistic understanding of an event or situation in question through inductive logic, reasoning from specific to more general terms (Huberman, 1984). Implementing a qualitative case study research project and including observational short- and long-term research techniques can be used to create a case study that demonstrates both reliability and validity.

Qualitative Research Applied to Art and Design

In the area of art and design, case studies and observational research are often referred to as "precedent studies" (Duerk, 1993; Pena, 1987). As noted above, precedent studies compare more than one location or example in a particular area. In the field of design, precedent studies are used extensively to evaluate all aspects of the built environment and those who occupy it. It is common to study what has been done in the built environment and learn what has been successful and what has not. The documentation of the findings then becomes the precedent study. Precedent studies in the applied arts typically document the inception of the design process and each phase of design, and then evaluate the success and failures of the space and those who inhabit it (Alexander, 1974; Duerk, 1993; Pena, 1987).

Educational Connoisseurship and Criticism

The art educator Elliott Eisner developed a form of evaluation called "educational connoisseurship and criticism." Here, **connoisseurship** is the process of being aware of the educational program and its meaning, goals, and objectives. To do this well, the connoisseur "must have expert knowledge of the program being evaluated" (Gall, Borg & Gall, 1996, p. 710). This form of educational criticism focuses on "describing and evaluating that which has been appreciated" (Gall, Borg & Gall, 1996 p. 710). The "evaluating" part, of course, is where the criticism comes in. This approach parallels the critique experience that is common in both academic and professional settings. The validity of educational connoisseurship and criticism relies heavily on the expertise of the evaluator. Criticism can be approached as the process of helping others to see the qualities of something that they did not see. Unfortunately, hearing the term "criticism," often generates negative feelings. However, within design, as outlined in Chapter 2, critique and criticism are integral parts of the process of design. Students are encouraged to seek criticism as a way of improving their design problems. Eisner (1998) states that "effective criticism functions as the midwife to perception. It helps it come into being, then later refines it and helps it to become more acute" (p. 6).

Many academic examples of qualitative studies within the applied arts are available via the online database resource ProQuest. Many academic institutions also have their own databases of theses and dissertations available.

Applying Quantitative Research

Quantitative research methods were originally developed in the natural sciences to study natural phenomena (CSU Writing Guide, 2002). Quantitative research, or positivist research, is grounded in the assumption that the features of the social environment constitute an objective reality that is relatively constant across time and place. The field of design has adopted many quantitative research methods for analyzing attitudes toward the built environment.

Survey Research Method

Questionnaires and **surveys** are quantitative research methods used extensively by designers. Often combined with interviews, both are very quick and effective ways to gather information from the users of a space.

According to Gall, Borg, and Gall, "The term survey frequently is used to describe research that involves administrating questionnaires or interviews. The purpose of a survey is to use questionnaires or interviews to collect data from participants in a sample about their characteristics, experiences, and opinions in order to generalize the findings to a population that the sample is intended to represent" (Gall, Borg, & Gall, 1996, p. 289).

When planning a research survey, Gall, Borg, and Gall state that the researcher needs to carry out eight steps to ensure thorough documentation. Table 4.2 outlines these eight steps.

The survey method is a research tool that includes questions that are either open-ended or close-ended. You can administer your survey orally, documented in an interview, or as a questionnaire. Your goal in compiling quantitative research in a survey is to "gain specific information about either a specific group or a representative sample of a particular group. Results are typically used to understand the attitudes, beliefs, or knowledge of a particular group" (CSU Writing Guide, 2002, Survey Research, ¶ 2).

Compiling Statistical Research

According to Gall, Borg, and Gall (1996), the last step in both the questionnaire and interview research methods is to compute data into descriptive statistics, or tabulate and analyze the quantitative data. Descriptive statistics describe the data that has been collected, which include statistics, frequency counts, ranges (high and low scores or values), means, modes, median scores, and standard deviations (CSU Writing Guide, 2002, Statistics Research, ¶ 5). The key point in using descriptive statistics is to understand the variables and distributions of the numbers.

Statistics are a set of tools used to organize and analyze data. Data must either be numeric in origin or transformed by researchers into numbers. Employing statistics serves two purposes—descriptions and prediction. Statistics are used to describe the characteristics of groups. These characteristics are referred to as **variables**. Data is gathered and recorded for each variable. Descriptive statistics can then be used to reveal the distribution of the data in each variable (CSU Writing Guide, 2002). Predictive statistics can be used to estimate future events with each variable. For example, by analyzing the demographics of an area, predictive statistics can help to determine the type of restaurant that would be the most profitable for a particular location.

Statistics can be used to analyze individual variables, relationships among variables, and differences between groups. For the purpose of employing a survey,

TABLE 4.2 EIGHT STEPS TO CARRY OUT RESEARCH STUDY USING A QUESTIONNAIRE

STEP	DESCRIPTION
1	Define Research Objective
2	Select a sample
3	Design the questionnaire format
4	Pre-test the questionnaire
5	Pre-contact the sample
6	Write a cover letter and distribute the questionnaire
7	Follow up with non-respondents
8	Analyze questionnaire data

Adapted from *Educational Research: An Introduction*, by Gall, Borg & Gall, (1996) p. 291.

questionnaire, or interview research method, analyzing differences between responses could be the means of statistical comparison.

Quantitative Research Methods Applied to Art and Design

Most of what exists in the field of design in advanced research pertains to the physical structure, and very little exists in the area of critical studies of the educational experience of design (AIA, 2015; ASID, 2015). Look to the interior environment and how it is sculpted to study further how space can be enhanced by focused research committed to these areas.

There is a need for future research in applied arts to build a solid foundation of historical data. Professional organizations have identified the lack of research in the applied arts and have teamed up with industrial partners to help fund further research. **The American Society of Interior Designers (ASID)** and the **International Interior Design Association (IIDA)** both have sections on their websites entitled Knowledge Center. This area is committed to research, sharing of information, white papers, and ongoing professional development for design professionals.

InformeDesign has been an instrumental source for obtaining research relating specifically to the interior design profession. InformeDesign is the first searchable database of design and human behavior research on the internet. The site contains "practitioner-friendly" research summaries of findings related to design and human behavior drawn from research literature in scholarly journals. All services on the InformeDesign website are available at no cost to visitors.

According to InformeDesign, "Good design, in the end, requires people with different experience, skills, and perspectives drawing on many forms of information in the pursuit of making creative and informed applications of knowledge as they generate and evaluate possible design solutions. Most important of all is a mindset that acknowledges that more information, including that generated through formally structured research processes, has the potential to generate plans and buildings that, as noted earlier, work synergistically on multiple levels" (2008).

Applying Mixed Method Research

The combination of qualitative research, including case study, observational short-term and long-term techniques, and quantitative methods of research, including survey and statistics, results in a mixed method approach. This combination of methodology fits into the definition as defined by Creswell (2003): "A mixed method approach: pragmatic knowledge claims collecting of both qualitative and quantitative data sequentially" (p. 12). The possibility of integrating both a qualitative and quantitative approach into one research method such as a questionnaire is an interesting approach (Labuschagne, 2003).

It is important to keep in mind that the purposes and functions of qualitative and quantitative data on questionnaires are different, yet complementary. The statistics from standardized items make summaries, comparisons, and generalizations quite easy and precise. The narrative comments from open-ended questions are typically meant to provide a forum for explanations, meanings, and new ideas (Labuschagne, 2003, ¶15). Integrating both qualitative and quantitative questions in one delivery method to gain insight into statistical and open-ended responses from the same participant is an appealing mixed method approach.

As a mixed method researcher, you need to be familiar with both techniques of research and have an understanding of the rationales for combining both forms of data (Creswell, 1998). Creswell also notes that a mixed method project will take extra time because of the need to collect and analyze both qualitative and quantitative data. Creswell also states that "mixed method research fits a person who enjoys both the structure of quantitative research and the flexibility of qualitative inquiry" (p. 23).

Mixed Method Research Applied to Art and Design

Integrating a mixed method research approach to study design amounts to a comprehensive study, as it encompasses both qualitative and quantitative techniques. Triangulation will validate findings within a mixed method approach as you implement multiple data collection methods.

In the field of design, most studies are committed to studying all aspects of the built environment. A mixed method research approach to analyze the built environment will improve programming and schematic design studies. It is another way of helping to eliminate biases opposed to relying exclusively on any one data collection method. Additionally, the analysis of information gathered can help you clarify your approach to the programming task.

DETERMINING THE METHOD FOR YOU

While absolute objectivity is impossible, it is essential that researchers enter the field or study group with an open mind, an awareness of their own biases, and a commitment to detach from those biases as much as possible while observing and representing the group. This will help as you begin to understand and apply the qualitative, quantitative, and mixed method research approaches that have been addressed in this chapter. Most designers are curious by nature and attempt to think outside the box. For the creative thinker, a research process is merely the organization of this instinctive form of exploration.

KEY TERMS
- Action research
- American Society of Interior Design (ASID; www.asid.org)
- Analyzing descriptive data
- Case study research
- Connoisseurship
- Critical instance case studies
- Cumulative case studies
- Ethnography
- Evidence-based design
- Exploratory case studies
- Formal and numerical methods
- Illustrative case studies
- InformeDesign
- Internal consistency reliability
- Internal Review Board (IRB)
- Inter-rater or inter-observer reliability
- Journal of Interior Design (JID)
- Laboratory experiments
- Mixed method approach
- Observational research
- Parallel-forms reliability
- Pilot studies
- Precedent study
- Program effects
- Program implementation
- Qualitative observational research
- Qualitative research
- Quantitative research
- Reliability
- Selective coding
- Statistics
- Survey
- Survey methods
- Test-retest reliability
- Thick description
- Thin description
- Triangulation
- Validity
- Variable

CHAPTER 5

Historical, Observational, and Interactive Research

CHAPTER OBJECTIVES

After reading this chapter, you should be able to:

- Conduct and document historical research.
- Conduct and document observational research.
- Conduct and document interactive research.
- Understand the value of conducting research.

What if a client asks you to design a coffee shop? Would you say, "I'm sorry, I've never designed a coffee shop before"?

As a trained designer, you must have the skills to apply good design to a diversity of design applications. You may not have the knowledge of specific technical requirements, but a good designer must have the ability to **research** and analyze the historical aspects of a design. A good designer must be able to assemble a plan to study the requirements and needs of any facility.

The beginning phase of design offers a wonderful opportunity for designers to take time out from everyday tasks and engross themselves in a new topic and in the type of design that new topic requires. In other words, research gives the designer time to gain insight into programmatic requirements and to learn about the type of design that would best serve those requirements. This chapter introduces skills and training to help you begin thinking like a researcher. Chapter 4, "Research Methods," introduced numerous research methods that you may utilize. This chapter focuses on several types of research most commonly used by interior designers. Chapter 7, "Precedent Studies," should round out your formal research for the programming document.

In business or the classroom, a client or professor assigns the projects. As a student, you may find yourself designing a restaurant or retail space for the first time. It is only natural to have many questions concerning what should go into the space, where the space is located, who will use it, and so on. Intense curiosity is key for the student, programmer, and designer. Asking questions is essential.

It's a good idea to break down this phase of the process into three key areas: historical, observational, and interactive research. Each of these areas will be discussed in this chapter.

BEGINNING THE RESEARCH PROCESS

First, put on your researcher's hat. Try not to have any preconceived notions of the design or solutions—a very hard but crucial concept not only for the designer but for the client as well. Designers are trained to solve problems. But prior to the problem-solving phase, which can encompass both practical and conceptual solutions, designers can learn from the past to redefine and improve applications and solutions thereby becoming even better problem solvers.

Often a client will contact a designer when he or she is ready to start a project. He may have a very specific idea in mind about how he envisions the end result to look. This is where it is imperative for you as the designer to educate the client about the process of design, as outlined in Chapter 2, "The Process of Design." By including an exploratory research component into your programming phase, you can now also use it as an extra incentive for your client— offering to include them in the process.

Start with an open mind and gather as much information as possible. At this point you are a sponge absorbing as much as you can until you hit your full saturation point.

Let's get to full saturation and learn about historical, observational, and interactive research techniques and how to analyze the data collected.

MORE THAN INFORMATION GATHERING

It is important to note that research is not merely information gathering. "Research is a systematic process of collecting, analyzing, and interpreting information (data) in order to increase our understating of the phenomenon about which we are interested or concerned" (Leedy, 2005, p. 2). This chapter is aimed as a primer for understanding and

employing some research methodologies that align in an instinctive application to the programming phase of design. It is not meant to substitute for or replace a comprehensive research project, but to identify and provide an overview of such methodologies. It can also serve as an introduction to research and various methodologies.

HISTORICAL RESEARCH

Starting the **historical research** aspect of your topic can be exciting and a tad overwhelming. In research terminology it can be compared to starting a **literature review** of the specific topic. The library might sound a bit old-fashioned, but it is the best place to begin the process of collecting historical research. Historical research, as it applies to interior design programming, is directly related to collecting information that is in print and documented. Books, periodicals, newspapers, and journals are some options for collecting historical research. A key factor in your success as a researcher is using the right tools. While starting the process, remember that it is imperative to have patience and not expect to find everything on your first trip to the library or through your first online search.

Library Research

Reference librarians are of great benefit when using a library. It is helpful to schedule a time to meet with the librarian to discuss your topic of research. Librarians have extensive knowledge on how to gather information using a multitude of venues and welcome the opportunity to aid you in your research. Some colleges and universities even have staff designated to work with specific schools and programs. These people have extensive knowledge as it relates to the discipline within the school. If you opt to visit your local library, you will also find that many have research librarians that can assist you.

Research librarians can be an important part of your research team. Often they come to a class, introduce themselves, and share an overview of how the library and its staff can aid students in their research. They are eager to assist and have great skills to help you with your research! Often they may invite you to call, text, or email them to schedule an individual appointment. At these appointments, you can discuss the specific design topic that you have in mind. Begin by doing a literature search that will develop into a literature review. The literature search involves identifying resources such as books, journal articles, dissertations, and previous interior design theses that relate to your selected design topic. This task involves searching databases related specifically to the field of interior design.

Once the books and articles are located, examine their bibliographies for additional works that may be relevant. This is a very useful step because it can help enrich your information on the topic. Often research librarians can help you request further information through an interlibrary loan.

Internet Research—CREDO Reference

Internet research is the next step. However, keep in mind that not all internet sites provide authoritative information. Articles, books databases, and research guides may be excellent resources, but they may not be entirely up to date.

A literature search should be as thorough as possible and include recent as well as historical material. A good tool is the CREDO Reference. This resource offers introductory information on a wide range of topics. Most students in design enjoy using the CREDO Reference Mind Map tool. It's an extremely intuitive visual tool. In Figure 5.2 the phrase "sustainable design" was inserted to start the search; this now becomes the center of a map of related concepts. Reference articles from your CREDO title list display on the right of the screen. But let's say you want to focus on a related concept to make that concept the center of a new map. You can continue building reference articles and a new central term will populate the sidebar.

When you click on an entry heading, a reference article will open the full text article in a new tab. CREDO Mind Map is a fabulous tool to help you begin your research. It also can help you easily organize main topic and subtopics. Lastly, CREDO can provide high-quality images that can be used in your research papers and presentations.

Document Research—Work Cited

Once the literature search is complete, you'll need to write up a literature review. The literature review involves evaluating the information found in the literature

FIGURE 5.1 **Take time to explore and gather as much information as possible.**

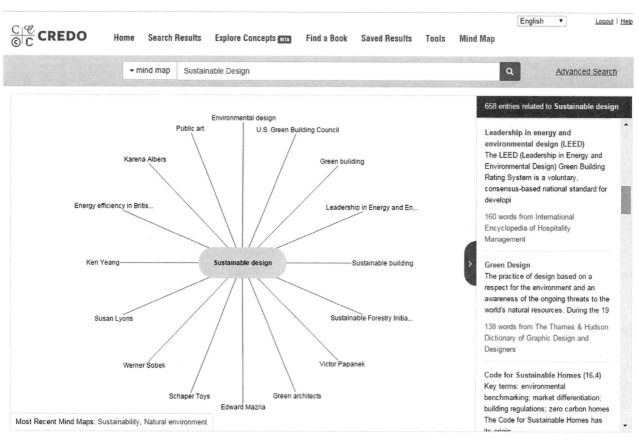

FIGURE 5.2 **Screenshot of CREDO Mind Map tool.**

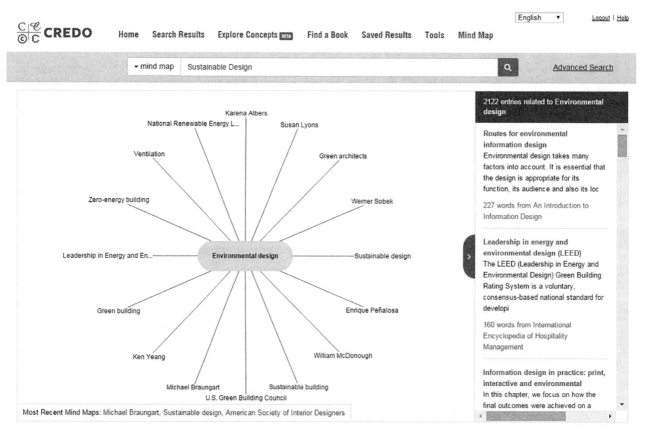

FIGURE 5.3 **Screenshot of CREDO Mind Map tool selection of related topics.**

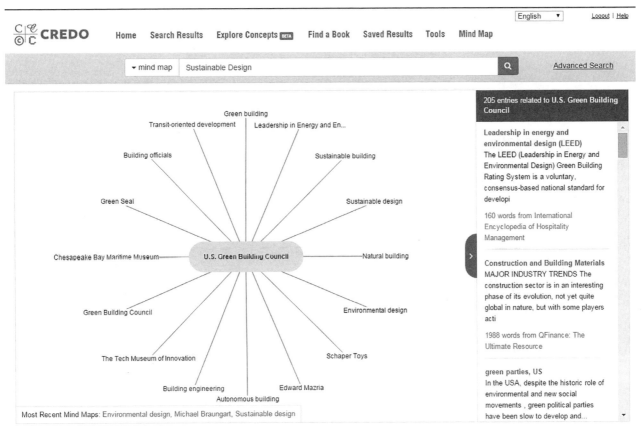

205 entries related to U.S. Green Building Council

FIGURE 5.4 Screen shot of CREDO Mind Map tool selection of related topics.

A project by interior design student Liz Carter demonstrates how you might begin the process. Here, a student chose to design a restaurant that encompasses a winery and brewery located in historic Kittery, Maine. The beginning of her data-collecting process started with a concise assessment of the history and involvement of breweries, wineries, and restaurants:

A watering hole for generation after generation, restaurants and breweries are gathering places for people of all ages because of their atmosphere, food, and beverages. The mix use of a restaurant-brewery-winery introduces a broad history of each subject as well as its concepts. A brief history of brewing will be introduced as well as how malt beverages are made,

what types there are, and the comings of micro-breweries. The history of wine-making will follow, with the process of how wine is made. The history of restaurants will be presented followed by the newly found market of brewpubs. To gather further information on all of these operations, observational research will be presented including how these mixed amenities can successfully work together. (Carter, 2007)

Carter's experience also demonstrates how research can turn up unexpected surprises:

Part of the historical research exposed me to the beautiful unique sustainable products that are being made from cork. When I located the product, I was able to save it and document it in my sketchbook to implement later in the design process. My design decisions and choices were heavily influenced by sustainability. Finding a product that fused my concept and sustainability with such accuracy was an unexpected and valuable find during the research process. (Carter, 2007)

Student Example: Starting the Research Process

Another student example, seen in Box 5.1, explores the design of a facility and safe haven for youth ages sixteen to twenty-four who have grown up in the foster system but are facing struggles associated with aging out of the system.

The proposed facility will help at-risk youth in continuing to grow as citizens of their community and learn independently. The facility will provide additional education, housing, food, medical services as well as guidance programs to youth at risk. A goal is to provide them a place to earn their G.E.D. if they have yet to receive a high school diploma. There will be programs to prepare youth for college and assist them in the enrollment process. Employment training as well as placement will also be a benefit of the facility. Upon aging out of the foster system it is known that 12–30% of foster children struggle with homelessness. A residential part of the facility will include a group home with 20 studio apartments and 15 one

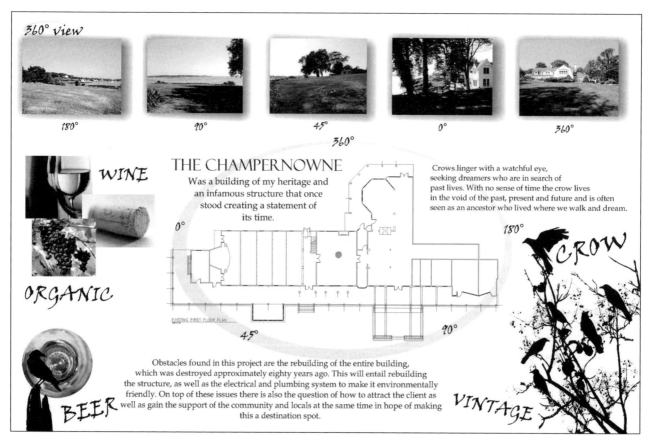

FIGURE 5.5 **Introduction to the site and the concept, Liz Carter, 2007.**

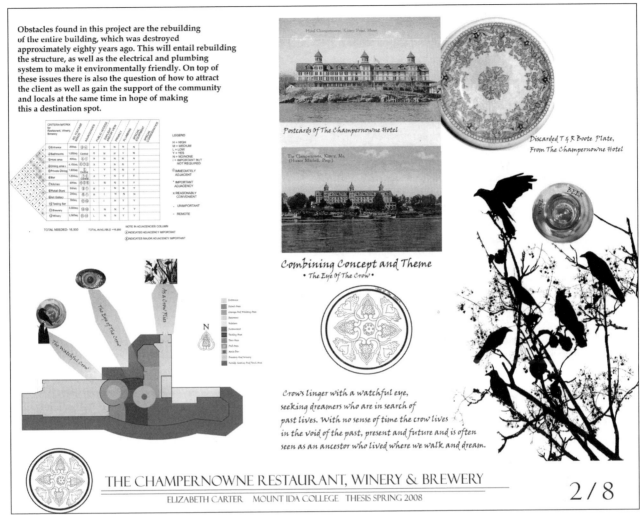

Obstacles found in this project are the rebuilding of the entire building, which was destroyed approximately eighty years ago. This will entail rebuilding the structure, as well as the electrical and plumbing system to make it environmentally friendly. On top of these issues there is also the question of how to attract the client as well as gain the support of the community and locals at the same time in hope of making this a destination spot.

Postcards Of The Champernowne Hotel

Discarded T & R Boote Plate, From The Champernowne Hotel

Combining Concept and Theme
• The Eye Of The Crow •

Crows linger with a watchful eye, seeking dreamers who are in search of past lives. With no sense of time the crow lives in the void of the past, present and future and is often seen as an ancestor who lived where we walk and dream.

THE CHAMPERNOWNE RESTAURANT, WINERY & BREWERY
ELIZABETH CARTER   MOUNT IDA COLLEGE   THESIS SPRING 2008

2 / 8

FIGURE 5.6
Concept board site with historical and contemporary images, Liz Carter, 2007.

bedroom apartment building complexes. The program will help provide the youth with money toward their rent, food or medical bills. (Westgate, 2013).

Key Topics Included in Historical Research
Historical research of a selected topic should usually include the following:

• Concise overview of topic
• Application of topic in the built environment
• Provide historical milestones as they relate to the evolution of the topic
• Historical and economic factors that might have influenced topic

• Brief synopsis of topic's application in today's societal and current research
• Identification of relevant building codes specific to topic
• Special technological requirements
• Universal design issues relating to topic
• Sustainability issues relating to the topic

As illustrated in Box 5.1, a brief historical introduction to the topic is followed by statistical information outlining the issues and documenting the need to explore the topic. Because the proposed location for this thesis was in California, further research was included that contained specific historical data regarding foster children in California.

BOX 5.1 HISTORICAL DOCUMENTATION FOR A THESIS TOPIC DESIGNING A FOSTER TRANSITIONAL HOUSING

Kasandra Westgate

HISTORY OF TOPIC

The placement of children in foster care homes is a concept that dates back to biblical times. A formal system first began in England under the English Poor Laws in the 1500s. These laws lead to development and eventual regulation of family foster care in the United States.

A law was created stating that poor children were able to be placed with wealthy families. In these families they were used as indentured servants and although in some cases it was an upgraded way of living than they were used to, it was still not the best living conditions for them. The first official foster child in the United States was Benjamin Eaton in 1636, he was seven years old (History of foster, 2012). In 1853 in New York a minister began The Children's Aid Society. When Minister Charles Loring Brace became aware of the exorbitant number of homeless immigrant children, he knew something must be done and began trying to find them homes. His initial idea was to send the children to the west and south to live with families who would provide them housing. As of result of this movement state governments and sectarian social agencies became involved in foster home placements. There were three states that were leaders in the movement: Massachusetts, Pennsylvania, and South Dakota (Harvard University, 2012).

Prior to 1865 Massachusetts began to pay board to foster families who cared for young children that could not be indentured. The first licensing law was passed in Pennsylvania in 1885. After this law it was a misdemeanor to provide care for two plus unrelated children without having a license. The Children's Home Society began receiving subsidies in South Dakota after it was organized in 1893 to benefit its public child care work. This all lead to what the foster care has grown into today.

The Foster Care Independence Act of 1999 established the John Chafee Foster Care Independence Program. This program allowed states to provide more funding as well as flexibility to help young people transition into adulthood. This also meant that states received increased funding and were permitted to extend Medicaid eligibility to former foster children up to age twenty-one. Figure 5.1a outlines the number of children in the foster care system from 1980 to 2012.

Present Day Foster System

Foster care is provided for children from birth until the age of eighteen and in some states up to twenty-one years of age. According to information provided by the Adoption and Foster Care Analysis and Reporting System, as of July 2013 there were 399,546 children in foster care. Of that number 101,719 children were waiting to be adopted and 58,587 of those children's parents have had their biological parental rights permanently terminated. Although the state should be working rapidly to place these children in an

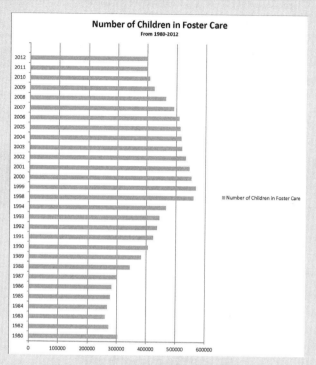

BOX FIGURE 5.1A **Chart outlining the number of children in the foster care system from 1980 to 2012.**

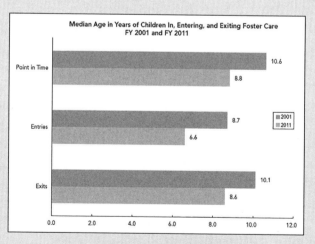

BOX FIGURE 5.1B **Adapted from Children's Bureau, 2011.**

adoptive home, the average time they have been waiting for an adoption is 23.6 months.

According to the 2000 census nearly 4 million people ages twenty-five to thirty-four live with their parents due to economic realities. When foster youth exit the foster system, they typically do not have the option to live with their parents until they can get on their feet, leaving them at extreme risk.

The following information is provided by the Children's Bureau based off of the most recent national statistical estimates for children in foster care. From 2001 to 2011 the overall median age of children in foster care has increased in every category. In 2011 the children entering the foster system had a median age of 8.7 years, and the number of children exiting had a median age of 10.1.

The majority of children in the foster system have been involved for one to twenty-three months. The amount of children in the system for a month or less increased from 12 percent in 2001 to 20 percent in 2011 ("Children Welfare Information Gateway," 2011). (See Figure 5.1c.)

From 2001 to 2011 all of the ethnicities decreased with the percentage of white children in the foster system decreasing from 41 percent to 38 percent. However, the

percentage of black children in the foster system increased from 27 percent to 38 percent. ("Children Welfare Information Gateway," 2011). (See Figure 5.1d.)

Somewhat consistently throughout the years, the male population has been more predominate than the female population in foster care. In 2012, 52 percent of the children in foster care were male and 48 percent were female.

When children are put into foster care, the majority of the children are placed in nonrelative foster family homes (47 percent). The second most common placement was in relative foster homes. Other placement settings for foster children include institutions, group homes, pre-adoptive homes, and trial home visits, runaway and supervised independent living ("Children Welfare Information Gateway," 2011). (See Figure 5.1e.)

Being that foster care is set up to be temporary placement for children, until they can find a stable home each foster child has a permanency goal. The ideal goal for placement is reunification with parents. Out of the 400,540 children in foster care as of September 30, 2011, 52 percent were aiming toward that outcome. (See Figure 5.1f.) In 2011 the number of children hoping to be reunified with their family, compared to the outcome remained the same. However, out of the 25 percent of children planning to be adopted, 20 percent actually were causing the other outcomes to slightly rise ("Children Welfare Information Gateway," 2011). (See Figure 5.1g.)

Although foster care exists in all of our states, it is more predominate in certain states as opposed to others. In 2012, according to the Children's Bureau, 29,605 children were in foster care in Texas. Texas was shortly followed by New York with 23,884 children and Florida with 19,530 children. California, however, greatly surpassed every state with an astonishing 54,250 children in foster care in 2012.

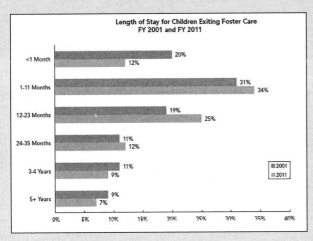

BOX FIGURE 5.1C **Length of stay for children exiting foster care.** Children's Bureau.

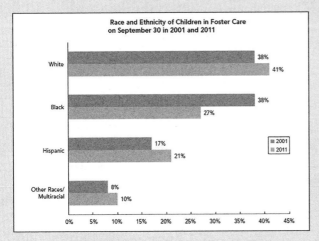

BOX FIGURE 5.1D **Race and ethnicity of children in foster care.** Children's Bureau.

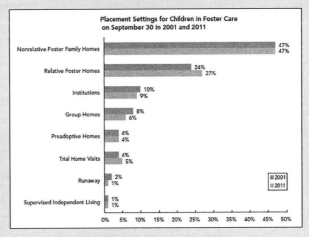

BOX FIGURE 5.1E **Placement settings for children in foster care 2001–2011.** Children's Bureau.

(continued on next page)

BOX 5.1 [ADD TITLE] *(cont.)*

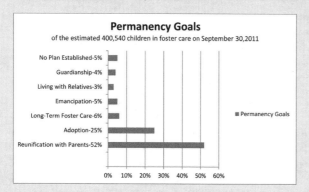

BOX FIGURE 5.1F **Permanency goals for children in foster care 2011.** Children's Bureau.

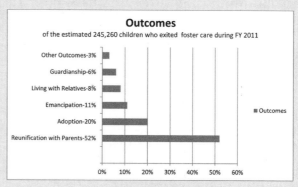

BOX FIGURE 5.1G **Outcomes of the estimated 245,260 children who exited foster care during FY 2011.** Children's Bureau.

Foster Care System in California

The proposed site for the thesis project will be in California. In 2003 the population of children in the foster system in California was at a high with 87,278 children. This is an unbelievable amount of children. In 2012 Newton, Massachusetts, where I attend college, the overall population was 86,307 people, just shy of the number in California foster care. The number of children in foster care in California has been consistently decreasing over the years; however, it still remains high above every other state.

They were removed from their parents because county child welfare departments, in conjunction with juvenile dependency courts, determined that these children could not live safely with their parents. However, most children for whom reports of maltreatment are received do not enter foster care. In FY 2008-09, just less than 1% of children in California had a report of abuse or neglect sufficient to meet the legal definition of maltreatment—and only about a third of these children entered foster care. (Public Policy Institute of California)

With California's new budget in 2013 the foster youth benefitted a great deal. It enforced that all schools, districts as well as county offices, are to be held responsible for the academic progress of their foster youth. They created a separate subgroup for foster youth under the state's Academic Performance Index. The Academic Performance Index (API) is used to measure schools' students as a whole, as well as in subgroups. Traditionally the subgroups would be based upon income, race, English learners, and disabled students. No other state has ever tracked the academic performance of foster youth according to the National Youth Law Center. Due to the small number of children in foster care in comparison to all of the other students in the state of California, they decreased the minimum number of students to fifteen to qualify as a subgroup. Other groups are required to have a minimum of thirty students. This is a huge step for foster

children, not only because typically they have learning delays, but also because foster children are such a minority that they tend to be invisible in the API's eyes. This will hopefully also boost the morale of foster youth because it shows that their academic success is of importance (Frey, 2013). According to a California Department of Education report nationwide only 45 percent of foster children graduate from high school.

The past ten years has given way for a decrease in the percentage of black children in foster care. However it still remained the most predominate ethnicity as of 2009 when there were 2.7 percent black children in comparison to 0.6 percent Hispanic, 0.5 percent white and 0.2 percent Asian/Pacific Islander children in foster care. Unfortunately we have also learned from past years that "black children typically remain in foster care for longer periods of time than other children." In 2008–09 in the state of California there was an estimated 4,500 children who aged out of the eligibility to receive foster care when they turned eighteen (Danielson, 2010). Since 2000 this number has increased, justifying the need for additional aid to ease the transition process into independence.

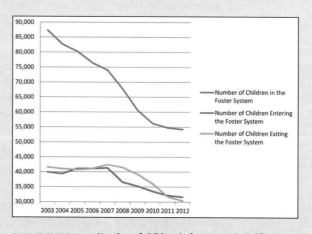

BOX FIGURE 5.1H **Number of children in foster care in California.** Children's Bureau.

OBSERVATIONAL RESEARCH

Observational research occurs when you take the time to visit locations relating to the type of application that you are studying, within natural settings. As noted in Chapter 4, "Research Methods," observational research techniques are often used within the field of design. The observer's role is to record group interactions and behaviors in the setting that you are studying as objectively as possible. For example, if you are designing a restaurant, visit restaurants that have a similar clientele, location, and the market that you are hoping to achieve and attract. Often the client will suggest places to you that he or she has seen and admired. Or as part of the research, you might go the client's location and observe that environment.

Observational research techniques solely involve the researchers making observations. There are many positive aspects of the observational research approach. Observations can be flexible or very structured.

How to Conduct Observational Research

Before forming a research question, many researchers choose to conduct observations first in order to help form that question (Social Science, 2008). When conducting an observational visit, keep in mind the following:

- Call ahead and schedule an appointment.
- Ask if you can take photos or a video.
- Bring your sketchbook.
- Remember that you must be able to observe what is relevant to your topic, so plan accordingly.

Many designers don't realize that observational research can be extremely time-consuming. It is important not only to think through the process but to plan for the experience prior to just showing up ready to observe.

Be mindful of your presence as the researcher. Because this form of research involves direct observation, people might see you watching them. This can make them feel and act differently than if you weren't there. Hence, it might be advantageous to visit the site at different times of the day and maybe even different days of the week. Randomly observing a space might give the researcher a more realistic idea of how the space is being used.

Recording (e.g., by voice recording or cellphone video) how people interact in the space is another observation tool. This can prove insightful regarding work productivity, especially in office and healthcare design and when observing way-finding paths or seeking efficiencies in user movement and interaction in space. Recordings can help identify different user groups, in order to clarify needs and program requirements for each group. In some cases, the programmer sets up a video camera to document the way the users work in the existing space. In this way, the research can analyze the flow of users (traffic, communication, and work flow can all be observed), adjacency, lighting, human factors, ergonomics, and anthropometrics. Any of these areas could warrant further observation and exploration to generate possible programmatic solutions to improve the function of the space. Tsoi/Kobus & Associates implements observational research as part of their programming documentation. Often they implement observational techniques in the naturalistic setting, utilizing photography, video recording, and simple observation with note taking. These research techniques were implemented for both the Boston Medical Center Moakley Building and Center for Transitional Research at the University Of Pennsylvania School Of Medicine. When working in the healthcare profession it is imperative to understand the process and complexity of task, states Associate Principal, Director of Interiors Kate

Wendt, IIDA. Observational research helps the design team early on in the process to gain a better understanding of the spaces that they are designing for.

Wendt reports that the design of the Johnson & Wales Cuisinart Culinary School is another good example of this. "The client's educational program is very comprehensive so the programming process was extensive. Faculty heads were integral in explaining the unique approach to a learning environment that they wanted to achieve. We toured existing facilities to field-verify all requirements and observed classes in session to better understand their needs and programmatic requirements. Their classes are a combination of 'hands-on learning,' lecture, and exploration."

Behavior Mapping

Behavioral mapping is the process of observing the current conditions of an environment. As you observe and study existing conditions, you gain insight. For example, you could observe how students enter a classroom and, based on the layout, what seats they might select first.

This is an extremely important tool to employ as you begin to understand a client's organization and the functions of that organization. Dr. Lennie Scott-Webber is an author and professor of interior design. Her research focuses on how the environment impacts behavior, learning, and knowledge sharing. Scott-Webber writes that the "behavioral mapping process is used to better understand people's behavior in an environmental setting. Often what people think they do and what they actually do are two different things" (p. 47).

When conducting an observational study focused on behavioral mapping, consider the following:

- What you need to know about the people using the space.

- The number of people, the users type, the amount of time each user is observed doing different activities, and the exact location of each user within the space. These factors are known as "user type specifications."
- Whether user activity is active or passive. Users of a specific space vary in their interaction and participation in that space. For example, the needs of a patient in a hospital room are very different than those of the doctors and nurses.
- Clues that indicate the physical interaction between user and environment.
- What the setting *tells* the users. Are they welcome to come right in, or are they greeted with visual barriers? (Scott-Webber, 1998; Duerk, 1993)

Traffic Mapping and Activity Mapping

Duerk identifies two basic types of behavior mapping: traffic and activity. **Traffic maps** show the paths people take through a space, while **activity maps** show what people are doing when they are stationary (p. 96). Once again, prior preparation by the researcher is crucial to conduct a behavior mapping study. Both Duerk and Scott-Webber recommend first constructing a template of the space to be studied. A predetermined coding system should also be generated to employ throughout the observation.

Figure 5.7 is a visual from a one-day circulation analysis study by Stephanie Scheivert for her graduate work at Corcoran College of Art + Design. In this study, Scheivert analyzed the circulation paths of individuals within a building in L'Enfant Plaza in Washington, D.C. While Scheivert's thesis project would propose major changes to the building interior, she wanted to ensure that critical circulation paths were maintained within the space, because it serves as a connection point to major office buildings and public transportation. One of the busiest

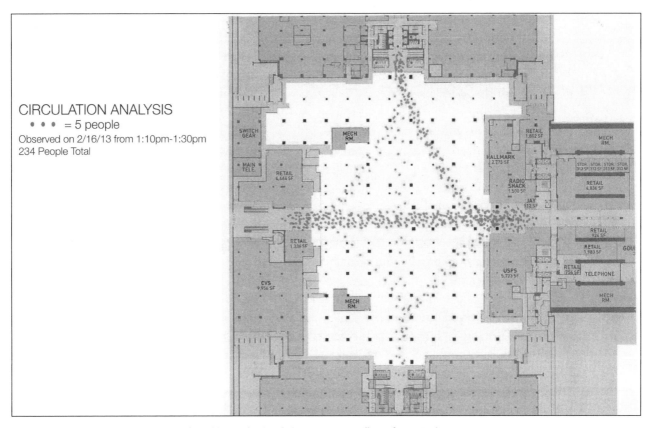

CIRCULATION ANALYSIS
• • • = 5 people
Observed on 2/16/13 from 1:10pm-1:30pm
234 People Total

FIGURE 5.7 Circulation analysis study conducted by Stephanie Scheivert, Corcoran College of Art + Design.

hours of the day in the building was lunchtime, so Scheivert chose to conduct some of her observational research during that time. Traffic mapping in the space ensured that her proposed changes did not complicate the necessary circulation patterns.

Putting Them All Together
Whether you're a professional designer or a student striving to learn more about a space and its functions, observational studies can be extremely valuable. Paired with historical research, observational research is a great way to start gaining insight into an application of design. The third key component is **interactive research**. If you plan ahead—budgeting enough time for your observational research visit, for example—you'll be able to fit this important area into your research as well.

INTERACTIVE RESEARCH
While observing a space, you might also conduct some interviews with the users of the space. This activity would fall into the realm of interactive documentation. When the researcher becomes more than just an observer, interactive research begins. The researcher begins to ask why certain things are done instead of just recording them and theorizing.

Approaches to Interactive Research
If you bring a list of questions with you to the space, then you might be able to elaborate on observed detail while interviewing a user of the space. When the researcher/programmer seeks input from others, interactive research can encompass a multitude of applications; it is—hence the term—"interactive."

Forging the interaction between two groups does not have to happen in person; with the advancements in technological applications, a growing variety of options include the following:

- Interviewing (over the telephone, in person, etc.).
- Questionnaires.
- Online surveys.
- Electronic mail correspondence.
- Traditional mail correspondence.
- LinkedIn.
- Listserv (used to communicate with a focused group of individuals who all have joined an automatic email list based on a common interest).
- Web logs. ("Blogs" vary in comment and documentation. Some are personal, while others address newsworthy content.)
- Web conferencing.

Strategize Before You Start

It is important to think first about where you want to retrieve information and what the most efficient means of obtaining it are. The instruments listed above should be carefully evaluated prior to using any of them. For example, if you decide to conduct a questionnaire, think about the type of questions you will be asking. Will they result in a quantitative (closed) or qualitative (open-ended) response? Consider administering two tools—for example, an interview and a follow-up survey. Also be mindful of how much time you have to implement and retrieve all the information. Think about how much time the respondents will need to complete the task. It is wise to keep the interactive research tool simple, with clear instructions and requiring minimal time from your participants.

Student Example of Observational and Interactive Research

A good example of a student who strategized before she started the process is Catherine Shibles. For her thesis topic Shibles was interested in the healthcare design of a neonatal intensive care unit. As you can imagine this would be a very difficult place to schedule an interview and employ interactive research strategies. Shilbles started by setting up an account on LinkedIn, the world's largest professional networking online source, with over 300 million members. She then began to connect to all types of individuals working in the realm of neonatal intensive care. She joined groups that included designers, healthcare providers, and facilities that specialized in this type of care. LinkedIn helped Shibles connect with Elliot Hospital Neonatal Intensive Care Unit in Manchester, New Hampshire. They invited her to tour their facility where Catherine could conduct her observational research. She also created a survey using Survey Monkey, and posted it to some of the groups she joined in LinkedIn. This fulfilled her interactive research and enabled her to collect information from nurses, doctors, and healthcare design professionals.

DOCUMENTING, ORGANIZING, AND ANALYZING THE DATA COLLECTED

After you have conducted your historical observational and interactive research, the abundance of material gathered can be overwhelming. You now need to sort through and organize your data so you can represent it through a quantitative or qualitative approach. For example, if you opted to conduct an online survey, the results can be downloaded and exported to an electronic spreadsheet. Such results are often documented in a quantitative approach. Following are two student examples that employ and document interactive skills. Both students were in the programming phase of their undergraduate thesis and were required to conduct interactive research for their proposed thesis topics. As in most cases, this was their first time using a formalized research method to obtain programmatic information.

Student Example: Interactive Research of Hostels, by Taylor Birse

Taylor Birse was inspired by her study abroad experience to design a youth hostel in Boston for her thesis. She was able to implement both a survey and interviews for her interactive research.

Her interactive research survey explored what youth are looking for in a hostel, as well as their experiences of being in one. An IRB form was submitted to the college for approval prior to pursing the research. The survey was linked to Facebook, a social networking website, as well as emailed to specific youth known to have visited hostels.

Birse interviewed a youth employee of Hostel International: Boston Downtown, shown in Figure 5.8. Information gathered from the interview described the real-life tendencies of guests as well as employees and will be helpful in the programming of the new building. A phone interview with Bob Sylvia, the general manager of Hostelling International for the Boston area, discussed ideal amenities, offering insight into Hostelling International's proposal for a new location.

Creating a Survey

Using the Survey Monkey website, Birse created and distributed a survey to gather responses from youth participants. Questions covered such areas as what guests expect from youth hostels concerning reservations, accommodations, and special amenities.

Create a simple overview that includes a brief introduction, something like:

My name is Taylor Birse, and I am a senior at Mount Ida College majoring

FIGURE 5.8 **Photo of main entrance of existing youth hostel in Boston.**

in interior design. For my thesis project I will be designing a hostel in city center, Boston, MA. By answering the following questions you are helping me understand what exactly youth want in a hostel, and what is expected in the experience. Thank you for your time.

Findings from the twenty-five individuals who responded to the survey are graphically represented below, in Figures 5.9–12. Not all questions are shown, only a sample. The following amenities were described by survey takers as "necessary":

- 24-hour reception
- Linen and towels
- Lockers in guest rooms
- Wi-Fi

The following amenity was described as "undesired":

- A curfew for guests

OBSERVATIONAL RESEARCH
Elliot Hospital Neonatal Intensive Care Unit
Manchester, New Hampshire
Catherine Shibles observed the neonatal intensive care unit (NICU) at Elliot Hospital in Manchester, New Hampshire, as part of her research. The primary goal was to observe a similar facility to gain further insight to the type of design that she selected for her thesis project. This is including with the programming and research document that is completed prior to the design phase.

Shibles documents that they are a newly renovated NICU floor with state-of-the-art equipment and design, making then a level III NICU. The facility was designed by an architect with the help of many staff, doctors, and nurses that work within the NICU. The NICU has a celestial theme that is carried throughout the entire space including the offices and behind the scenes spaces. To enter the NICU there is a security point that you have to go through, all staff on that floor carries keyless entry cards that they "tap" on a sensor in order to be allowed onto the NICU floor, visitors have to be escorted to that floor by hospital faculty. Security was a main focus at this particular NICU, they strongly enforce all security systems to ensure the babies safety and parent's anxiety of having a newborn. This NICU was recently designed based on the recommended standards for a newborn in an intensive care unit. They took into consideration noise, lighting, aroma, infant development, and the relationship between infant and parent. The floor is designed with single patient rooms but has the capabilities to house two to three babies at one given time in each room. They wanted to make each room feel more like a hotel room and give the parents and other family members the comfort of being "home away from home" and have a

level of independence with their newborn while they were in the unit. There are many places designated specifically for the parents of the newborns as shown in Figures 5.2c and d: they have a room where there is laundry, internet, a living room space with a TV to enjoy, and a kitchen area to bring food or they provide some foods that the hospital café supplies.

All patient rooms are fitted with at least one or two incubators and/or cribs to lay the baby in. The first thing I noticed when I entered the babies' personal room was this glowing red light on the ceiling that was turning on and off. This light was meant to let people in the room know when they were speaking too loud and that it was affecting the baby. The staff shared with me that newborns should not be placed in a loud environment when premature babies are still developing. They need to be in a serene place where little noise is produced. At the head of the baby's bed along the headwall (in every room) there is a decibel reader, this determines if the red light glows or not. If the meter reads above 57 decibels, the red glow would appear and meant that those in the room needed to quiet down to be sure not to disturb the baby, but if it wasn't on then the room was at an adequate sound level for the newborn. Each baby is monitored at all times by a device they are hooked up to that tracks their vitals, and this information can be accessed at many points throughout the floor, including their room. There are monitors in the hallway to notify if a baby is having problems or needs attention. There are also stations throughout the halls called POCs that let the nurses have access to the information too, also at these stations there are other supplies such as diapers, pacifiers, syringes, and other needs, sinks to wash for hand washing, along with safety equipment such as a "westie," which was a fireproof

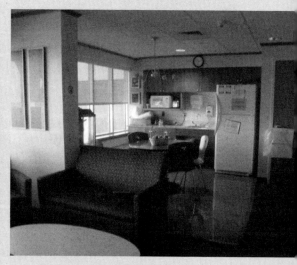

BOX FIGURE 5.2A **Hall way to critical care rooms, Elliot Hospital Neonatal Intensive Care Unit, Manchester, New Hampshire.**

BOX FIGURE 5.2B **Entrance and reception desk, Elliot Hospital Neonatal Intensive Care Unit, Manchester, New Hampshire.**

BOX FIGURE 5.2C **Family center kitchen, Elliot Hospital Neonatal Intensive Care Unit, Manchester, New Hampshire.**

BOX FIGURE 5.2D Family center living room, Elliot Hospital Neonatal Intensive Care Unit, Manchester, New Hampshire.

FIGURE 5.2E Family overnight room, Elliot Hospital Neonatal Intensive Care Unit, Manchester, New Hampshire.

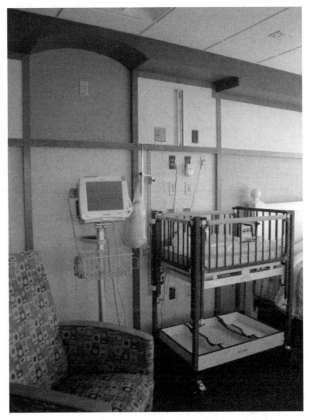

FIGURE 5.2F Family baby zone in family overnight room, Elliot Hospital Neonatal Intensive Care Unit, Manchester, New Hampshire.

vest that has large pockets in the front of it to place the babies if there was ever a fire and evacuation was required. Behind the baby's incubator or crib is a head wall where nurses can access electrical, oxygen, air, or vacuum outlets, which run most of the equipment required for a NICU. The rooms were zoned for different activities that take place in the one space: there was a place for the parents to relax and store their personal belongings; a place for the nurses to place their belongings that they are carrying at the time; the babies' space, with a place for storage of supplies that the nurse may need at any given time; and a space to make the baby's room feel like their own by those who visit or parents that want to leave notes for the nurse.

The NICU floor at Elliot Hospital not only has private rooms, but they also have rooms specifically for parents who

come from long distances and need to spend more than one night at a time at the hospital. These rooms are equipped with a queen size bed for the parents and a place for the baby to be placed in an incubator and be able to have all the necessary hookups. The room also has a TV and area for a dining table shown in Figure 5.2e.

Other areas of the NICU included a room called the "milky way" where the nutritional supplies, such as breast milk and formula, were kept. It was nice to see how the concept was carried out throughout the facility. The unit also has a private room designated to give a place for a mother to breastfeed or pump breast milk in private. The room is equipped with everything mothers' would need, such as a chair, pumps, pillows, and entertainment to read or watch. There is a serenity area for parents and family members to retreat to when they needed to relax and step away from the reality that their baby is in the NICU. On the employees side of the NICU the design continues and there is a space for offices and conference rooms, as well as staff lounges with small resting areas and eating spaces. Each employee has his/her own locker to place their belongings during their shift at work. The layout was a large horseshoe

(continued on next page)

BOX 5.2 CATHERINE SHIBLES *(cont.)*

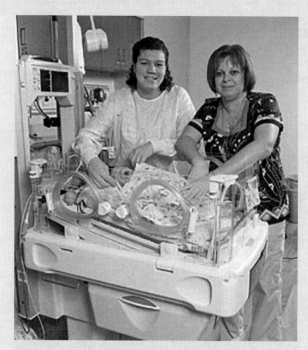

FIGURE 5.2G **Staff members at Elliot Hospital Neonatal Intensive Care Unit, Manchester, New Hampshire.**

shape with hallways connecting in the middle. Also the center was a gathering circle for anyone who may want a space to socialize. Overall the space caters to everyone's needs and was a very serene place that lowered anxiety and created comfort for all.

Interactive Research

It's important to cater to the needs of everyone occupying the space and also to get ideas of how previous designers have designed NICUs. Their input will help me further my research and program details. LinkedIn.com was an excellent source to reach out to other nurses and designers to get their input on certain areas of the NICU and their thoughts about the design of the current NICU they were working in or designing. A post was made and announced in different groups on the website where people could comment. Comments were made by others, such as grieving spaces are very important and places for prayer and meditation should be easily accessible for those in a difficult time. A survey was created and distributed to many nurses and doctors that work within a NICU, as well as designers in the field of institutional design to get their

opinions on certain aspects of the NICU. Unfortunately it is nearly impossible to interview the patients but those who work in the space were very generous with their time and sharing information with me.

Both staff and designers were asked the same questions to evaluate the differences in the answers and create a knowledge based on what is best to create a level III NICU. In my findings I found that most survey takers responded with the patients' needs first and what is best for the growth of the baby, relating everything back to how the baby feels and what they are reacting positively to. Very few mentioned things such as staff needs or hospital needs. Although the staff needs and hospital needs are important, they put the patient first and made sure to comfort their every wish. All nurses emphasized that they wanted to create an environment that was based around the patient (baby) but also catered to the parents' comfort and the relationship between them and the baby.

Summary of Findings

- Creating a way to control natural light in a space.
- Making circulation throughout the entire floor to help it move smoother.
- Having interaction spaces for staff and parents to communicate.
- Finding ways to reduce noise levels.
- Promoting private rooms with plenty of family space.
- Using soothing colors to be easy on the infant's eyes, not to many yellows.
- Offering more office spaces and storage spaces.
- Creating family community areas, activity spaces, and spaces to take the parents mind off of the baby for a while.
- Finding ways to reduce disease transfers between babies.

Catherine Shibles' observational and interactive research was very specific and relative to her area of design. She was able to connect with staff at Elliot Hospital Neonatal Intensive Care Unit in Manchester, New Hampshire, via LinkedIn. She was able to request a tour and conduct an observational study and concurrently interview staff. She was also able to create and issue a survey attracting experts via LinkedIn. Both of the above techniques proved to be a wonderful way to gather research and build upon the historical literature review that was conducted first. Many of her outcomes will become invaluable information as she begins the design phase of her thesis.

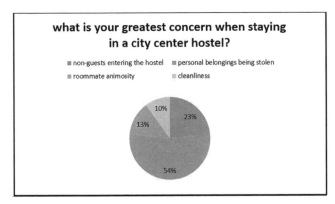

FIGURE 5.9 Graphic chart identifying results to: "What is your greatest concern with staying in a city center hostel?"

FIGURE 5.11 Graphic chart identifying results to: "What is your largest reservations about staying in a hostel?"

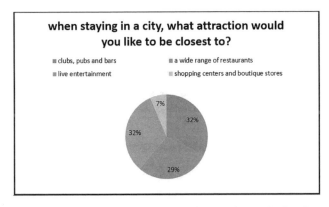

FIGURE 5.10 Graphic chart identifying results to: "When staying in a city, what attractions would you like to be closest to?"

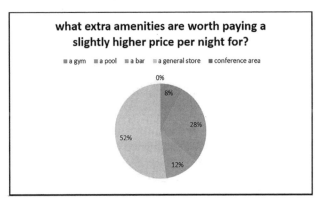

FIGURE 5.12 Graphic chart identifying results to: "What extra amenities are worth paying a slightly higher price per night for?"

Conducting Interviews

Interviews with an employee of the Boston Downtown Hostel and the general manager of Hostelling International enabled the designer to better understand the needs of employees and the concerns of management. Both interviews provided useful information to be used throughout the design process.

Employee Interview

While collecting information from the existing Hostel International: Boston Downtown, an impromptu interview was conducted with a youth employee. Information gathered from this interview will help determine the placement of employee quarters and common areas. The following points were discussed:

- Guests don't spend time in common areas that don't have Wi-Fi or food
- Employees need easy access to the kitchen and place to hang close to the reception desk
- The living space should be locked and only accessed with a key
- No visitors allowed in the living quarters
- Guests are always looking for someplace to go, close by
- Common areas: few and large; that way people hang together and don't have to go looking for a group
- Employees in 24-hour reception get bored; common areas near reception are appreciated
- There's not much of a "back house"

General Manager Interview

As the general manager of Hostelling International in Massachusetts, Bob Sylvia knows all the ins and outs of hostels, as well as the Boston area. During the phone interview, besides sharing ideas for a "no limits space" that could be designed, a main topic of conversation was the proposal for a new location for Hostel International's Boston Downtown that had yet to be advertised to the public.

Ideal amenities predicted to be included in the new building are as follows:

- Large common room
- Large group kitchen
- Wii room
- Library
- Silver LEED certification
- Informational TV instead of bulletin boards
- A laundry chute for soiled linens
- A Wi-Fi room
- A fireplace in a larger common room
- A projector in every common room, for meetings and to show movies

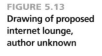

FIGURE 5.13
Drawing of proposed internet lounge, author unknown

INTERNET LOUNGE
5·4·2010   StA/PA

- The new hostel will sleep 468, making it the second largest hostel in the network

During the interview Sylvia explained that he "hopes the new location will incorporate sustainable design concepts, and further engage its hostellers into the city of Boston. Hoping to achieve a large hostel feel in a small building, the new hostel will have an entire floor of common space divided into smaller specialized areas. For example: a room specifically for Internet usage or a room with TVs just for video games." The image shown in Figure 5.13 is a rendering of the proposed internet common area of the anticipated hostel.

Analyzing and Drawing Conclusions from the Findings

Based on her observational research, Birse felt that big city hostels lose their personality, while small town hostels don't offer as many amenities. This was a valuable piece of information to retain while moving into the schematic design phase. Travelers are able to socialize better in a smaller environment; lots of space doesn't always mean happier guests. It was also discovered that thought given to what activities guests will be doing while at the hostel will greatly improve the space. During interactive research, the survey uncovered what youth think about hostels: concerns about staying in a hostel, ideal locations, what extra amenities are worth paying for, concerns about staying in a city hostel, as well as necessary and undesirable features. Information shared in the section was thought to be important to the development of the project. The interviews provided a wealth of information about what amenities would be ideal, as well as shedding light on the upcoming building process of a new Hostel International: Boston Downtown. Crucial to the progression of a fully functioning design, historical and interactive research should not be excluded from any program development.

Student Example: Interactive Research: Survey to Rumford Community, by Erin Anthony

Interior design student Erin Anthony opted to hand-deliver a questionnaire, seeking input from individuals that lived in the community (See Box 5.3).

Questionnaire 2

The student example is based on a questionnaire given to residents of the Rumford Community in Rhode Island. In total, eighteen people participated, and respondents varied in age as well as gender.

Interpreting Data from Questionnaire 2

The graph in Figure 5.14 presents three important values gathered from the survey. The first is the number of participants, the second is the number of female to male participants, and the last is the average number of years the participants have lived in the district of Rumford. This graph shows the overall scope of the survey.

Question Two: "Do you find the Rumford Chemical Works site to be a convenient location?" This question received overwhelming support from the participants. Figure 5.15 demonstrates that 98 percent of them felt that the location was convenient, while 2 percent did not.

Questions Three and Four: Very important aspects of the survey, these questions gave insight into how the residents of Rumford feel with regard to their current retail options. Of the eighteen participants, only one felt that Rumford already has a diverse mix of retail options. The remaining participants gave a variety of answers to Question Four, "What kind of stores would you like to see?" Figure 5.16 depicts the response percentages graphically.

BOX 5.3 SAMPLE QUESTIONNAIRE

Dear Rumford resident,
My name is Erin Anthony, a Rumford resident, studying interior design at Mount Ida College in Newton, MA. I am currently working on my senior thesis project. This project will entail the design of a retail store located on the Rumford Chemical Works (Rumford Baking Powder) site. As part of my preliminary stages of the design process, I am required to complete an interactive research component. This will help in gathering valuable information to make my project the best it can be! It would be *GREATLY* appreciated if you could take five minutes of your time to answer these quick survey questions. Thank you so much for all your input!

SURVEY QUESTIONS

1. How long have you been a resident of Rumford?
2. Do you find the Rumford Chemical Works site to be a convenient location?
3. Are there any types of stores that are NOT present in Rumford currently?
4. If you answered *yes* to the above question, what kind of stores would you like to see?
5. Are there any special characteristics you expect to see in a store while shopping?
6. Is customer service an important aspect of your shopping experiences?
7. When shopping, do you take time to notice the overall design of the store?
8. If so, what qualities make you recognize the store as one that is well designed?
9. Would you enjoy seeing the historical elements of the building incorporated within the store design?
10. Would knowing that the design of a store is earth-friendly have an impact on your shopping experience?

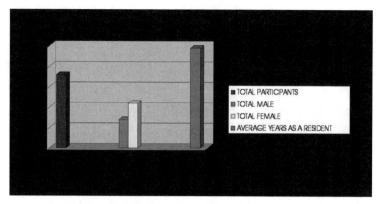

FIGURE 5.14 **Graphic chart identifying survey participants.**

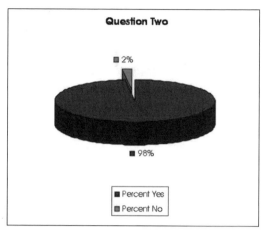

FIGURE 5.15 **Response to Question Two: "Do you find the Rumford Chemical Works site to be a convenient location?"**

TABLE 5.1 ANALYSIS OF REPEATED WORDS

In Questions 5 and 8, the participants were asked, "Are there any special characteristics you expect while shopping?" and "What qualities make you recognize the store as one that is well designed?" Table 5.1 shows words that were most frequently used in their answers to these questions. The first part of the survey asked questions that would generate quantitative responses. The second set of questions focused on qualitative responses.

Identifying common themes in the repetition of words is an excellent way to begin to take the research and start to think how it will begin to translate itself into the final design.

WORD	NUMBER OF TIMES USED
Lighting	10
Cleanliness	6
Color	4
Open	3
Space	3
Layout	2
Flow	2
Bright	2
Airy	2
Music	2
Atmosphere	2
Not overcrowded	2
Décor	1
Style	1
Organized	1

Source: Erin Anthony, 2008.

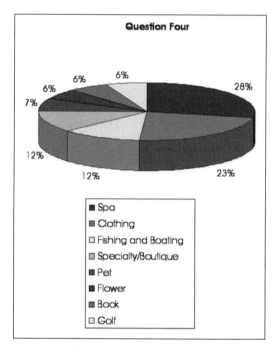

FIGURE 5.16 **Response to Question Four: "If you answered yes to the above question (Are there any types of stores that are NOT present in Rumford currently?), what kind of stores would you like to see?"**

Questions Five and Eight: In Questions Five and Eight, the participants were asked, "Are there any special characteristics you expect while shopping?" and "What qualities make you recognize the store as one that is well designed?" The similarities of these two questions require them to be analyzed using a form of qualitative research. A word search was conducted to tabulate repeating words used most frequently by the respondents when they answered the questionnaire, as seen in Table 5.1. This technique of identifying words and how many times they were repeated was employed to see if themes began to emerge from the data collected.

Drawing Conclusions from Questionnaires 1 and 2

The most influential data gathered within this interactive research came from the surveys (Questionnaires 1 and 2) given to community members of Rumford. The answers the participants provided shed light on what they expected, needed, and would enjoy seeing in a retail space within their hometown. But most importantly, based on their responses, the decision to design a spa as the retail space for the proposed thesis project was validated (Anthony, 2007).

Student Example: Interactive Research of Stakeholders, by Lucrecia Ela Ebang

Another student example is outlined in Box 5.4. For her graduate thesis topic, Lucrecia Ela Ebang proposed to explore design solutions in response to the housing crisis in Equatorial Guinea. Her interactive research *of the stakeholders* was employed differently, based on working with an international location and design.

The student examples outlined above— The neonatal intensive care unit, Boston youth hostel, Rumford Chemical Works, and housing in Equatorial Guinea—employed different types of interview and questionnaire techniques to obtain information from potential users. Interestingly, they all were looking for indicators to help them design elements and ascertain programmatic requirements of proposed design projects Design firms include these techniques as part of their research and programming. Tsoi/Kobus & Associates'

philosophy "manifests itself in a design approach that is both innovative and practical, collaboratively rooted in our clients' missions."

PROFESSIONAL EXAMPLE: TSOI/KOBUS & ASSOCIATES

Tsoi/Kobus & Associates was founded in 1983 on the belief in the power of technology and the promise it holds for buildings of all kinds. Since then, they have sought to apply rigor and beauty in equal measure to the design of technologically complex projects for clients in healthcare, science and technology, colleges and universities, and commercial real estate. This principle has guided their search for design solutions that accommodate intensive technical demands while demonstrating sensitivity to human needs for comfort, dignity, and inspiration.

As architects, planners, and interior designers, they believe that their primary role is to lead their clients to solutions that not only address their building needs but also advance their strategic goals. Their philosophy manifests itself in a design approach that is both innovative and practical, that is rooted in their clients' missions, that relies on intensive collaboration, and that ends with smart architecture rather than celebrating smart designers. They create spaces that support the delivery of compassionate healthcare that accelerates discovery, that promotes learning, and that enhances the quality of human interaction. Currently, TK&A has a staff of nearly one hundred architects, interior designers, planners, and administrative professionals, making it one of the largest design firms in the Boston area.

Kate Wendt discussed the programming process in their firm. With nearly thirty years of experience in Boston and Chicago, Kate is a strategic and versatile interior designer who has worked for an array of

Graduate student Lucrecia Ela Ebang was exploring a design solution in response to the housing crisis in Equatorial Guinea. She is from Equatorial Guinea a country located on the west coast of Africa between Cameroon and Gabon. In the 1990s Equatorial Guinea made a discovery that would forever change the country—oil had been discovered off the coast of the country. As a result, the government decided to invest the new found wealth into improving the country's infrastructures, water, electricity, roadways, and educational system. As news was sent that the living conditions were improving, many people decided to move back to the country.

The need for more housing began as soon as more people were moving back into the country. For years the country has been looking for a solution, but housing never seems to be enough to satisfy the demand. During a recent trip to the countryside, Ela Ebang noticed that the residents were living in homes made out of either wood, bamboo, or clay bricks. The houses seemed easy to build, fast and reliable, but the government noted that the lack of housing became a serious concern because residents were building inadequate shelters or wooden shacks, which caused several issues such as safety issues and health issues. Ela Ebang embraced this as an opportunity for her to possibly answer and address the demand and to propose modern day solutions for residents.

FIGURE STUDENT EXAMPLE: INTERACTIVE RESEARCH: GATHERING INFORMATION FROM VARIOUS STAKEHOLDERS
Triangular Axial Coding
From the three different research tools the data collected was analyzed using the following techniques. A qualitative analysis looked at the repetition of themes and words. The analysis of the word search was to review all data collected and identify words repeated within the reoccurring phrases. Straus and Corbin (1998) refer to this step as "axial coding." In axial coding, categories are related to their subcategories to form more precise and complete explanations about phenomena" (p. 24).

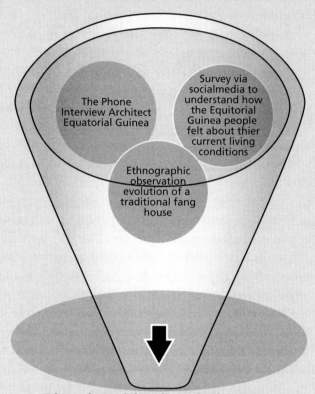

Triangular Axial Coding of Information

BOX FIGURE 5.4A Triangular axial coding.

This cross analysis of identified words was then categorized into main themes. Straus and Corbin (1998) refer to this process as selective coding. Synthesis of the data—looking for common themes:

- Ethnographic observation: evolution of a traditional fang house
- The phone interview with Hazem Ali, an architect and Arab contractor working in Equatorial Guinea

FIGURE 5.4B Traditional Equatorial Guinea house (circa 1980s).

FIGURE 5.4C Traditional Equatorial Guinea house (circa 1990s).

- Survey via social media to understand how the Equatorial Guinea people felt about their current living conditions

Synthesis of the Data—Looking for common themes
The words below have been identified through the data.

House	22
Safe	18
Sustainable	15
Wood	12
Reliable	12
Modern	10
Demand	7
Change	6
Construction	5
Progress	3

Based on the feedback from the data, it is clear that the resident of Equatorial Guinea want a house that has modern features. They did not favor wooden houses in the capital, but they suggested that it was only appropriate in the rural towns.

BOX FIGURE 5.4D **Creation of a word cloud graphically represents important themes that emerged from the research.**

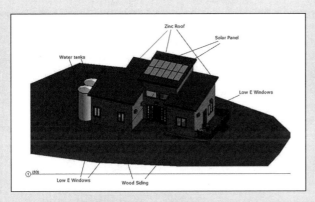

BOX FIGURE 5.4E **House design proposal.**

The design of the proposed house would be a combination of both traditional and modern style. Wood would be the main building material for its availability and it is a reference to the traditional house except that it would be treated, recycled wood. The house would have a private and public area, the public area would be open, again a reference to the traditional style. The design will include sustainable features such as a water tank for water storage and a solar panel for electricity production and storage. Adding these features allow residents to living independently in a secluded area.

BOX FIGURE 5.4F **Design proposal—floor plan.**

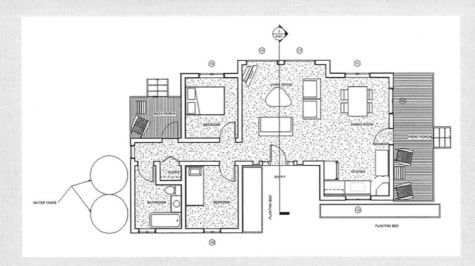

FIGURE 5.17 Kate Wendt IIDA, NCIDQ Certificate # 5547.

top-tier healthcare, science and technology, college and university, and commercial clients. Kate is especially skilled at leading multidisciplinary teams and overseeing quality assurance. An engaging and effective communicator, she is adept at translating client needs into attractive and functional designs. Kate's interactive approach to the design process has resulted in sophisticated, award-winning, flexible interior environments for a variety of users and projects.

TK&A's Approach to Programming

According to Wendt, the firm's approach involves the client as part of the team from the outset. Wendt defines programming as information gathering with clients to learn about their organization and the needs they have for a new or renovated space. A good programming process is progressive in the level of detailed information gathered. Generally, the initial program is a macroprogram that identifies basic space types and the amount of square footage required. In many cases, the client has already completed this phase of the program as a part of its overall facility capital planning process. "We acknowledge the value and importance of the information they may have assembled to date and try to incorporate this into our process," says Wendt.

The method of collecting and reporting program information is based on surveys, observation, and personal interviews. (See Appendix E: E.3, "Individual Questionnaire," and E.4, "Department Questionnaire.") Information is gathered from different levels within an organization in order to understand the needs of all of the potential users of the space. This top-down and bottom-up technique often reveals variations in responses and can point out the need to reach agreement and bring clarity to the information. "This process has changed a lot over the years as we are no longer using any pre-determined survey questionnaires. Instead we have been conducting our meetings in a workshop format to gather information and begin initial design concepts with user input. Today, clients are more engaged in co-creation of their work environments. They are interested in how the space can support their business goals, corporate culture and brand, and provide an optimum place to innovate new ideas and products."

It also begins with senior leadership and selected key individuals of each division of a company, and continues with the direct user groups through design development.

In addition, it creates an opportunity to communicate with the employees of an organization to discuss anticipated facility changes and the beneficial impact of changes on the corporate goals and objectives of the organization. Wendt states that they have found that this procedure yields the most accurate and appropriate information possible in an expedient time frame.

TK&A's Process Steps

Once the higher-level strategic planning intent has been defined and the goals and objectives are established, the actual programming process can begin. Wendt and her team consider this an opportunity to learn about the client's organization and have fun in the process. Their commitment is to make the experience one that is collaborative, without being a burden to the client or their staff. "We are doing even more benchmarking and tours with clients prior to conceptual design. More time is spent on understanding their corporate culture and in visioning the user experience." Therefore, they have broken this effort down into a number of clear and concise steps:

- Prior to Kick-Off Meeting—Distribute List of Information Required (See Appendix E: Tsoi/Kobus & Associates Programming Forms: E.1, "Understanding Your Organization," and E.2, "Background Information.")
- Orientation/Kick-Off Meeting
  - Project Introduction and Orientation
  - Organizational Committee Review
  - Project Communications
  - The Future—What Is the Business Plan?
- Tour of Facilities
  - Data Gathering—On-Site Work at Your Facility
  - Personal Interviews
  - Surveys
  - Observation
- Existing Conditions Documentation
  - Program Report Generation
  - Analysis of Information
  - Preliminary Presentation of Results
  - Modeling, Revisions, and Scenarios
  - Final Program Report, Presentation, and Subsequent Information Added

TK&A's Program Document
As discussed in Chapter 3, "Defining a Topic and Structuring Your Program Document," a program document analyzes and reports information on a number of strategic levels. The reports detail criteria based on information essential to the planning effort and to the client's decision-making process. The typical structure of the report is as follows:

- **Executive Summary**
  - Overall Planning Mission Statement
  - Image and Identity
  - Quality of Work Life Goals
  - Schedule and Budget Parameters and Objectives
- Design Criteria
  - Recommended Typical Workstation
  - Room Data Sheets
  - Site and Building Design Criteria
  - Technical Building Systems and Engineering Requirements
  - Security and Access Criteria
  - Special Requirements
- Spatial Requirements
  - Work Areas
  - Ancillary, Common, Support, and Special-Use Areas
  - Equipment Space Requirements
  - Circulation Requirements

"It is an automatic assumption that clients will do the basics and beyond, when incorporating sustainability into their new visions. Our firm always aims at LEED Silver as a minimum," states Wendt. "We have a very high standards for all of our interior selections and utilize several software programs to evaluate them. We are also reviewing criteria to design spaces toward the WELL Building Standard."

Summary of TK&A Interview
Wendt explains that as a designer it is important to recognize that just as business styles differ, there are different ways to obtain the information needed to design spaces. Using a variety of information-gathering tools can provide a better opportunity for accuracy of the data. In general, Wendt finds personal interviews and observation of existing facilities to be the most beneficial and the use of preprinted survey forms to be the least effective method of gathering the information. Photography, especially video, can be very helpful in situations where the

activities occurring within the space are complex or vary with the time of the day.

The programming process and time frame will vary with the level of complexity of the organization and of the space usage, both the Boston Medical Center Moakley Building was a very complex project which required extensive research to create the programming document. Boston Medical Center is a consolidated cancer care center that advances the hospitals mission to provide "exceptional care without expectation" by streamlining access to state-of-the-art services for some of Boston's most vulnerable residents.

TK&A Architects state the following about the Boston Medical Center Moakley Building Project:

• Designed to support interrelated clinical, research, and teaching programs.
• Transforms the hospital campus and provides a visual connection to the

historic South End neighborhood, as seen in Figure 5.18a.

• Clinics are organized around zones of varying degrees of openness and density from open public areas to private and service zones.
• Public circulation and waiting areas are organized along the perimeter of the atrium to capitalize on the natural light and views to the exterior, as seen in Figure 5.18b.

Programming for healthcare projects is often a specialized service performed by those specializing in healthcare planning. The technical, characteristics of these spaces, often highly regulated, as well as guidelines for best practice need to be considered when programming and planning healthcare spaces.

Programming for the public spaces within a healthcare facility often involves focus group meetings with patients and

FIGURE 5.18A
Boston Medical Center Moakley Building.

FIGURE 5.18B **Boston Medical Center Moakley Building.**

FIGURE 5.18C **Center for Transitional Research, University of Pennsylvania School of Medicine.**

their families. Precedent studies from other institutions are gathered to help validate the space types and space requirements.

Programming for university projects often includes interviews and focus group meetings with student representatives along with the faculty and administration of the university. Sometimes, the decision-making process for a university project may take a little longer than for other projects due to multiple levels of decision-making. Additionally, universities tend to take a longer assessment of their facility needs, and there may be several program scenarios developed as a part of a long-term master plan for the university.

In summary, the process and program document outlines supplied by TK&A are provided as guidelines and should be modified to meet the specific needs within a market type, project type, and the organization's style and structure of decision-making to provide the best information for design planning.

FIGURE 5.18D **Center for Transitional Research, University of Pennsylvania School of Medicine.**

THE VALUE OF GOOD RESEARCH SKILLS

When historical, observational, and interactive research skills are employed and documented, you can begin to build a solid foundation of knowledge regarding a specific type of design. Whether you're observing a residential, commercial, or institutional type of design, the data that you collect becomes of great value as you create your program and move further into the design process.

Information extracted from research can then be employed in a multitude of applications and aid in evidence-based program and design criteria outcomes. With knowledge gleaned from research, you can begin to formulate program requirements and creative ideas. Always keep your sketchbook with you during the research phase because when something triggers, or "clicks," you will want to document it so you can return to it at a later date and not lose that idea or thought.

The data obtained from the research should help a client, student, or design professional make intelligent decisions based on quantifiable information. Your observations and research will be compared with that of other similar design types in your precedent studies, as we will discuss in Chapter 7, "Precedent Studies."

KEY TERMS

- Activity map
- Behavioral mapping
- Historical research
- Interactive research
- Literature review
- Reference or works cited
- Research
- Traffic mapping
- WELL Building Standard

CHAPTER 6

Exterior, Interior, and Site Analysis

CHAPTER OBJECTIVES

After reading this chapter, you should be able to:

- Document an overview of the state and town where the site is located.
- Document exterior building and site conditions.
- Document interior building and site conditions.
- Identify design constraints and limitations related to the building and site.

Both the building and the specific site are vital elements to consider during the programming phase of design. The location can significantly impact decisions when you are evaluating programmatic requirements.

When considering the location, you'll need to address several factors:

- Is there an existing location?
- Is it the best site for the potential use?
- Should more than one site be explored and evaluated?
- How do you locate a site to use as a project while you are still in school?

If the site is specified, you should conduct an extensive site study analysis. If the site is still to be determined, you should conduct an exploratory site analysis. This chapter will help you perform an exploratory site study, which can be a pivotal point for the decision making involved in a specific site location.

WHAT IS A SITE STUDY?

The site is the location where your design project will be located. As a student you might be able to select your own site. Or often your instructor will allocate one for the class. A site study is an evaluation of a proposed location to determine its suitability for a particular purpose or use.

The Role of the Interior Designer

It is important that an individual who is trained in interior design be included in the site study process. Typically engineers, developers, architects, and landscape architects are also part of the team that begins to evaluate the proposed site or possible sites. As the interior designer, you must be involved in this process early on as well.

Interior designers bring a different set of skills and viewpoints to the table. This chapter addresses the large-scale issues of site evaluation as well as the details; this is also referred to as "a macro-to-micro approach to site analysis."

Professional Example: Christine Shanahan Managing Director of Design, HVS DESIGN

Christine Shanahan ASID, points out the importance of addressing regional connections. Shanahan is managing director of design, HVS DESIGN.

HVS Design is an international, hospitality-based interior design firm headquartered in Washington, D.C. Dedicated to the principles of innovation, excellence, and service, HVS Design takes a pioneering approach to the design process—blending the creativity and imagination of an experienced hospitality design firm with the financial and operational expertise of HVS, the leading global consulting and services organization focused on the hotel, restaurant, shared ownership, gaming, and leisure industries.

One of the key elements in hospitality design is the regional connection a project will have to its location and culture. According to Shanahan, "We will perform

FIGURE 6.1 Christine Shanahan managing director of design, HVS Design Group.

studies on local flavor, spirit, and interest in order to incorporate elements into the guest's experience." The programming for that, she says, may include physical visits to the geographic area, internet research, interviews with the front desk personnel and concierge on local highlights (if existing), and tours of the competition.

Shanahan finds the market audience of the hotel is a critical component. Programming for this area would include a brand analysis of target audience, interviews with the site (if existing) to determine existing clientele, an interview with ownership to determine desired clientele, financial analysis to formulate the market through rate, and research to determine what are the determining factors for a guest in booking at this location (e.g., a conference center next door or vacation attractions).

Preliminary research is a crucial step in the process and helps to prepare a comprehensive program. Like Shanahan, all of the designers interviewed for this book agreed that without the parameters discovered in the context of preliminary research, they could not come up with solutions that they believe are feasible or even good. Without preliminary research, all agreed that their time and the client's time would be wasted because vital information would either continue to turn up throughout the project, causing them to go back and repeat themselves over and over, or it would be missed altogether. Students conduct their preliminary research in their historical, observational, and interactive research outlined in Chapter 5 and the precedent study outlined in Chapter 7.

Explore Community Statistics

Take another careful look at your proposed topic. Compare the design proposal to the current demographics and socioeconomics in the community. When reviewing a proposed site and data, take into consideration growth, economic forecasting, and master planning for the proposed locality. Most of this information can be found by conducting an online search of the community's website or the United States Census Bureau. If your site is nearby, you can inquire at the local library or town hall.

Say your topic is a boutique hotel. Would this fit into all communities? What communities would help make the location successful? The right choice may be a major metropolitan city or a tourist location and maybe not a suburban town with little tourist appeal. This might sound like common sense, but you can use this as a reminder to look at the demographics and average income of the community. It could, for example, help you determine the build-out per square footage cost for the space and help you analyze price points for a restaurateur contemplating a specific location. Looking at the demographics and average income of a community not only helps with design decisions but also provides a realistic "snapshot" for you to give to a client who might be choosing between two or three locations.

Student Example: Sustainability Educational Center, by Monica Mattingly, 2007

This example of community statistics exploration is from interior design student Monica Mattingly, who was exploring the best possible location for a sustainability educational center. The education sector has had a large impact in the city of Boston., Figure 6.2 shows the effect of this large number of schools on the local economy, while Figure 6.3 indicates the locations of the colleges currently located in Boston. The education sector's portion of the local economy is equal to that for business and for natural resources.

In-depth knowledge of proposed locations is extremely important. This can be

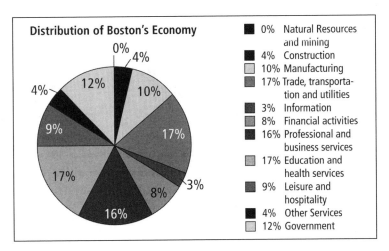

FIGURE 6.2 Distribution of Boson's economy.

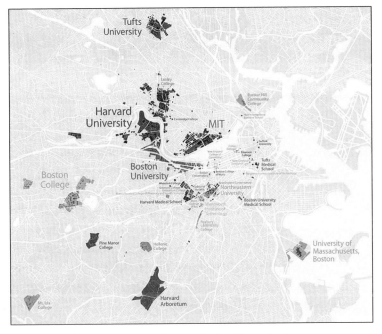

FIGURE 6.3 Proximity of Boston's colleges and universities to the site.

seen in the student example. According to the student, Monica Mattingly, "The size of Boston was greatly increased throughout the nineteenth century by a series of landfill projects that added a total of 1,071 acres to the original peninsula of only 487 acres" ("The History of Landfill in Boston," 2007). The choice of a building site on a landfill will affect the construction and needs to be considered carefully.

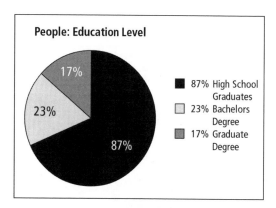

FIGURE 6.4A **Education level in the community.**

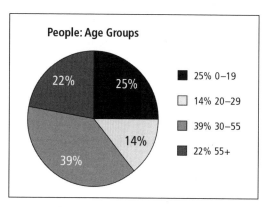

FIGURE 6.4B **Age groups within the community.**

As an example of demographics playing a role in the decision-making process, Mattingly states that, due to the high percentage of educational facilities, there is a high ratio of young people in the city, as well as a high ratio of educated population (Mattingly, 2007). Projects geared toward this demographic would have a higher probability of success.

The research and statistics in Figures 6.4a and 6.4b help validate the site location decision. They also help in identifying other potential options based on the demographics of the community.

Location Overview
Another reason to look at the site early and on a large scale is to see if the proposed site is adequate in size for the planned use. Is it too large or small? Will it allow for further expansion or reduction if needed? This is especially true when exploring a tenant fit-up facility for a client. Once these decisions have been evaluated, there should be an overview of the location. A **location overview** can consist of the following:

- State and country
- Introduction with maps
- Major forms of transportation (e.g., air, train, highway)
- Environmental features

The overview does not have to be extensive, but it should cover a bit about the state and include some maps so that one can visualize the site in a larger context. What is gained from this exercise is extremely valuable as you begin to think about and visualize the design from a different vantage point. Is there a water view? Is there any view? Are views important? Where is it in relation to public transportation? Is this important to your design? Will it affect the use of the space? Will customers be able to get to your location via public transportation, highways, or plane? What are the parking requirements? Is the site subject to flooding? The questions are endless.

Student Example: Art Therapy Retreat
Interior design student Nicole Stewart provides an excellent example of a location overview. Stewart wanted to establish an art therapy retreat in an area located in a country atmosphere in Greenwich, New York. With green rolling hills that the local farmers use for their crops, dense woods filled with wildlife, and friendly agricultural livestock roaming about, the community has a secluded and relaxed environment. As a large city flourishing with residents and business life, Greenwich is an ideal area for an art therapy retreat location.

Stewart anticipates that her choice of geographical location will thrive off of the serene immediate surroundings and provide a peaceful environment away from everyday life. She hopes that her design for a retreat, where people may experience a serene and peaceful atmosphere, will help individuals improve and become stronger, well-balanced, and composed people (Stewart, 2006). It is important for the project that transportation to the location be easy and convenient. Also, the journey to the site could aid in the therapeutic experience. Relaxation can begin as the customer leaves the fast-paced, hectic city for the calm tranquility of the country setting.

Overview of the State

The State of New York is located in the northeastern United States. New York borders with Canada to the north; Vermont, Massachusetts, and Connecticut to the east; New Jersey, Pennsylvania, and a bit of the Atlantic Ocean to the south; and Lakes Ontario and Erie to the west. Geographically, the state is the center of the Northeast. Because of the dense populations in the southern tip of the state, areas in New York are typically referred to as Downstate and Upstate.

Downstate, including New York City and its immediate suburbs, is densely occupied by commercial and retail spaces and closely knit residential areas. By contrast, the Upstate area is more open and rural; towns are typically separated by green rolling hills and open skies. Commercial businesses are still common and well developed, but there is more of a chance to easily escape the fast-paced life of the city than in the denser region to the south. Greenwich is located in the Upstate region, near Albany, the state capital.

State Transportation

Finding your way in and around New York State can be rather simple at times and a bit challenging at other times. The Upstate area and more specifically the capital region

FIGURE 6.5 **Scenic view of Greenwich, New York.**

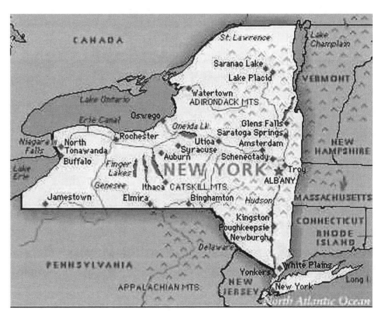

FIGURE 6.6 **Map of New York State.**

have Albany International Airport for convenient air travel. The major highways of New York seem to branch out from Albany to the extents of the state (see Figure 6.7). The routes travel in different locations, allowing easy accessibility from other surrounding states. Other common forms of transportation within New York State are train and bus (see Figure 6.8; Stewart, 2006).

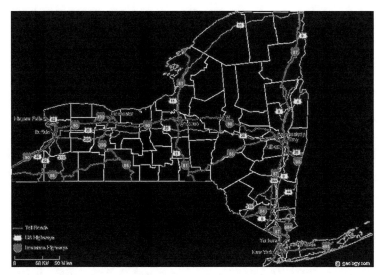

FIGURE 6.7 **New York State road and highway map.**

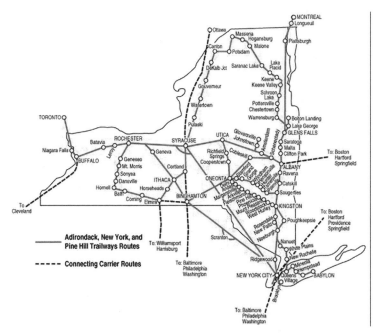

FIGURE 6.8 **New York State route map.**

In most scenarios, analyzing travel to the site can be an insightful exercise. Issues might surface that warrant documentation. In the example above, the experience is a therapeutic one. Conversely, think about traveling by car to a large city; it might have the opposite effect as you begin to deal with a faster pace, traffic, and more noise. You might begin to see very tall buildings.

The massive structures reaching to the sky have a monumental feeling about them. Theoretically, this might indicate that they are very important structures with significant activities occurring inside them. This same experience can be applied in numerous ways when you think about traveling to a location by foot. An example could be when one enters a hospital setting and travels by foot through corridors or walkways between buildings to a final destination inside that setting. This experience is referred to within the interior design profession as **way-finding**. If it is a children's hospital, the travel experience is catered to a child's eye and perspective. Colorful diagrams on the floor may help guide the way. Focus points such as fish tanks may be strategically placed at a child's eye level to engage and relax him or her in this unfamiliar setting. Both interior and exterior travel experiences can affect decision making of programmatic requirements.

Overview of the Town

Documentation of the town where the project is located gives you important, in-depth details about the town, population, and community. When you are gathering an overview of a town, the following should be addressed:

- A written overview of the town where the project is located.
- Statistical information about the community.
- Places of particular interest (include both text and images)—it is important to keep this focused and not to digress or attempt to document too much. The places of interest that you select should relate to your topic or be of some value. If your topic is a banquet facility that hosts private parties such as weddings, you might consider documenting the area's religious structures, florists, and scenic locations for photography.

When you document the above, it is important to try and capture the essence of the community in order to deliver a realistic picture of the area and what it encompasses.

WHEN STUDENTS WORK WITH CLIENTS

Often students will work with actual clients for a thesis project and have access to the town and community information via these clients. On occasion, members of the community will seek out students for design services. In many cases this can be a win-win situation for both parties, especially when both parties enter the arrangement with realistic expectations and goals. The student will have immediate access to a client, location, building, and the users of the space. This can create a real-life scenario in which to experience the programming process. The client can benefit from numerous options being explored, especially if more than one student is working on the project. A client that embraces and participates in the academic experience will walk away with many ideas.

Student Example: Pastry Shop

One such experience was a company entitled Dessert Works, currently located in Norwood, Massachusetts. Jen Cilano, an interior design senior contemplating what to do for her thesis, opted to work with Kristen Repa, owner of Dessert Works.

Through interviews, Cilano learned that Repa began her career more than fifteen years ago at Konditor Meister, a bakery known for its fine European pastries. Later, she worked as an apprentice pastry chef for the Ritz-Carlton in Boston, and then in 2001 she founded Dessert Works, a shop specializing in unique cakes and pastries (Dessert Works, 2016). While working at the Ritz, she met fellow chef Leonardo Savona, who is now her husband and business partner.

She went on to perfect her talents at Gerstner, the world-renowned pastry shop in Vienna, Austria, before opening Dessert Works.

Repa owned and operated Dessert Works in Medfield, Massachusetts, until November 2004, when she relocated to Norwood. In her three and a half years in Medfield, Dessert Works sales increased by 575 percent and quickly grew out of the space (Dessert Works, 2006). The Norwood site currently has a much larger retail space than Medfield, but Dessert Works is quickly growing out of it as well. The current location in Norwood is not easily noticed when passing by. It is in a strip mall that is situated away from vehicle and foot traffic. Repa told Cilano that her goal was to find a new location that would draw in more customers due to foot traffic as well as visibility and accessibility of the main road. She wanted to attract more walk-in customers, promoting the store name and brand.

Cilano could identify that Repa had specific programming needs: the building will be used for multiple purposes, including on-site baking, bakery sales, baking classes, wedding consulting, special-order cakes, and a café-type space. The clientele is typically high-end, which led to the reasoning behind the relocation to Wellesley, Massachusetts, a more affluent community.

After educating herself about her client's needs, Cilano can then turn to the community to see if it is, in fact, the right fit. The best sources to begin obtaining this information would be the town hall, the town's website, and the local library.

Wellesley is a town located in Norfolk County, Massachusetts, United States. The population was 26,613 in the 2000 Census. It has the reputation of being one of the most affluent and prestigious suburbs of Boston. It consistently ranks among the top five wealthiest towns in the state.

FIGURE 6.9
Kristen Repa, owner of Dessert Works.

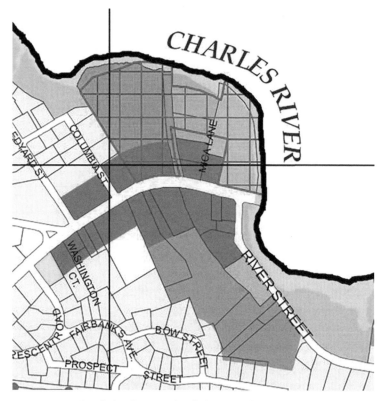

FIGURE 6.10A **Detail of zoning map of Wellesley, Massachusetts.**

FIGURE 6.10B **Color key** for **zoning map of Wellesley, Massachusetts.**

Through the foresight of the town fathers who, in 1914, made Wellesley the first town in America to adopt zoning laws, Wellesley grew into a beautiful town by the 1920s. It was then recognized as one of the leading suburbs of Boston. Filene's, the major department store, opened its first branch in Wellesley, where it then became a center for shopping.

The map in Figure 6.10 shows Wellesley's current zoning. Each zoning district is designated by a separate color. Essentially, a **zoning map** acts as a blueprint for a community's future development, showing how the land is divided to accommodate varied development interests. For example, this zoning map shows where Wellesley intends to place houses (i.e., residential buildings) and businesses (i.e., retail, commercial/industrial buildings) and their relationship to each other (Massachusetts EOEA, ¶10).

Washington Street, the potential site on the zoning map, is included in the Industrial A zone as well as the Lower Falls Village Commercial District.

Another area for Cilano to explore is the town's demographics. Will the community be able to sustain such a facility?

The median age of Wellesley was thirty-eight years old according to the 2000 census. This indicates that approximately 20 percent of Wellesley's population consists of young professionals. The median income for a household in the town of Wellesley was $113,686, and the median income for a family was $134,769. The average income for males was $100,000, while it was $53,007 for females. Only 3.8 percent of the population in Wellesley was below the poverty line, and that included 4.0 percent who were under the age of eighteen and 2.1 percent of those who were sixty-five years old or older (City-data, ¶2).

The site, image, and statistical documentation demonstrate that the proposed location of the Dessert Works facility in

Wellesley appears to be a good fit—it meets the client's needs and goals (Cilano, 2006).

EXTERIOR AND INTERIOR SITE DOCUMENTATION

The observational documentation of a site should start with the exterior. Then documentation should move into the building. When you are documenting the site, it is helpful to have a floor plan to make notations and document the dimensions. Also take a number of photos from various viewpoints. In many cases the space might be occupied, so you need to be efficient and courteous with your presence and that of others in the space.

Overview of the Site

Where is north? It may sound simple, but it's one of the most important questions. Do surrounding buildings cast shadows that will affect your interior space? Think about the earth elements and environmental factors. Can you easily implement the use of natural resources? What is the annual precipitation? Is there potential to harvest wind power? A brief introduction to the structure is imperative. It is essential to obtain a clear understanding of existing conditions.

Document the location and street. This can be done very easily online using internet search tools such as Google Earth or MapQuest. Once you have saved the image, you can then insert the map into Photoshop and add arrows or otherwise highlight specific areas that you might want to reference.

Typically the following should be documented:

- Location and street (text and images)
- Surrounding structures (text and images)
- The exterior of the building (text and images)

TABLE 6.1 EDUCATIONAL DEGREES OF WELLESLEY RESIDENTS

In 2000, those at least 25 years old:

High school degree or higher	97.6%
Bachelor's degree or higher	75.9%
Graduate or professional degree	41.2%

Source: Adapted from Department of Housing and Community Development, 2000.

TABLE 6.2 HOUSEHOLD CONFIGURATION OF WELLESLEY RESIDENTS

In the year 2000, there were 8,594 households in Wellesley, which included:

Children under the age of 18 living in the household	39.9%
Married couples living together	67.2%
Female householder with no husband present	7.1%
Someone living alone who was 65 years old or older	10.5%

Source: Adapted from Department of Housing and Community Development, 2000.

TABLE 6.3 HOUSEHOLD AGES OF WELLESLEY RESIDENTS

In 2000, the average household size was 2.70 and the average family size was 3.14. The average age of a person living in Wellesley was:

Under age 18	25.1%
18-24 years old	13.9%
25-44 years old	22.9%
45-64 years old	24.2%
65 years old and older	13.9%

Source: Adapted from the Department of Housing and Community Development

- Interior of the building (text and images)

Student Example: Rumford Chemical Works Site

Interior design student Erin Anthony explored the reuse and renovation of an old warehouse. The entire Rumford Chemical Works property is located at the intersections

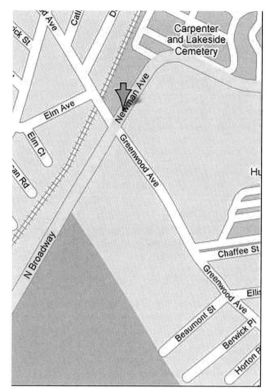

FIGURE 6.11A & B Map and bird's eye view of proposed project street location.

of North Broadway, and Greenwood and Newman Avenues in Rumford, Rhode Island. The street map and aerial view in Figures 6.11a and b pinpoint the exact location of the site.

Student Example: Waltham Street Site

Kristen Patten, also an interior design student, demonstrates her work in Figure 6.12. Patten's is another example of how to

FIGURE 6.12 An internet search provides a satellite view of a proposed project.

document an overview of a site location on Waltham Street, a few miles from Lexington Center in Massachusetts. The aerial map is shown with color-coded blocking overlaid. The transparency of color is a clever way to indicate where the building is in relation to surrounding structures.

Site Interior Documentation

When documenting the interior, you should place yourself at specific locations that can then by keyed into the floor plan for future reference. Figures 6.13a–e diagram examples of where you should place yourself. From these locations, document what you see visually, and with your written word, capture your experiences when moving through the space. A digital camera or cell phone is probably the most vital tool to use. Some documentation of the site can be taken via video, although for detail and further documentation, digital images truly are the best.

FIGURE 6.13A Front façade of site.

FIGURE 6.13D Rear façade, view 3, of site.

FIGURE 6.13B Rear façade, view 1, of site.

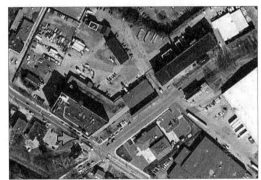

FIGURE 6.13E Satellite view of site.

FIGURE 6.13C Rear façade, view 2, of site.

Remember, it is important to be prepared when you go to the site. Call ahead to schedule an appointment. Bring all the tools you might need, including camera, graph paper, tape measure, and a friend or two to help. It would be advantageous to first document the location via Google Earth or other map application and have a printout of the aerial view. There are features with Google Earth such that you can import the site and get a fairly accurate measurement of the perimeter of the structure.

Although in some cases you may have selected a building that is in a different city or even country. You still can obtain information about the structure and surroundings using Google Earth. Google Earth Pro has advanced business tools in addition to all the easy-to-use features and imagery of Google Earth. (https://www.google.com/earth)

- Utilize data layers to locate your target demographic
- Compute distances and areas using measurement tools
- Use Movie Maker to produce collateral media
- Print high-resolution images for presentations and reports
- Import large vector image files to quickly map GIS data
- Map addresses with the Spreadsheet Importer

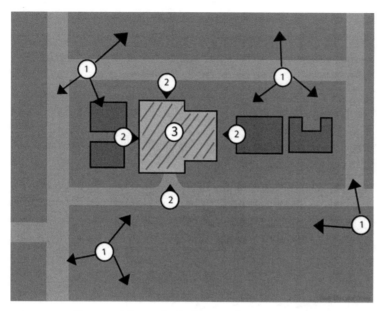

FIGURE 6.14 Diagram to help you visually document the site.

Student Example: International Community Church, Allston, Massachusetts

For her thesis project, interior design student Nicolette Gordon chose to collaborate with her church—The International Community Church.

This building is located at 30 Gordon Street, Allston, Massachusetts. The main street that the original church front faces is Cambridge Street, but after a renovation about five years ago the new main entrance is now located on Gordon Street. Figure 6.15 is a map of the location with a street view and means of transportation.

At the Cambridge Street entrance there is a flight of stairs leading up to the large wooden doorway entrance, centered by two plots of open grass lawn. The Gordon Street entrance has a small flight of three steps before entering the building. The opposite side of the building to Gordon Street is gated off to separate the space of the neighboring building; it consists of large trees. There is a small driveway located at the rear of the building, which can only hold about three cars in a row. The Gordon Street building entrance gains the most sunlight and foot traffic.

In Figures 6.16a–d, Gordon documents the visual surroundings of her selected site. This was accomplished by using Google Earth.

Gordon documented the interior wayfinding difficulties and general building conflicts in Figure 6.17. The floorplan identifies problematic issues in specific spaces in the structure. The exterior and site of the ecclesiastical structure that International

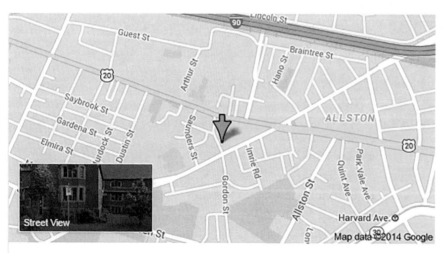

30 Gordon St Boston, MA 02134

Transit: Cambridge St @ Gordon St

Get directions

FIGURE 6.15A, B Google map of location & means of transportation.

Transportation

 9 bus routes within in a 5 minute walk

 10 minutes from Mass Turnpike

 Off a Bicycle Trail and 15 minute walk from Shopping area

FIGURE 6.16A Exterior observation: A view of the church entrance on Gordon Street.

FIGURE 6.16C Exterior observation: A view of the right side of Gordon Street, showing the houses across the street from the church.

FIGURE 6.16B Exterior observation: A view of both sides of Gordon Street, with the International Community Church on the left-hand side.

FIGURE 6.16D Exterior observation: A view of the church's original main entrance on Cambridge Street.

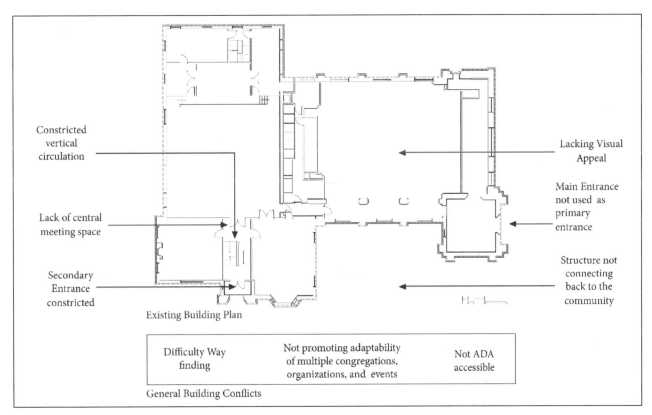

FIGURE 6.17 Floorplan of existing building.

Community Church occupies, which was built in 1930. Then she begins to document the interior of the structure with the same level of detail.

The structure consists of three stories, encased in a brick masonry envelope. The design is traditional, with high vaulted ceilings, hardwood floors, and large stained glass windows. Currently the existing structure holds many multi-purposed rooms of various sizes and a main sanctuary used for services. The four main areas on level one of the church are all common spaces, including an auditorium, the main sanctuary, the "little chapel," and the children's Sunday school space. The auditorium, as seen in Figure 6.18a, and the main sanctuary are used mainly for religious services, while the "little chapel" and Sunday school room are used for smaller meetings. The second level is designed for use as office space, laid out in cubical form with designated storage spaces. The lowest level of the church contains a dining function space, a "No Name Room," the "Basement Lounge," and the teen center. The structure also has allowances for a residential unit on the top floor, previously occupied by the building maintenance caretaker.

Gordon states that the various options for spaces in the building are ideal for incorporating multiple occupants. The traditional concept of the church will help to guide the design techniques used throughout the programming process. What is key to the development process is understanding the varying needs of each space in order to allow for maximum possible usage. Observations of the interior details of the space are the greatest piece of information needed, and will be documented during an on-site visit by taking photographs. It will be critical to acquire the building plans, and do additional measurements to ensure that building documents are drawn precisely and accurately. One of the only limitations that this structure may experience is its possible classification as a historical building, and the consequent guidelines for development and programming.

Gordon's final thesis presentation can be seen in Appendix F. The presentation incorporated many elements of the site's interior and exterior documentation that was conducted during the programming phase of design. Gordon was fortunate to be able to visit her site and tour and observe the interior and exterior in person. Often students select buildings in locations that are too far to visit for an observational study.

Student Example: Historic Building Not Easily Accessible

An example of this is Domeny Anderson's senior thesis. She selected the Divine Loraine Hotel located in Philadelphia, Pennsylvania. She was able to find an abundance of information online about this historic hotel. As seen in Box 6.1, she was able to document this succinctly without actually visiting the site. Obviously this is not ideal when you are working with a client—but for thesis and studio project documentation this is completely acceptable.

Locating Floor and Site Plans

Locating floor and site plans is an important exercise for students selecting a potential building and site for a project. The town

FIGURE 6.18A
Interior observation: The auditorium.

FIGURE 6.18B Interior observation: Main sanctuary ceiling detail.

FIGURE 6.18C Interior observation: Main sanctuary ceiling structure and balcony.

FIGURE 6.18D Interior observation: Main altar view from on top of the balcony.

FIGURE 6.18E Interior observation: Original sanctuary organ.

FIGURE 6.18F Interior observation: Narthex at rear of sanctuary.

FIGURE 6.18G Interior observation: Original stained glass.

FIGURE 6.18H **Interior observation: Baptism pool.**

FIGURE 6.18I **Interior observation: Sanctuary 2.**

hall, in most cases, is where the building department is located, and you can obtain existing site and floor plans for some structures there. Another option is to contact the owner, developer, builder, or architect of the structure directly. If you state that you are using the plans solely for academic purposes, in most cases people will be helpful. Also, many plans for public and historical buildings can be found online by conducting a detailed search. One very clever student found a building that was for sale and contacted the real estate broker, seeking a copy of the plans and requesting a visit to the site. When the student explained he was seeking to explore alternative retail uses for the tenant space, not only did the realtor agree, but he also requested a copy of the final project to put on display for potential clients to think about alterative retail options for the space.

Needless to say, it is helpful to think outside the box. Many benefited from the example above. The student gained access to a building, the realtor obtained a unique tool to help lease the space, and the student also gained some exposure from having work on display. If your building has some historical significance, you could call the local town historical society and visit the town hall. Most historians are eager to help and share their knowledge.

FIVE STEPS NEEDED TO DOCUMENT EXTERIOR AND INTERIOR SITES

This chapter aimed to share a variety of approaches to documenting a site analysis. A complete site analysis should include both visuals and written descriptions. It should encompass the following five steps:

BOX 6.1 A BARRIER FREE BOUQUET HOTEL

Step 1: Overview of the State
- Introduction (text)
- Maps (images)
- Major forms of transportation (air, train, highway)

Step 2: Overview of the Town
- Introduction (text)
- Information about the community (text and images)
- Places of particular interest (text and images)
- Demographics

Step 3: Overview of the Site
- Introduction to the structure
- Location and street (text and images)
- Visual Documentation: as diagramed in Figure 6.14.
- Surrounding structures—noted as 1 in Figure 6.14
- Exterior of the building—noted as 2 in Figure 6.14
- Interior of the building—noted as 3 in Figure 6.14
- Zoning and building codes

Step 4: Analysis and Documentation of the Building's Exterior
- Identify design constraints and limitations related to the exterior of the site.

Step 5: Analysis and Documentation of the Building's Interior
- Identify design constraints and limitations related to the interior of the site

Pulling It All Together

The best resources to retrieve this information are found on the website of the town where the project site is to be located. You can then review any local codes. You might also refer to **International Code Council**. Its website (www.iccsafe.org/index.html) currently has a map that shows where the **International Building Code (IBC)** has been adopted at the state or local level. Other such codes include the following:

- **International Residential Code (IRC)** is adopted at the state or local level in forty-six states plus Washington, D.C.
- **International Fire Code (IFC)** is adopted at the state or local level in forty-one states plus Washington, D.C.
- **International Plumbing Code (IPC)** is adopted at the state or local level in thirty-five states and Washington, D.C.
- **International Mechanical Code (IMC)** is adopted at the state or local level in forty-seven states and Washington, D.C.
- **The International Fuel Gas Code (IFGC)** is adopted at the state or local level in forty-six states and Washington, D.C.

(http://www.iccsafe.org/government/adoption.html, 2008).
- **ADA codes** and guidelines can be retrieved from the website www.access-board.gov/.

At this stage, try to identify design constraints and limitations that might have surfaced at this point relating to the site. It might be that the existing building has limited views, or that it's a historic structure, or that it isn't in ADA compliance and ramps and elevators need to be added. Observations to a site can be included here as well; these might include vehicular flow patterns and views from interior locations to exterior and vice versa. Daylight analysis encompassing various times of the year is another factor to explore and document.

Your clients might ask you to compare two sites from which they will select one, basing their decision on your analysis. As programmer, your goal is to give the reader, client, and designer a holistic picture of the town, community, site, and conditions at the point you document them.

KEY TERMS
- ADA codes
- International Building Code (IBC)
- International Code Council (ICC)
- International Fire Code (IFC)
- International Fuel Gas Code (IFGC)
- International Mechanical Code (IMC)
- International Plumbing Code (IPC)
- International Residential Code (IRC)
- Location overview
- Zoning map

CHAPTER 7

Precedent Studies

After reading this chapter, you should be able to:

- Select appropriate precedent studies that represent a global perspective.
- Analyze precedent studies.
- Document information gleaned from the precedent study to help formulate programmatic requirements.

Imitation may be the highest form of flattery; it's also one of the best ways to learn. We can learn from successes and failures alike, but as designers, our goal is not to imitate success but to learn from and improve upon it. When a researcher examines successes and failures in something that already exists in order to create something better, it's called a **precedent study**. Researching examples of what already exists in the realm of one's design topic is a natural process for a designer who's looking to gain insight into a new project.

You would be remiss to approach the design process without taking the time to study what already exists and learn something from it. The goal in performing a precedent study of your specific type of design application is to learn from the examples you collect. Thus, analysis of both the strengths and weaknesses of each design are important to document. In order to bolster your project with knowledge gleaned from these previous successes and failures, a precedent study should be performed before embarking upon the programming phase of a project.

An example of a precedent study within the built interior environment might be an examination of the various types of color used in educational settings and their potential impact on the users. Another example might be a review of circulation patterns in retail design to examine the relationship between consumer paths and sales. Numerous studies have been completed on topics related to virtually every existing aspect of interior design.

THE VALUE OF PRECEDENT STUDIES

Within the design curriculum, it is required that students undertake a precedent study analysis during their education. By studying precedents that parallel the type of design that you are employing, you can glean insights from the analysis of various

BOX 7.1 FLORIDA STATE UNIVERSITY FACULTY MARLO RANSDELL, PHD: OVERVIEW OF THE VALUE OF PRECEDENT STUDY ANALYSIS DURING THE PROGRAMMING PHASE OF DESIGN

Marlo Ransdell is an associate professor at Florida State University and specializes in the creative process within design education and the application of technology.

She is the director of graduate studies and oversees Studio D: Design and Fabrication Lab. Dr. Ransdell teaches furniture design, research and programming, research methods, and design fundamentals. Her research centers on the application of technology in design education and enhancing critical thinking among interior design students.

Research and programming is a central aspect of creating a successful and vital master's degree of study. At Florida State University, all graduate students create a programming document to guide their master's thesis and project outcomes. This document allows students to explore the needs of their topics and justify their design decisions. The difference in this and a standard design studio is that students are given full responsibility of defining the program requirements for their individual projects. This allows each student to become the "expert" of content in their area of study while relying on faculty for advice and guidance.

Uncovering precedents studies for studio work is an important part of student research, but what is really valuable is the justification of the precedent studies themselves. Students identify previous precedent studies but take that a step further and justify each against

FIGURE 7.1A
Marlo Ransdell PhD

literature within the interior design body of knowledge. Students are able to look at precedent studies through the lens of previous research to identify successes and limitations of designs and learn from them for their own projects. This experience teaches students how to justify their design decisions beyond their own likes, dislikes, and preconceived notions and asks them to identify aspects of design that relate to proven research. This process serves each student well as they go into the professional field and take these introspective skills with them.

design solutions to the same type of problem. Your analysis and critique of existing design solutions can take place at many levels, and will create a useful foundation that you can use throughout your professional design career.

A PRECEDENT STUDY MODEL

The following is a model to use when selecting, documenting, and analyzing precedent studies. As outlined in Chapter 4, "Research Methods," there are many qualitative and quantitative methods that could be applicable in analyzing any given precedent study. You can modify the following model to meet your needs for any given design project.

- **Step 1: Introduction**—List an overview of each project or site that you have selected to analyze as parts of your precedent study. Identify each by name, address, state, and country of location.
- **Step 2: Description of Each Site**—Write a description for each site. Discuss the same kinds of observations from each site for consistent data comparison, and include a written analysis.
- **Step 3: Qualitative Analysis of Each Site**—Employing a thick or thin description in your analysis, analyze the written content that has been collected from the sites. Identify common and recurring themes that emerge. Examples of a thematic analysis are discussed later in this chapter.

- **Step 4: Quantitative Analysis of Each Site**—Analyze the site's programmatic requirements and create a chart or matrix that outlines the spaces included within each requirement. The matrix chart could expand to include not only physical requirements but also amenities offered; examples of this are included in this chapter.
- **Step 5: Summary of Findings**—Document what was gleaned from the above information and analysis.
- **Step 6: Conclusion**—From the precedent study analysis, how and what will impact your design topic and programmatic requirements.

The model shown in Figure 7.1 is a suggested approach to help you synthesize all of the information that you have collected. Many designers and students have not only implemented this model but have also adapted it to meet their needs.

SELECTING YOUR PRECEDENT STUDY

Students should select examples of sites that represent a **global perspective**. As a design student, you should be aware of world views and design considerations that are relevant and can be embraced by all, while also noting cultural and regional differences. The precedent study should examine operations, design layouts, features, amenities, and anything that the researcher feels would help in designing a similar space.

In general, it is advantageous to pick five to eight sites. You will then have accumulated a substantial amount of data to be analyzed.

Select examples from all over the world. There are numerous ways to obtain this information. Whenever possible, make site visits to specific locations, where you can employ an observational research method

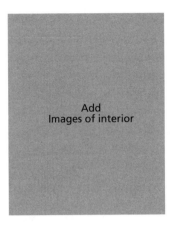

Precedent Study #
Location:

Description of
Space and List
of Amenities
Exiting spaces
Outside spaces
Square footages
Capacity
Lighting
Handicap Accessible

Add
Images of interior

Add
Any other special features that you might be documenting
A mission statement
Customers review of space
Specific Branding images

Add
Drawing/sketch of floor plan
Identify circulation
Traffic patterns
Means of egress
Natural light
Indicate a north arrow

FIGURE 7.1 **A visual diagram of a precedent study template created by Rose Mary Botti-Salitsky.**

that includes interviews and photos; this might then culminate in a thick description of your site observation. You can also obtain further information by generating a questionnaire and sending it out to target groups. You can always gather information from books, journals, and magazines, when you are trying to represent a global perspective. The internet is a great resource as well.

To locate precedent study examples, it is imperative to search all areas of information thoroughly, from locally accessible library reference books and magazines to reliable online databases. To narrow your search, it is helpful to use descriptive words

FIGURE 7.2
An exterior view of Boston City Hall (right).

FIGURE 7.3
An interior view of Boston City Hall (below.

by city employees who must work in the building and might feel otherwise. It can be interesting to compare different authors' viewpoints of the same site.

When you feel a sufficient amount of data has been collected, it is important to read through each piece, noting key facts and information related to your design focus. Generally, the more noteworthy the resources are, the more likely you are to be able to find the research cited in other works.

Once you have compiled all of the data to analyze from the sites, make sure that you study comparable information from each one. You want to be absolutely sure your analysis plan will be a feasible task. In doing so, be sure to perform the following steps:

from your key focus areas. Some locations may have been the subject of more than one study. Sometimes you may need to explore how a site has changed through time or how it is considered from alternative perspectives. For example, City Hall in Boston was built in the Brutalist Modern style during the 1950s to the 1970s (Figures 7.2 and 7.3). It is viewed very differently by designers, who appreciate its style, and

- Document the location, size, and interior spaces, as well as the exterior.
- Identify what is unique about your example.
- Document your response using a "thick description" technique.
- Use visuals.

- List all the amenities.
- Document unique features.
- If a website is available, look to see if the company has a mission statement.
- If it is a public space, look to see if customers have written reviews.

Try to consolidate all the information for each site into a template. The template suggested here is very generic, as the applications of design can vary tremendously. When you create your template, be sure that you will be able to retain the same information from each site in order to allow for consistent data comparison.

Precedent Study Student Example

Katie Timmerman, a graduate student at Florida State University, compiled a graduate thesis programming and research document on the topic of MILLENNIALS + HOME: Understanding the Needs of the Millennial Generation in Their Living Environment. A challenging issue for Millennials (the generation born roughly between the early 1980s and 2000s) is the lack of available housing that meets their needs, and the difficulty of building an emotional connection to their homes and surrounding community (Jones, 1995). In order to accommodate this desire for emotional connection to their surroundings, and to better understand their housing needs, it is essential to understand the Millennials' meaning of home. Determining what attributes Millennials include in their view of home can help designers understand how to enhance emotional connections to their living spaces, to establish a personal identity through "sense of place" and a social identity through "sense of community" (Jones, 1995).

The purpose of Timmerman's project is to provide a design solution that meets the needs of the Millennial generation in relation to housing and emotional connections

within their surroundings. Millennials are currently the largest population to be moving away from home to new cities due to personal or career changes (PRC, 2010). Without any emotional ties to their new locales, Millennials must form a connection with their surroundings that supports a balance between personal and social identities (Jones, 1995). This project explored the role of mixed-use design as it impacts the development of personal and social identity through sense of place and sense of community. The final solution was the design of a mixed-use housing environment tailored to the physical and social needs of this generation.

The site selected was Downtown Los Angeles, the main business district in Los Angeles, California. Approximately 50,000 people reside in Downtown LA, and over 500,000 people work/commute to downtown on daily basis. The Arts District occupies the eastern side of Downtown LA. This district's borders are Alameda Street to the west, the 101 Freeway to the north, the LA River to the east, and the 10 Freeway to the south. Older industrial warehouses and railroad buildings comprise the majority of the Arts District. In 1981, the city passed an Artist in Residence ordinance, allowing formerly industrial buildings to be transformed into artist studios and residences. The Arts District is a vibrant, community neighborhood filled with artist lofts, restaurants, trendy bars, art galleries, retail stores, and many live entertainment venues. Home to an abundance of artists, creative businesses, and architecture students, this up-and-coming district is also a popular film location.

Prior to starting designing, Timmerman researched previous studies of similar designs to the one she was embarking on. Figure 7.4 lists twelve different precedent studies identified in phase one of the research.

PHASE 1

RESEARCH
design considerations
precedent study 1- 16M
precedent study 2- 2000 ave. of stars
precedent study 3- the domain
precedent study 4- limelight
precedent study 5- 261 city road
precedent study 6- manhattan lofts
precedent study 7- WKL
precedent study 8- confidential
precedent study 9- spring tower lofts
precedent study 10- brockman lofts
precedent study 11- 8th + hope
precedent study 12- one santa fe
precedent study general comparison
precedent study amenities comparison

PROGRAMMING
general programming info
general adjacency matrix
special considerations matrix
circulation diagram level 1
circulation diagram level 2
circulation diagram level 3
circulation diagram level 4
circulation diagram rooftop
stacking diagram
furniture needs
technology needs
lighting needs

FIGURE 7.4 **List of precedent studies identified during phase one of research, by Katie Timmerman, Florida State University graduate student.**

To organize the data collected for all of her precedent studies, Timmerman created a standard template, seen in Figures 7.5 and 7.6, to synthesize her data on each one. Her template consisted of a one-page sheet with images running along the top, listing the location, levels, square footage, building category, architect, and interior designer. A brief description, list of amenities, and some noteworthy design considerations were also included.

Student Example: Millennial Homes
Above in Figure 7.4 Timmerman outlined the precedent studies in a one-page format.

In the chart seen in Figure 7.7, she takes each precedent study and synthesizes its information even further, allowing for a quick comparison of some of the design attributes between the twelve precedent studies.

Figure 7.8 is a chart Timmerman created to look at the amenities offered in each precedent. It outlines some of the standard amenities that one would assume all facilities would contain, but after a quick scan of the quantitative analysis, the results are interesting. Not one of the amenities totals 100% for each precedent study, these findings are thought-provoking and can help the design evolve while planning the programmatic requirements.

A MIXED METHOD APPROACH TO PRECEDENT STUDIES
Through each step of your precedent study, always keep in mind that your goal is to gain greater insight into the type of design that you are researching. Also be mindful that the knowledge gained here will continue to be of value throughout the next phases of the design process. This cannot be overstated.

It is wise to keep a sketchbook as a way to visually document ideas, or inspirations that might surface, so you can capture the essence of your insights for later use. When analyzing the data collected from the research, you should look at the information using both quantitative and qualitative skills.

Quantitative Analysis to Precedent Studies
At this point in the project, most students are very curious about the existing program requirement for each space. Identifying core requirements is a common approach to analyzing the different precedent examples. Unique spaces might also be identified that could make the difference in a design. Including a simple matrix in your precedent

PRECEDENT STUDY 1:

16M
Location: Denver, Colorado
Levels: 10
Square Footage: 330,000
Category: Mixed-use
Architect: Gensler
Interior Designer: Philip Nimmo Designs

Description: 16M is comprised of ground floor retail, four floors of luxury apartments, five levels of office space, and three levels of below grade parking. This mixed-use building is located in the heart of Downtown Denver, and caters to the live-work-play community.

Amenities:
Reception/Concierge
Community rooftop terrace
Fitness center
Office/Workspace
Resident Lounge
Bike storage
Parking
Walkability
Retail

Design Considerations:
-Architecture and interiors are designed to fit seamlessly into Denver's neighborhood context; exterior space overlooks local downtown environment
-Apartments are located within close proximity to in-building amenities and amenities located within walking distance
-Outdoor terraces are provided for public and private use, successful integration of interior and exterior spaces
-Large windows allow for natural lighting
-Grouped seating in lobby

FIGURE 7.5 Example precedent study using standard template. Created by Katie Timmerman, Florida State University graduate student.

PRECEDENT STUDY 2:

2000 AVENUE OF THE STARS
Location: Los Angeles, California
Levels:
Square Footage: 750,000
Category: Commercial Office, Mixed-use
Architect: Gensler
Interior Designer: Gensler

Description: 2000 Avenue of the Stars, contains over 750,000 square feet of office space, as well as retail, restuarant, cultural amenities, and below grade parking. The building was devloped on a sustainable approach, and is one of the most energy efficient buildings in Los Angeles.

Amenities:
Reception/concierge
Office/workspace
Bike storage
Parking
Retail
Cafes
Walkability

Design Considerations:
-Architecture and interiors are designed to incorporate state of the art facilities
-Campus amenities are located within walking distance and close proximities
-Large windows allow for natural lighting
-Design is contemporary

FIGURE 7.6 Example precedent study using standard template. Created by Katie Timmerman, Florida State University graduate student.

	PS1	PS2	PS3	PS4	PS5	PS6	PS7	PS8	PS9	PS10	PS11	PS12
NAME	16M	2000 Ave of the Stars	The Domain	Limelight	261 City Road	Manhattan Lofts	WKL	Confidential Project	Spring Tower Lofts	Brockman Lofts	8th + Hope	One Santa Fe
LOCATION	Denver, CO	Los Angeles, CA	Austin, TX	Ontario, Canada	London, UK	London, UK	Kuala Lumpur	San Francisco, CA	Los Angeles, CA	Los Angeles, CA	Los Angeles, CA	Los Angeles, CA
SIZE	Medium	Large	Large	Medium	Medium	Large	Large	Medium	Medium	Medium	Large	Large
FUNCTION	Mixed Use Residential Retail Hospitality	Mixed Use Corporate Office Retail Hospitality	Mixed Use Residential Retail Hospitality	Residential	Mixed Use Residential Retail Hospitality	Mixed Use Residential Retail Hospitality	Mixed Use Commercial Residential Hospitality	Residential	Residential	Residential	Residential	Residential
LIGHTING	pendants, overhead fixtures, recessed lighting, contemporary fixtures	contemporary fixtures, good variety of overhead lighting	good mixture of overhead and ambient lighting	contemporary, highly designed fixtures, good variety of overhead and ambient lighting	good variety in lighting fixtures, including pendant, overhead and task lighting, ample daylighting	good variety in lighting fixtures, including pendant, overhead and task lighting, ample daylighting	contemporary, highly designed fixtures for pendant and overhead lighting	bright lighting, contemporary fixtures, natural light	small variety in lighting fixtures, minimal task lighting, ample overhead lighting	bright lighting, cove lighting, contemporary fixtures	bright lighting, contemporary fixtures, large variety of fixtures, ample natural light	bright lighting, contemporary fixtures, natural light
COLOR PALETTE	brick, metal, wood, glass, neutral color palette	glass, metal, stone, neutral color palette	stone, wood, neutral color palette, pops of color	stone, wood, glass, neutral color palette, pops of color in finishes	glass, metal, stone, neutral color palette	glass, metal, stone, wood, neutral color palette	glass, metal, stone, wood, neutral, rich color palette	stone, wood, glass, neutral color palette	brick, concrete, metal, monochromatic color palette	brick, concrete, neutral color palette	glass, metal, stone, wood, neutral	stone, concrete, glass, neutral color palette, pops of color
FURNITURE	Contemporary furniture, and arrangements that promote comfort and socialization	Contemporary seating and office furniture	Contemporary furnishings, and large quantities of seating and arrangements	Contemporary furnishings arranged similar to living room settings to promote comfort and socialization in intimate settings	Contemporary, high end furniture, and arrangements that promote comfort and socialization. Hospitality style: functional furniture	Beautiful contemporary, and end furnishings and finishes. Fixtures and finishes have Asian influences	Contemporary furnishings, and large quantities of seating and arrangements	Contemporary furnishings arranged similar to living room settings to promote comfort and socialization in intimate settings	traditional furnishings, sparse arrangements	contemporary furnishings and finishes	Contemporary furnishings, and large quantities of seating and arrangements to promote socialization	Contemporary furnishings arranged to promote comfort and socialization

FIGURE 7.7 Chart comparing size, function, lighting, color palette, and furniture of twelve precedents. Created by Katie Timmerman, Florida State University graduate student.

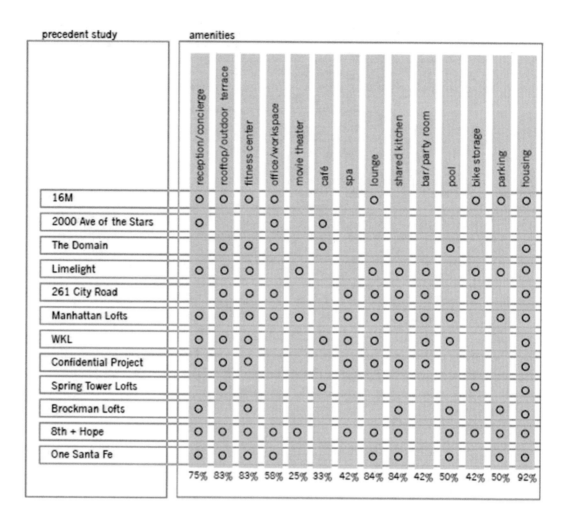

FIGURE 7.8 Chart comparing specific amenities offered by twelve precedents. Created by Katie Timmerman, Florida State University graduate student.

study to analyze the locations seems to work best in this application.

For example, say you have chosen to design a jazz club for your senior thesis. Prior to designing, you should look at other jazz clubs and learn what makes them successful and where areas of improvement can be incorporated. After deciding on the feel of the jazz club, you might set out to find locations that combine jazz clubs with a modern-style bar and lounge. You might choose these two aspects to research because you wish to combine the feel of jazz with a modern style in the final design. Your precedent studies would be chosen from all over the world, so you could get a fuller idea of the programmatic requirements and design aesthetic that could be included in the design of your jazz club.

After you determine the sites for your precedent study, you gather all the functions of the study—the color palette, furniture style, what seemed to work and what did not, and the lighting of all the studies. After these are determined, you organize your findings by employing various charts. These charts allow you to take a holistic view of the sample that was examined.

Six sites were selected for the precedent study (PS) review. Representing a global perspective, these include Page, Tokyo, Japan (PS-1); Crow Bar, Auckland, New Zealand (PS-2); Mandarin Bar, London, England (PS-3); Buddy Guy's Legends, Chicago, Illinois (PS-4); Iridium Jazz Club, New York, New York (PS-5); and Stampen, Stockholm, Sweden (PS-6) (N. Heerdt, 2007). Once you have collected the data, both quantitative and qualitative, for each site, you document an analysis of them all. After gathering information from each, you then take a closer analysis, looking at location, function, design details, and similarities between them, if any. In doing so, you are integrating both the qualitative and quantitative research as part of your analysis.

Student Example: Jazz Club

Nicole Heerdt is an interior design student exploring a jazz club for her senior thesis project. For a first step, Heerdt decided to generate a comparison chart showing the location of each site in her precedent study. In total, they represented a worldwide study. This comparison chart also organized and focused on the design details of each location; these details included lighting, color scheme, and the furniture found throughout each bar.

Comparison charts help organize the design aspects of each site. In this case, the chart demonstrates that some jazz clubs provide an additional source of entertainment for their customers, such as dancing. It also identifies from the selected sample that the most popular color scheme was neutral with accents. The lighting in all the locations featured an array of techniques, all of which focus on an intimate and relaxing atmosphere for customers.

Heerdt's "Amenities" chart differs from the comparison chart in that the former aims to identify programmatic spaces that are included within each of the sites (see Table 7.2).

In most cases these sites have common programmatic spaces. They all featured bars, and half of them either had lounges or stages. This comparison proved very useful, as it identified that only two in the sample group had a dance floor, and one included

TABLE 7.1 COMPARISON CHART: SIX SITE STUDIES

	PS- 1	PS- 2	PS- 3	PS- 4	PS- 5	PS- 6
NAME	**PAGE**	**CROW BAR**	**MANDARIN BAR**	**BUDDY GUY'S LEGENDS**	**IRIDIUM JAZZ CLUB**	**STAMPEN**
Location	Tokyo, Japan	Auckland, New Zealand	London, England	Chicago, Illinois	New York City, New York	Stockholm, Sweden
Function	Bar and Lounge	Bar and Lounge	Bar and Lounge	Bar	Bar and Club	Bar
Lighting	Pendants, Table lamps, Uplighting	Spotlights, Wall sconces, Candle, Pendants	Uplighting, Accent Lighting, Recessed Lighting	Recessed Lighting, Track Lighting	Pendants, Track Lighting	Pendants, Candle, Track Lighting
Color Scheme	Neutral: Beige and Black	Accent: Rich Red Neutral: Black	Neutral: Variations of Browns and Ochres Accent: Deep Rich Orange	Black	Pale Rose	Neutral: Taupe
Furniture	Modern Leather Armchairs and Couches	Modern Leather Booths	Art Deco Inspired Bar Chairs and Armchairs	Wooden Dining Style Tables and Chairs	Wooden Dining Style Table and Chairs	Wooden Bar Style Stools and Tables
Entertainment	None	Dancing	None	Live Music	Live Music	Live Music, Dancing

Source: N. Heerdt, 2007.

TABLE 7.2 AMENITIES CHART FOR PRECEDENT STUDY

AMENITIES	PS-1	PS-2	PS-3	PS-4	PS-5	PS-6	PERCENTAGE
2 or more floors	No	Yes	No	No	No	Yes	33.33%
Bar	Yes	Yes	Yes	Yes	Yes	Yes	100%
Lounge & stage	Yes	Yes	Yes	No	No	No	50%
Kitchen	Yes	No	No	Yes	Yes	No	50%
-If Yes, kind of food	Appetizers	—	—	Louisiana Style	Tapas	—	—
Dance floor	No	Yes	No	No	No	No	16.67%
Gallery	Yes	No	No	No	No	No	16.67%
Pool Room	No	Yes	No	No	No	No	16.67%

Source: N. Heerdt, 2007.

a cigar divan. Such information will be invaluable in developing the programming requirements of the potential space; when looking for typical requirements, the designer can also explore what might be included as a unique feature in the space.

Student Example: Sustainable School

For her senior thesis project, Samantha Roblee, an interior design student, explored primary and secondary school environments that were also sustainable and LEED compliant.

For this project, Roblee focused on academic structures and employed sustainability to their environments. The selection and focus encompassed two topics that might not always be found simultaneously; hence, the approach was slightly modified. In order to analyze and depict what was successful and where improvements were needed, she divided her precedent study into two equal sections. The academic precedents were strictly limited to renovated school structures, while the sustainable section of the

precedent study included both new and renovated school structures that applied sustainable design attributes.

The academic sites (APS) included the Grand View Elementary School in Manhattan Beach, California (APS-1) and the Ben Davis High School in Indianapolis, Indiana (APS-2). Additionally, information was compared and contrasted between the Buffalo, New York-based East Aurora Senior High (APS-3) and the North Warren Central School in Chestertown, New York (APS-4). The sustainable sites for the precedent study (SPS) included Diébédo Francis Kéré's Gando Primary School, Gando Vilage, Burkina Faso, a West African nation (SPS-1); the Newton South High School in Massachusetts (SPS-2); the Bamboo Primary School in Vietnam (SPS-3); and the Druk White Lotus School in India (SPS-4) (Roblee, 2007, p. 57).

The information that Roblee selected to compare in this sample group specifically focused on two issues: sustainability and educational K–12 facilities. Roblee chose to focus on these issues because sustainability was a key factor that she was aiming to learn more about from her precedent study analysis.

The sustainable precedent study matrixes showed that the most substantial contribution to "green" considerations was through use of simplistic systems and local and/or recycled materials. **Passive sustainable systems,** including natural lighting, energy-efficient utilities and fixtures, solar heating and cooling, natural ventilation, and site orientation, were clearly the easiest to adapt to an array of varying environments. However, LEED qualifications would maintain the foundation for further sustainable enhancements (Roblee, 2007, p. 73).

TABLE 7.3 COMPARISON CHART: FOUR SITE STUDIES

	SITE STUDY #1	SITE STUDY #2	SITE STUDY #3	SITE STUDY #4
	NEWTON SOUTH HIGH SCHOOL	**GANDO PRIMARY SCHOOL**	**L'ÉCOLE SAUVAGE / BAMBOO PRIMARY SCHOOL**	**DRUK WHITE LOTUS SCHOOL**
Site Location	Newton, MA	Gando Village, Burkina Faso, West Africa	Luong Son Village, Nha Trang, Vietnam	Shey, Ladakh, India
SUSTAINABILITY				
Solar Power	*			*
Local Materials	*	*	*	*
Site Orientation		*	*	*
Recycled Materials	*	*	*	*
Carpet Tiles	*			
Low-Zero VOCs	*	*	*	
Natural Ventilation		*	*	*
Natural Lighting	*	*	*	*
Energy Efficient Utilities/Fixtures	*	*	*	*
Rain Water Collection System				*
Low-Flush Toilets	*			
Gardens		*		*
Solar Heating Cooling Insulation		*	*	*
LEED Qualification: Schools Registered Certified Gold Platinum	Registered	N/A	N/A	N/A
Collaborative for High Performance Schools (CHPS)	Best Practices Manual	N/A	N/A	N/A

Source: S. Rooblee, 2007.

TABLE 7.4 COMPARISON CHART OF SUSTAINABILITY APPLICATIONS IN THE FOUR SITE STUDIES

SUSTAINABILITY	NUMBER RATIO	TOTAL PERCENTAGE
Solar Power	2:4	50%
Local Materials	4:4	100%
Site Orientation	3:4	75%
Recycled Materials	4:4	100%
Carpet Tiles	1:4	25%
Low-Zero VOCs	3:4	75%
Natural Ventilation	3:4	75%
Natural Lighting	4:4	100%
Energy Efficient Utilities/Fixtures	4:4	100%
Rain Water Collection System	1:4	25%
Low-Flush Toilets	1:4	25%
Gardens	2:4	50%
Solar Heating Cooling Insulation	3:4	75%
LEED Certification:	1:4	25%

Source: S. Roblee, 2007.

Student Example: Spa

As Erin Anthony, an interior design student, began to explore program requirements necessary in designing a spa, her precedent study focused on day spas in the United States and abroad in order to gain a global perspective on the subject. The five sites selected were SenSpa of San Francisco (PS-1); Rain Spa of Quebec (PS-2); Villaggio Day Spa of Fishers, Indiana (PS-3); Adamina Spa of London (PS-4); and the Maui Spa and Wellness Center of Boca Raton, Florida (PS-5).

The first table focuses on the various types of treatment rooms, including the quantity and facilities offered by each spa (see Table 7.5). The second analysis of the five selected sites focused on the types of treatments and services offered to customers by each spa (See Table 7.6). This is an essential part of the research, as it alludes to what needs to be included in the proposed project in order to make it a successful business.

The goal of this precedent study analysis was to gather valuable information by studying projects similar to the one being proposed as a senior thesis project. With data analysis, valuable information was acquired as to what should be included in the program and design of the proposed spa project. Key indicators identified that the following facilities should be included in the program: treatment rooms, relaxation rooms, retail areas, cafés, and exercise areas. Also, it was important to include in the proposed project a wide variety of treatments,

TABLE 7.5 TYPES OF TREATMENT ROOMS AND FACILITIES AT FIVE SPAS

ANALYSIS OF TREATMENT ROOMS/ FACILITIES	SENSPA SAN FRANCISCO, CA	RAIN SPA QUEBEC, CANADA	VILLAGGIO DAY SPA FISHERS, IN	ADAMINA SPA LONDON, ENGLAND	MAUI SPA AND WELLNESS CENTER BOCA RATON, FL
Treatment Rooms	N/A	N/A	N/A	6	10
Sauna	N/A	N/A	N/A	N/A	1
Steam Room	N/A	N/A	N/A	1	1
Relaxation Rooms	N/A	N/A	2	1	1
Changing Rooms	N/A	N/A	N/A	2	N/A
Retail Space	N/A	1	N/A	1	1
Nail Rooms	N/A	1	1	1	1
Salon	N/A	N/A	1	N/A	1
Check- In/ Reception	1	1	1	1	1
Café	N/A	N/A	N/A	N/A	1

Source: E. Anthony, 2007.

ranging from massages to herbal medicine. Based on the study, the treatments on offer should fall under three basic categories: facial care, body care, and aesthetics.

Additionally, the proposed project should incorporate and focus on themes such as relaxation, rejuvenation, and the body, each similar to those seen in the precedent study. The design, as well as the business, should evoke relaxation, wellness, rejuvenation, and tranquility within its clients. Overall, the space should consist of soothing qualities and atmospheres to ensure that customers can focus on rejuvenating their body, mind, and spirit (Anthony, 2007 p. 48).

As seen in the preceding precedent studies, when students look at programmatic requirements of existing designs based on what they are aiming to achieve, a quantitative analysis of program spaces is helpful in creating and justifying the program.

Qualitative Analysis to Precedent Studies

Exploring a qualitative analysis to the precedent study exposes many issues that can significantly influence design decision making as well. Analyzing written content that has been collected from the precedent study can help identify significant common and recurring themes. The thematic analysis process starts with the collection of data. Once the data is organized, "patterns of experiences can be listed [which] can come from direct quotes or paraphrasing common ideas" (Aronson, 1994, ¶4). Once the data is coded, themes derived from patterns serve as a focus (Aronson). Eisner (2002) refers to this as identifying the thematics of the data. This method would be a considered a qualitative approach to analyzing data. Chapter 4 reviews this research method, as well as other qualitative approaches.

TABLE 7.6 TYPES OF SERVICES AT FIVE SPAS

ANALYSIS OF TREATMENTS AND SERVICES	SENSPA, SAN FRANCISCO, CA	RAIN SPA, QUEBEC, CANADA	VILLAGGIO DAY SPA FISHERS, IN	ADAMINA SPA, LONDON, ENGLAND	MAUI SPA AND WELLNESS CENTER, BOCA RATON, FL	PERCENT YES FOR ALL SPAS
Massage	Yes	Yes	Yes	Yes	Yes	100%
Facials	Yes	Yes	Yes	Yes	Yes	100%
Peels	Yes	No	No	Yes	No	40%
Waxing	Yes	Yes	No	Yes	Yes	80%
Hot Stone	Yes	No	Yes	Yes	Yes	80%
Microdermabrasion	Yes	Yes	Yes	Yes	No	80%
Mud Therapy	Yes	No	Yes	No	No	40%
Acupuncture	Yes	No	No	No	Yes	40%
Herbal Medicine	Yes	No	No	No	Yes	40%
Body Scrubs	No	No	Yes	No	Yes	40%
Body Wraps	No	Yes	Yes	Yes	Yes	80%
Hair Removal	No	Yes	No	Yes	No	40%
Manicure/Pedicure	No	Yes	Yes	Yes	Yes	80%
Reflexology	No	Yes	Yes	No	Yes	60%
Gentleman Services	No	No	Yes	Yes	Yes	60%
Couples Services	No	No	Yes	No	Yes	40%
Mom-To-Be Services	Yes	No	Yes	Yes	Yes	80%
Salon Services	No	No	Yes	No	Yes	40%
Meditation	Yes	No	No	No	Yes	40%
Exercise Programs	Yes	No	No	No	Yes	40%
Total Yes	12	8	13	11	16	- - -
Total No	8	12	7	9	4	- - -

Source: E. Anthony, 2007.

Student Example: Vineyard

Liz Carter is an interior design student, exploring the topic of a winery for her senior thesis project. In her precedent study for her winery project, Carter used the Microsoft Word search tool to tally repeating words, phrases, and passages. It is important to make sure that you can obtain comparable information from each site that you are analyzing. Repeated words are identified and can be assigned a color. Carter selected five different sites: Nashoba Valley Winery,

Bolton, Massachusetts (PS-1); Wagner Vineyards, Lodi, New York (PS-2); The Round Barn Winery, Baroda Michigan (PS-3); Embudo Station, Rio Grande Valley, New Mexico (PS-4); and Vintara Estate, New Zealand (PS-5). Content was taken from the main web page of the vineyard corresponding to each site. The description of each winery was then copied and pasted into a Word document. Once the document was formed, a word search was conducted identifying recurring words, aiming to characterize common themes throughout the study. As seen in Figure 7.9 and Table 7.8, the most common words found were noted, keyed in, and color-coded. They were then categorized and charted from the most prevalently repeated words down to the least repetitive. Also noted were the number of times the word appeared. This was executed to identify common themes that emerged.

The data identified that the most common theme between the sites was wine; it was used at least thirty times in all the opening statements. "Other themes found between these sites were in the words winery, beer, brewery, and restaurants" (L. Carter, 2007, p. 49). These themes could have a significant impact in identifying programmatic requirements, as well as design aesthetic.

Student Example: Loft Space

Ashley Benander, an interior design student, used a qualitative approach to explore the topic of residential loft spaces for her senior thesis project. She analyzed five sites for her precedent study, the first three representing a global perspective, with the remaining two located within the United States: Oliver's Wharf, London, England (PS-1); The West Shinjuku Lofts, Tokyo, Japan (PS-2); The New River Head Lofts, London, England (PS-3); The O'Malley Residence, Avoca, Pennsylvania (PS-4); The Bay Loft, San Francisco, California (PS-5); and The Pavonia Loft, Jersey City, New Jersey (PS-6).

TABLE 7.7 WRITTEN ANALYSIS OF THICK DESCRIPTIONS: IDENTIFYING RECURRING WORDS IN THE PRECEDENT STUDY

WORD	# OF TIMES USED
Wine	30
Winery	9
Beer	6
Brewery	5
Restaurant	5
Tour	4
Unique	4
Distill	3
Tasting	2
Variety	2
Gourmet	1
Learn	1

Source: Liz Carter, 2007.

TABLE 7.8 WRITTEN ANALYSIS OF THIN DESCRIPTIONS: IDENTIFYING RECURRING WORDS-CONCEPTS IN THE PRECEDENT STUDY

REPEATING WORDS THAT WERE IDENTIFIED	NUMBER OF TIMES USED IN DESCRIPTIVE ANALYSIS OF LOFT
Space	14
Original	12
Warehouse	8
Contemporary	6
Kitchen	6
Light	6
Steel	5
Modern	3
Exposed	2

Source: A. Benander, 2007.

Nashoba- Located in the heart of Massachusetts' apple country, Nashoba Valley Winery is a stunning hilltop orchard overlooking the charming town of Bolton. Always growing and ever-beautiful, we are open daily throughout the year, with the exception of The Fourth of July, Thanksgiving Day, Christmas Day and New Year's Day. Since first producing superior fruit wines in 1978, Nashoba Valley Winery has earned wide acclaim as a pioneering winery orchard and a premier destination for visitors seeking excellent wine, exquisitely prepared food, and a gorgeous country setting. The family-owned orchard, winery & restaurant, set on 52 rolling acres, boasts a state-of-the art wine-making and distillation facility, an exceptional wine and gift shoppe, a brewery, and a gourmet restaurant.

With over 100 national and international medals to its credit and accolades from such noteworthy publications as "Boston Magazine", "Wine Enthusiast", "Cooking Light", "Food & Wine", "The Yankee Magazine" 2003 Editors Choice, and "Community Newspaper Company 2004 Readers Choice Award, Nashoba Valley Winery is the ultimate destination for any wine connoisseur. We take the art of winemaking seriously. And with over 20 varieties of wines, a variety of hand crafted beers and distilled spirits, Nashoba Valley is dedicated to quality and is recognized as a premium producer. From its beginning until today, Nashoba Valley remains a family owned winery with our focus on quality and value at the forefront of all we do. Plan a visit to a truly unique American farm and learn why Nashoba Valley was selected as one of the ultimate destination places on the east coast.

Wagner- Wagner offers the most comprehensive tour of any Finger Lakes winery. The tour encompasses all facets of the winemaking operation as well as the viticultural practices important to the production of quality wine grapes. A tasting of a wide selection of our wines and non-alcoholic grape juice follows the tour. Visitors can also take a self-guided brewery tour and taste our craft-brewed beers. **Pub Nights on the Brewdeck** are held every Friday from Memorial Day weekend through Labor Day weekend, with live entertainment, great wine, beer & food on the brewery deck. Visitors can then browse in our retail wine shop where all of our wines and beers are available for sale.

The Round Barn- The Round Barn Winery is a family-owned and operated winery, distillery and brewery and is nestled in the rolling hills of the Southwest Michigan countryside. We specialize in hand-crafted wines, fruit brandies, vodka and microbrews.

Our tasting room is located in a turn of the century post and beam bank barn originally built in 1881 while our still and Banquet/Wedding facilities are housed in our unique Amish-built round barn.

Embudo- At the Embudo Station restaurant you might choose to enjoy our succulent barbequed ribs, charbroiled steaks, grilled chicken, or a variety of authentic New Mexican dishes. People travel for miles to enjoy our unique oak smoked rainbow trout. There are many vegetarian choices, as well as salads, on our menus. Lunches feature choices of sandwiches, including our famous Brisket Sandwich. Along with these choices, try one of our fresh brewed beers or a glass of award winning local wine.

Vintara Estate - Vintara is operated by Lisa and Michael Murtagh. Michael and Lisa were born just down the road (Michael literally married the girl next door) from the Vintara vineyard, having worked in the wine business for over 20 years both in Australia and in many parts of the world, they returned to setup Vintara and reside in the Rutherglen region.

Michael makes the beers and the wines as well as managing the 50 hectares of vineyards, Lisa manages the office and general operations.

Gavin Swalwell, our chef, moved from Melbourne six years ago to run the kitchen at a renowned local restaurant and has never looked back. Gavin's love of traditional flavours, using local products and then presenting them in a contemporary way lifts the food at Vintara to great heights.

Steve Wallace our cellar door and brewery bar manager has over 25 years experience in managing Rutherglen cellar doors and his expertise in our wines and those of the region make him a great guy to talk to about wine and the region, where to stay and what to do.

Alicia Martin is our Restaurant front-of-house and functions manager - give her a call or drop in to see what we have to offer those looking for a unique and pleasurable function experience.

FIGURE 7.9 **Analyzing and identifying reoccurring words. Created by Liz Carter.**

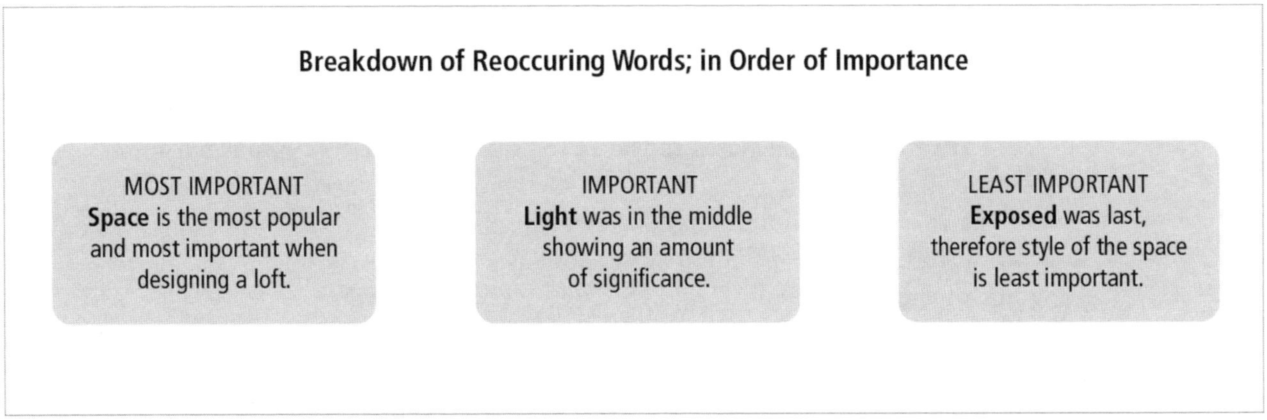

Breakdown of Reoccuring Words; in Order of Importance

MOST IMPORTANT
Space is the most popular and most important when designing a loft.

IMPORTANT
Light was in the middle showing an amount of significance.

LEAST IMPORTANT
Exposed was last, therefore style of the space is least important.

FIGURE 7.10 **Identification of common themes. Created by Ashley Benander.**

Table 7.7 lists words that Benander found and the number of times they repeated throughout the six sites. "The first word identified within the table is 'Light,'" which showed up six times. This was not unexpected, as many clients in the precedent study expressed the need for "natural light, a lot of light and a light feel to the environment."

Another recurring word was "space"; this word showed up the most out of all identified words from the sample. This is important when you consider lofts and how one occupies them. "Warehouse" was identified eight times, which displays a uniting factor of historic origins, as many of the spaces had been converted from warehouse industrial use to residential-home use. Another popular word found was "original." This could be reflecting the occupants' desire to maintain the "original" integrity of the building as a high priority among loft designers/owners (Benander, 2007. p. 41).

The next step was to not only look at words and the amount of times they were repeated but to then also try to generate common themes. The chart in Figure 7.10 aims to prioritize the words found and shows visually where these words fall in the realm of importance. "Looking even further into these findings one could conclude that the actual design of the space, the flow

of the rooms and structure are most important. Atmosphere is second to this, such as light and views. And last is the actual style the space is designed in" (Benander, 2007, p.45). Straus and Corbin (1998), who refer to this step as **axial coding**, state that "in axial coding, categories are related to their subcategories to form more precise and complete explanations about phenomena" (p. 124). Chapter 4 explains in more detail this form of research and other approaches. Employing this method of organizing data is very comfortable for designers. As visual thinkers it helps to see things graphically.

ANALYZING THE INFORMATION

Once all the data has been sorted and analyzed, it is important to see and document what you have discovered. A synopsis statement should be included as a conclusion to your precedent study. It could reinstate some of the expected outcomes but also identify any unexpected issues that might have surfaced during the precedent study analysis process. It should reflect the five to eight examples that you selected as a sample to study, and document a mixed method approach.

The critique of existing design solutions is common in the design educational experience and within the profession. It is important to train the designer's eye not only in design aesthetics but also in analytical skills that can critique spaces objectively (i.e., to remove personal biases and begin to learn from precedents).

This is a perfect time to predict what you might choose to include in your program of the space you will design based on what you have learned from the precedent study analysis. If you are conducting a precedent study for a client, this is a useful tool for analyzing existing competitors. The client might aim to emulate some of the programmatic requirements, learning from what exists and planning for future possibilities. This also might be where you include some conceptual and aesthetic findings that surfaced during the study.

KEY TERMS
- Axial coding
- Global perspective
- Passive sustainable systems
- Precedent studies

CHAPTER 8

Generating the Program

After reading this chapter, you should be able to:

- Generate overall program requirements.
- Generate requirements for each space in your program.
- Calculate square footage and the circulation of a space.

Once the site is selected and you have completed a precedent study, the general programmatic requirements can be outlined. The client's program requirements have been identified, and you can compose a list that includes any special features. By program requirements, we mean all the spaces that are needed in order for the space to function. When generating the program for a space, there are a few key aspects to keep in mind. First and foremost are the client's needs and wants, the "must-haves" and the "would-like-to-haves." Second is the data and analysis from the research that you conducted before you began creating this program. These were discussed in previous chapters. Synthesizing both of these factors will help create a program that should

meet existing requirements, and anticipate change, such as future growth, or reduction.

The knowledge that you gleaned from the precedent study analysis should be reflected in your program. Your research in the precedent study helps determine necessary spaces to be included in the programmatic requirements. Together, the quantitative and qualitative analyses discussed in the prior chapter should help you create the ideal program for your space.

THE PROPOSED PROGRAM

The program begins to take form as you start to list all the program requirements, determine the circulation, calculate the required square footage, document the existing square footage, and analyze specific needs. Each of these steps is discussed below.

TAKING THE MACRO VIEW

As you may have noticed by now, most programmers find it advantageous to look at everything on a large scale first before delving into the details. Only after gaining knowledge of the "big picture" do programmers begin to work their way through the project until every detail has been addressed. This should be an instinctive skill for an interior designer, who is accustomed to observing a space first and then planning for its occupants.

Listing the Program Requirements

The programmer's first task in generating a program is to make a list of program requirements. Most likely at this point in the programming phase, you will have a fairly good idea of what needs to be included from the client's request, interviews, observational studies, and analysis of your precedent study.

Remember, by "program requirements," we mean all the spaces that are needed in order for the site to function. When approaching this list, you can look at this task from several vantage points:

- Is there an existing space?
- What is the total square footage of anticipated requirements?
- How much is factored in for circulation?
- How much is factored in for core requirements?
- Do the potential users have projections of growth or downsizing for the next two to three years?
- Are there any special requirements?
- What are the codes that need to be considered?

Document Your Information

To get started, document everything. You need to think of all the individual spaces as well as all necessary support spaces. For example, if you are programming for a retail store, how much space will be allocated for the merchandise? What are the display options? Are the displays freestanding or hanging? What about storage, cash, wrapping, checkout area, circulation,

office space, and bathrooms? Sometimes it is easy to overlook details. If, for example, the retail space were specifically set up for apparel, one would need to add dressing rooms and maybe even a seating area to the program requirements. Document this information in a chart outlining the requirements for your space, including the quantity for each item on this list. A simple equation in Box 8.1 can help you organize this information and estimate the square footage. Using computer spreadsheet software, like Microsoft Excel, is a great way to organize the material. Design firms typically employ their own standardized templates for organizing this material, as seen in some of the interviews from the design firms throughout the text. Consider Allegro Interior Architecture and Spagnolo Gisness & Associates, both discussed in Chapter 1; Tsoi/Kobus & Associates in Chapter 5; and MPA | Margulies Perruzzi Architects in Chapter 9. For an academic exercise, however, the template in Box 8.1 should be sufficient to get you started.

Determining the Circulation

It is important to determine the circulation or space to be allotted for people to move around. Depending on what percentage is needed for circulation, it can have a significant impact of the size of your other spaces. Typically, circulation should be factored in between 22 to 40 percent. This will vary depending on the type of design project. A low circulation number is often associated with good, efficient space planning. But many factors weigh into this scenario, the most significant being the application for which the space is being designed.

Calculating the Square Footage

Calculating the square footage of your proposed space is important because it gives you a realistic idea of the site and how much room you have to work with.

BOX 8.1 GENERIC TEMPLATE FOR SQUARE-FOOTAGE CALCULATIONS

SPACE	QUANTITY	EST. SQ. FT	TOTAL SQ. FT
ADD SPACE	HOW MANY	ADD #	ADD TOTAL #
TOTAL			#
% OF PROGRAM FOR CIRCULATION			#
TOTAL REQUIRED SQUARE FOOTAGE			ADD TOTAL #

Once you have the program requirements, you can total them. This will give you the total programmatic requirements needed for your site. Then you can figure out how much is remaining and determine the circulation or, if there is extra space, decide how it should be allocated.

Most likely, when you conducted the historical, observational, and interactive research, you probably gathered a great deal of relevant information that can help determine the appropriate square footage for each space.

Calculating the square footage of a space can vary based on what formula you employ. It might sound a bit odd that there is not one formula that everyone uses, but there are many factors that come into play, and so formulas must vary to accommodate these differences. For example, if the building is a tenant fit-out and there are common spaces, the landlord would employ a formula that would include a percentage of the "shared spaces" and include this in the square-footage cost. If, on the other hand, the building is freestanding and the client owns it, the client will be very aware of every space and how it is going to be used.

Floor Usable Area and Gross Measured Area

It is important to understand what the usable space of a building entails and how to measure that area properly. This calculation can vary based on the type of space you are dealing with and the core components of the space. Following are definitions from the U.S. General Service Administration Facilities:

- **Floor usable area**—Floor usable area is the sum of all office, store, and building common usable areas. Floor usable area is the floor rentable area minus floor common areas that are available primarily for the joint use of tenants on that floor.
- **Gross measured area**—Gross measured area is the total area within the building minus the exterior wall.

Documenting the Existing Square Footage

Documenting the existing square footage of the space allows you to see if the program requirements are going to fit into the proposed site. If a few sites are being considered, the total programmatic square-footage requirements plus circulation will help you determine what the right space should be. It is helpful to see all the requirements outlined in a list format with the total square footage needed for each space. You can then compare the existing square footage against the proposed square footage and make adjustments where needed.

Helpful Resources

Resources that can help you find space square-footage standards for specific design applications include the following:

- **American National Standards Institute (ANSI)**—www.ansi.org
- **Building Owners and Managers Association (BOMA)**—www.boma.org
- **The International Facility Managers Association (IFMA)**—www.ifma.org

Student Example: Domestic Violence Shelter

Katrina Rutledge, a graduate student at Florida State University, completed her precedent study analysis, seen in Figure 8.1. Looking at precedent studies and their amenities is extremely useful to help identify what program requirements to include.

FIGURE 8.1 **Phase one of research and programming, by Florida State University Graduate Student Katrina Rutledge.**

It also will help identify unique spaces you may not have thought about. This is outlined in Chapter 7. Rutledge is designing a domestic violence shelter in the city of New Orleans, Louisiana. Domestic violence is a widespread problem that affects over one million women each year (Tjaden & Thoennes, 2000). According to the Violence Policy Center (2013), Louisiana has often ranked in the top ten states, with a number one ranking in 2007, for the highest percentage of female homicide victims murdered by male perpetrators. Of the victims, 94 percent knew their killers personally, and 61 percent were killed by a current or previous intimate partner. There is currently a need for a large domestic violence shelter in New Orleans. There are existing small shelters and programs in surrounding areas; however, these shelters are often not easily accessible to women needing immediate shelter within New Orleans. The need for safe emergency and transitional housing for victims of domestic violence is great.

During Rutledge's first phase she completed the precedent study research and then implemented that information to create her program. As noted in Figure 8.1 she generated the following:

- General programming information
- Square footage of spaces
- Adjacency matrix
- Special considerations matrix
- Circulation
- Furniture needs
- Lighting & technology needs
- Code considerations

This creates quite an extensive and comprehensive document prior to embarking on the design.

The general programmatic requirements for the major spaces are identified in Figure 8.3. Below in Figure 8.4 the minor spaces have been identified with the estimated square footage.

Phase 1:

Research
General Design Considerations From Literature
Precedent Study 1:Domestic Abuse Intervention Services
Precedent Study 2: Homesafe
Precedent Study 3: Baylor Boarding School
Precedent Study 4: Annie Wright Boarding School
Precedent Study 5: Saint John's Rehabilitation Hospital
Precedent Study 6: Sister Margaret Smith Treatment Center
Precedent Study 7: Groot Klimmendaal Rehibilitation Center
General Precedent Studies Comparisons
Precedent Amaenities Compariosons
Programming
Square Footage of Spaces/Adjcency Matrix Circulation
Furniture Needs/Lighting and Technology Needs
programming
General Programming Information
Square Footage of Spaces
Adjacency Matrix
Circulation
Furniture Needs
Lighting and Technology Needs
Code Considerations

	PS1	PS2	PS3	PS4	PS5	PS6	PS7	TOTAL %
Name	DAIS	Home Safe	Baylor	Annie Wright	Saint John's	Marharet Smith	Groot Klimmendaal	
Resident Rooms	yes	yes	yes	yes	yes	yes	yes	100%
Offices	yes	yes	yes	yes	yes	yes	yes	100%
Health Clinic	no	no	yes	yes	yes	yes	yes	71%
Kitchen/Cafeteria	yes	yes	yes	yes	yes	yes	yes	100%
Group Rooms	yes	yes	yes	yes	yes	yes	yes	100%
Courtyard	no	yes	yes	yes	yes	yes	yes	85%
Serenity Garden	yes	no	yes	no	yes	no	no	42%
Fitness	no	no	yes	yes	yes	yes	yes	71%
Library	no	no	yes	yes	no	no	yes	43%
Arts Facilities	no	no	yes	yes	no	no	yes	43%
Daycare	yes	yes	no	no	no	no	no	28%
Children's Play	yes	yes	yes	yes	no	no	yes	71%
Chapel	no	no	yes	yes	yes	yes	no	57%
Classrooms	no	no	yes	yes	no	yes	no	43%

FIGURE 8.2 **Amenities comparison, by Florida State University Graduate Student Katrina Rutledge.**

Major Spaces	Estimated Sq. Footage
Resident Rooms	40 Rooms x 300 sq. ft. each = 12,000
Resident Bathrooms	20 Bathrooms x 64 sq. ft. - 1,280
Kitchen(s)	4 Kitchens x 200 sq. ft. - 1,200
Dining Area	4 Dining x 480 sq. ft. - 1,920
Living Room(s)	4 Living x 600 sq. ft. = 2,400
Group Rooms	4 Group x 600 sq. ft. = 2,400
Children's Daycare	1 Daycare Center = 1,500
Children's Play	1 Indoor Children's Play = 1,000
Courtyard	1 Interior Courtyard = 2,500
	Total = 26,200

FIGURE 8.3 **General programming major spaces, by Florida State University Graduate Student Katrina Rutledge.**

Minor Spaces	Estimated Sq. Footage
Entry	600
Intake Area	600
Offices	10x200-2,000
Classrooms	4x300=1,200
Clinic Room	500
Serenity Garden	500
Art Class	1,000
Fitness Areas	500
Community Room	500
Storage (Donations)	500
Storage (Residents)	300
Storage (Staff)	300
Pantry	300
Pet Kennel	1,000
Reflection (Room(s)	3x200=600
Spa	1,00
Public Restrooms	200
Children Outdoor Play	500
Laundry	4x250=1,000
Hotline Office	700
	Total=13,800

FIGURE 8.4 **General programming minor spaces, by Florida State University Graduate Student Katrina Rutledge.**

	Entry	Intake	Offices	Group Rooms	Classrooms	Clinic	Daycare/Play	Courtyard	Arts	Fitness	Community Rooms	Serenity Garden	Office Storage	Pet Kennel	Reflection Rooms	Spa	Public Restrooms	Outdoor Play	Hotline Office	Resident Rooms	Resident Baths	Laundry	Living Rooms	Kitchens	Dining Rooms	Donation Storage	Resident Storage	Pantry
Entry		^	v	v	v	v	X	X	X	X	X	X	X	^	X	v	^	X	X	X	X	X	X	X	X	^	X	X
Intake			v	v	X	^	v	X	X	X	v	X	X	^	X	X	^	X	X	v	v	X	X	X	X	X	X	X
Offices				v	v	X	O	X	X	X	X	X	^	O	X	X	^	O	^	X	X	X	X	X	X	v	X	X
Group Rooms					v	X	v	X	v	v	v	X	X	O	X	^	v	X	v	v	X	X	X	X	X	X	X	X
Classrooms						X	v	X	X	X	v	X	X	v	X	^	O	X	X	X	X	X	X	X	X	X	X	X
Clinic							O	O	v	X	X	X	^	X	X	X	^	X	X	X	X	X	X	X	X	X	X	X
Daycare/Play								v	X	X	X	O	X	O	X	^	^	O	O	X	X	X	X	X	X	X	X	X
Courtyard									v	X	v	^	X	^	v	X	^	^	X	v	X	X	v	X	v	X	X	X
Arts Facilities										X	^	v	X	X	X	v	^	X	X	X	X	X	X	X	X	X	X	X
Fitness											^	O	X	X	X	v	^	X	X	X	X	X	X	X	X	X	X	X
Community												v	X	X	X	X	^	^	X	X	X	X	X	X	X	X	X	X
Serenity Garden													X	X	^	^	^	O	X	X	X	X	X	X	X	X	X	X
Office Storage														X	X	X	X	X	X	X	X	X	X	X	X	X	X	X
Pet Kennel															O	O	^	v	X	v	X	X	X	X	X	X	X	X
Reflection Rooms																v	v	O	X	v	X	X	v	X	X	X	X	X
Spa																	^	O	X	X	X	X	X	X	X	X	v	X
Public Restrooms																		v	v	X	X	X	v	X	v	X	X	X
Outdoor Play																			O	X	X	X	X	X	X	X	X	X
Hotline Office																				X	X	X	X	X	X	X	X	X
Resident Rooms																					^	v	^	^	^	v	^	v
Resident Baths																						v	v	v	v	X	v	v
Laundry																							X	X	X	v	X	X
Living Rooms																								^	v	X	X	X
Kitchens																									^	v	X	^
Dining Rooms																										v	v	^
Donation Storage																											v	v
Resident Storage																												v
Pantry																												

FIGURE 8.5A Adjacency matrix, by Florida State University Graduate Student Katrina Rutledge.

Legend

^ High Adjacency
v Medium Adjacency
O Undesirable Adjacency
X No Adjacency Needed

FIGURE 8.5B Legend for adjacency matrix, by Florida State University Graduate Student Katrina Rutledge.

The adjacency matrix in Figure 8.5 is a great tool to help synthesize all of the information into one chart prior to starting bubble diagramming.

The special consideration matrix also helps to consolidate all of the information into one location. This is a wonderful tool. Once generated, you can print out and review it prior to working on bubble diagrams.

Figures 8.7, 8.8, and 8.9 show how Rutledge takes the data and begins to translate it into circulation studies for each floor.

During phase two of her research Rutledge repeats the process with more focused detail on the specific spaces she will be designing.

Student Example: High-Quality, Small-Scale Hotel

Ashley Johnson, an interior design student, researched and prepared the programmatic requirements for a high-quality, small-scale hotel. The information that she gathered from the precedent study helped generate programmatic requirements. Table 8.1

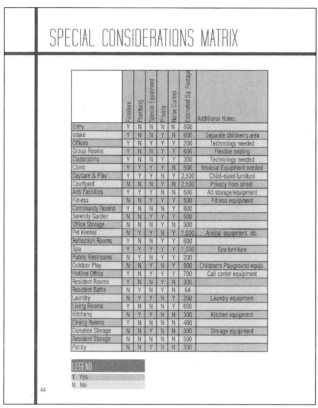

SPECIAL CONSIDERATIONS MATRIX

	Furniture	Plumbing	Special Equipment	Privacy	Noise Control	Estimated Sq. Footage	Additional Notes:
Entry	Y	N	N	N	N	600	
Intake	Y	N	N	Y	N	600	Separate children's area
Offices	Y	N	Y	Y	Y	200	Technology needed
Group Rooms	Y	N	N	Y	Y	600	Flexible seating
Classrooms	Y	N	N	Y	Y	300	Technology needed
Clinic	Y	Y	Y	Y	N	500	Medical Equipment needed
Daycare & Play	Y	Y	Y	N	Y	2,500	Child-sized furniture
Courtyard	N	N	N	Y	Y	2,500	Privacy from street
Arts Facilities	Y	Y	Y	N	N	500	Art storage/equipment
Fitness	N	N	Y	N	Y	500	Fitness equipment
Community Rooms	Y	N	N	N	Y	800	
Serenity Garden	N	N	Y	Y	Y	500	
Office Storage	N	N	N	Y	N	300	
Pet Kennel	N	Y	Y	N	Y	1,000	Animal equipment, etc.
Reflection Rooms	Y	N	N	Y	Y	600	
Spa	Y	Y	Y	Y	Y	1,000	Spa furniture
Public Restrooms	N	Y	N	Y	Y	200	
Outdoor Play	N	N	Y	N	Y	500	Children's Playground equip.
Hotline Office	Y	N	Y	Y	Y	700	Call center equipment
Resident Rooms	Y	N	N	Y	N	300	
Resident Baths	N	Y	N	Y	N	64	
Laundry	N	Y	Y	N	Y	250	Laundry equipment
Living Rooms	Y	N	N	N	Y	600	
Kitchens	N	Y	N	N	N	300	Kitchen equipment
Dining Rooms	Y	N	N	N	N	480	
Donation Storage	N	N	Y	N	Y	500	Storage equipment
Resident Storage	N	N	N	N	N	500	
Pantry	N	N	Y	N	N	300	

LEGEND
Y Yes
N No

44

FIGURE 8.6 Special consideration matrix, by Florida State University Graduate Student Katrina Rutledge.

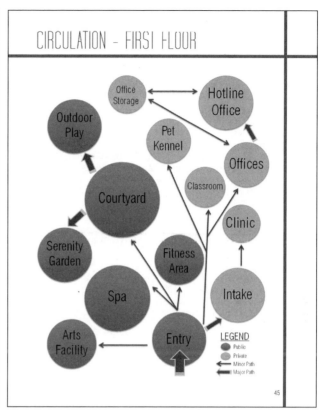

CIRCULATION - FIRST FLOOR

45

FIGURE 8.7 Circulation—first floor, by Florida State University Graduate Student Katrina Rutledge.

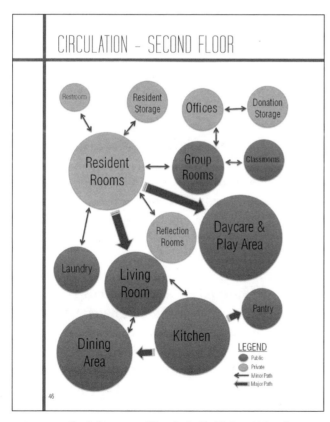

CIRCULATION - SECOND FLOOR

46

FIGURE 8.8 Circulation—second floor, by by Florida State University Graduate Student Katrina Rutledge.

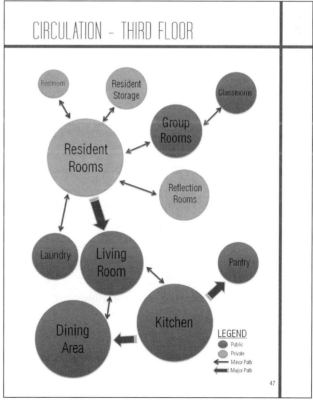

CIRCULATION - THIRD FLOOR

47

FIGURE 8.9 Circulation—third floor, by Florida State University Graduate Student Katrina Rutledge.

Phase 2:

Catergory A: Children's Daycare/Play
Research General Design Considerations From Literature Precedent Study A:-1:Aegis Precedent Study A:-2: Early Childhood Precedent Study A:-3: Big Smile Precedent Study A:-4: Chesapeak Child Development Center General Precedent Studies Comparisons Precedent Amenities Comparisons Programming Square Footage of Spaces/Adjcency Matrix Circulation Furniture Needs/Lighting and Technology Needs
Catergory B: Residents Rooms
Research General Design Considerations From Literature Precedent Study B:-1:Warsaw Apartment Precedent Study B:-2: Sao Paulo Small Apartment Precedent Study B:-3: Generator Hostel Precedent Study B:-4: Hich Line Hotel General Precedent Studies Comparisons Precedent Amenities Comparisons Programming Square Footage of Spaces/Adjacency Matrix Circulation Furniture Needs/Lighting and Technology Needs
Catergory C: Dining/Kitchen
Research General Design Considerations From Literature Precedent Study C:-1:Pakta Restaurant Precedent Study C:-2: Saison Restaurant Precedent Study C:-3: Ella Dining Room & Bar Precedent Study C:-4: Jing Restaurant General Precedent Studies Comparisons Precedent Amenities Comparisons Programming Square Footage of Spaces/Adjacency Matrix Circulation Furniture Needs/Lighting and Technology Needs

FIGURE 8.10 **Phase two of research and programming, by Florida State University Graduate Student Katrina Rutledge.**

TABLE 8.1 PROGRAMMIC REQUIREMENTS

MAJOR SPACES	ESTIMATED SQUARE FEET
Check-in/Lobby	870
Lounge/Dining	1,207
Guestrooms (44)	13,860
Kitchen	370
Pool/Hot tub Area	1,045
Employee Office/Lounge	950
Laundry/Storage	1,185
MINOR SPACES	
Public Restroom	41
Fitness Room	508
Gaming/Leisure Room	522
Boiler/Furnace Room	223
Vending/Ice Machine	128
Elevator (1)	64
Stairwells (3)	290

Estimated Square Footage Total: 21,263
Circulation 30%: 6,379
Relevant Codes: Residential Occupancy (R-1), Assembly
(A-3), Business (B), Cal. 133,
NFPA 701, ADA compliant, ICC/ANSI standard
Source: Ashley Johnson, 2008.

shows the areas that are to be included in the proposed hotel. The criteria matrix in Figure 8.11 lends insight into adjacencies and the space-planning phase of design.

Johnson blocked out in concept both the first and second floors with the estimated proportion that should be allocated to each space. Also note that she inserted a gray phantom corridor to allocate the circulation. A square footage can then be allocated to this (Figure 8.12).

Analyzing Specific Needs
Once each space and the square-footage requirements have been determined on a macro scale, break down each space to analyze the specific needs and document them. For example, within a reception space for an office, you might need to include seating for a certain number of people, a coat closet, a reception desk, task seating, storage, and the like.

Programming for Future Needs
When generating your program, flexibility of design is needed for the optimum use of the total square footage. You might be programming for a longer-range plan that could realistically extend out three to five years.

CRITERIA MATRIX FOR PROPOSED HOTEL IN CATSKILL, NY	SQ. FOOTAGE NEEDS	ADJACENCIES	PUBLIC ACCESS	DAYLIGHT AND/OR VIEW	PRIVACY	PLUMBING	SPECIAL EQUIPMENT	SPECIAL CONSIDERATIONS
① CHECK-IN/LOBBY	870	CENTRAL	H	Y	N	N	N	HISTORIC CHARACTER
② LOUNGE/DINING	1,207	① ④ ⑧	H	Y	N	N	N	
③ GUESTROOMS	15,860	⑨⑩⑪⑫⑬⑭	L	Y	H	Y	N	UNIQUE & SPECIALIZED, NOT COOKIE-CUTTER
④ KITCHEN	370	②	L	N	H	Y	Y	
⑤ POOL/HOT TUB AREA	1,045	① ⑨ ②	M	I	M	Y	N	
⑥ EMPLOYEE OFFICE/LOUNGE	950	①	L	I	H	Y	N	
⑦ LAUNDRY/STORAGE	1,185	② ⑬ ⑭	L	N	H	Y	N	
⑧ PUBLIC RESTROOM	41	① ②	H	N	N	Y	N	
⑨ FITNESS ROOM	508	⑤ ②	M	I	M	Y	Y	
⑩ GAMING/LEISURE ROOM	522	⑤	M	I	M	N	N	
⑪ BOILER/FURNACE ROOM	225	REMOTE	L	N	L	Y	N	
⑫ VENDING/ICE MACHINE	128	②	M	N	L	Y	N	
⑬ ELEVATOR	64	① ②	H	N	N	N	N	
⑭ STAIRWELLS	290	① ②	H	I	N	N	N	

ESTIMATED S.F. TOTAL: 21,263
CIRCULATION 30% : 6,379

NOTE: IN "ADJACENCIES" COLUMN ② - INDICATES ADJACENCY IMPORTANCE
② - INDICATES MAJOR ADJACENCY IMPORTANCE

LEGEND
H = HIGH
M = MEDIUM
L = LOW
Y = YES
N = NO
I = IMPORTANT BUT NOT REQUIRED
◉ = IMMEDIATELY ADJACENT
● = IMPORTANT ADJACENCY
× = REASONABLY CONVENIENT
• = UNIMPORTANT
— = REMOTE

FIGURE 8.11
Criteria matrix.

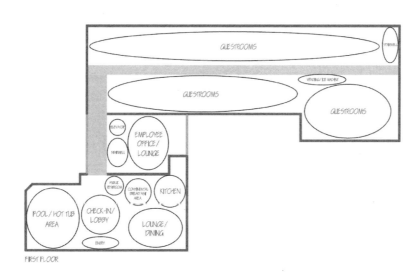

FIRST FLOOR

FIGURE 8.12
Blocking out requirements with the phantom corridor indicating circulation.

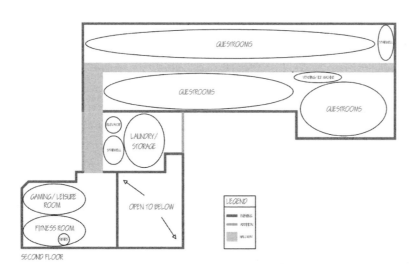

SECOND FLOOR

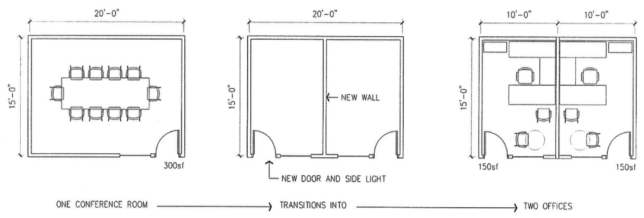

FIGURE 8.13 **Anticipating change.**

Space Utilization Studies

Often the programmer is asked to think ahead, planning for the optimum use of space and its utilization. An example of this can be found in the professional example on Spagnolo Gisness & Associates in Chapter 1, "What Is Programming?" SGA analyzes client needs while listing and reflecting on the observational and interactive data that it previously collected. In this case, the client needs a conference room; however, the client's anticipated growth indicates that he will in fact also need more office space within the next few years. Figure 8.13 help the client see how to allocate 300-square-foot spaces for potential future expansion.

Space utilization studies often combine written analyzed data that has been gathered with visual concepts. As you begin to document each space with its programmatic requirements, set up a template to help you work your way through each program requirement. Begin by introducing how decisions were made resulting in the final program requirements. Then document your findings.

Student Example 1: Writing the Program

For a proposed renovation of a residence hall facility, interior design student Jeanna Richard first documents that from her precedent study research she was able to outline the amenities and square footages that will be required for students to live comfortably in her proposed residence hall. Table 8.2 is a chart that outlines the proposed space, how many residents it would house, and the total square footage it would require. At the bottom of the chart, the total square footage is documented with the estimated percentage of circulation.

Richard includes a descriptive written introduction as an overview of the program requirements:

The renovation will include suite-style rooms, a fitness facility, offices of residence life, a study lounge, kitchens, a laundry facility, entertainment lounges, and apartments for residence life staff. The six residence halls studied in the sample have an average of three hundred and sixty-three square feet of living space available per resident. Currently the Residence Hall has one hundred and seventy square feet of living space per student. To create a more comfortable environment and allow for more privacy, the overall resident occupancy will be lowered from three hundred and thirty students to approximately two hundred students. The addition of social areas will promote community building within the residence hall, and the use of quality,

TABLE 8.2 FACILITIES AND SPACE REQUIRED FOR MALLOY HALL		
AMENITIES REQUIRED	**# & LOCATIONS IN BUILDING**	**TOTAL SQUARE FEET NEEDED**
Double-occupancy student rooms	96	225 per room 21,600 total
Restrooms within suite-style living spaces	1 per suite; 24 total	180 per suite; 4320 total
Lounges (within suites)	1 per suite; 24 total	300 per suite; 7200 total
Lounge for entertainment	3 (one/floor)	450 per floor; 1350 total
Lounge for study	1 (ground floor)	400
Staff apartments	3 (one/floor)	350 per apartment; 1050 total
Single occupancy suites (Resident assistants)	3 (one/floor)	180 per room; 540 total
Kitchen	3 (one/floor)	300 per floor; 900 total
Fitness area	1 (ground floor)	350
Offices of residence life	1 (ground floor)	400
Lobby/reception area	1 (ground floor)	300
Laundry facility	1 (ground floor)	250
Building storage and maintenance	3 (1/floor)	360 per floor; 1,080 total
Circulation	+30% of total	12,000

TOTAL SQUARE FEET REQUIRED FOR MALLOY HALL 50,020

TOTAL SQUARE FEET AVAILABLE IN MALLOY HALL 56,000

Source: Jenna Richard, 2006.

attractive, durable finishes, materials, and furnishings will allow students to enjoy these spaces for many years to come. (Richard, 2006)

After the written introduction and the program space requirements, as noted in Table 8.2, the chart outlines the proposed space. Adjacency studies in Figures 8.14 and 8.15 are visual examples of bubble diagramming that take the required space and represent it in the appropriate size and relationship to other spaces. The criteria matrix in Figure 8.16 visually synthesizes the program requirements, space, sizes, and adjacency requirement into one diagram.

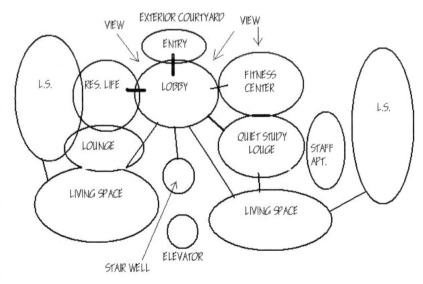

FIGURE 8.14 **Bubble diagrams: ground floor adjacencies.**

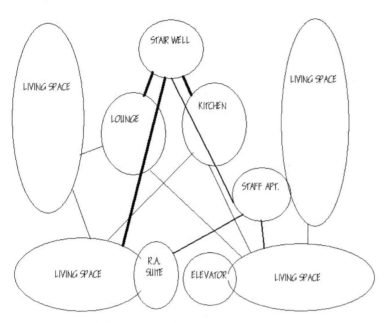

FIGURE 8.15 **Bubble diagrams: second and third floor adjacencies.**

Some programmers like to include conceptual images; specific code requirements that might relate to the space, lighting, and furniture; and maybe even a written description of how the space should feel. A descriptive statement will help set the tone when the program begins to evolve into the schematic design process.

For example, the following might describe a reception area of a spa:

When one enters the spa the sound of water should be heard, embracing nature to relax and calm customers when they enter. Water in concept is a purifying experience and the spa customers will hear the therapeutic sound, then experience it later when in treatment rooms. The seating is to be soft, embracing the customers and absorbing and muffling the outside sounds that might enter through the main entrance. The ceiling can also be lowered over the seating area to help facilitate a sense of intimacy and relaxation while encouraging a peaceful and tranquil experience. A fireplace will be placed in the reception for warmth and visual tranquility.

Table 8.3 is a suggested one-page template to use when outlining your requirements for each space. Richard used this template as she documented her program for the proposed residence hall. First, she

FIGURE 8.16 **Criteria matrix: outlining residence hall adjacency requirements.**

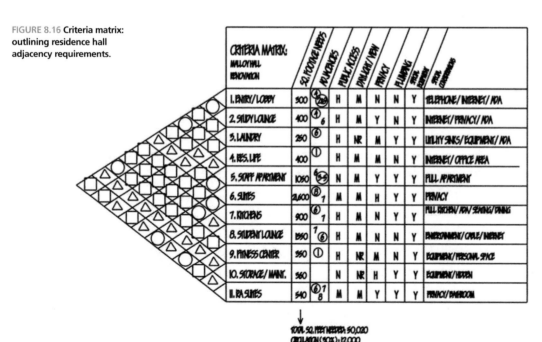

Legend

H-High
M-Medium
L-Low
NR-Not Required
P-Partial
N-No
Y-Yes
O - Important
□ -Low Importance
△ -High Importance

TABLE 8.3 TEMPLATE PAGE FOR EACH PROGRAM REQUIREMENT EXAMPLE ONE PAGE TEMPLATE FOR EACH SPACE

Name of Space:

Insert space with visual adjacency requirements.

List all of requirement for space.

Add some conceptual images that you might have found during your historical, observation, or interactive research.

Objects, furniture, words, and poems all can be placed here to help one begin to envision the space at a glance.

Add a brief concept statement about the space. Add Codes to keep in mind that directly apply to this specific space.

took the space that she was documenting and placed it onto the top of the page. She included a visual adjacency diagram with the program requirements listed next to it. She also included some conceptual images with a written description of how the space might feel. Notice how the template in Figure 8.17 is the same as that of Figure 8.18; only the content has changed, as Richard inserted each space with its own requirements, needs, and features.

This exercise outlined for Figures 8.17 and 8.18 may be time-consuming, but it produces a comprehensive snapshot of each space to be designed. Typically, in an academic setting the student generates the program and then designs the final solutions. This is not always the case within the profession, where sometimes the programmer and the designer are different people who may not even work in the same office. Hence, it is imperative to be as detailed and comprehensive in your documentation as possible.

Professional Example: Lisa C. Bonneville, FASID, NCIDQ

Bonneville Design Creates Living Environments to Last a Lifetime

Lisa Bonneville founded Bonneville Design, an award-winning independent interior design firm that has served a residential, corporate, healthcare, and retail clientele in Manchester-by-the-Sea, Massachusetts, since January 1981. She continues to work with many of her original clients to create new "homes" for them, time and time again. Her inspired approach to the process of spatial planning and aesthetic impact provides fresh creative solutions on every project. She encourages collaboration within her project teams and improves outcomes by ensuring timely and transparent communication. This distinctive approach, coupled with a high level of organization and project management expertise, makes her a valued resource to her clients, vendors, and colleagues in the trade.

FIGURE 8.17
Student example: residence hall facilities and space required for residence hall lobby, reception and office, by Jeanna Richard.

FIGURE 8.18 **Student example: residence hall facilities required for suite-style living area, double-occupancy, and private rooms, by Jeanna Richard.**

Lobby/Reception Area & Offices of Residence Life

MAIN ENTRY TO BUILDING THROUGH
EXTERIOR COURTYARD

LOBBY/RECEPTION
300 SQ.FT.

OFFICES OF
RESIDENCE LIFE
AVAILABLE BY ALL
CAMPUS USERS

FITNESS CENTER
ACCESSIBLE BY OTHER
CAMPUS USERS

ACCESS TO STUDENT
ROOMS & ELEVATOR

QUIET STUDY LOUNGE
ACCESSIBLE TO
NON-RESIDENTS FOR STUDY
GROUP MEETINGS

Lobby Requirements:

- Occasional seating & tables
- Way-finding signage
- Reception/security desk

Conceptual Images:

Image 1

Image 2

Image 3   Image 4

The lobby should feel bright, spacious and accommodating. The main entrance to the building through the exterior courtyard will become the central hub of the building's activity. Offices of Residence Life will remain accessible directly from the outside by all campus users. Seating will be provided for social interaction and waiting areas for the adjacent offices. The atmosphere should be comforting yet reflect upon the busy excitement of collegiate life in Malloy Hall.

Resident Student Suite Style Living Area

Double Occupancy Private Rooms

CORRIDOR

BATHROOM
180 SQ.FT.

DR.
225 SQ.FT.

DR.
225 SQ.FT.

DOUBLE ROOM
225 SQ.FT.

LOUNGE
300 SQ.FT.

DR.
225 SQ.FT.

Student Room Requiremen

- Two dressers
- Two desks w/chai
- Two x-long twin b
- Two closets
- Built in shelving
- Full-length mirror
- Microfridge
- Wireless connectivity, podcasting, cable television

Conceptual Images:

Image 19

Image 21

Image 20

Student rooms serve as sleeping rooms, living rooms, and study areas. Residents should be able to make their rooms as personal as possible. Color palettes will remain neutral, durable, and easily cleaned. Ample general and task lighting will be provided to ensure that the space is as functional as possible. Furnishings will be flexible for ease of rearranging. Comfort is of the utmost importance; residence halls are home to students nine months a year and should provide the same sense of relaxation

Bonneville is steadfast in her commitment to creating people-centered living environments that focus on universal design, accessibility, style, comfort, and efficiency. Her mission is to help people plan ahead to age at home—for a lifetime. She is widely published locally and nationally for her design projects and professional practice and is author of the book *The Safe Home, Designing for Safety in the Home.*

Lisa Bonneville is a member of the Council of Fellows of the American Society of Interior Designers, an inductee into the New England Design Hall of Fame, and the recipient of the 2014 Irene Winifred Eno Grant from the ASID Foundation

FIGURE 8.19 Lisa C. Bonneville, FASID, NCIDQ.

for evidence-based research into the costs of upgrading a house to age at home versus moving to an assisted living facility. In 2015 she authored a webinar entitled "Planning Ahead to Age at Home, A Price Tag with a Happy Ending."

- We are committed to human-centered design and apply the Standards of Universal Design on every project.
- We design homes to be accessible for all people, regardless of age, size, or physical ability.
- We integrate the principles of Biophilic Design to enrich lives with vital connections to nature and light.
- We create lifelong homes through careful planning with "home" owners, realtors, builders, contractors, and vendors.

Always a strong advocate for the physically and mentally challenged, Bonneville incorporates the Standards of Universal Design into her project solutions and works with clients to heighten awareness of the importance of safety and mobility within the

home while achieving optimum living environments for themselves, family members, and friends who frequent their homes. Her most recent work focuses on creating lifelong interiors.

Bonneville states: "Home is the most treasured place we inhabit in our lifetime. It is where we spend time with family and friends and where we include our most prized possessions. It is designed to suit uniquely individual preferences and lifestyle and has increasingly become a multipurpose, highly technological enjoyment center." In Box 8.2 Bonneville shares her process and approach to programming and research as a residential designer.

GENERATING YOUR PROGRAM

After reviewing the various examples, you can now take all the spaces that have been identified as programmatic requirements

FIGURE 8.20 Gloucester residence, designed by Bonneville Design.

BOX 8.2 PROGRAMMING FOR RESIDENTIAL PROJECT

Author: Lisa Bonneville, FASID, NCIDQ,
Founding Principal, Bonneville Design

Residential interior designers are a unique breed. In no other specialty within the practice of interior design does the practitioner become more intimately aware of each individual client's lifestyle preferences, interpersonal dynamics, idiosyncratic methodologies, physical capabilities and specific personal preferences and requirements. The level of interaction necessary to successfully create optimal environments for each client requires finely honed skills, astute fact finding, creative research, analysis of design solutions, and presentation skills that successfully communicate to the individual and to the family as a whole. (The Safe Home, Designing for Safety in the Home, author Lisa Bonneville, FASID 2007)

Residential interior design firms establish their unique brand through not only the clientele they attract but also the projects they accept. It is most often the vision, together with the personality of the firm and specifically the owners or principal designers, that connects them with their clients and ensures ongoing projects and referrals that sustain their future. Firms must weigh their internal capabilities with the requirements of a project, as well as the alignment of brand reinforcement and monetary value. People typically hire residential designers because they are too involved in their own fields of expertise to have the time or the ability to transform their living spaces to coincide with their personal vision of "home." Designers create comfort, convenience, beauty, and style while preserving their clients' health, safety and welfare on every project. These services are integral components in the "tool belt" of the professional interior designer and are the foundation of successful programming with their clients.

The ability to create a shared language around the client's vision is the foremost goal in residential programming. Phrasing the questions to ask in the initial interview and then applying feedback to create a client profile can literally determine the success of a project and begin the development of trust in the client-designer relationship and, ultimately, the future success of the firm. In the process of programming, the picture of the real project becomes clear. It is never about what the designer may want or imagine—it is always the client's project. What are the client's vision and expectations? How will the designer deliver the client's vision—on time and within their budget? Reaching an understanding as early in the design process as possible ensures timely and appropriate decision making throughout the project.

Organizing a residential interior design firm that projects a collaborative nature will simultaneously create a safe and comfortable atmosphere in which to encourage clients to share their most personal stories about hopes and dreams, needs and preferences, and personality differences between other residents within the same home. Multigenerational living environments that define homes today require an understanding of the adjustability and flexibility of use required within the same spaces and/or rooms by people of varied ages, sizes, and abilities. Design solutions that embrace diversity within a household is the goal of successful design solutions and careful programing provides the parameters that lead to those solutions. Designers collect, interpret, and apply a considerable amount of information that, time and again, becomes historic memory that can be carried from project to project for the same client(s). Repeat business in residential design is the highest compliment and establishes the strongest firm identify.

Programming begins with the first contact a potential client makes to a design firm. This underscores the importance of training all staff to understand the importance of this first contact and participate in achieving the goals of this initial opportunity to gain and share information that will begin a meaningful dialog with the caller. This cordial conversation with any staff member includes questions that begin to build a picture of the client and their project:

> *"Would you care to leave a brief message to describe what design services you are looking for? Where is your home located? How did you hear about Bonneville Design? What is the time frame of your project? When is a good time for our principal to reach you? Thank you for calling Bonneville Design!"*

Every subsequent contact with a client is orchestrated into a design process that continually reinforces a collaborative brand and the organization, superior customer service and creative design solutions of the firm or sole proprietor designer. At Bonneville Design this process of fact finding has been organized into a series of project phases. Within each phase are steps that fall into a sequence that guides the progress of a project. Although each client introduces uniquely different projects to the firm, this orderly sequence provides a framework in which to monitor the flow of the project—the time to issue a services contract, the appropriate times to meet with clients for presentations and ongoing programming, the time to invoice clients for work to be performed and product to be ordered, opportunities for review, etc. Managing these steps in a time efficient manner contributes to the firm's financial stability. Time is money!

INTERIOR DESIGN PROCESS MATRIX
Phase I: Strategic Planning, Design Assessment, Concept Development, and Analysis

This phase begins with the *client on-site interview*. All decision makers and end users of each space to be considered in the scope of services is requested to be present for this initial exercise in defining the goals of the proposed project.

- Define the project parameters and priorities
- Identify building and fire code requirements
- Identify project design team with contact information and preferences
- Determine project procedure and preferred communication standards
- Outline project budget

Information gathered includes introduction to all residents of the house and description of frequent visitors/relatives/friends (this focuses on physical size, ability, preferences, interactions, etc.); reason for calling a designer, definition of how the designer will help them reach their goals, and what they perceive the project to include; which rooms will be involved; what changes will be made in each room; the history of the building and length of time the current owners have lived there; listing of structural issues; listing of spatial issues to be addressed; deadlines that pertain to the project completion timeline; listing of team members to be involved in the project, including the trades and consultants, and what their role and responsibilities will be; budget parameters and anticipated phasing due to budget or timing; ability to read architectural drawings; preferences for hands-on participation; will other designers be interviewed for the project; and long-range planning for the future.

It is very important that all stakeholders be present for this fact- finding meeting during which the designer is observing the interpersonal interactions and dynamics between family members, identifying the leader(s) of the household, beginning with each individual, determining the decision makers.

This meeting is followed by a proposal for design services, as outlined in the interview. It is accompanied by a cover letter that numerates the goals and priorities of the project, uses the client's exact descriptive words, and outlines the sequence of meetings and presentations that comprise the process steps implemented by Bonneville Design. This is accompanied by the Proposal for Interior Design Services that specifically lists the precise tasks that will be performed by the designer by room. Included in this outline are the cost worksheet and project sequence outline that are incorporated into every project performed by Bonneville Design. These tools make it possible for the designer and client to know at all times throughout the project what is to be accomplished during a given week and how the current financial status appears.

Phase II: Design Development and Specification

Once the proposal is accepted, a contract is signed between Bonneville Design and the clients (if a couple, both names are on the contract) in order to proceed with the well-defined project. A deposit to begin services is received, and the programming continues to include the details of style and color preferences, an accessibility audit is conducted (short and long term), and maintenance preferences are delineated.

During *meeting one*, site measurements and photographs are taken of each space/room to be impacted during the project for use in design and as a "before" view of what might be used in marketing once the project is complete. Furniture is inventoried for reuse, and site conditions are reviewed in detail for code compliance and durability. Mechanical services are checked for support of any changes that the new design may require. This information is gathered in a systematic way in order to preserve an organized methodology. With multiple projects underway simultaneously, it is important to proceed as organized as possible.

- Gather and review input and information
- Prepare preliminary design options
- Identify revisions and adjustments
- Prepare design documents (architectural drawings, CDs)
- Specify furnishings, fixtures, finishes, and accessories

A *preliminary presentation* is made to the client with plans of existing conditions overlaid with drawings of design solutions for each area involved in the project. They include floor, furniture, and lighting plans; elevations and sections; window treatment layouts; a sampling of detailing; furniture; light fixtures; plumbing fixtures; fabrics; finishes like tile and carpeting; coverings; and accessories that suggest color palette. During this meeting the direction is confirmed for architectural finishes, furniture placement and style and the color scheme is agreed.

(continued on next page)

BOX 8.2 PROGRAMMING FOR RESIDENTIAL PROJECT (cont.)

THE INTERIOR DESIGN PROCESS REMODELING / RETROFITTING / REDECORATING

THE TEAM: CL: CLIENT D: DESIGNER A: ARCHITECT CO: CONTRACTOR	PHASE	DESCRIPTION	SERVICES INCLUDE
CL, D, A	I	STRATEGIC PLANNING, DESIGN ASSESSMENT, CONCEPT, DEVELOPMENT AND ANALYSIS:	outline client goals & objectives define project parameters and priorities identify building code requirements identify project design team determine project procedure outline project budget
CL, D, A	II	DESIGN AND SPECIFICATION:	gather and review input and information prepare preliminary design sketches identify revisions and adjustments prepare design documents (architectural drawings) specify furnishings, finishes, coverings, and accessories
CL, D	III	SELECTION AND COST ANALYSIS:	select and price designer's product to complete the design prepare designer's product cost worksheet
CL, D, A, CO	IV	BID PROCUREMENT:	outline project management requirements prepare contractor work order listings identify procurer of permits review contractor bids select contractor & sub-contractors
CL, D, A, CO	V	PROJECT IMPLEMENTATION, PRODUCT ACQUISITION:	define role of each project team member sign contracts with contractor team members establish communication system w/in project team issue purchase orders for products and services
CL, D, A, CO	VI	*PROJECT SCHEDULING:* *PROJECT MANAGEMENT:*	*outline project process to completion* *identify all deadlines to a master project time line* *schedule all contractors and subs* *determine timing for site visits and progress checks* *outline construction process* *coordinate inspections* *verify design adherence* *prepare change orders* *review project additions* *maintain scheduled site visits and check points* *maintain ongoing communication* *determine and conduct project team meetings* *verify construction completion* *install contractor supplied finishes, fixtures & furniture*
CL, D	VII	PROJECT INSTALLATION & MOVE IN:	deliver and install window treatments & carpets deliver and place furniture, accessories, artwork, and interior landscaping acquire project photos for designer's file
CL, D, A, CO	VIII	POST OCCUPANCY EVALUATION, FINAL PROJECT REVIEW & FOLLOW-UP:	post occupancy evaluation of products and services outline maintenance requirements for finishes determine final follow-ups

Additional meetings may be required to complete this step. Clients are taken to furniture vendors to confirm the "fit" of selected pieces and experience as much of the product that will be installed in their home as possible. It is advisable never to surprise a client ,so expectations must match reality.

Phase III: Selection and Cost Analysis

Communication between designer and clients may be ongoing during the entire design phase and updated information may result in revisions to the preliminary designs until the final drawings are approved for production. Once this milestone is reached, edits to the designs are considered "back stepping" and result in an hourly increase to the contracted services amount. The *final presentation* is made to all residents of the home for the final sign-off before plans are put out to bid by contractors and the trades.

- Price designer-selected product to complete the design
- Prepare a project cost worksheet

Next Steps

Before proceeding with the project implementation, after the design phase is completed and the full scope of the project is finalized, Bonneville Design discusses the process that will be involved to the completion of the client's project, in detail and plotted on a timeline. Vacations of both client and designer are plotted, lead times for product to be ordered are outlined, and RFP lead times are confirmed with contractors. The availability of contractors and even product, in some cases, may determine who and what is included on the project, if timing is a strict parameter to completion.

Phase IV: Bid Procurement

Phase V: Project Implementation, Product Acquisition

Phase VI: Project Scheduling & Management

Phase VII: Project Installation & Move In

Phase VIII: Post Occupancy Evaluation

Remodeling and renovation projects can be an overwhelming experience for homeowners. Expert guidance and organization through this detail-infused process is highly regarded and brings most residential designers their best clients. The ability of the interior designer to map out a step-by-step sequence that prepares clients for the work to be done on their home, the team members that will be participating, and when to anticipate potential obstacles to insure a smooth process and excellent finish is what is of the highest value to clients. This comes through experience from repeated projects.

Today, design of the homes focuses not only on style and beauty but on function, relevance, and systems that preserve the health, safety, and welfare of all people, for all residents in the home as well as their visitors. Bonneville Design strives to incorporate the standards of universal design and accessibility on every project, not only to improve the lives of current residents but for all future users—for the life of the home.

Nothing effects home design today more than technology. Homeowners are well informed with daily access to the internet and the ability to directly acquire furnishings, fixtures, finishes, and all manner of accessories. They are subscribers to online resources that pull together thousands of images of completed interiors for every room in the house and even provide design advice and chat sessions on numerous social media. Many clients use the images from these sites to communicate their vision to their designer. This time-saving resource is another tactic to be used during programming that can create the shared language and collaborative trust between designer and client.

This Bonneville Design was established over thirty years ago through the commitment of founding principal, Lisa Bonneville, to help clients create their favorite place to be—their own home. Today, the firm and its trusted vendors focus on providing accessible housing for people of all ages and abilities—birth to death. They term them "lifelong" interiors. Baby Boomers reaching retirement age has created a housing crisis in America. Over 88 percent want to age in their homes, yet their houses are not prepared for them. Most remodeling and new construction is initiated by homeowners in their 50s and 60s. Research shows that upgrading a home to the standards of universal design and accessibility costs less than moving to an assisted living facility where independence is forfeited for services that can be obtained in the home.

FIGURE 8.21 **Gloucester residence designed for a family with a wheelchair user: mantle view.**

FIGURE 8.22 **Manchester-by-the-Sea residence designed for a couple to age at home, designed by Bonneville Design.**

FIGURE 8.23 **Manchester-by-the-Sea residence master bath, for a couple to age at home, designed by Bonneville Design.**

for your design project and assign the required square footage to each space. Once the requirements have been documented in a chart with the square-footage requirements and circulation needs, you will have a clear picture of how much space will be needed to facilitate the design.

It is important to take the time to document each space, including its own internal requirements, features, and codes. This step is often overlooked during the programming phase, perhaps because it's a time-consuming task. But the time invested in documenting and visualizing each space as you implement the template model diagrammed in Table 8.3 will help you and your client begin to visualize the space very early in the process of design. To make changes at this stage in the programming phase is a manageable task. Making changes at this stage should actually be encouraged. Changes in later design phases can be problematic. Let's say your client requests an extra office space or lounge. When in the design process could that request best be implemented? At some point, such a request could be very problematic to the design and maybe not even an option. The time invested at the start in developing a comprehensive program is time well spent. It gives the client and the design team a complete document to implement, and it gives the program requirements good design solutions.

KEY TERMS
- American National Standards Institute (ANSI)—www.ansi.org.
- Building Owners and Managers Association (BOMA)—www.boma.org.
- Floor usable area
- Gross measured area
- Space utilization studies
- International Facility Managers Association (IFMA)—www.ifma.org

CHAPTER 9

Written and Visual Analysis

CHAPTER OBJECTIVES

After reading this chapter, you should be able to:

- Review and analyze data collected to date.
- Understand the importance of building codes and documenting the information.
- Plan for energy conservation and sustainability.
- Understand the visual language of diagramming.
- Translate written data into visual data.
- Create bubble and blocking plans.
- Create stacking plans.

For this book, many interior designers shared their thoughts as well as the processes they use to solve clients' problems. Much of that data has been synthesized into these pages, and we can see how many of these designers approach programming in a similar manner that varies only slightly. This should not be surprising: the purpose of programming, as we have seen, is to take a look at a given type of design and explore user needs in relation to space. What varies

considerably more are the numerous types of spaces that interior designers program as they aim to meet all sorts of needs, codes, requirements, and tastes. In other words, there may be an infinite number of ways to solve design problems, but designers can rely on a relatively straightforward process for arriving at the best solution. Another recurring theme in our design firm interviews is that good design solutions come from really understanding the client's needs. Each firm we spoke with stressed the need to interact with clients through a multitude of interview and data-gathering techniques.

REACHING SOLUTIONS THROUGH IDENTIFICATION AND ANALYSIS

As we have seen from previous chapters, the first important step toward reaching your design solution is to gather as much data as possible. The next phase after generating the programmatic requirements and working with the square footage needs and other requirements can be compared to putting together a jigsaw puzzle. Once you have all of the pieces of the puzzle in play, you move them around until they begin to fit together in the arrangement that best suits your client's needs. All the pieces need to fit together properly or the puzzle will not come together. Have you ever tried to fit a piece of a puzzle into a space, knowing it was the wrong one but insisting that if you just turn it or flip it, you can make it fit? This frustration can parallel the experience of taking the requirements from the **adjacency matrix** and beginning to translate them into visual blocking or bubble diagrams. If your data is organized and you have documented each space and are working with the appropriate square footage, eventually all the pieces will fit, and your space will come together.

IDENTIFYING YOUR DATA

After you've gathered your data (itself a multistep process, as we've seen in the previous chapters), you can begin to sort your findings into the various categories that meet the needs of the project. You may also need to conduct further research in order to identify information critical to finding your solution. Typically, you'll need to identify the following:

- State and local codes
- Sustainability requirements
- All of the facets that make up your problem statement, as discussed in Chapter 3
- Your precedent study, as discussed in Chapter 7
- The needs of your client

To home in on information necessary for your particular project, you may also look to **comparative case studies**, interviews, and observation research.

Identifying State and Local Codes

Local and state code requirements need to be researched prior to any programmatic or design decisions. Codes act as boundaries for your design options. Therefore, full awareness of all codes is a crucial foundational element to making solid design decisions for any client.

At this time, also look for any idiosyncratic or site-specific information. For example, when you look out the window, are you greeted by a scenic or obstructed view? Research for site-specific information includes studying site plans, plot maps, building restrictions, historical information about the site, and the area around the site that might help with design decisions. Much of this may have already been documented when you completed your interior and exterior site analysis in Chapter 6. However, it is wise to revisit the information that you documented and organize it within your programmatic document. It is important to note that code requirements may vary by state and should be used as a basis of your research for the applicable code in your area.

Student Example: Documenting Code and Special Considerations

Florida State University student Katrina Rutledge generated a table of code considerations that includes general code considerations, as well as occupancy loads and occupancy types.

In Figure 9.2, Rutledge organizes the egress requirements for the type of use. All the information in the table was retrieved from IBC 2009.

In Figure 9.3, Rutledge outlines code considerations for plumbing and for fire suppression and flame spread of finishes.

Student Example: Documenting Code and Special Considerations

Florida State University student Katie Timmerman generated the matrix in Figure 9.4. Timmerman took each of her spaces and described their location, occupancy category,

CODE CONSIDERATIONS

Construction Type: **IIB**   Number of Stories: **3**   Sprinkler Presence: **Yes**

Square Feet per Floor: First: 15,600 sq. ft.
                        Second: 15,135 sq. ft.
                        Third: 8,923 sq. ft.
                        TOTAL: 39,658 sq. ft.

Percent Gross Area Assumed for Circulation: **40%**

Circulation square feet total: **15,863 sq. ft.**

Square feet gross area available after circulation: **23,795 sq. ft.**

Occupancy Loads and Occupancy Types:

Space Type	Occupancy Category	Estimated Sq. Feet	Load Factor	Max # of Occupants	Notes
ASSEMBLY Community Spaces Art, Classrooms, Fitness, Spa, Group rooms	A-3	6,300 Gross	÷ 15 net	= 420	2 hr. firewall required between A-3 and B. 1 hr. firewall between A and I.
BUSINESS Offices, related storage and support areas	B	4,600 Gross	÷ 100 gross	= 46	2 hr. firewall required between A-3 and B. 1 hr. firewall between B and I.
INSTITUTIONAL Resident rooms, bathrooms, kitchen, dining, living rooms	I-1	23,600 Gross	÷ 200 gross	= 118	Walls separating I and A, B require 1 hr firewall. Walls separating dwelling/ sleeping units must be fire partitions. Floors separating dwelling/ sleeping units must be horizontal assemblies.
INSTITUTIONAL Daycare	I-4	2,500 Gross	÷ 35 net	= 71	Walls separating I and A, B require 1 hr firewall.
				Total # of Occupants: 655	

FIGURE 9.1 Florida State University graduate student Katrina Rutledge generated a table of code considerations.

CODE CONSIDERATIONS: EGRESS

Minimum Number of Exits: **2**

Min. Distance Apart for Two of the Exits: **113 feet**

Min. Width of Corridors and Stairs: **44"**

Corridor Width for Assembly Areas:

Floor 1	Total Occupancy Load		Width Factor-Corridors		Minimum width (may be superseded by other codes)		Corridor width to be used
Assembly (A)	420	x	0.2	=	84"		84" min.

Exit Access Travel Distance For Sprinklered Building:
Assembly: 250'   Business: 300'   Institutional: 250'

- The common path of egress travel will not exceed 75' in length.
- Minimum corridor width for 2 passing wheelchairs per ADA 60" minimum.
- Minimum door opening width per ADA 32" minimum.
- Doors, when fully open, will not protrude into the path of travel more than 7". Also cannot reduce the required path of travel by more than one half.
- Doors have push/pull flat, unobstructed wall space next to the latch side of minimum 24" (18" in special exception cases as outlined in ADA p. 11.67)
- Dead end corridor maximum length = 20'
- No object protrudes from vertical plane more than 4" between 27" and 80" AFF.
- Wheelchair turning radius = 60"
- Means of egress doors must swing in direction of exit travel. Exceptions: Doors leading to areas of occupancy for 50 or less persons.
- Elevators are minimum 54" wide x 68" deep. This assumes the door is to one side of the car.

Floor Level Changes:
- Ramps- Minimum width: 36"   Slope & Rise = 1:12
- Landings are at least 60" x 60" at a direction change.
- Handrails are necessary on both sides if ramp longer than 72"
- Handrails must extend minimum of 18" beyond stair/ramp end.
- Handrails must be between 34" and 28" AFF.

Stairs:
- Minimum riser = 4"   Maximum riser = 7"   Minimum tread depth = 11"
- Minimum headroom within stairwell = 80"

FIGURE 9.2 Florida State University graduate student Katrina Rutledge organizes the egress requirements for the type of use.

use classification, estimated size, load factor, and occupant load. This matrix synthesizes the information into one document.

Code documentation and research is a critical step when preparing your programming document. As outlined in Chapter 5, the library and its resources are an imperative component of your process—especially when you need to obtain code information. One of the best databases is MADCAD.com. Some of the information requires membership to access, but some of the information is free. A free app allows you to download and search for local building codes: simply type in the location of your site, and it identifies the local codes and standards. This is great for codes in the United States. If you are working with a site outside the country, the International Code Council ICC is the go-to database for codes (http://www.iccsafe.org).

CODE CONSIDERATIONS

Plumbing:

Space Type	Category	Water closets	Urinals	Lavatories	Bathtub or shower	Quantity Accessible	Water Fountains	Service Sink
Assembly spaces	A-3	M: 1	not required.	M: 1 (1 per 200)	0		1	1	1
occ. 420 Assume female has more of occupancy number		F: 4		F: 3 (1 per 200)				
Business	B	M: 1	not required.	M: 1	0		1	1	1
occ. 46		F: 2		F: 2			(1 per 100)	
Institutional	I-1	F: 12	N/A	F: 12	16		1	1	1
occ. 118		occ. 118 (1 per 10)		occ. 118 (1 per 10)	occ. 118 (1 per 8)			
	I-4	M: 2		M: 2	0		1	1	1
occ. 71		F: 2 (1 per 15)	N/A	F: 2 (1 per 15)				

- Walls with plumbing/drainage are 10" in thickness.
- Consideration is given, as possible, to grouping plumbing within floor plates as well as across floors for economy.
- Water fountains conform to ADA figure 11.27a for approach and height.

Fire Suppression/Flame Spread of Finishes:
- Every point on a floor lies within reach of a 30' stream from the end of a 100' fire hose.

Space type: Sprinklered	Vertical Exit and Exit Passageways	Exit Access Corridors & Other	Rooms & Enclosed Spaces
A-3	B	B	C
B and I-1	B	C	C
I-4	B	B	B

Other:
- Existing columns are retained in their current location and size.
- Walls respect window openings: no wall abruptly ends at a window opening.
- All transaction counters have an accessible portion that is minimum 30" in length and maximum 48" in height for accessibility.

FIGURE 9.3 Florida State University graduate student Katrina Rutledge outlines code considerations for plumbing and for fire suppression.

_____ **CODE RESEARCH**

OCCUPANCY LOADS

Section 1004 - Occupancy Loads. Occupancy Types + Existing

1004. 1 Design Occupant Load.
In determining means of egress requirements, the number of occupants for whom means of egress facilities shall be provided shall be determined in accordance with this section

space	level	occupancy category	use classification	estimated size (sq.ft)	load factor	occupant load
lobby	1	assembly - A	A-3	1000	15 net	66
reception	1	business - B	B	400	100 gross	4
lounge - lobby	1	assembly - A	A-3	800	15 net	53
workspace	2	business - B	B	2750	100 gross	27
shared kitchen	3	assembly - A	A-2	1400	15 net	93
bar/party	3	assembly - A	A-2	2400	15 net	160
seating/lounge	3	assembly - A	A-3	600	15 net	40
residential	2,3,4	residential R	R-2	40,000	200 gross	200
rooftop/outdoor	5	assembly - A	A-3	3000	15 net	200

FIGURE 9.4 **Florida State University graduate student Katie Timmerman generated an occupancy load matrix.**

Energy Conservation and Sustainability

Energy concepts have been a concern of programmers for many years. The study featured in Figure 9.5, for example, demonstrates the implemented energy concepts for a structure in Manila designed by The Architects Collaborative (TAC) in the early 1980s. TAC was committed to energy-conscious building design. At the time, during a worldwide energy crisis, governmental agencies throughout the world were establishing guidelines to regulate the amount of nonrenewable fuels (i.e., electricity, gas, and oil) a building could utilize (TAC, 1981, p. 54).

The energy conservation goals included in the programming document were as follows:

Provide natural ventilation.
• Promote the best use of natural breezes for cooling.

Maximize the use of daylight.
• Minimize energy consumption of artificial lighting throughout.
• Maximize the use of natural daylight by locating the majority of office areas within 15 meters of windows, and by locating program elements not requiring daylighting toward the interior.
• Provide natural daylighting opportunities for natural ventilation, ensuring that office operations can continue during brown- and blackouts without creating undue reliance on emergency power.

Protect against solar heat gain.
- Minimize east and west exposures.
- Shade glass areas.
- Insulate walls and roof.
- Install rooftop plantings.
- Use "active" solar systems where possible for air conditioning of selected areas and heating of domestic hot water.
- Use automated building management systems for maximum efficiency in energy systems operation and lighting control.

By using diagrams in the final program document, the environmental aspect of the building is recorded; this helps the design team and the client understand and visualize the programmatic requirements. It's a good idea to look at site location, longitude and latitude, solar angles, orientation, average wind velocity and direction, and geological information. This information will prove relevant when it comes to alternative energy generation and collection.

In Box 9.1, Mount Ida College professor Stephanie McGoldrick shares an overview of key elements influencing environmental and sustainability issues to include during the programming phase.

Note that when seeking input to include and plan for energy concepts, an excellent place to start is at the United States Green Building Council (USGBC) website (www.usgbc.org). This site encompasses an abundance of information. It also lists local chapters where more relevant regional data can be obtained.

Revisiting Your Research and Programmatic Documentation

When beginning the process of identifying the problem statement, as addressed in Chapter 3, it is important to include all the facets of the problem. Be mindful that, realistically, more problems will emerge as you

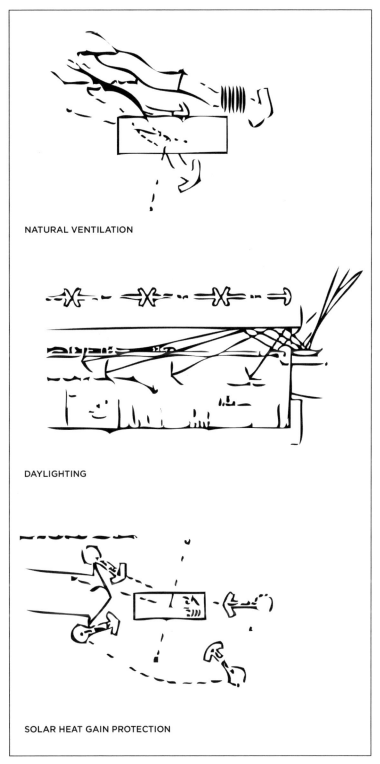

NATURAL VENTILATION

DAYLIGHTING

SOLAR HEAT GAIN PROTECTION

FIGURE 9.5 **TAC energy conservation concepts views and solar issues.**

BOX 9.1 PRELIMINARY SUSTAINABILITY EXPLORATIONS

Stephanie McGoldrick is an assistant professor at Mount Ida College and specializes in sustainability, lighting, and universal design. She is a LEED-accredited professional and is very passionate about sustainable design. Educating students on sustainability early in the research and programming phases is critical in her teaching.

The process of understanding sustainability and its integration into a design project begins with research and evaluating precedent studies, locating similar project types that contain viable sustainable solutions. The LEED (Leadership in Energy and Environmental Design) certification process is a useful starting point for students to develop awareness of potential sustainable strategies. The next steps include visually representing how these strategies may be effectively integrated into their specific project, through sketches and diagrams.

Daylighting is a critical sustainable strategy for students to consider in the programming phase of their designs. Research supports that natural lighting contributes to the well-being and productivity of individuals using a space. Integrating the use of natural lighting into a design involves considerations of site, building orientation, and lighting control methods, and these components of the design must

BOX FIGURE 9.1A
Stephanie McGoldrick, LEED AP BD+C, assistant professor | Interior Architecture + Design Mount Ida College.

be analyzed early in the design process by sketching and noting possible sustainable approaches.

Example A: This sketch completed by a sophomore student, Nicole Handzel, represents her analysis of the orientation of the building and its relationship to the sun, as well as how that will affect the interior space. Additionally, she shows potential control methods for this office space, such as lighting sensors and light shelves (panels).

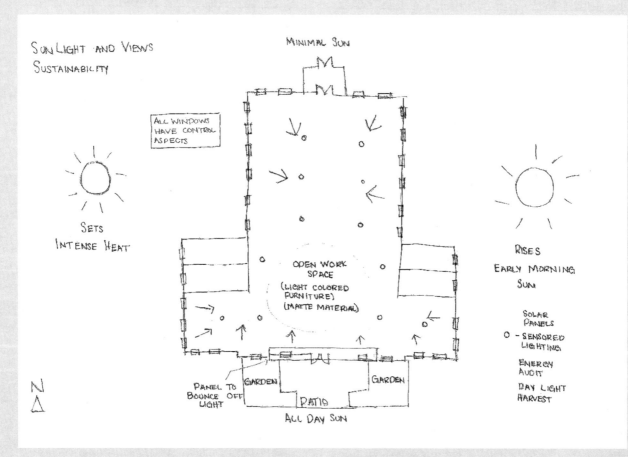

BOX FIGURE 9.1B **Sophomore student, Nicole Handzel, sun analysis.**

Example B: Individual spaces within a building may be analyzed to consider use of natural lighting with appropriate control methods. In this sketch by student Mary Kate Reidy, she considers use of a light shelf and reflective materials to appropriately integrate daylighting into the office interior and distribute that light throughout the space.

While analyzing a building site, students may also discover other sustainable strategies directly correlated to the LEED credits, such as access to quality transit, surrounding density and diverse uses, reduced parking footprint, heat island reduction, and rainwater management.

Example C: This site diagram developed by student Kerri LaBerge shows the building's close proximity to public transportation and amenities, as well as a variety of potential sustainable strategies, including collection of rainwater on the roof and use of porous pavement.

In the early phases of the design process, it is important that students are encouraged to explore as many sustainable solutions for their project as possible. These early diagrams may not provide all of the details for implementation, but the technicalities can be worked out during a later phase in the process. Sustainability must be a consideration from the beginning to ensure it is not overlooked, and diagrams like those shown in the examples, provide evidence of early understanding of sustainability within the programming phase of design.

BOX FIGURE 9.1C
Sophomore student Mary Kate Reidy, sketch of light shelf and reflective materials.

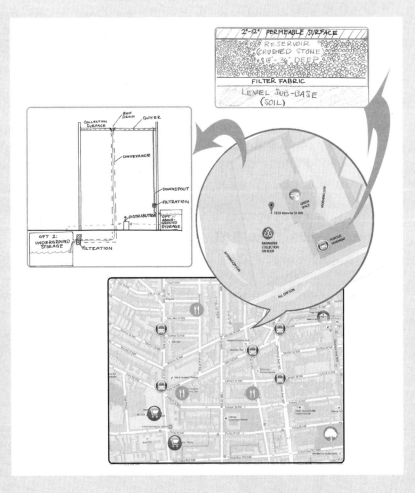

BOX FIGURE 9.1D
Sophomore student Kerri LaBerge, site diagram & exploring sustainable strategies.

engross yourself in conducting the historical, observational, and interactive research techniques. These can be introduced as sub-problems. Implementing and/or adapting a research method to help identify a phenomenon should be part of the process. Documenting and learning from research benefits not only the designer but also the community at large.

At this point it is wise to take a step back from all of the data collected, analyzed, and documented and reflect on it as a whole. Ask yourself the following questions: *Did I outline everything I was aiming to in my original problem statement, as outlined in Chapter 3?* If not, maybe you need to go back and update that statement. *Did the historical, observational, and interactive research identify areas that I did not think of as a result of my work in Chapters 4 and 5?* If so, go identify them now. *Was the interior and exterior site analysis I conducted in Chapter 6 sufficient? Are there gaps? After studying and conducting precedent study analysis in Chapter 7, was I able to generate the programmatic needs for my project, as outlined in Chapter 8?*

As you fill in the voids, you will prepare yourself to move forward with the visual documentation of your programming.

ANALYZING YOUR WRITTEN DATA

After you have gathered your data and identified how it relates to your design problem, you can begin to see how it all fits together and leads to your solution. In analyzing the data, there are several tools you can use. These include interviewing and observation, both of which were discussed in Chapter 5 and will be explored further here; matrix studies; bubble and stacking diagrams; and diagramming studies. All of these will be discussed in this section.

Graphic Format to Simplify Written Information

For years, the design profession has transferred written information into various graphic formats. It is a logical step in the design process and helps everyone visualize and interpret the data, both two dimensionally and three dimensionally. Many other professionals apply this same technique to their work. A great example is Edward Tufte, a statistician, artist, and professor at Yale University. His books are all focused on data visualization. Many of the techniques are innate to what we do as designers, but Tufte outlines the reorganization of information for graphical statistical inferences. This is very similar to an infographic that takes complex information and visually represents it for all to have a clear understanding of the facts. Cassidy Dickeson, a sophomore in the Interior Architecture + Design department at Mount Ida College, prepared an infographic as part of her research exploring resilient strategies when designing for a school. Her infographic in Figure 9.6b combines statistical information, precedent study findings, and some recommendations. This is not meant to replace comprehensive research practices but rather give a quick snapshot to engage participants enticing them to look deeper into a particular subject.

Edward Tufte's work is not only relevant to this section but also to Chapters 4, 5, and 7. In Figure 9.6b, Tufte looks at "a map metaphor of connected bubbles (with acronyms inside each bubble) similar in structure to the 1933 Czechoslovakia Air Transport Schedule" from the book *Envisioning Information*, page 102. The map has not only a 2D spatial orientation but also includes another variable: time. (*http://www.edwardtufte.com/bboard/q-and-a-fetch-msg?msg_id=0000XG*) This diagram from 1933 looks a lot like the bubble diagrams

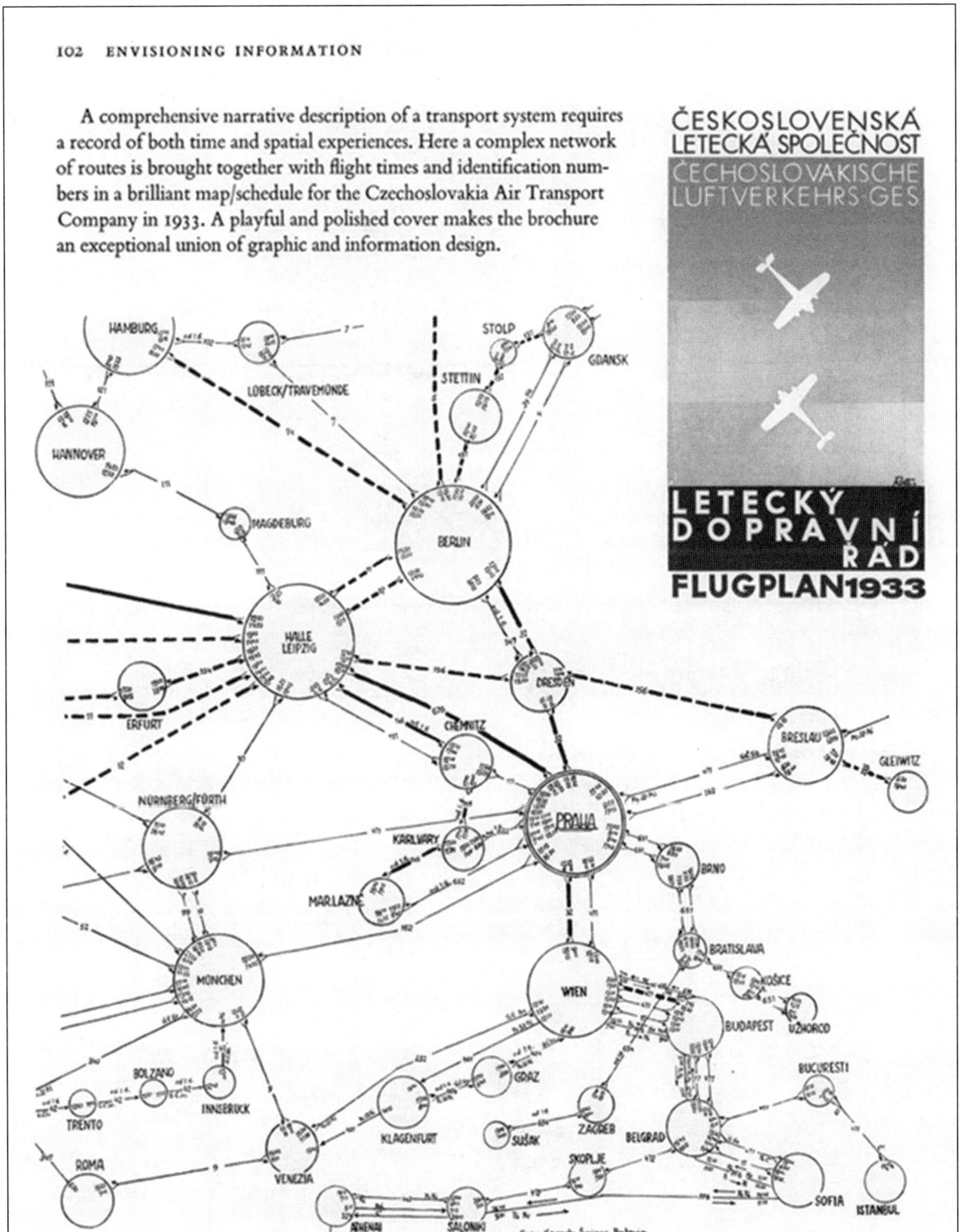
102 ENVISIONING INFORMATION

A comprehensive narrative description of a transport system requires a record of both time and spatial experiences. Here a complex network of routes is brought together with flight times and identification numbers in a brilliant map/schedule for the Czechoslovakia Air Transport Company in 1933. A playful and polished cover makes the brochure an exceptional union of graphic and information design.

FIGURE 9.6A Edward Tufte—*Envisioning Information.*

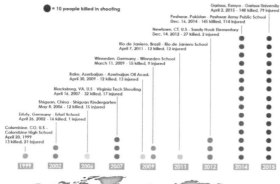

INTEGRATING RESILIENT STRATEGIES FOR SCHOOL DESIGN

TOP 10 WORST SCHOOL SHOOTINGS SINCE 1999 - WORLDWIDE

● = 10 people killed in shooting

Garissa, Kenya - Garissa University
April 2, 2015 - 148 killed, 79 injured

Peshwar, Pakistan - Peshwar Army Public School
Dec. 16, 2014 - 145 killed, 114 injured

Newtown, CT, U.S - Sandy Hook Elementary
Dec. 14, 2012 - 27 killed, 2 injured

Rio de Janeiro, Brazil - Rio de Janiero School
April 7, 2011 - 12 killed, 12 injured

Winnenden, Germany - Winneden School
March 11, 2009 - 15 killed, 9 injured

Baku, Azerbaijan - Azerbaijan Oil Acad.
April 30, 2009 - 12 killed, 13 injured

Blacksburg, VA, U.S - Virginia Tech Shooting
April 16, 2007 - 32 killed, 17 injured

Shiguan, China - Shiguan Kindergarten
May 8, 2006 - 12 killed, 15 injured

Erfuly, Germany - Erfuel School
April 26, 2002 - 16 killed, 1 injured

Columbine, CO, U.S -
Columbine High School
April 20, 1999
13 killed, 21 injured

1999 2002 2006 2007 2009 2011 2012 2014 2015

Gun Law Control After Disaster World Wide

Australia
35 people died from a single gunman
- twelve days after, gun laws changed

United Kingdom
16 people were killed and a dozen injured by one armed man using a pistol.
- Firearms (Amendment) Act 1988 - making registration mandatory for owning shotguns and banning semi-automatic and pump-action weapons.

16 five and six year-olds were shot by a single gunman
- All private ownerships on handguns were banned

Finland
8 students were killed after a teen opened fire at a school.
- Gun Law changed the minimum age was raised from 18 to 20

10 people were killed on a college campus in the same year.
- All people applying for a gun must be prove they were in a gun club for a year.
- In response to new laws, gun purchase went down **30%**

Norway
69 people were killed in a shooting at a youth camp.
- Gun control enforced that semi-automatic weapons were banned.

The United States holds the record for 88.82 firearms per 100 people, compared to the next highest at 32 firearms per 100 people in Norway

Changes in the environment to create Resiliency

Positive School Body Language
- Created through Decor and Culture
- In return, creates more of a connection with others and the building
- Can be created using murals, student artwork and the use of color schemes

Natural Surveillance
- Agressors are afraid when people will be able to see their actions
- People are able to see each other and they are able to be seen by others without the using of technology
- Creates a more positive environment with students, feeling connected to the outside

Safer Lockdowns Rooms
- Important to include in all areas including; offices and storage rooms
- Lockdown technology should be reasonable to secure areas safely and quickly
- Wall construction, type of door, room layouts, additional one-way exit doors should be integrated into every area.
- Emergency food, water and supplies should be accessible in all areas along with school's crisis plan.
- Use of AE System's new lockdown technology; strategically placing "emergency activation buttons" throughout schools
- The integration of Bilco's new product "The Barracuda" which is an easy, safe, and efficient way to securely lock all doors types.
- Incorporating bulletproof glass in all doors and windows in the building.

Roof Access Features
- Reduces the factors of break-ins which include; low roof sections, catwalks, exposed, gutters, utility boxes, and railings
- Commonly gained through loose items; pallets, milk crates, and ladders

Advanced Technology
The development of new technology is the best way to prevent the amounts of casualties that have taken place in the past.
- University of Connecticut took the initiative to integrate a system where when there is a gun shot, authorities are immediately notified.
- The system shows the pin point location of the shooter in order to identify the location and speed up response time.
- "The military-grade gunshot detector created by Dr. Socrates Deligeorges of BioMimetic Systems uses artificial intelligence and ultra-sensitive acoustic sensors to distinguish between gunshots, explosions, and non-lethal sounds..."
- Overall, the development of this technology and its possibility to save lives is exactly why it should be integrated into all schools, while not being limited to any public facilities.

References
http://www.garybaxter28.com/category/2nd-amendment/
https://en.wikipedia.org/wiki/List_of_school_massacres_by_death_toll
http://www.cnn.com/2013/10/31/us/virginia-tech-shootings-fast-facts/
http://www.history.com/topics/columbine-high-school-shootings
http://www.cnn.com/interactive/2012/12/us/sandy-hook-timeline/
http://www.doe.in.gov/sites/default/files/safety/sevenimportantbuildingdesignfeaturestoenhanceschoolsafetyandsecurity-isssa2014.pdf
https://everytownresearch.org/school-shootings/
http://www.huffingtonpost.com/2013/09/17/mass-shootings-2013_n_3941889.html
http://www.theatlantic.com/international/archive/2016/01/worldwide-gun-control-policy/423711/
http://www.cnn.com/2015/10/02/world/can-legislation-prevent-mass-shootings/

CASSIDY DICKESON - GLOBAL DESIGN - SPRING 2016

FIGURE 9.6B Mount Ida College student Cassidy Dickeson infographic—integrating resilient strategies for school design.

we use to help interpret space, adjacencies, and information.

Using Matrix Studies

For some designers, the use of an adjacency matrix is imperative. It is a tool that varies in its application and approach. A simple adjacency matrix can be created to illustrate, confirm, and clarify a client's needs and wants, while in a corporate or institutional setting, significant relationships must be documented and can sometimes prove difficult to manage. An adjacency matrix is a helpful tool in the development and analysis of special relationships. In complex situations, it is helpful to be able to refer back to the tool to be sure that the design is accomplishing the documented complex relationships and the goals associated with them. The example in Figure 9.7a is the work of a student who studied adjacency requirements by converting the bubble diagram in Figure 9.7b into a simple matrix while illustrating functional relationships for interaction and communication (Gouveia, 2005).

The example in Figure 9.7b is conceptual. The level of detail and complexity these diagrams can evolve into are endless. The student whose work appears in Figure 9.7a and b is now working in the profession as an interior designer; she notes that research, programming, and adjacencies are very important to her design process, and something that she thoroughly enjoys (Gouveia, 2008).

Research allows designers to dig deeper and?learn about the project, and it helps them generate ideas. Sometimes an image will help you create a motif or parti for your design that you may not have thought about. This often is referred to as imagineering or inspirational research. These initial ideas can develop into a strong concept later in schematic design and in the development of the design. Refer back to

	STAFF	SUPPORT	HEALTH	RELAXATION	PUBLIC	ACTIVITY	FITNESS
STAFF							
SUPPORT							
HEALTH							
RELAXATION	†		†				
PUBLIC	†	‡		†			
ACTIVITY	‡	†	†	†			
FITNESS	‡	†	†	†			

Adjacency Requirements Matrix indicating proximity with representing critical location to each other, † standing for desirable adjacency, and ‡ meaning as long as it is accessible. By Marcia A Gouveia

FIGURE 9.7A Adjacency model. Marcia Gouveia.

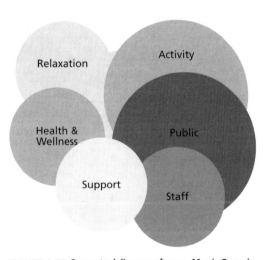

Fitness

FIGURE 9.7B Conceptual diagram of space. Marcia Gouveia.

Chapter 3, Box 3.2 to refresh your memory about the design process as outlined by Courtenay Dean Wallace.

Programming allows you to figure out who the users are and what their needs may be. Once you know who the users are, adjacencies allow you to?utilize bubble diagrams and matrices to create the layout and refine it. This allows you to create a better project for the client and the end user

Often departmental adjacency and matrix charts are very detailed. The example in Figure 9.8, implemented as a weighing system from very desirable to undesirable, is an interpretation of a modified **Likert scale**. Developed by Rensis Likert, a sociologist at the University of Michigan from 1946 to 1970, this method of scaling and evaluating responses is commonly referred to as a Likert scaling. Figure 9.8 shows the departmental adjacency matrix that was completed by the various department heads, and the chart that was subsequently created to summarize that data.

This type of summary chart records detailed adjacency requirements between specific areas within the various units. The department that provided the information

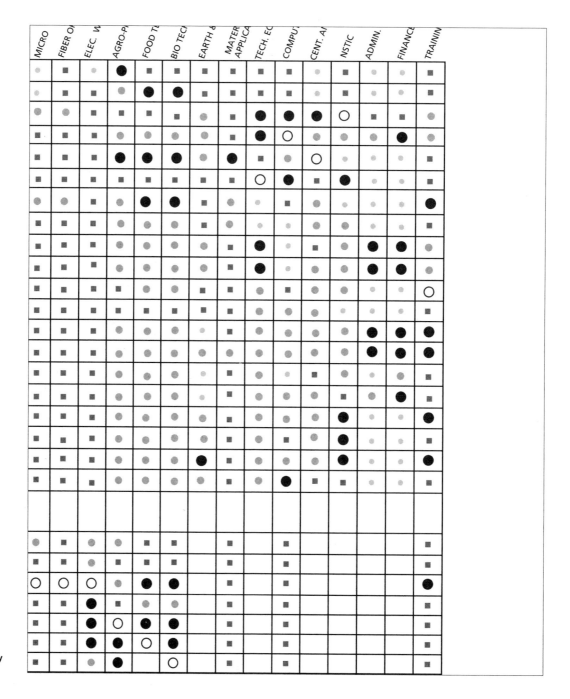

FIGURE 9.8
TAC departmental adjacency model diagram. Redrawn by Grace Herron.

is identified at the top of the chart, and the relationship of each department to the other departments or functions is recorded in the vertical column. Researchers used this information to help them develop the adjacency for a master plan; it was valuable in establishing the interdepartmental relationships for the schematic phase of design. The chart demonstrated that there was a great deal of interaction between units and among the various research departments. Therefore, a walking relationship between all research departments, technical support functions, and management was necessary to encourage informal exchange of ideas and to provide convenient access for collaboration between researchers (TAC, 1981).

Although this adjacency model was created in 1981, many of the same concepts are still used today. **Lean design** offers a great example of this. With lean design, interior designers evaluate the adjacencies and effectiveness of a specific function as well as the overall layout. Lean planning is extremely common in healthcare design, as it aims for efficiency and improved workflow for the user and patient experience.

Laurie DaForno, AIA, LEED AP BD+C, an architect with Tsoi/Kobus & Associates and an expert in lean design, she outlines some strategies of implementation in Box 9.2

Blocking: Bubble, Stacking, and Diagramming Studies

Diagramming is a powerful tool. Using diagramming, the designer conceptualizes the relationships of spaces discovered in client interviews, adjacency matrices, and **flow diagrams** and converts this information to either a bubble or a blocking diagram (Figures 9.9 and 9.10). Using relative bubbling or blocking of sizes based upon the relative square footage of the space allows a designer to get a good idea of size requirements. But the main purpose of the diagram

is to indicate the special relationships spaces have to one another. It is imperative at this point to keep your ideas conceptual. Diagramming is a great tool to execute this task; it allows you to move quickly and explore numerous scenarios.

S. Christine Cavataio, NCIDQ Certificate #9741, is an interior designer with thirty years of professional experience on both commercial and residential projects. She is the author of *Manual Drafting for Interiors* and is an associate professor at Newbury College. Cavataio has aided many designers through the study and preparation for their NCIDQ exam. Cavataio notes that color is often used to illustrate data, with

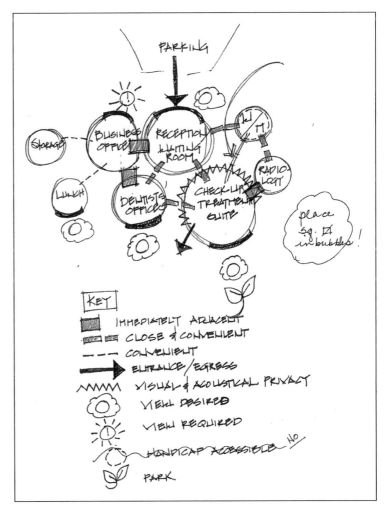

FIGURE 9.9 **Bubble diagramming plan.**

BOX 9.2 LAURIE DAFORNO, AIA, LEED AP BD+C

Laurie DaForno is a project architect with Tsoi/Kobus & Associates located in Cambridge, Massachusetts. She works on healthcare and laboratory projects that feature complex and technically challenging programs and components. She implements lean design to ensure an integrated and process-driven approach to programming and design, which oftentimes parallels the client's own internal efforts toward greater levels of efficiency and effectiveness. Engaging in lean design ensures a high energy and engaging programming experience for all participants. Laurie recently obtained a certificate of achievement in Lean Six Sigma Black Belt from Villanova University.

DaForno explains:

Lean design is an overarching philosophy that many organizations adopt in order to improve efficiency and effectiveness. Lean activities, such as value stream mapping, paper doll exercises, spaghetti diagramming, and mock ups, can be implemented into the programming and planning phases of the design process. Usually lean design is an inclusive process, involving end users in a series of lean activities geared toward a deeper understanding of their unique space needs and arrangement. The high energy meetings generate buzz and excitement, foster engagement throughout the organization, and help with change management.

Paper doll exercises are a dynamic way to engage end users in establishing relationships between program groups (i.e., adjacencies). Pieces of paper or cardstock are created to accurately represent the space program; they are furnished to the end users so that they can freely arrange them on a base plan and experiment with varied adjacencies. Natural light, columns, and other constraints or considerations can be illustrated on the base plan, or you can just free-form brainstorm with the end users to help generate out-of-the-box ideas. Indicating common modules like workstations or in-patient rooms helps illustrate the scale of the spaces.

BOX FIGURE 9.2A **Laurie DaForno, AIA, LEED AP BD+C, architect Tsoi/Kobus & Associates.**

Spaghetti diagramming is the visual representation of movement across a plan—movement of people, assets, specimens, or whatever is deemed the most important functional aspect of the project. A marker is placed at the start point and the line is drawn in a continuous path until the rational end point is reached. The diagrams should be multilayered, studying all important aspects of the project in overlapping colors or patterns. Analysis of the final diagrams is quite intuitive: bottlenecks, density, multiple crossovers, or long strands are all clearly visible and create a picture of space utilization. Oftentimes spaghetti diagramming is performed on top of multiple options of paper doll arrangements. This helps with greater understanding of the pros and cons of multiple adjacency diagrams.

Lean design is an inclusive process so the results are oftentimes fresh, creative, and unique, coming from individuals who don't necessarily have a background in design. Solutions must always be validated against physical limitations such as code constraints, constructability, and aesthetics. Amazing collaborations happen when learning occurs across both sides of the table.

BOX FIGURE 9.2B **Paper doll materials.**

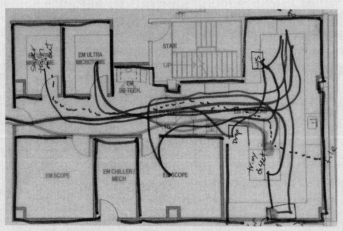

BOX FIGURE 9.2C **Spaghetti diagram.**

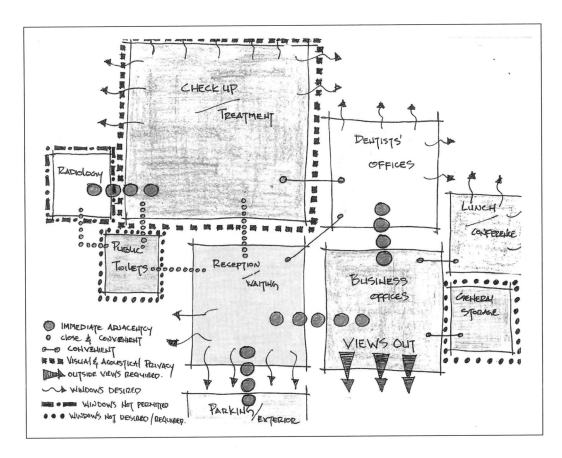

Inside the figure:

CHECK UP

TREATMENT

DENTISTS' OFFICES

RADIOLOGY

LUNCH CONFERENCE

PUBLIC TOILETS

RECEPTION / WAITING

BUSINESS OFFICES

GENERAL STORAGE

VIEWS OUT

PARKING / EXTERIOR

Legend:
- IMMEDIATE ADJACENCY
- CLOSE & CONVENIENT
- CONVENIENT
- VISUAL & ACOUSTICAL PRIVACY
- OUTSIDE VIEWS REQUIRED.
- WINDOWS DESIRED
- WINDOWS NOT PERMITTED
- WINDOWS NOT DESIRED / REQUIRED.

FIGURE 9.10 Color blocking plan.

a color key included. Would-be interior designers need to be able to take their clients' statements about existing conditions and spatial requests and turn these into a layout. Being able to diagram the written program information before attempting to plug it into a floor plan is a very valuable tool. By completing this intermediate step, the NCIDQ exam candidate who is working under a tight time frame will be more likely to accurately retain the spatial requirements in the finished layout. This can be the difference between passing or failing. Test-takers will be immediately disqualified if any of the space-related programming requirements are omitted.

Diagram-Making Exercise
Cavataio states:

> To practice this diagram-making exercise, I have students draw circles to

indicate rooms or areas listed in the written program and then symbols to represent the relationship that this space has with other nearby or adjacent spaces. The immediacy of each adjacency can be usually simplified into three levels; high for immediate access, medium for somewhat close, or low for distant rooms or those spaces that don't require easy access to the other areas.

As students feel comfortable creating these simple diagrams, we move to the next step which is to extract additional information from the written program statement that pertains to other aspects that will likely impact interior design, such as square footage, views, orientation, special equipment, and so forth. The goal is for the designer to be able to use the diagram without need to return to the written statement while moving onto space planning with the given floor plan. This approach seems to work well, saving exam takers precious time, because the underlying assumption is that all designers are visual learners and therefore seem to more quickly see information in diagrams than from reading words. (Cavataio, 2008)

Bubble Diagramming

There are numerous approaches to articulating the concept of bubble diagramming. Many implement color coding as a key to help delineate space and identify specific areas. In making use of these categories, the designer can discover and document when existing spaces and their relationships don't make sense, and then conceptualize ways in which spaces and their relationship to one another might make sense in the future. Figures 9.11 and 9.12 are freehand bubble and blocking studies exploring adjacency and space requirements. These freehand exploratory studies can be generated very quickly, allowing for fast movement and quick discovery of what is working and what is not.

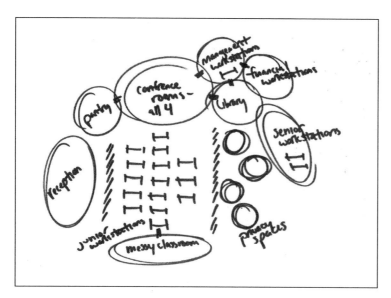

FIGURE 9.11
Endicott College student example of a freehand sketch.

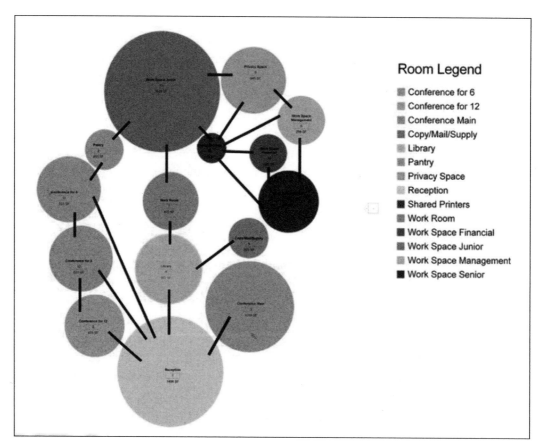

FIGURE 9.12
Endicott College student example of a bubble diagram.

BOX 9.3 STUDENT EXAMPLE: SUSTAINABILITY CENTER, BY MONICA MATTINGLY

Monica Mattingly generated the programmatic requirements for the sustainability center. She then compiled them into a chart containing the written programmatic requirements and an example of the criteria matrix, seen in 9.3a.

Then a final diagram for the first floor that blocks out space meeting adjacency and programmatic requirements was created. The final blocking plan was computerized and included the square footage for each space.

The last example takes the blocking diagram and demonstrates how it evolves into a floor plan, with a gray path indicating a phantom corridor for circulation.

CRITERIA MATRIX

	SQUARE FT NEEDS	ADJACENCIES	PUBLIC ACCESS	DAYLIGHT/VIEW	PRIVACY	PLUMBING	SPECIAL EQUIP.	SPECIAL CONSIDERATIONS
LOBBY	200	H	I	N	Y	N		XXXX / XXXX
AUDITORIUM	1280	H	N	N	Y	N		
SMALL CONFERENCE	320	H	Y	N	N			
INTERACTIVE DISPLAY AREAS	1920	H	Y	N	N	Y		
STUDIO/ WORKSHOPS	1280	H	Y	N	N	Y		
BREAKOUT/ PREEVENT AREAS	200	H	Y	N	Y	N		
CONSULTATION OFFICES	500	M	Y	N	N	N		
BROKER OFFICES	200	M	Y	N	N	N		
SITE MANAGER OFFICE	150	L	Y	L	N	N		
ELEVATOR/ STAIRS	XX	H	N	N	N	N		
RESTROOMS	400	H	N	N	Y	N		
DINING AREA	640	H	Y	N	Y	N		
TOTAL REQUIRED	7090							
CIRCULATION	1772							

LEGEND

⊖ IMMEDIATE ADJACENCY H HIGH
⊖ IMPORTANT ADJACENCY M MEDIUM
◉ REASONABLY CONVENIENT L LOW
– UNIMPORTANT ADJACENCY Y YES
× REMOTE N NO/NONE
 I IMPORTANT, NOT REQ'D

BOX FIGURE 9.3A Criteria matrix.

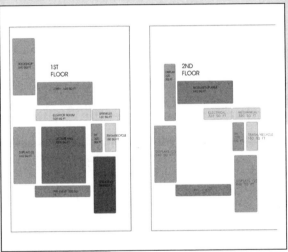

BOX FIGURE 9.3B
Blocking plans.

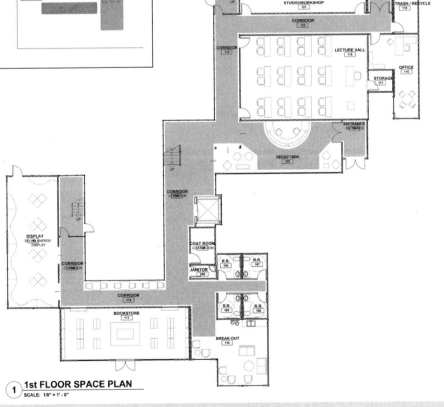

BOX FIGURE 9.3C
**Floorplan with
phantom corridor.**

1 **1st FLOOR SPACE PLAN**
SCALE: 1/8" = 1' - 0"

TRANSFERRING INFORMATION

There is no one single size or style that will fit everyone's needs. Many of the graphic interpretations of data will vary depending on style and office standards. Many are purely based on the designers' preferences.

Student Examples from Endicott College

Professor Michael Fior has been working as an interior designer for the past thirty years. Over the past ten years he embarked on a new focus as an educator. After completing his MFA, he now is enjoying teaching. Fior states that it is a difficult task to help students take their programmatic requirements and transform them into two-dimensional thinking. Working in Microsoft Office, design students are given programmatic requirements and a building. Examples of Professor Fior's student work in figures 9.11 and 9.12 and 9.14 and 9.15, demonstrating a sequential progress from freehand sketches to clear delineation of spaces.

The first stage might look something like Figure 9.11, a loose, freehand sketch starting to identify spaces and relationship of spaces.

In the second stage, students begin to refine their adjacencies a bit more. Now, the sketch might look like the bubble diagram in Figure 9.14.

In stages three and four, students are fine-tuning square footage and applying options directly to the footprint of the building. In Figure 9.15 Kelsey Creamer's example is of the final designation blocking diagram.

Stacking Plans

Stacking plans are another tool that programmers implement for the study of space both horizontally and vertically. It is important to identify vertical relationships and how they might need to interact. Does there need to be a visual connection? Adjacency takes priority; the visual connection (e.g., open stairs or the creation of two-story spaces) is developed after you figure out the adjacency of the vertical stack. Acoustical concerns are also a factor when evaluating vertical relationships.

Professional Example: MPA | Margulies Perruzzi Architects

Dianne A. Dunnell, IIDA, NCIDQ certificate # 015756, is a senior interior designer and director of interior design associate partner at Margulies Perruzzi Architects, a multidisciplinary firm in Boston, Massachusetts. According to Dunnell, her firm emphasizes the importance of studying the space from many vantage points. Below, she outlines a step-by-step approach to programming.

STEP 1:
Interview senior leadership for their goal and objectives. Some of the questions included in the interview are:

- Why now?
- What level of change is appropriate? On a level of 1 (no or minimal construction change, paint and new carpet)

FIGURE 9.13
Michael Fior, NCIDQ, LEED IDEC, IIDA, ASID.

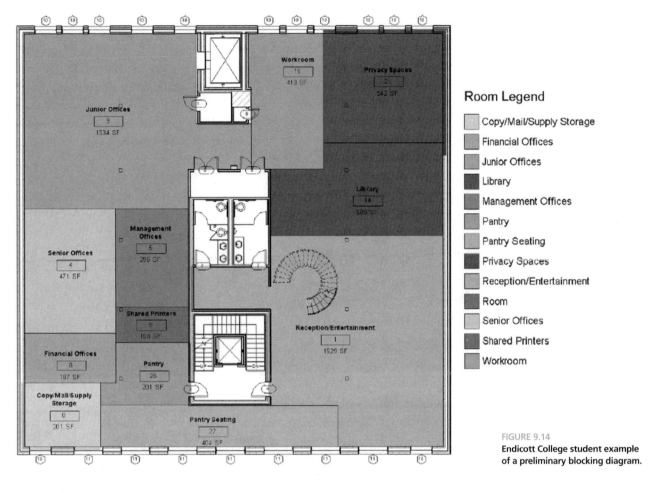

Room Legend

Copy/Mail/Supply Storage

Financial Offices

Junior Offices

Library

Management Offices

Pantry

Pantry Seating

Privacy Spaces

Reception/Entertainment

Room

Senior Offices

Shared Printers

Workroom

FIGURE 9.14
Endicott College student example of a preliminary blocking diagram.

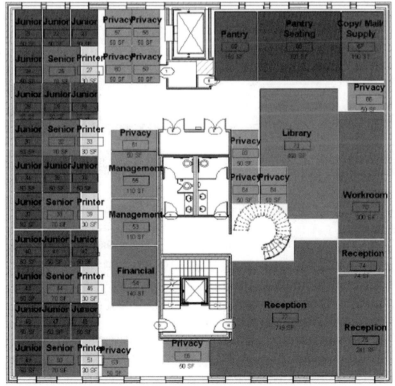

GUEST SPACE

WORK SPACE

EMPLOYEE SUPPORT

PRIVATE SPACE

FIGURE 9.15 Endicott College student Kelsey Creamer's example of a final designated blocking diagram.

FIGURE 9.13
Dianne A. Dunnell, IIDA, NCIDQ certificate # 015756.

FIGURE 9.17A Initial brainstorming session with focus group. MPA | Margulies Peruzzi Architects.

to level 10 (gut and redesign the entire space), what level of change is desired?

- How do you work today vs. how do you see yourself working in the future?
- What are the adjacencies and work styles within your company? Do you see this changing in the future?
- What are the business drivers?
- What is your current state?
- Review of trends/technology:
- Office/workstation ratio (current vs. desired):
- Change management:
- Furniture:
- Branding:
- Project schedule:

The above questions and information gathering aim to obtain a large overview of the client and overall goals. While they are critical it is only the beginning.

STEP 2:

Often a focus group meeting will be held to better understand how the company works. The focus group will be asked specific questions. (They can be seen in Appendix G.)

Figure 9.17a is from a series of design-related topics noted on a large sheet. The focus group members are given five pink and five blue Post-its and can place them on any of the topics listed on the sheets in the room that they think are important. This is a quick technique to address important issues and gain feedback from a cross section of employees. As seen in Figure 9.17b, this particular question gauged the need to increase collaborative areas: the response tallied at fifty-nine. This weighted response on important issues is a great research-gathering tool that can then translate to generating a program that reflects the users of the space.

STEP 3:

Obtain current headcount by department and growth factors for the next five years from the Human Resources (HR)

	Would work for our department	Might work for our department
Increase to the number of of ces	9.09% 4	25.00% 11
Reduction to the number of of ces	0.00% 0	48.84% 21
Elimination of of ces	0.00% 0	45.24% 19
Of ces removed from the exterior window well	43.18% 19	38.64% 17
Lowered height panels at the workstation	47.73% 21	25.00% 11
Reduced, universal workstation size	2.33% 1	60.47% 26
Open plan Benching (minimal or no panels)	2.27% 1	65.91% 29
Touchdown spaces for the visitors and adjunct workers	59.09% 26	36.36% 16
Huddle rooms (3-4 person private) meeting space)	84.09% 37	13.64% 6
Phone rooms (1-2 person private meeting space)	75.00% 33	11.36% 5
Open Collaboration Spaces (2-6 people)	77.27% 34	18.18% 8

FIGURE 9.17B
Brainstorming session response to questions. MPA | Margulies Perruzzi Architects.

department. Typically, when working with large clients the HR department will give the project designer information about growth and expansion plans. When the firm first receive the program document, Dunnell says, it is helpful to conduct a site visit to observe the space and double-check all the written data. In some cases the documents include inaccurate head count information, and many times the non-staff requirements are overlooked. These spaces (e.g., copy room, coffee areas, storage space) need to be identified and planned for because they not only take up space, but they are also essential in facilitating that daily tasks run smoothly. Often when observing a space, Dunnell adds, she will observe and ask the users who they interact with on a daily basis, both internally within their own group and department but also with others external to their group, such as departments from other floors or visitors from outside the company.

From the information obtained above, Dunnell's firm will begin to develop a program document. The current program

FIGURE 9.18

Example of a master program summary from MPA | Margulies Perruzzi Architects.

CLIENT NAME   **DESIGN FIRM NAME**

Issued:
Revised:

MASTER PROGRAM SUMMARY

Department name: B77 DE group
Representative: Jane Smith
Adjacencies: WF Group

Periods			Current	Year 1	Year 2	Year 3	Year 5
Most Likely growth		Office		1%	1%	0%	TBD
		Cube		4%	9%	4%	TBD

Comments:
Current B77 cube vs office counts from Jane Smith
Current flex staff counts from Jane Smith

Year 1 growth % from Jane Smith. (1% office/ 9% Flex growth.)
Client to confirm the Year 2 growth %
Year 3 growth not to exceed 500 as noted from Jane Smith
Year 5 growth counts are TBD.

Non office components qty/pp= industry standard.
Non office components SF= industry standard.

Average Current SF/PP: 138

Head count per office/workstation

Offices	SF		Current	Year 1	Year 2	Year 3	Year 5
Sizes varies	SF	TBD	56	-	-	-	-
Office/Cube		TBD	-	-	-	-	-
Visitor		TBD	-	-	-	-	-
shared- 2p		150	-	-	-	-	-
shared- 3p		225	-	-	-	-	-
Total			56	57	57	57	TBD
Workstations							
Sizes varies		TBD	330				
Staff (6x7)		42	-				
Contractors/interns (6x7)		42	-				-
Touchdowns (6x4.5)		27	-				-
Flex		TBD	46				-
Total			376	391	426	443	TBD
Subtotal			432	448	483	500	TBD
Total SF for staff			59,445	61,591	66,512	68,858	TBD

Non-office component
Ratio: (qty/pp)

			SF	Qty				
1	500	Assembly 40+	1500	1	1	1	1	TBD
1	100	Large Conference (12-20 people)	300	4	4	5	5	TBD
1	50	Medium Conference (8-12 people)	150	9	9	10	10	TBD
1	25	Huddle room (4-6 people)	100	17	18	19	20	TBD
1	10	Enclosed Workspace (2 person)	49	43	45	48	50	TBD
1	40	Filing	150	11	11	12	13	TBD
1	40	Copy/print	150	11	11	12	13	TBD

Required area

Non-office component SF	10,973	11,369	12,277	12,710	TBD

Grand Total SF required	70,417	72,960	78,789	81,568	TBD
SF for staff + Non Office components

FIGURE 9.19

Example of a master department summary from MPA | Margulies Perruzzi Architects.

CLIENT NAME   **DESIGN FIRM NAME**

Issued:
Revised:

MASTER PROGRAM SUMMARY

			Proposed OPTION 5	Proposed OPTION 6	Required IN 5 YRS
Ratio:	Office		5%	5%	TBD
	Wrkstg		95%	95%	TBD

Comments:
Est. Carpetable SF
B77 areas 1-10

B77 Floor 1 SF:					12,500 SF
B77 Floor 2 SF:					56,000 SF
Total					68,500 SF
B71 Floor 1 SF:					2,000 SF
B71 Floor 2 SF:					9,000 SF
Total					11,000 SF
B71 & B77 SF combined					79,500 SF
No. of pilot layout repeats in B77 & B71 combined					14.5

Head count per office/workstation

Offices			Proposed	Proposed	Required
10x10			0	0	TBD
10x11			3	0	
Total in pilot plan			0	3	
			3	3	
Est total number of offices in B77 & B71 (based on repeat qty)			44	44	TBD

Worksettings					
5x6 ABW benching			60	0	TBD
6x6 ABW benching			0	21	
6x6 Non ABW benching			0	30	
Add'l 6x6 ABW benching possible (in 13.5 repeat)			0	9	
Total in pilot plan			60	60	
Est total number of worksettings in B77 & B71 (based on repeat qty)			870	861	TBD

Total seat counts (B77 & B71)			**914**	**905**	**869**
Seat count difference from 2020 req'd count			45	36	

Total Non Office components (to be provided in B77 & B71)
Ratio: (qty/pp)

			SF	Req'd	Provided	Req'd	Provided	Req'd
1	500	Assembly 40+	1500	2	0	2	0	2
1	100	Large Conference (12-20 people)	300	9	0	9	0	9
1	50	Medium Conference (8-12 people)	150	18	0	18	0	17
1	25	Project/ Huddle room (4-6 people)	100	37	44	36	18	35
1	10	Silence/ Quiet Rms (2 person)	49	91	44	90	73	87
1	40	Filing	150	23	0	23	0	22
1	40	Copy/print	150	23	15	22.61	15	22

Common Areas req'd in 5 years

Archive/storage	1	500
4 Network Closets	1	320
Mechanical rm	1	700
Computer rm	1	900
Other		TBD
TOTAL SF		2,420

Additional Non Office components SF required

			Proposed	Proposed
Assembly 40+ (qty 1 add'l reqd)			1,500	1,500
Large Conference rm (12-20 people)			2,700	2,700
Medium Conference (8-12 people)			2,700	2,700
Filing (Assumed not req'd in new ABW layouts)			0	0
Common areas (see listing on right column)			2,420	2,420
Total SF required			9,320	9,320

SF of pilot plan	4,972	5,568
No. of pilot layout repeats in B77 & B71 combined	14.5	14.5
Total SF of office components in B77 & B71 combined	72,094	80,736
Total SF for additional program spaces	9,320	9,320
Grand total SF required:	81,414	90,056
(Note: This excludes SF for building common elements.)		
B71 & B77 est SF (carpetable SF) (Excludes SF for building common elements.)	79,500	79,500
Est SF/Person per option	87	88

SF Difference	-1,964	-10,556
Note: Add'l SF maybe desired for increased qty of non-office components

document is outlined in Figure 9.18. It includes the master page—a summary with the entire building's requirements.

Also, each individual department would have a summary. All of that information is rolled into the master page (Figure 9.19).

In most cases, the program document seems to be a moving target of sorts. Dunnell states that as she and her colleagues analyze the space in anticipation of specific head counts, the head counts can change, for example, when the company's new quarterly reports are issued from the HR department. Hence, the program must be updated as needed. This is a realistic scenario for a large project aiming to meet an ambitious move-in date.

STEP 4:
Hold interviews with key members of each department to:

- Verify head count
- Identify unique needs and wants
- Identify meeting room usage
- Identify adjacencies
- Understand how they work today and how they will work in the future

STEP 5:
Adjust program document and reissue to client for approval.

STEP 6:
Develop schematic test fit & schematic 3Ds, for larger projects this involves developing two phases for a project.

- Phase 1 PILOT PLAN: includes developing a pilot plan first that captures the office layout within a few thousand square feet. This allows the client to test various design solutions and furnishings to ensure they meet the needs of all departments vs. rolling out a single design throughout the building only

to learn it does not function well for some departments (i.e., transparency levels, workspace sizes, lighting and branding strategies).
- A schematic master plan of the entire building using the pilot area layout as a repeated element throughout the building is drawn to estimate overall seat capacity.
- The sample test fit attached is for a 5,000SF+/- pilot area developed and the pilot area is built out.
- Various departments sit in the pilot area for a number of weeks and evaluate how well the space and furnishings function for them.
- Phase 2 MASTER PLAN: In this phase, the pilot plan is rolled out, with the revisions made based on the feedback from the users who tested the pilot office space, throughout the entire building.

Often, Dunnell says, "we will be projecting for three to five years out with anticipated growth. The programming and schematic designs in this scenario are running tandem to each other. Typically, a series of generic test-fit designs will be conducted so they can get the big picture as they await the remaining programming documents. The goal is to understand and know each floor's total staff counts when studying various percentages of offices per test fit." Figure 9. 20 demonstrates an example of a stacking test fit with sixty-one offices equaling 76 percent of the space being allocated to offices. Figure 9.21 is a test fit with fifty-six offices equaling 64 percent of the space being allocated to offices. Finally, Figure 9.22 demonstrates the same space test-fitting forty-seven offices, or 48 percent of the space being allocated to offices.

When analyzing projects of this magnitude, Dunnell says, the firm *must study the space vertically*. Stacking studies help

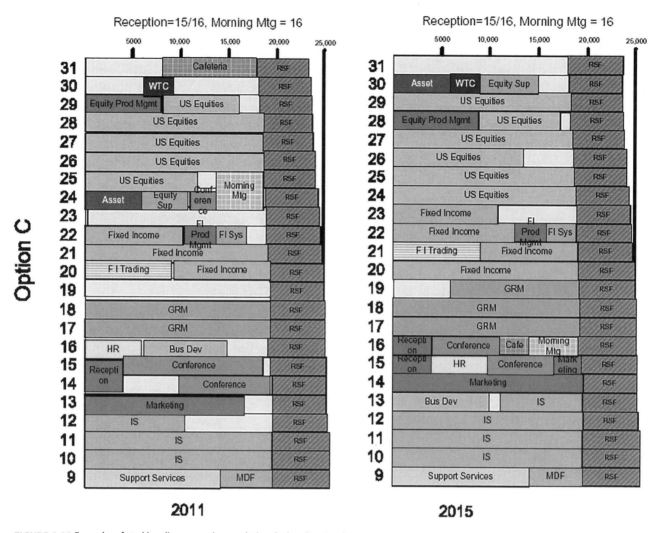

FIGURE 9.20 Examples of stacking diagram options exploring the best location for program requirements. These are typically used for a large projects. The space is represented in a vertical, cross section to visually see the stacking of requirements on multiple floors. From MPA | Margulies Peruzzi Architects.

visually articulate to the client how many floors and the adjacency relationship to each department. Also other issues need to be addressed regarding the hierarchy of space in a high-rise structure, such as these: What division should be on top with prime view? Who has secondary views? Not only are preferences and hierarchy issues addressed but pragmatic ones as well; for instance, who needs to be on a crossover floor with access to both elevator banks? Stacking electrical spaces is an efficient decision, as copper is expensive and the consolidations and vertical stacking can be a significant cost savings.

Figures 9.23–9.26, are stacking plans that explore the percentage of space each function needs based on the head count and programmatic requirements.

These examples have been created implementing Microsoft Excel or Microsoft Visio. The diagrams analyzed each floor, stacking floors 9 through 31, and forecast out for the years 2011, 2012, and 2013, with a 3 to 7 percent growth rate.

Clients not only want to see the numbers but the beginning of the actual design. Many three-dimensional test fits are generated to help the clients begin to visualize the spaces. These are created using Revit.

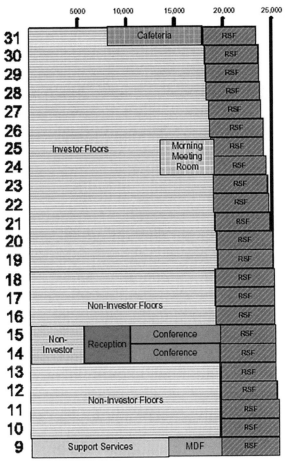

2011

FIGURE 9.21 Examples of stacking diagram options exploring the best location for program requirements. These are typically used for a large projects. The space is represented in a vertical, cross section to visually see the stacking of requirements on multiple floors. From MPA | Margulies Perruzzi Architects.

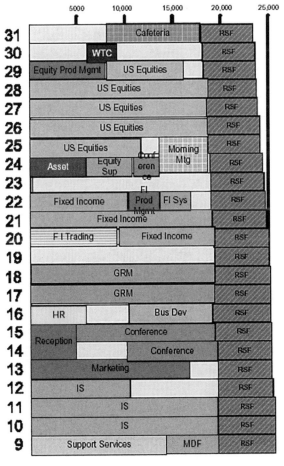

2011

FIGURE 9.22 Examples of stacking diagram options exploring the best location for program requirements. These are typically used for a large projects. The space is represented in a vertical, cross section to visually see the stacking of requirements on multiple floors. From MPA | Margulies Perruzzi Architects.

3-0-00_alloc 3 stacking study-DD

stacking diagram
(based on Allocation 3- Year 2011)
5/8/2008
Growth rate: 7% growth

(based on Allocation 3- Year 2011)

Floors		key:	Flrs req'd:		Leased flrs:
31	conference center & recept	conf center	1.5		
30	multi purp	marketing (& equity prod mgmt)		* captured in marketing no.	
29		IM groups	8.07		
28		MMR flr	0.5		
27		GRM	2.10		
26		BD & Admin & Inv. Admin.	0.80		
25		marketing	1.82		
24	MMR	IS	3.03		
23		Service flr & Curators space	1		
22		security & lobby			
21	trading flr?	growth space			
20	trading flr?	flrs on hold			
19		TOTAL	18.82		19
18					
17					
16		notes:			
15	cross over flr	1. The FI open office/trading flr originally was designed for flr 20 & 21- should it move to flr 22 &23?			
14		2. Will the service flr need more then 1 flr?			
13	on hold	3. There is limited growth space			
12	on hold	4. There are not enough floors for all the IS groups. 2 floors are provided and 3.03 flrs are needed.			
11	on hold	5. This stacking diagram does not include the space needed to imbed some of the divisions into other divisions such as the IM group.			
10	on hold	6. This stack does not include space needed for additional specialty spaces.			
9					
lobby					
P1					

2011 stacking- alloc 3-7% / 2012 stacking- alloc 3-7% / 2013 stacking- alloc 3- 7% / copy of alloc 3- 7% grow

stacking diagram
(based on Allocation 3- Year 2012)
5/8/2008
Growth rate: 7% growth

Floors		key:	Flrs req'd :	(based on Allocation 3- Year 2012)	Leased flrs:
31	conference center & recept	conf center	1.5		
30	multi purp	marketing (& equity prod mgmt)		* captured in marketing no.	
29		IM groups	8.64		
28		MMR flr	0.5		
27		GRM	2.25		
26		BD & Admin & Inv. Admin.	0.85		
25		marketing	1.95		
24	MMR	IS	3.24		
23		Service flr & Curators space	1		
22		security & lobby			
21	trading flr?	growth space			
20	trading flr?	flrs on hold			
19		TOTAL	19.93		19
18					
17					
16		notes:			
15	cross over flr	1. The FI open office/trading flr originally was designed for flr 20 & 21- should it move to flr 22 &23?			
14		2. Will the service flr need more then 1 flr?			
13	on hold	3. There is no growth space for all the groups except a limited amount for IM.			
12	on hold	3. There are not enough floors for all the IS groups. 2 flrs are provided and 3.24 flrs are needed.			
11	on hold	4. This stacking diagram does not include the space needed to imbed some of the divisions into other divisions such as the IM group.			
10	on hold	5. This stack does not include space needed for additional specialty spaces.			
9					
lobby					
P1					

2011 stacking- alloc 3-7% \ 2012 stacking- alloc 3-7% / 2013 stacking- alloc 3- 7% / copy of alloc 3- 7% grow

FIGURE 9.23 Stacking plan 1, using Microsoft Excel, example from MPA | Margulies Perruzzi Architects.

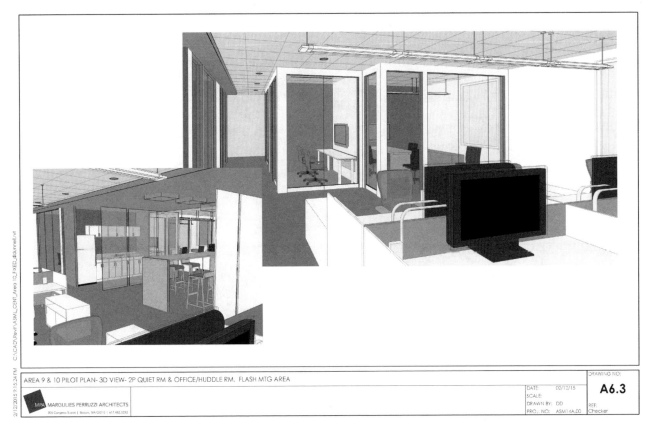

FIGURE 9.24 Three-dimensional Revit test fit; neighborhood zone example from MPA | Margulies Perruzzi Architects.

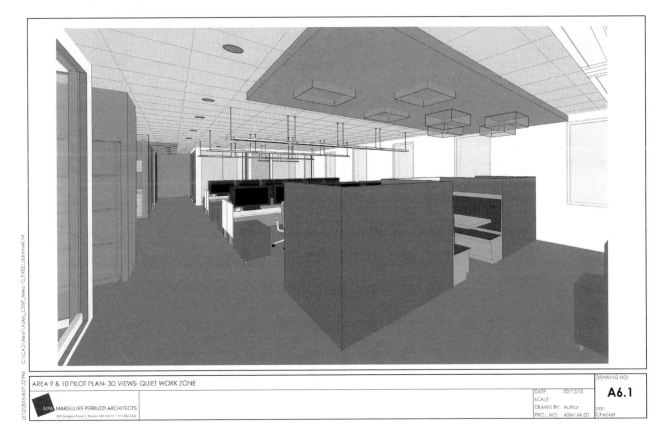

FIGURE 9.25 Three-dimensional Revit test fit; office huddle room example from MPA | Margulies Perruzzi Architects.

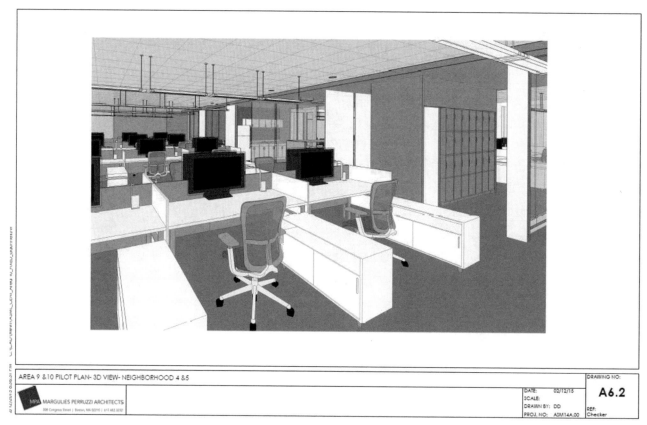

AREA 9 &10 PILOT PLAN- 3D VIEW- NEIGHBORHOOD 4 &5

MARGULIES PERRUZZI ARCHITECTS

DATE:	02/12/15	DRAWING NO:
SCALE:		**A6.2**
DRAWN BY: DD		REF:
PROJ. NO:	A5M14A.00	Checker

FIGURE 9.26 **Three-dimensional Revit test fit; quiet work zone example from MPA | Margulies Perruzzi Architects.**

These quick test-fit computer drawings help the client to visualize and share their thoughts during the beginning of the phases of design.

identified programmatic requirements and have begun to visually translate them into a diagramming format that will become the foundation for the final design solutions.

REACHING DESIGN SOLUTIONS

Numerous issues can be studied and considered easily and quickly with blocking, bubble, stacking, and diagramming studies. These can be documented and included as part of the programming study. By completing this task, you have taken the

KEY TERMS

- Adjacency matrix
- Comparative case study
- Flow diagram
- Lean design
- Likert scale
- Stacking plan

Challenging Your Thinking

After reading this chapter, you should be able to:

- Periodically review the process of programming in order to sharpen your skills and knowledge about programming for interior design.
- Review the material that is included in a programming document to assist you in creating one.
- Appreciate the advantages of programming and how it enhances your design decisions.
- Understand how programming fits into your design career.

Remember how you revisit your concept statement after exploring its possibilities in order to sharpen its focus? And recall how you review various parts of your program in light of results for your research, or how you pore through precedent studies of old projects in order to create new designs? You can apply these same approaches to your reading of this book to sharpen your understanding of programming and research for interior design.

CHALLENGING YOUR THINKING

This book has given you a holistic overview of programming. Its goal is to help you integrate programming and research skills into your work as a student and design professional.

To explore how and why programming is used in the interior design profession, a variety of firms have shared how they incorporate programming into their design process. This book brings into the academic setting programming skills that are currently employed in the profession. Chapter by chapter, it has guided you through the process, striving to help you build skills and knowledge and increase your comfort level in developing your own program. Even after you put these skills and knowledge into practice, you can continue to sharpen them by revisiting all that you've learned in light of each new experience in your career.

Think about how we defined programming in Chapter 1. What is the role of programming in the design profession? We will return to this discussion at the end of this chapter.

Chapter 2 provided a step-by-step overview of the process of design. How does the process of design in the academic experience differ from that in the professional world?

Chapter 3 showed you how to define a topic and structure your program document, whether you chose your topic or had it assigned to you. Throughout your academic experience and professional life, refer back to the programming document template included in Chapter 3. Use it as an example to compare against the ones that you are creating now and will create in the future.

Think about the different research methods introduced in Chapter 4. Consider which one(s) would fit best for your project.

Chapter 5 focused on three specific forms of research: historical, observational, and interactive. How can you build a solid foundation of knowledge about a specific type of design using each of these research skills, both individually and combined?

Chapter 6 focused on conducting a building and site analysis. Why is it important to document such factors as the environment of a design project (e.g., its state and town), exterior building and site conditions, interior building and site conditions, and design constraints and limitations?

How are precedent studies, as discussed in Chapter 7, relevant to programming for interior design? How do you select and analyze them? How do you document the information gleaned from a precedent study to help formulate programmatic requirements?

Finally, consider the written and visual analysis used during the programming phase of design, discussed in *Chapters 8 and 9*. How do visual diagramming, bubble and blocking, and stacking plans contribute to the unique style of this analysis?

PUTTING YOUR PROGRAMMING DOCUMENT TOGETHER

Programming documents come in many shapes and sizes. For students and professionals alike, variations occur because of the infinite range of potential projects. The reality of client constraints is another major mitigating factor.

The academic experience offers a great opportunity to prepare yourself for the myriad possibilities and challenges that programming will provide for your design career ahead. Introduce yourself to the various aspects of programming in gradual and sequential stages, building your knowledge with each new experience. You might first explore the research component as a group project, with each group sharing all of its data. Taking it one step at a time will help build knowledge, expertise, and confidence to implement the skills on your own. Generating a complete programming document will validate your decision-making abilities in the field of design.

Programming documents, which in some cases might be referred to as "pre-thesis reports," in many design schools typically include and are devoted to original research. Thus, creating this document is a research- and writing-intensive experience.

Typically, students should follow APA guidelines when generating this document. Make sure that everything is referenced properly, including all of your images. Becoming familiar with the APA guidelines is important. When you enter the profession, programming reports can be essential in obtaining external funding; they require a standard of style. For this and many other reasons discussed in this book, good writing skills and attention to detail will serve you well.

Take full advantage of the writing center on your campus. Have your drafts reviewed and edited. Writing centers offer a great opportunity to work on the clarity of your thoughts and the organization of your content. Emulate the process of writing a paper for an English class: numerous revisions and reviews will help you craft a final result that is exponentially better than your first draft. As your thoughts and documentation take form, so will the clarity of your ideas.

In their interviews for this book, many professionals stated that the program document became the primary reference at the beginning of the design process. Students who have completed a comprehensive programmatic research document enter the schematic design phase with less anxiety and more confidence. Typically, the schematic design phase begins with lucid ideas that form from knowledge gleaned during the programming experience.

Now, as an intelligent designer who has completed a full program on the space that you will be designing, you become the "expert." Design options are most likely already floating around in your head, and you are visually able to see numerous solutions!

APPRECIATING THE ADVANTAGES OF PROGRAMMING

By implementing research methods in the programming phase, you are able to provide solid documentation of your findings. Conducting historical, observational, and interactive research on your topic emulates the triangulation process as outlined in Chapter 4. Not only will using multiple data-collection methods help validate your

findings, but it will also help prevent any biases that might result from relying on a single data-collection method (Gall, Borg, & Gall, 1996).

Applying research methods to the design process should not be limited to the programming phase of design. As addressed in Chapter 2, the whole process encompasses a series of steps to the final solution. Numerous research methods can be employed throughout the phases of design. Programming is a fundamental place to begin. Another very pragmatic time to implement research methods is once the client has occupied the space and you are conducting a post-occupancy evaluation (POE). A POE offers the potential to analyze many research themes, such as technologies, health and care of patient environments, effective learning environments, energy in use, lighting, the social and economic aspects of the design, and way-finding evaluation. This is a small sample of the potential areas that can be studied. By evaluating and documenting the spaces after they have been occupied, the results can be documented and added to the body of knowledge within the interior design profession. Cumulatively this knowledge will benefit future designs and the public as a whole. Your work can then be cited by others in their precedent studies!

According to Dohr and Guerin, "Knowledge of research methods is useful in any business, and the practice of design is ever evolving. Currently, changes seem embedded in our 'information society.' Clients want information in addition to design. They want to know the substance of decisions, the 'why' behind what you designed. While the design community has long held that programming is design research, researchers maintain that design research in its academic interpretation complements not only programming but other stages of the design process as well" (Dohr & Guerin, 2007).

With the research and facts to validate your decision making, the process of design becomes less subjective and more pragmatic. A career in interior design continues to be a popular educational path. Popular culture and business forecasts indicate that this trend will continue as more students are exposed to the applied arts as a viable career path. The media interpretation of interior design, however, has caused some confusion about interior design as a career path (Waxman & Clemons, 2007). It is important to emphasize that both research and critical thinking are employed in design solutions; decisions are not based on "I like it," or "that's a nice color." Effective programming and research can help the client at the front end of the project to have a realistic idea of budget and timing and to prepare for long-range planning. Also, interior design is a service-driven profession. What better skills to implement than strategies that will meet the needs of clients while demonstrating innate understanding of their business practices? Analyzing and observing clients' work patterns, behaviors, and habits allow you to design programming for efficient and aesthetic work environments that can be enjoyed by users now and in the future.

PURSUING A CAREER IN PROGRAMMING

Typically, you will conduct some aspect of programming in all applications of the interior design profession. Programming is a comprehensive task; it involves identifying all requirements prior to design. In addition, because it is the first phase of design, you will need to retain the data needed to move to the next phase. In an informal sense, we all program in some form or another within the profession. Edward T. White,

author of *Project Programming: A growing architectural service*, states; "Whether we call it programming or not, we all collect and process information for our design decisions. Programming, in this sense does not have to result in a polished report. It can take the form of a conversation with a client, hand-scribbled notes, or minutes for a meeting or project files. It is helpful to hold an expanded view of what programming is rather than to define it narrowly" (1982, p. 6).

Private Firms

Some large firms and companies have their own in-house facility manager whose job is solely focused on programming. Developers or real estate firms also employ individuals just for their programming skills. Some firms interviewed for this book stated that they employ individuals to work solely on the programming requirements for specific clients. This is more prevalent in healthcare and institutional design, but most design firms offer programming as part of their services to clients.

It is probably inconceivable that you will be working in the profession without implementing programmatic skills in one form or another.

NELSON is a global architecture, design, engineering, and consulting services firm. For nearly forty years, NELSON has been providing clients with strategic and creative solutions that positively impact their ideas, goals, objectives, and environments. It has an integrated service delivery model that includes thirty-five locations. Part of NELSON's programming, and a standard NELSON methodology, is referred to as "the Playbook." The NELSON approach to generating a programming document, aka "the Playbook," is a collaborative way of gaining pertinent information, says David Stone, director of design at NELSON Boston.

BOX 10.1 USING A PLAYBOOK TO DESIGN FOR THE CASUAL COLLISION AND THE DESTINATION WORKPLACE

David D. Stone

David is responsible for design quality and excellence across multiple projects , while supporting business development efforts in the region. His thirty-plus years of experience in the interior architecture + design profession is focused on workplace development, and is composed of local, national, and international projects for commercial, hospitality, healthcare, retail, and government clients. His portfolio includes creating effective brand-based environments for a worldwide athletic company, two global bio-pharma companies, the leading internet search engine provider, an educational publisher, and a number of well-known international software/hardware developers, among others. David has served as the IIDA New England chapter president, as a director on NCIDQ's/CIDQ's Board and on the GBCI's Credential Steering Committee as the interior design representative. He continues to participate as a volunteer with the NICDQ Exam and IIDA as well as a guest lecturer at numerous educational institutions and industry trade shows.

BOX FIGURE 10.1A
David D. Stone, IIDA, LEED AP ID+C. NCIDQ. design director at NELSON Boston

The Destination Workplace

Pearson engaged NELSON [in 2011] to assist with a 310,000 square foot (sf) restack of its space at one of their main Boston locations. This workplace transformation—taking their current staff from a space populated with large perimeter offices, featuring 80+ sf workstations with high panels and lacking amenities to a more collaborative, open work space reflective of the UK-based parent company's home office—was being undertaken in three East Coast sites simultaneously.

NELSON developed multiple scenarios to accommodate Pearson's evolving real estate strategies, which coincided with lease terminations and consolidations within their multibuilding Back Bay Boston campus. The ultimate goal was to reduce square footage per person to a range of 150 to 175 sf.

Coinciding with these planning studies were conceptual design studies on the look and feel of the new offices and amenities, specifically the "magnet" hubs envisioned as

BOX FIGURE 10.1B **Pearson: destination location.** Photography © Halkin Mason Photography LLC.

(continued on next page)

focal points spread about the work place based on the newly restacked planning approach. Image studies of these hubs depicting the various attributes and services to be present in the space were included as part of the real estate strategy package.

This exercise resulted in NELSON being asked to develop a full design and construction package, including furniture fixtures and equipment (FF+E) services, for the first of potentially four floors that housed a more digitally oriented, younger workforce deemed more in-tune with the changes proposed.

Flexibility in NELSON's design was paramount to the project's success. Pearson faced two main issues: 1) they are in a publishing business that is rapidly moving from traditional paper/print media to one more digitally based, and 2) the parent company is not American based and has very different expectations on real estate. Pearson staff that work with print media (aka "books") and those that do digital media work very differently. They have very different expectations on private and collaborative space as well as work processes. Regarding the real estate side, Pearson was being told they needed to reduce their overall real estate portfolio with the expectation that all staff would be moving into much smaller open benching style work spaces. So how do you reduce a portfolio? You give everybody less space. This directly related to the second issue but not the first: dealing with work processes and products.

Stone elaborates that Pearson's facilities staff had been tracking usage of their spaces by employees on a daily basis for about two years. This data had a direct impact on the planning as they discovered that on any given day, their spaces had a maximum occupancy of 80%. Pearson asked "why are we giving everyone a desk? We'll plan the

new space at 60% occupancy, asking more people to take advantage of the 'work at home' initiative" that would allow more people to use less space. The new space designed by NELSON introduced teaming spaces at a significantly higher proportion spread throughout the new office. The workplace vs. meeting space (the "I" vs. "We" concept) ratio is better than one collaborative seat to one desk seat, allowing people to find appropriate places to do their jobs as they transition throughout the day.

Pearson brought other technology on-line to facilitate this change, including a VOIP phone system that allows calls to be picked up virtually anywhere, including another office or even home, and a policy of supporting any device an employee choices to use (laptop, tablet, Android, or iOS). The NELSON designed space provides quiet "alone" spaces; one-on-one, small group, or "huddle" spaces; open collaborative lounges; and other numerous informal and formal meeting spaces, letting the Pearson employees work better, smarter, and faster.

"I" vs. "WE" Space

Stone goes on to say that many initial discussions with clients are based on the same issues Pearson faced: how to fit more people into less space yet still provide that collaborative atmosphere that research says helps generate new business ideas, products, and processes. And one of the ideas he and the NELSON team talk about is the concept of "I" vs. "We" space. "I" space is that personal, assigned "desk" location that you call your office home. It's assigned to you. The "We" space are those locations when two or more people can engage in discussion, dialogue, and conversation. The past office setup, much like Pearson's was to provide everyone with large "I" spaces, some with "owned" meeting areas, with few and large traditional meeting spaces (aka conference rooms). What NELSON's own practice-based research is seeing is that the "I" space is becoming smaller and the "We" bigger in proportion, almost to the point of a 50/50 mix. The square footage being reduced from the personal work space is being aggregated together to create new, team-based collaborative areas in numerous layouts, none of it bookable. What makes a space successful is to dramatically increase the availability of these informal, "of the moment" meeting areas and place them in immediate proximity to the work or "I" space to a quantity where you sometimes have, for every single desk seat, one or even more collaborative seat.

This concept is creating a paradigm shift in how more mobile, agile, workplace-for-the-future companies and clients are thinking about office design. As one colleague put it, the new hypothesis is that your "desk" is becoming where you perform collaborative work with your colleagues and you are now going to these collaborative areas to actually get away and do "alone time" work, basically hiding

BOX FIGURE 10.1C **Pearson: the "I" vs. "we" workplace.** Photography © Halkin Mason Photography LLC.

BOX FIGURE 10.1D **Pearson: paradigm shift in how one works.** Photography © Halkin Mason Photography LLC.

in plain sight. Think of the local coffee shop or college lounge: multitudes of single people in a shared workspace doing individual work unrelated to each other.

The Casual Collision in the Workplace

Another client of NELSON's facing similar situations is Biogen. Biogen and NELSON have a relationship that spans more than ten years and numerous projects, including a move of their corporate headquarters from their MIT-adjacent research and production facilities in Cambridge, MA, to a suburban campus in Weston, MA, in 2010. With the arrival of a new CEO shortly after the move, there was a recognition that separating management and sales from R+D staff was hampering their ability to bring new products to market faster. By separating these two related workforces, the "casual collision" that leads to so many radical new business ideas was lacking. To increase this activity, the decision to return back to Cambridge was made. But how do you make the business case for a move back to more expensive real estate so soon after a major move? By being able to place more people in less space, achieving a net "loss" in rentable space and showing that this enhances the ability to bring more product ideas successively to market.

NELSON was asked to help with this effort starting with prelease services for Biogen's return to Cambridge. Comprising two built-to-suit low-rise buildings totaling 507,000 sf, the larger property includes two small historic structures that underwent extensive adaptive reuse for incorporation into the project.

This larger building houses the traditional corporate services support group while the other building, immediately adjacent to an existing R+D Lab building, houses R+D

administrative groups. This second structure was connected to the existing lab by a NELSON designed two-story "bridge" building to enhance horizontal circulation.

During the design and construction process, the Biogen corporate management team fully embraced the new collaborative workplace concept. To help inspire innovation, Biogen abandoned a twenty-year-old conventional office standard for a new model that is cross-functional with a totally open plan that is more supportive of teaming and collaboration. A change management and visioning process also was orchestrated to allow employees to be actively engaged in planning the design details for their new work environment. The final result responds directly to the collective employee wish list.

BOX FIGURE 10.1E **Pearson: collaboration.** Photography © Halkin Mason Photography LLC.

BOX FIGURE 10.1F **Biogen casual work location.** Photography © Halkin Mason Photography LLC.

(continued on next page)

BOX 10.1 USING A PLAYBOOK TO DESIGN FOR THE CASUAL COLLISION
AND THE DESTINATION WORKPLACE *(cont.)*

BOX FIGURE 10.1G **Biogen menu of furniture.** Photography © Halkin Mason Photography LLC.

Stone explains that Biogen is a very interesting exercise about how one collectively designs office space that is flexible to the user group's wants and needs. At the beginning of the design process, during programming discussions, Stone and his colleagues sat down with each group and asked the usual quantitative questions: "how many people/space do you have/need" (and some other things) to assign the actual floor space but went even further by asking what type of worker made up each group and what kind of work each type actually did. Using outcomes from the change management processes, NELSON then went back to the groups to ask them to actually decide on the type (style of workstation, size/configuration of enclosed collaborative space, aka "meeting" rooms, etc.) and quantity of these spaces that would be included in their area.

NELSON and the Biogen facilities team also created a "kit of parts" handbook with multiple set-ups and layouts for each room type. This allowed the user group to use the menu of furniture pieces to set up rooms (i.e., they could have a six-person traditional meeting table, or it could be set up with lounge furniture for six). The idea is that it's the user group's space tuned to their needs, so you don't need to go hunting and poaching space from other groups. The concept is that if you all have done it right, you don't need to go far from your desk as the quantity and diversity of places is high enough in your own realm for you to do your work.

The Playbook Process

What worked for Biogen, and is now a NELSON standard methodology for other clients, is referred to as the Playbook. It collects the programming discussions and outcomes along with the corporate facilities planning goals, and guidelines into a document that users can use to customize and personalize work space without creating extra costs and efforts. It allows meetings between the design and facilities team with the users to be much more conversational and less adversarial. It allows the employees to take more interest and ownership in creating their own space, raising the success of such a drastic workplace change. Programming no longer becomes a "fill out this form" exercise with just numbers of employees/spaces, but instead it is about work styles and what is needed to support the work processes. It's about how the design of the space supports productivity and how that productivity can be directly enhanced through the collaborate process.

Biogen embraced this all the way to the top. No one—from the CEO and senior executive suite on down—sits in an enclosed work space; everyone is in an open, low-height work station that is flexible in layout. Everyone now sits along the perimeter of the floors with the non-bookable, collaborative two-, four- and six-person spaces adjacently located in/along the building's core. Bookable traditional meeting spaces are kept to a minimum and in the same places on successive floors, for easy access, while at the same time keeping intrusions into user group's spaces to a minimum. Large, informal, multiuse lounge and coffee areas are centrally located, serving as mini, large group, ad-hoc discussion, celebration and assembly places. And "flexible" work spaces are strategically located within the floor. NELSON designed these last areas with preplanned lighting and HVAC controls to allow walls to be added/removed in multiple room sizes over a weekend.

BOX FIGURE 10.1H **Biogen visual connection.** Photography © Halkin Mason Photography LLC.

Enhanced and Improved Productivity

Both Pearson and Biogen continue to see positive results from their new workplace designs. In Pearson's case, the acceptance of the new planning approach is meaning more groups want the new layouts. The density of the floorplate has increased to the point where additional toilets are needing to be added to accommodate a larger-than-code workforce count. And it is proving financially viable enough that the reduced real estate savings is allowing the design to be applied to the remaining floors.

For Biogen, the ability to be agile has resulted in a number of new drugs being brought to late-stage trials or even to market in areas not traditionally part of their portfolio. Employees across the board have responded to post-occupancy surveys with a resounding 90-plus percent approval rate. Groups who balked at the proposed spatial arrangements are now asking for even more openness and collaboration, even in areas dealing with legal and HR

topics. Even traditional R+D laboratory spaces are being reworked to incorporate collaborative areas and open work stations, something traditional scientists are less inclined toward. This acceptance has allowed the company to experience unprecedented growth.

Lessons Learned

What NELSON has learned through these and other client's project work is that the nature of workplace design continues to evolve. The ever-increasing number of office generations, new demands from Millennials entering the workforce, and their new work styles demand highly flexible and adaptive planning and design. Success requires a high degree of inclusivity and "change management" support, both tangibly and technologically. It requires discussions rather than dictates. It's about embracing a whole new generation of workers . . . and their revolutionary, ground-breaking and innovative ideas about *WORK* . . . into the physical work *PLACE*.

BOX FIGURE 10.1I **Biogen casual and formal collaboration.** Photography © Halkin Mason Photography LLC.

Public: Government Agencies

The U.S. Office of Personnel Management Interior Design Series 1008, Individual Occupational Requirements, shows the large percentage of tasks falling in the realm of programming. The position classification flysheet for interior design series, GS-1008, states:

This series includes positions the duties of which are to perform, supervise, or manage work related to the design of interior environments in order to promote employee productivity, health, and welfare, and/or the health and welfare of the public. Typical duties include investigating, identifying, and documenting client needs; analyzing needs, proposing options, and working with the client, developing specific solutions; developing design documents, including contract working drawings and specifications; and, as appropriate, managing design projects performed in-house or by contract. The work requires applying knowledge from a variety of such fields as:

- Interior construction—includes building systems and components, building codes, equipment, materials, and furnishings, working drawings and specification, and codes and standards.
- Contracting—includes cost estimates, bid proposals, negotiations, contract awards, site visits during construction, and pre- and post-occupancy evaluations.
- Facility operation—includes maintenance requirements, traffic patterns, security, and fire protection.
- Aesthetics—includes sense of scale, proportion, and form; color, texture, and finishes; style and visual imagery.

- Psychology—includes privacy and enclosure, and effects of environmental components (e.g., color, texture, space).
- Management—includes design project and resource coordination. (OPM, 1991)

Public: State Agencies

Each state has its own agency that oversees the programming and construction of its capital projects. The Massachusetts state agency is the Division of Capital Asset Management and Maintenance (DCAMM). "It is an agency within the Executive Office for Administration and Finance (A&F), and is responsible for major public building construction, real estate services, and facilities management and maintenance for the Commonwealth of Massachusetts. The agency was created by the legislature in 1980 to promote quality and integrity in the management and construction of the Commonwealth's capital facilities and real estate assets"(Massachusetts Government, 2016).

"DCAMM directly manages 5.5 million square feet of state buildings and hundreds of millions in capital construction projects each year, and more than 500 active leases comprising 7 million square feet of privately-owned lease space housing state offices. Further, our agency is also responsible for the disposition of surplus real estate owned by the Commonwealth" (Massachusetts Government, 2016).

Shirin Karanfiloglu, AIA, Director of Programming Services at DCAMM shared her experiences overseeing such large and complex projects. Karanfiloglu shares that her team oversees many complex projects and works to ensure the projects are on task. Programming services include all pre-design activities as required by statute for state building projects and public development initiatives including strategic long-range capital planning. The Office of Programming oversees the development of a wide range of project studies, including architectural programs, master plans, agency capital development plans, and feasibility studies. Project studies seek to:

- Define the scope of the project in terms of space needs, required space program, maintenance and operational costs, construction costs, and scope of work for final design.
- Identify issues, needs, and technical requirements for the particular activities for which space is required. This involves close work with client agencies throughout the study process.
- Address problems of **feasibility: site constraints** and **opportunities; permit requirements; technical concerns,** such as utilities and engineering; and potential cost premiums.

- Determine total project cost (TPC) and schedule.
- Establish a basic **framework for more detailed design decisions** that must be made in subsequent phases of the project.

As noted in Figure 10.1, their scope of construction and investment focus cover a variety of program areas.

The Guidelines for the Preparation of Studies for Building Projects for the Commonwealth of Massachusetts State Agencies Building Authorities Counties, 2000, is a document that provides guidelines for the preparation of studies and programs for building projects by state agencies, counties, and building authorities. Karanfiloglu points out that "Chapter Seven of the Massachusetts General Laws (MGL) requires the Division of Capital Asset Management & Maintenance (DCAMM) to establish

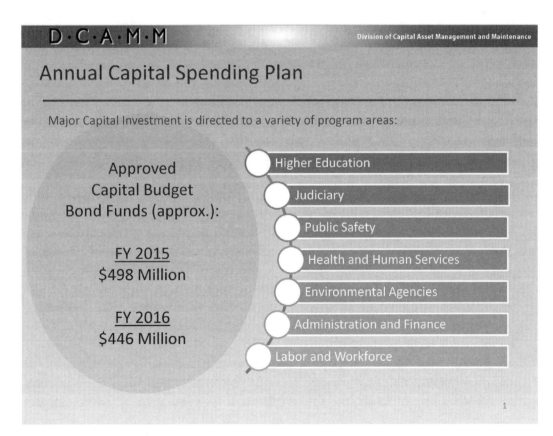

FIGURE 10.1
DCAMM annual capital spending.

these guidelines and to supervise the preparation of studies and programs" (Massachusetts Government, 2016).

The executive summary states the following:

> Studies and programs are a critical component, and MGL requires the following for all state building projects for state agencies:
>
> 1. A study must be prepared prior to contracting for the design or construction.
> 2. The study must be certified by the Commissioner of Capital Asset Management & Maintenance prior to contracting for final design services and construction.
> 3. The designer preparing the study must be selected by the Designer Selection Board, and can be appointed by the DCAMM Commissioner to perform final design services for that project subject to the approval of the Designer Selection Board. (Massachusetts Government, 2016, p. 2)

State agencies are required to have completed the studies before they request appropriations for the final design and construction.

> The purpose of studies is to investigate, justify and define projects before design begins. The legislature can then make better-informed decisions prior to appropriating funds for design and construction. As a result unnecessary and wasteful projects will be avoided. Thus, the preparation of a study is not a guarantee of eventual construction, since a study may result in a recommendation not to proceed into design and construction. In addition, the legislature may decide not to appropriate design and construction funds. (p. 3)

Karanfiloglu shares that the agency staff at DCAMM are skilled to oversee such vast projects, collaborating with other business units, secretariats and user agencies and overseeing often large consultant teams comprising architects, programmers, planners, engineers, and cost estimators. In some cases they are able to handle small projects in-house.

The DCAMM *Designers Procedures Manual* (2008) outlines instructions for designers to compete for public construction, which allows the program designer to complete the study phase of the project. The study phase of design is in essence a programming document. Some firms participate only in the study phase, while others complete the entire scope from study to construction.

DCAMM utilizes a project management and accounting system for all study and design project-related activities, this is fairly common in state and federal agencies to implement such software, as it helps keep track of large projects.

Refer to Appendix H, which outlines the *Guidelines for the Preparation of Studies for Building Projects for State Agencies*; these requirements address the variety and nature of projects (e.g., from an entirely new facility, to a partial renovation), each study will vary as to its specific requirements. These requirements of a study should be determined during the initial conferences, after which the designer should prepare a more detailed scope of work for the approval of DCAMM and the operating agency.

There is also the *Designers Procedures Manual* that defines and describes the designer's contractual tasks and obligations. These tasks encompass all project phases

BOX 10.2 COLLEEN LOWE, NCIDQ INTERIOR DESIGNER U.S. DEPARTMENT OF VETERANS AFFAIRS

Working as an interior designer for the U.S. Department of Veterans Affairs (VA) is a very rewarding experience. I am able to take part in the design of a broad range of design specialties (i.e., complex healthcare, offices, commercial spaces, leases, signage, and artwork). Through these designs, I am creating a healing space to honor those that have served our country. The VA has many regulations, guidelines, and standards for VA facilities and architectural/engineering firms for use on construction projects and daily in-house maintenance and repairs. Within those regulations there is ample opportunity as the interior designer to utilize my skills to make the spaces unique and attentive to the needs of the population of the veterans that we serve.

As a designer for the medical facility, I am intimately involved with the projects, from programming and concept development to completion. I'm invested in the success of each project, by actively being engaged as both the designer and end-user role. It's a unique role, as you pay close attention to how things will maintain and function for years to come after completion. Projects do not start and end with the development of the construction documents. For the facility designer, it can start as an idea or need from the clinical end-user or facility staff and end when the occupants move into and function in the space.

BOX FIGURE 19.2A
Colleen Lowe

As an interior designer for a regional team of designers, I am also involved in reinforcing the VA brand in our region to create consistency between medical centers, as well as creating interior design standards for the facilities. Included in that team role is creating and developing a design approach to support a patient-centered, sustainable, healing environment.

from the award of the contract for study through the occupancy of the facility by the user agency. The *Designers Procedures Manual* has a checklist for the study phase process, this can be seen in Appendix H.

At first glance, working with state agencies can appear cumbersome and overwhelming with paperwork and guidelines. But, with practice the process and guidelines become familiar and appreciated. Working in a state agency can be very rewarding knowing that you are contributing to structures that will have a direct impact on the public.

Colleen Lowe an interior designer for the U.S. Department of Veterans Affairs, shares her experience working for the government in Box 10.2.

Case Study/ Professional Example: The Salem Probate and Family Court Renovation

The Salem Probate & Family Court renovation is a case study of a project that completed extensive programming. The project consists of a complete interior rehab of an existing building, the demolition of the 1979 addition, and the construction of a smaller addition tailored to the present day and future program needs of the court that is keeping with the style and scale of the original building. The combined building's new interior was completely reprogrammed.

Gross Square Footage: 77,000
Courtroom Total: 4
Estimated Completion: 2017

Total Project Cost: $55 million
Est. Construction Cost: $36 million
Designer: Perry Dean Rogers | Partners Architects

This case study includes the following key players: Perry Dean Rogers | Partners Architects, DCAMM, and the Office of Court Management (OCM), under the Executive Office of the Trial Court. Perry Dean Rogers | Partners Architects (PDR) is a Boston-based firm founded in 1923, with a national reputation for service to academic and cultural institutions. Today, PDR maintains a focused architectural practice with

special emphasis on planning and design of academic buildings for many institutions of higher education across the country. In addition, renovation and historic restoration work continues to be an important part of PDR's contemporary practice.

Anne Brockelman, AIA, LEED AP BD+C, is the project manager for the Salem Probate & Family Court renovation. She is an architect with over sixteen years of experience in the design profession, and she also leads the sustainable design focus at PDR. She graduated from Wesleyan University with a bachelor's degree in art history and studio art, and she holds a master's degree

FIGURE 10.2
DCAMM Salem Probate & Family Court renovation.

Salem Probate & Family Court Renovation

Salem Probate & Family Court Renovation

Salem Probate & Family Court Renovation
36 Federal Street, Salem

The Salem Probate & Family Court Renovation consists of a complete gut rehab of the existing Federal Street building, the demolition of the 1979 addition on Bridge Street, and the construction of a much smaller addition more in keeping with the style and scale of the original building. The building's interior will be completely reprogrammed to meet current courthouse circulation standards.

Current Status (3-24-2014): The project has completed the Design Development Phase. Perry Dean Rogers Architects and their consultants (engineering, structural, mechanical and security) are conducting in-depth site visits to learn more about the existing conditions and to formulate preliminary recommendations for the new renovated structure.

Gross Square Footage: 77,000	Total Project Cost: $55 million	Designer: Perry Dean Rogers
Total Courtrooms: 4	Est. Construction Cost: $36 million	Contractor: W.T. Rich, Co., Inc.
Total Holding Cells: 2	Funding Source: C. 304 of 2008	Estimated Completion: 1Q 2017

in architecture from Harvard University's Graduate School of Design. Her diverse experience has included all project phases from planning, programming through construction, and various project types, such as campus master plans, academic libraries, and institutional projects such as a museum and courthouse.

Brockelman was involved with the Salem Probate & Family Court project from its inception—from the Designer Selection Board interview, to completion of the DCAMM Certifiable Building Study, through the project's construction—a process that took over four years.

Brockelman states that programming is not a linear process but rather an iterative one that has many moving parts.

Brockelman explains that the planning, programming and design phases involved multiple meetings with key stakeholders—the Massachusetts Trial Court's OCM, DCAMM, the Probate & Family Court staff (including the Register of Probate and chief probation officer), judges, along with input from Massachusetts Historical and local agencies, such as the Salem Historical Commission. It is worth noting that the owner (DCAMM) and the user agency (OCM) are separate entities, thus forming a "triangular" relationship with the design team (PDR and its consultants). Every decision had to be vetted and agreed upon by both agencies, unlike a typical relationship between design team and single client entity.

Figure 10.4 identifies the team that collaborated on this project. Some of the participants have been on board since the inception, while others have joined the team as their expertise was needed (for example, during construction administration phase).

Presentations were given to the multiple stakeholders at key milestones, for example upon completion of programming and start of schematic design. Brockelman explains that the project's vision and scope were

FIGURE 10.3 Anne Brockelman, AIA, LEED AP BD+C, is the project manager for the Salem Probate & Family Court renovation.

often reiterated as a way to provide context to the discussion. Figures 10.5 and 10.6 are examples of this.

Brockelman points out that the program needed to meet a diversity of requirements, and DCAMM issues a very precise set of guidelines for courthouses, called the Courts Program Prototype. This document was used as a starting point, with final design decisions made from consensus-building conversations weighing the building's existing physical constraints, functionality, and court operations. The main program spaces include four courtrooms and accompanying judicial offices, the Register of Probate, and the Probation Department. The renovated facility exemplifies the current trend toward more pro se representation, flexibility, and the need for more meeting, conference, and hearing rooms instead of large courtrooms. The building also houses the headquarters of the Facilities Management Department for all Essex County courthouses, which resulted in expanded back-of-house program spaces, such as the maintenance workshop. Figures 10.7 and 10.8 outline the program and meeting the program requirements.

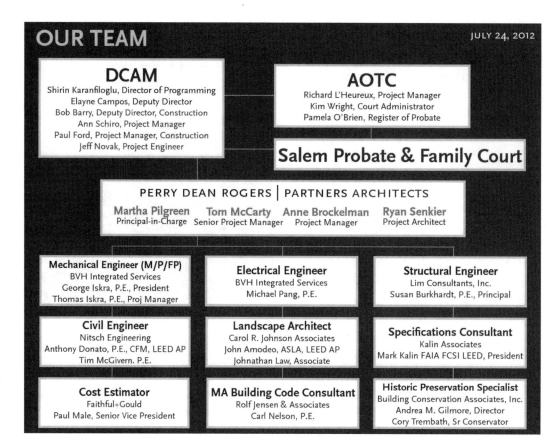

FIGURE 10.4 **Project team members for the Salem Probate & Family Court renovation.**

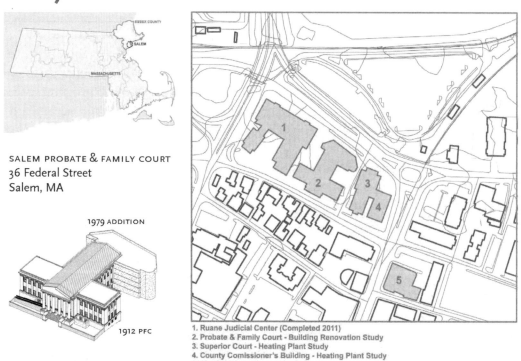

FIGURE 10.5 **Project location—Perry Dean Rogers | Partners Architects.**

UNDERSTANDING THE VISION

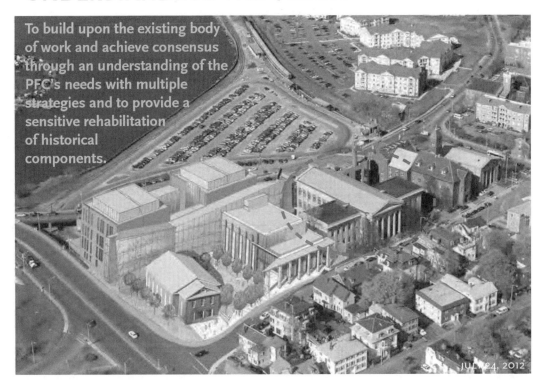

To build upon the existing body of work and achieve consensus through an understanding of the PFC's needs with multiple strategies and to provide a sensitive rehabilitation of historical components.

JULY 24, 2012

FIGURE 10.6 The project vision—Perry Dean Rogers | Partners Architects.

MEETING THE PROGRAM

KEY ISSUES IN CONTEMPORARY COURTHOUSES

- Diverse user groups
- Separate zones of circulation
- Multiple entry points
- Security

- Alternative Dispute Resolution
- Un-represented Litigants (Pro Se)
- Information Technology
- Social Services

SALEM PFC ISSUES:

- Department of Revenue - "DOR Day"
  - Must accommodate large surge of patrons every other week: shared, dual-use spaces
  - Use Hearing Room, Pre-Trial Conference Rooms, Waiting Areas
- Family Law / Pro Se Center
  - Reliance on Registry of Probate staff to oversee Public Research Area; share conference rooms
  - Share/combine Public Waiting/Transaction areas with Probate
- Detainees
  - Low anticipated detainee use;
  - Share secure circulation (corridor & elevator) with judges & staff

JULY 24, 2012

FIGURE 10.7
Meeting the program—Perry Dean Rogers | Partners Architects.

PROGRAM DEVELOPMENT

DEPARTMENT	DEPARTMENT GROSS SQ FT	
Court sets (4 Courtrooms)	11,875	*(2 large courtrooms @ 2,000 sf seating 50-60 spectators 2 small courtrooms @ 1,400 sf seating 25-30 spectators)*
Court Support & Holding	696	*(includes Court Officers; Detainee Holding)*
Judicial Offices & Support	3,931	
Register of Probate	11,544	*(includes approx 4,000s sf high-density Records Storage)*
Probate Probation	7,618	
Entry / Lobby Area	1,279	
Supplemental Operations	1,635	*(includes Pro Se/Family Law Center, DOR)*
Secure Waiting	455	
Building Support	6,003	
TOTAL	45,036 Dept GSF	

1912 Probate & Family Court:	50,000 GSF
1979 Addition	27,000 GSF
=	77,000 GSF TOTAL EXISTING
=	58% Target Efficiency

JULY 24, 2012

FIGURE 10.8
Program development— Perry Dean Rogers | Partners Architects.

As outlined in Chapter 6 it is important to document the site, exterior and interior of the building. PDR completed an existing conditions analysis of the exterior and interior of the 1909 court house.

Building Conservation Associates (BCA), the design team's historic preservation specialist, helped identify the building's character-defining features that would need special treatment in order to preserve the historic integrity of the building.

As noted in Figures 10.9a and 10.9b, BCA identified the interior historic features and spaces that were to be restored or replicated.

The existing interior and historic spaces and elements were also documented. Noted in Figure 10.10a, an exploded isometric drawing indicated where the historic elements are located on each floorplate. With an existing building there were many key constraints and limitations. Some of the key ones are outlined in Figure 10.10b

Figure 10.11 is a pie chart that represents how the overall gross square footage was divided up by departments.

Brockelman shares that balancing the DCAMM requirements, ADA and universal design compliance and the physical constraints of the existing building were challenging. For example, only two smaller courtrooms could fit within the main north wing, prompting the need for a new addition, which could accommodate a larger, higher-capacity courtroom.

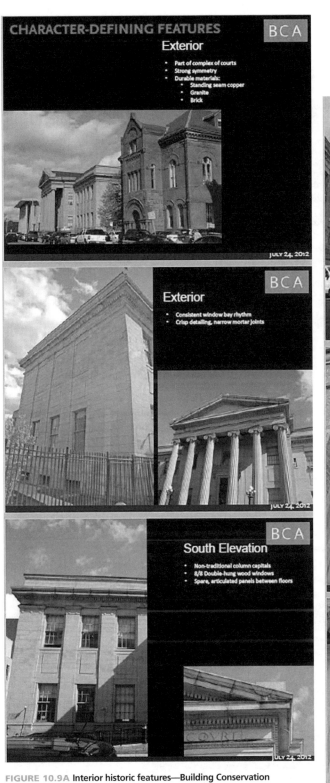

FIGURE 10.9A Interior historic features—Building Conservation Associates.

FIGURE 10.9B Interior historic features—Building Conservation Associates.

EXISTING CONDITIONS
Historic Spaces and Elements

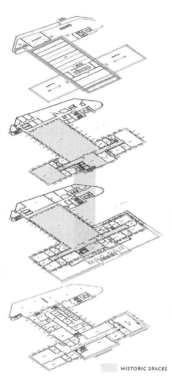

HISTORIC SPACES

FIGURE 10.10A
Existing interior
historic locations and
features—Perry Dean
Rogers | Partners
Architects.

CHALLENGES / CONSTRAINTS

PROGRAMMING ISSUES:

- Right-sizing; affirming the PFC's
  needs in the context of Essex County
  and the Ruane Judicial Center

- Accommodating large, contemporary
  courtrooms in existing historic envelope

- Secure circulation: maintaining
  separation of public, staff & detainees
  - New stair locations

JULY 24, 2012

FIGURE 10.10B
Challenges and
constraints—Perry
Dean Rogers | Partners
Architects.

PROGRAM DEVELOPMENT | Depts by Size (GSF)

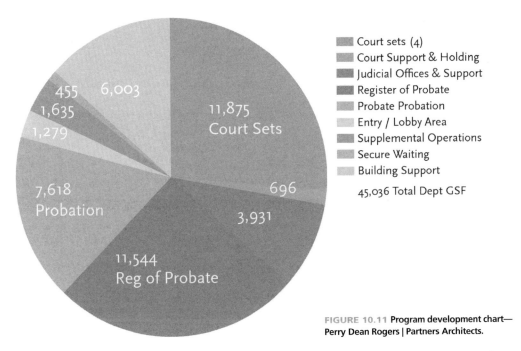

Court sets (4)
Court Support & Holding
Judicial Offices & Support
Register of Probate
Probate Probation
Entry / Lobby Area
Supplemental Operations
Secure Waiting
Building Support

45,036 Total Dept GSF

FIGURE 10.11 **Program development chart—Perry Dean Rogers | Partners Architects.**

Brockelman explains that the development of the preliminary adjacencies were created using Revit. DCAMM requested the use of BIM from the beginning. The advantage was that the big-picture relationship between gross and net square footage (and thus the efficiency factor) could be readily understood as individual spaces were adjusted or fine-tuned within the constraints of an existing building footprint. The data could be viewed both qualitatively (graphically, in plan view) and quantitatively (exported into spreadsheets) and analyzed in both ways.

PDR developed very detailed program adjacencies for each space that begin to help look at the entire space and circulation. The programmatic requirements are documented in the Courts Program Prototype, which was used as a starting point to test-fit space requirements into the existing building shell. This also included the courtroom mock-up plans, which had been commissioned by DCAMM to determine

optimal courtroom layouts, taking into account sightlines and accessibility, among other priorities.

Refer to Appendix I for further examples of Program Adjacencies Judicial Space, Register of Probate, and Probate Probation Department.

The courtroom mock-up template is seen in Figure 10.12. Brockelman shared that each courtroom had to be precisely designed with regard to sightlines, dimensional clearances for accessibility, and circulation. Over the years DCAMM, has conducted in-depth research that included full-scale spatial models that helped determine the state's programmatic needs and standards for courtrooms. The Salem Probate & Family Court utilized these spatial guidelines, adjusting them to the specifics of the project, such as the lack of a Jury Box requirement.

Another important aspect of courthouse programming is understanding the complex circulation requirements—the

PROGRAM ADJACENCIES

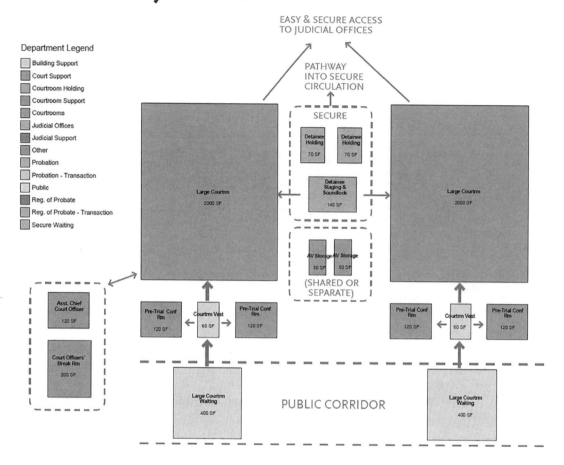

FIGURE 10.12
Program Adjacencies for Courtroom—Perry Dean Rogers | Partners Architects.

need for separation and access control between at least three groups: public circulation, staff circulation, and secure circulation (such as that of judges and detainees, separately). The separation and coming together of these three circulation paths needed to be defined and designed. Sightlines are also very important and critical to the experience of the facility by users. At the Salem Probate & Family Court, the C- or H-shaped waiting area allows two parties that may be in dispute to use the waiting room without seeing each other, while still receiving oversight from probation staff at the centrally located transaction counter.

In addition to serving as project manager for the project, Brockelman is also PDR's

director of sustainable design and led the project's sustainable design focus. In evaluating potential sustainable design strategies, the goals of energy efficiency had to be balanced with protection of the history property's character-defining features and materials. The project is tracking LEED Gold certification. Sustainable design was a priority for the Salem Probate & Family Court renovation, as outlined in Figure 10.14a and Figure 10.14b.

Many schemes were explored, with one key question being whether the 1979 addition could be feasibly renovated and repurposed (it was not). Figure 10.15 shows a figure-ground of the schemes that were explored thoroughly, including cost estimates of potential designs.

COURTROOM MOCK-UP TEMPLATES

※ NO JURY BOX NEEDED FOR PROBATE & FAMILY COURTROOM

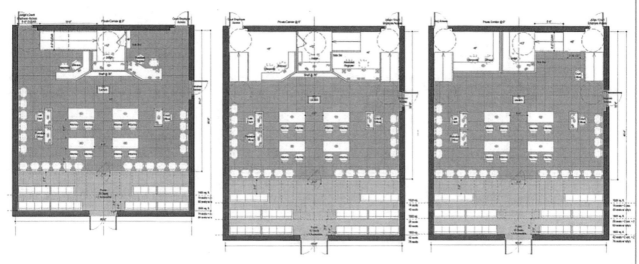

FIGURE 10.13A Courtroom mock-up template—DCAMM.

FIGURE 10.13B Rendering interior of courtroom—Perry Dean Rogers | Partners Architects.

SUSTAINABLE DESIGN | Summary of Strategies

SITE
- Encourage use of public transportation:
  - MBTA commuter rail & bus lines
- Maintain low parking capacity
- Provide bicycle storage. Share showers & changing rooms available at Ruane Ctr.
- Mitigate Heat Island Effect:
  - Site - SRI of hardscape materials
  - Roof - SRI of new flat roofs
- Light pollution reduction - site lighting
- Re-introduce trees to front (south facade)

WATER
- Water-efficient landscaping
- Reduce water use by 30%. Specify Low-Flow fixtures, possibly Dual-Flush for staff toilets
- Stormwater runoff quality control by mechanical means - install stormceptor

Not viable:
- Stormwater quantity control / Water reuse/ recycling / Rainwater harvesting - not enough demand for water use

ENERGY PERFORMANCE
- Improve by a minimum of 20% (existing building renovation)
- Building envelope improvements
- Renewal Energy - use of Solar PV's on flat roofs - under consideration
- Building Commissioning
- Enhanced refrigerant management
- Separate Metering - Measurement & Verification plan - under consideration
- Energy modeling to test / verify performance of options explored

Not viable:
- Geothermal / Ground Source Heat Pump - constricted site
- Green Power - State would need to contract

SUSTAINABLE DESIGN | Summary of Strategies

MATERIALS & RESOURCES
- Recycling - Collection & Storage
- Re-use existing building components
  - Document: Walls, Floors, Roof
- Reuse / Restoration of historic, decorative items
- Design Team to specify materials:
  - Recycled content materials
  - Regional materials
  - Rapidly-renewable materials
  - Certified wood

INDOOR ENVIRONMENT
- CO_2 monitoring in high-occupancy spaces
- Use low-emitting materials:
  - paints, coatings, flooring, composite wood
- Lighting: User-controlled at staff work spaces
- Thermal Comfort: Operable windows for staff spaces
- Thermal Comfort: post-occupancy survey
- Daylight - maximize natural light; use borrowed light
- Views - maximize where possible

Not viable:
- Enclosed copy rooms; Permanent walk-off mats

FIGURE 10.14A AND B Sustainable design summary of strategies—Perry Dean Rogers | Partners Architects.

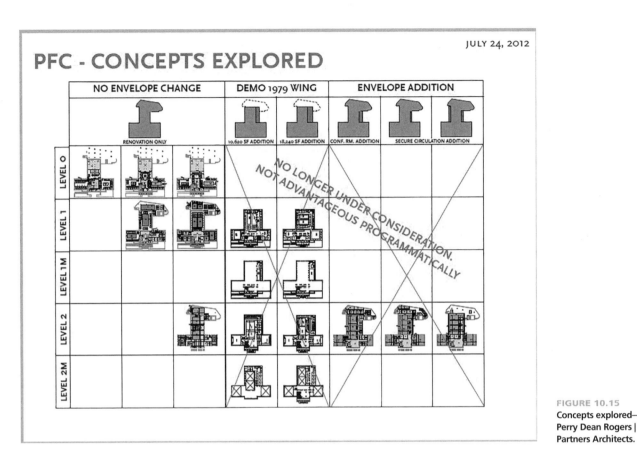

PFC - CONCEPTS EXPLORED

JULY 24, 2012

FIGURE 10.15
Concepts explored—
Perry Dean Rogers |
Partners Architects.

Salem Probate & Family Courthouse Renovation & Addition. Rendering by Perry Dean Rogers.

FIGURE 10.16
Rendering of
courthouse interior—
Perry Dean Rogers |
Partners Architects.

Refer to Appendix I to see the enlarged schemes that were explored.

This project has been active for over four years, states Brockelman, and is planned for completion in 2017. As outlined above, Perry Dean Rogers | Partners Architects worked very closely with DCAMM to plan a program that addressed a multitude of programmatic requirements. The result of this collaboration is a beautifully restored, designed, and well-functioning public structure.

PASSION FOR RESEARCH AND PROGRAMMING

As you apply the knowledge that you have learned in the academic setting to a professional one, educate your client about the benefits of programming and research. Learn from historical, observational, and interactive data, not only for the project at hand, but for future applications as well. Commit yourself to lifelong learning. Always seek information that will benefit your core body of knowledge, and be intensely curious throughout your career as you implement research and programming skills to benefit good design for everyone who occupies the spaces you create.

Appendices

The Appendices have been included for your reference. It is helpful to see the tools and approaches to collect and organize pertinent information from clients. The forms should be modified to fit the project and your style.

NCIDQ Exam Distribution That Falls in the Scope of Programming

Interior Design Professional Exam (IDPX)

CONTENT DISTRIBUTION

1.	Knowledge of and skill in analyzing and synthesizing programmatic information	10 Questions 6.7% of test
2.	Knowledge of and skill in the application of code requirements, laws, standards, regulations, accessibility and suustainability	20 Questions 13.3% of test
3.	Knowledge of and skill in integration with building systems and construction	13 Questions 8.7% of test
4.	Knowledge of and skill in selection, specification, use and care of furniture, fixtures, equipment, interior finishes, materials and lighting	22 Questions 14.7% of test
5.	Knowledge of and skill in development and use of construction drawings, schedules and specifications	15 Questions 10% of test
6.	Knowledge of and skill in interior design documentation and contract administration	23 Questions 15.3% of test
7.	Knowledge of and skill in project coordination and the roles of related design professionals	20 Questions 13.3% of test
8.	Knowledge of and skill in application of professional ethics and business practices	27 Questions 18% of test

APPENDIX A.1 **NCIDQ IDPX.**

Practicum

CONTENT AREA WEIGHT

1.	Knowledge of and skills in developing a design concept: • Programming • Design theory	10%
2.	Knowledge of and skills in design communication methods and techniques: • Written design communication methods and techniques • Visual design communication methods and techniques	15%
3.	Knowledge of and skills in measuring, drafting and technical drawing conventions: • Construction drawings and schedules • Architectural woodwork • Specifications • Lighting	30%
4.	Knowledge of and skills in analyzing and synthesizing the programmatic information: • Theories about the relationship between human behavior and the designed environment • Building construction • Sustainable design practices • Building systems • Interior finishes and materials	30%
5.	Knowledge of and skills in space planning: • Code requirements, laws, standards and regulations • Site analysis procedures • Furniture, fixtures and Equipment, including window treatments and textiles	15%

APPENDIX A.2 **NCIDQ practicum.**

Floorplan of Allegro Interior Architecture Furniture Plans for Asset Management Company Project

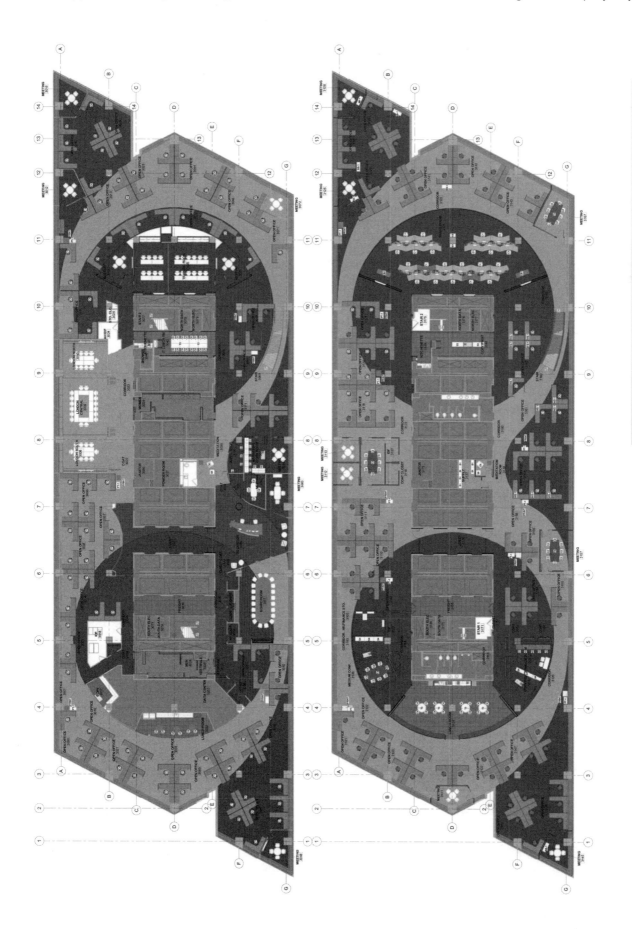

Asset Management Company

30TH AND 31ST FLOOR PLANS

ALLEGRO
Interior Architecture

Resiliency Example
Monica Johnson,
Interior Architecture + Design
Mount Ida College 2013

APPENDIX C.1 The final board presentation boards for the example in Chapter 2, Box 2.4.

Environmental + Interior Design Program at Chaminade University of Honolulu— Student Group Project

Kapiolani Medical Center for Women & Children
Children's Oncology Play Area

Lo'i

The design for the Kapiolani Medical Center for Women and Children's Oncology play area and display space is based on the representational and functional components of the taro patch (lo'i) and the taro plant. In a taro patch, rainwater from the mountains fills the lo'i and provides the optimal conditions needed for the taro plant to thrive. As the stream flows into the taro patch, it nourishes and provides sustenance to the community.

With the same intention, Pu'uwai O' Kāle'a ("heart of joy") and Pu'uwai O' Ka'āina ("heart of the land"), foster healing, growth, joy and community. With the use of natural finish materials; a color palette inspired by nature; and patterns, textures and motifs inspired by the lo'i; an inviting environment is created where patients or guests can be expressive, unrestricted (as much as possible), and curious. The design of Pu'uwai O' Kāle'a and Pu'uwai O' Ka'āina expresses the various attributes of the taro plant in a way that improves the the well - being of guests, patients, and staff.

Pu'uwai O' Kāle'a
Heart of Joy

Pu'uwai O' Kāle'a houses, a small office area for several staff members who oversee the oncology department's patient rooms and play area. Upon entering the space, guests are greeted by a wall of frames with interchangeable artwork made by the patients in the playroom. This area provides a more comfortable space where patients can be creative and relax indoors.

Open sight lines from the office area to the entrance and outdoor playspace gives staff the ability to supervise children's activities with confidence. Soft earth tones in the finishes mimic the natural landscape of the lo'i, while the light finishes brighten up the overall space.

Inspiration

Outdoor Play Area

Office

Floor Plan

Creative Space

Office

Creative Space

Entrance

Office Wall Covering   Bench Seat Upholstery   Office Casework

Tsoi/Kobus & Associates Programming Forms

1. UNDERSTANDING YOUR ORGANIZATION

Figure E.1 is an example of the programming services that Tsoi/Kobus & Associates offers to its clients. Kate Wendt, IIDA, director of interiors, shares this information with the client up front so they are aware of the process and are active participants. For more information on the firm and how it uses these forms, see Chapter 5, "Historical, Observational, and Interactive Research."

Understanding Your Organization

Survey • Interview • Observe • Document

TK&A ⎪⟋ T S O I / K O B U S & A S S O C I A T E S
            A R C H I T E C T S

APPENDIX E.1 Tsoi/Kobus & Associates: Understanding Your Organization.

Understanding your Organization
Programming and Strategic Facility Planning

Approach and Philosophy

Programming is the name we use for the process of getting to know your organization and understand your needs. This basis of this knowledge allows us to develop a series of facility solution options worth of consideration, final decision-making and action.

Our approach involves your team from the onset. We acknowledge the value and importance of the information you have assembled to date. Together we will now continue to support the planning process. Categories are outlined in later sections of this document with the anticipated date they will be required.

The method of collecting and reporting information is based on surveys, observation, and personal interviews. Examples of survey and interview questionnaires are included in this booklet. Our top down and bottom up survey technique often reveals variations in responses and can point out the need to reach agreement and bring clarity to the information. Additionally, it creates an opportunity to communicate to the employees anticipated facility changes and their beneficial impact on the corporate goals and objectives. We have found that this procedure develops the most accurate and appropriate information possible in an expedient time frame

Tsoi Kobus & Associates

Understanding your Organization
Programming and Strategic Facility Planning

Process Steps

Since the higher level strategic planning intent has been defined and the goals and objectives are established, the actual programming process can begin. We consider this an opportunity to learn about your organization and have "fun" in the process. Our commitment is to make the experience one that is collaborative, without being a burden to you or your staff. Therefore, we have broken this effort down into a number of clear and concise steps.

- **Prior to Kick Off Meeting – Distribute List of Information Required**
  (A detailed list of items is attached with key dates required.)

- **Orientation/Kick Off Meeting**
  Project Introduction and Orientation
  Organizational/Committee Review
  Project Communications
  The Future—Where are you going?
  Tour of Facilities

- **Data Gathering-On site work at your facility**
  Personal Interviews
  Surveys
  Observation
  Existing Conditions Documentation

- **Program Report Generation**
  Analysis of Information
  Preliminary Presentation of Results
  Modeling, Revisions and Scenarios
  Final Program Report, Presentation, & Subsequent Information Added

Tsoi Kobus & Associates

Understanding your Organization
Programming and Strategic Facility Planning

The Program Document

Your program will analyze and report information on a number of strategic levels. Reports detail elements based on the information critical to our planning efforts and your decision making process. The typical structure of the report is as follows:

- **Executive Summary**
    Overall Planning Mission Statement
    Image and Identity
    Quality of Work Life Goals
    Schedule and Budget Parameters and Objectives

- **Design Criteria**
    Recommended Workstation Typicals
    Site & Building Design Criteria
    Technical Building Systems & Engineering Requirements
    Security and Access Criteria
    Special Requirements

- **Spatial Requirements**
    Work Areas
    Ancillary, Common, Support & Special Use Areas
    Equipment Space Requirements
    Circulation Requirements

TSOI / KOBUS & ASSOCIATES

ARCHITECTS

Understanding Your Organization:
Programming and Strategic Facility Planning

Background Information Required From Your Executive Management

	Date Required	Date Received
1. Overall goals and direction for the project		
2. Direction on project-related communication; routing and degree of confidentiality required		
3. Pending organizational changes that will affect the planning process and/or outcome: staffing reductions, reorganizations, computer automation additions, process improvement plans, etc.		
4. Overall budget direction, including any criteria for budget distribution or allocation as well as all items that are a part of the budget (including those that are an owner expense), so that amounts available for construction and furnishings can be determined; also, is cost-center tracking required, and if so, to what degree?		

APPENDIX E.2 Tsoi/Kobus & Associates: Background Information Form.

Understanding Your Organization:
Programming and Strategic Facility Planning

Background Information Required From Your Facility or Operations Department

	Date Required	Date Received
1. Current, existing-conditions floor plans with furniture: Indicate boundaries for all departments and job titles, clearly mark all common or shared work areas or rooms, and indicate if they belong to a specific department		
2. Existing or requested known adjacencies or mandatory locations for certain functions (i.e., computer room to be located on the first floor)		
3. Write-up of workflow or process functions		
4. Proposed or mandated space or furniture standards, if known; procurement procedure		
5. List of any existing furniture or equipment to be reused		
6. Type of facility security system requirements you have or will require		
7. List of common areas shared by all departments, noting any areas that have special requirements for floor loading (i.e., vaults) or equipment (i.e., training rooms with special audio/visual requirements)		

Understanding Your Organization:
Programming and Strategic Facility Planning

Background Information Required From Your Human Resources Department

	Date Required	Date Received
1. Organization charts for all groups within the scope of this study		
2. List of all personnel by department (names with titles or functions); list of job categories		
3. Approved staffing plans for the next 3 to 5 years		
4. In-house telephone directory		

Background Information Required From Your Data Systems or MIS Department

	Date Required	Date Received
1. List of areas requiring special HVAC conditions for equipment, i.e., areas requiring 24-hour air conditioning and defined humidity, other than typical office areas; include all local area network closets or telephone equipment rooms in addition to the data center		
2. Individual workstation area requirements for computers or other equipment such as printers, plotters, and fax machines		
3. Future requirements for automation: Define any new systems that are planned or are in the process of being implemented; include time frames for implementation if known		

Understanding Your Organization:
Programming and Strategic Facility Planning

Additional Background Information Required

	Date Required	Date Received
1. Identification of all office equipment other than that already identified by the MIS group (examples: copiers, specialty equipment for mail processing and/or check writing, ATM machines); completed data sheets on all pieces of unique equipment with manufacturer's specifications attached (locations for all equipment will be reviewed by the coordinator for facilities and the individual department representative)		
2. Telephone system requirements; include information on individual responsible internally and externally for coordination		
3. Paging/intercom and or white noise required		
4. Cafeteria and kitchen requirements (these will be determined in a separate series of meetings with your foodservice vendor, the foodservice consultant, and both our design team and your planning team)		

Understanding Your Organization:
Programming and Strategic Facility Planning

Background Information Required From Each Department
(These topics will be covered in individual meetings with department head)

	Date Required	Date Received
1. Description of department function and discussion of required adjacencies to other groups or function areas		
2. List of current and future personnel		
3. Discussion of any proposed changes to work process, work flow, or staffing		
4. Review of specific departmental shared areas, such as file rooms, equipment rooms, or conference rooms used solely by their group		
5. Review of key personnel within their group to be interviewed		

Individual Questionnaire

Part 1 - Background Information (Required)

1. Your current department

   _____

2. Your job title

   _____

3. How long have you worked for the company?

   _____ yrs

4. Which of the following best describes your work setting?

   Private office

   Open workstation

   Team room

5. During a typical week in the office, how much time do you spend in the following locations?

   At your desk

   Somewhere else in the group/team area or nearby

   Elsewhere in the building/in meetings

   At off-site activities (e.g. client, etc.)

   Total (should equal 100%)

6. Do you use alternative work sites? Please list them below.

   _____
   _____
   _____
   _____

APPENDIX E.3 **Tsoi/Kobus & Associates: Individual Questionnaire.**

7. How much time do you spend per week in these situations:

In meetings at your desk or in a conference room dedicated to your group   [   ]

Working with a computer   [   ]

On the telephone   [   ]

Impromptu, face-to-face conversations with colleagues   [   ]

Writing reports/notes and filling in forms   [   ]

Reading/thinking/research/quiet work   [   ]

Sorting papers, filing, photocopying, faxing, mail, general paper management   [   ]

Other   [   ]

Total (should equal 100%)   [   ]

8. List up to three groups, other than your own, with whom you need to interact to perform your work most effectively. For each group, indicate whether interaction is scheduled in advance, unscheduled, or both.
Also indicate how often you interact with the group and how important the interaction is to performing your work.

Group 1 Name: _____

| ( ) Scheduled interaction
( ) Unscheduled interaction
( ) Both | ( ) Interact one/more times a day
( ) Interact on a weekly basis
( ) Interact on a monthly basis | ( ) Critical interaction
( ) Important interaction
( ) "Nice to have" interaction |

Group 2 Name: _____

| ( ) Scheduled interaction
( ) Unscheduled interaction
( ) Both | ( ) Interact one/more times a day
( ) Interact on a weekly basis
( ) Interact on a monthly basis | ( ) Critical interaction
( ) Important interaction
( ) "Nice to have" interaction |

Group 3 Name: _____

| ( ) Scheduled interaction
( ) Unscheduled interaction
( ) Both | ( ) Interact one/more times a day
( ) Interact on a weekly basis
( ) Interact on a monthly basis | ( ) Critical interaction
( ) Important interaction
( ) "Nice to have" interaction |

Part 2 - Workspace Performance

These questions ask for your opinion of how different features of the office workspace perform. You are also asked to rate the importance of each item, whether or not it applies to you at the moment.

Use the following scales when rating each item:

Performance		**Importance**	
Very good	4	Important	4
Good	3	Somewhat important	3
Adequate	2	Not very important	2
Poor	1	Not important	1
N/A	0		

First: Choose the number that comes closest to reflecting your opinion regarding performance for a specific item in your current workplace or setting. If you think the question is irrelevant to you, mark "not applicable".

Then: Rate the importance of the item for you, even if it does not apply to your current situation.

1. Accommodating Work Activities
How well does your office workspace accommodate the following activities?

Performance   Importance

a. Working with a computer
b. Conversing on the telephone
c. Informal communication and interaction with colleagues
d. Meetings and interviews
e. Writing reports, filling in forms
f. Reading/thinking/research/quiet time/creative time
g. Paper management: filing, faxing, photocopying, mail
h. Comments:

2. Your Desk
How satisfied are you with the following features of your office or desk?

Performance   Importance

a. Worksurface area of the desk
b. Space around the desk
c. Accommodation for meetings at the desk
d. Ability to arrange monitor and keyboard/mouse to suit your needs
e. Ability to adjust work surface to suit your needs
f. Ability to adjust chair to suit your work needs
g. Comments:

3. Filing and Other Reference Materials
How well does your office workspace perform in the following areas?

Performance   Importance

a. Quantity of storage space for filing materials at your desk
b. Quantity of storage space for filing materials near your desk
c. Access to central, shared filing
d. Usefulness and topicality of reference materials
e. Security for confidential hard copy documents
f. Display space
g. Storage for personal items
h. Comments:

4. Office Equipment

What is your view on the performance of your office equipment?

	Performance	Importance
a. Access to a computer when needed		
b. Access to a printer when needed		
c. Access to a LAN connection/data line		
d. Access to a photocopier		
e. Access to a fax machine		
f. General suitability of the above equipment		

g. Comments:

5. Meeting Facilities

How do you rate the performance of meeting facilities available to you?

	Performance	Importance
a. Availability of conference rooms when required		
b. Suitability of equipment and furniture layout in conference rooms (e.g. LAN connections, PCs, teleconferencing projectors)		
c. Suitability of lighting and acoustics in conference rooms		
d. Availability of informal team/project meeting areas		
e. Availability of break areas (e.g. pantry areas, lunch room)		

f. Comments:

6. Communicating with Others

How well do you rate your office workspace in fostering communication?

	Performance	Importance
a. Ability to communicate with colleagues in person		
b. Ability to communicate with your immediate supervisor or manager		
c. Ease of making and receiving confidential phone calls		
d. Ease of arranging one-to-one confidential interviews		
e. Suitability of space for one-to-one confidential interviews		

f. Comments:

7. Overall Performance of Workspace

How well does your office environment perform in general?

	Performance	Importance
a. Allowing concentration on work		
b. Minimizing noise and distractions		
c. Encouraging team working		
d. Providing a sociable atmosphere		
e. Enhancing productivity		
g. Fostering high quality work		

h. Comments:

8. If you have any comments about issues that were not addressed in the survey but you feel deserve special attention, please write these in the space below.

_____
_____
_____

9. Please note below any ways your workspace could be made better or more effective: suggestions, ideas for future space, etc.

_____
_____

TK&A V TSOI / KOBUS & ASSOCIATES
ARCHITECTS

Departmental Questionnaire

Your Name: _____ Date: _____

Position: _____ Division: _____

Present Location: _____ Dept.:_____

A. Introduction

Tsoi Kobus & Associates is conducting a planning study of your space needs. We need information about the areas in which you and your coworkers function in order to assure that you will have the space you need to do your job during the upcoming relocation. This is only possible if we have accurate information.

When you are completing the section entitled "General Department Information," please fill in the blanks and check all spaces that apply. To complete "Adjacency Requirements" and the remaining individual sections, please read over the worksheets before filling them out. Complete all spaces pertinent to your department, and leave blank all items that do not apply.

Attach additional sheets of paper if you need to. If you feel that any multiple choice answers do not adequately cover unique situations that may exist in your area, please feel free to write in any comments you may have.

All of your responses will be vital to the success of the study and to you and your department. Please give each question your most careful consideration.

1. What are the strategic objectives of your group? _____

_____

2. What type of physical space will you need to support your business objectives?

_____

TK&A   V   TSOI / KOBUS & ASSOCIATES
ARCHITECTS

B. General Departmental Information

1. Departmental subgroups, square footage, and number of personnel in each:

2. Hours of operation:
   ___ 8-hour day   ___ Weekday overtime
   ___ Weekend overtime   ___ Night shift (12AM +)
   ___ Evening shift (7-12AM)   ___ Other

3. Space requirements for additional persons: Indicate number of personnel.
   ___ Part-time personnel   ___ Seasonal personnel
   ___ Outside consultants   ___ Visitors from other facilities
   ___ Outside visitors   ___ Other
   ___ None

4. Requirements for visitors:
   ___ Average number of visitors per day
   ___ Use of shared reception area   ___ Use of separate reception area
   ___ Other   ___ None

5. Considerations: Level of Security
   ___ Low: standard facility security
   ___ Medium: verification required before admittance of outside visitors
   ___ High: area restricted to personnel only
   ___ Maximum: area restricted to specific personnel only

   Reasons:
   ___ Confidential activities
   ___ Confidential materials, documents, or equipment
   ___ Valuable materials or equipment
   ___ Valuable documents
   ___ Other _____

Comments:
_____
_____
_____
_____

TK&A TSOI / KOBUS & ASSOCIATES
ARCHITECTS

C. Adjacency Requirements

1. Primary modes of communication within this department
   - ___ Face to face
   - ___ Phone calls
   - ___ E-mail
   - ___ Spontaneous meetings
   - ___ Group meetings
   - ___ Memos
   - ___ Teleconferencing
   - ___ Other

2. Primary modes of communication with other departments/groups:
   - ___ Face to face
   - ___ Phone calls
   - ___ E-mail
   - ___ Spontaneous meetings
   - ___ Video conferencing
   - ___ Group meetings
   - ___ Memos
   - ___ Teleconferencing
   - ___ Other

3. Departments or special equipment that should be located adjacently (e.g. color copiers):

   _____
   _____
   _____

4. Departments or special equipment that should not be located adjacently:

   _____
   _____
   _____

5. Can any portions of your department be remotely located?

   _____
   _____
   _____

Comments:

   _____
   _____
   _____
   _____
   _____
   _____

TK&A   **V**   TSOI / KOBUS & ASSOCIATES
ARCHITECTS

D. Support Spaces

List shared departmental support spaces, such as reception areas, display spaces, equipment rooms or areas, computer rooms, libraries, training rooms, copy rooms, pantries/lounges, etc. (Shared departmental filing and storage space will be covered in another section.) Note appropriate quantities of these spaces in future projections. Indicate any equipment, storage units, or files contained within these spaces.

Support Space (Description)	PROJECTIONS (# OF SPACES)	Remarks
Equipment		Storage

Support Space (Description)	PROJECTIONS (# OF SPACES)	Support Space (Description)
Equipment		

Support Space (Description)	PROJECTIONS (# OF SPACES)	Remarks
Equipment		Storage

Comments:

_____

_____

_____

_____

_____

_____

TK&A   TSOI / KOBUS & ASSOCIATES
ARCHITECTS

E. Conference Space

Check off all general conferencing information as it applies to your department. Indicate sizes of required conference spaces by number of participants typically in attendance (e.g., 6-8 persons, 10-12 persons). Note whether a conference room can be shared with another department. List projection based on number of rooms required.

1. Types of meetings:
   ___ Staff meetings   ___ Client meetings / presentations
   ___ Project work sessions   ___ Outside vendors / consultants
   ___ Seminars / training   ___ Other _____

2. Frequency of use:
   ___ Daily   ___ 1-3 meetings / month
   ___ 1-3 meetings / week   ___ Other _____

3. Types of Meetings:
   ___ Audiovisual   ___ Computer interface
   ___ Tackable surfaces   ___ Chart rails
   ___ White boards   ___ Flexible furniture layout
   ___ Coffee service   ___ Storage
   ___ Video conferencing   ___ Teleconferencing
   ___ Other _____

4. Conference room size:

Conference Room (By # of Participants)	Shared YES	NO	Room Size (Sq. Feet)	Remarks

Comments:

_____

_____

_____

_____

_____

TK&A V

TSOI / KOBUS & ASSOCIATES
ARCHITECTS

F. Filing and Storage

1. Please answer the following questions as they apply to your departmental group filing requirements. Do not include working files kept at individual workstations or in offices. Refer to the drawings below.

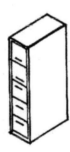   

2, 3, 4, 5 high <u>Vertical File</u>   2, 3, 4, 5 high <u>Lateral File</u>
Letter (15" wide), Legal (18"wide)

a. How many vertical or lateral file <u>**drawers**</u> are in use in your department / group today? Provide actual <u>**drawer**</u> count, not cabinet total count.

_____

b. How many <u>**drawers**</u> do you access regularly every day?

_____

c. How many <u>**drawers**</u> do you access one to three times per week?

_____

d. How many <u>**drawers**</u> do you access more than once a month but less than once a week?

_____

e. How many <u>**drawers**</u> are accessed less often than once a month?

_____

G. Equipment

On the following schedule, indicate by item number all equipment used in your department. Indicate any projected equipment as "future," and enter quantities if there is more than one of a certain piece of equipment, such as personal computers and typewriters.

Check the appropriate columns indicating whether the equipment is used by an individual, by more than one person, by a department, or by more than one department.

If a piece of equipment is used by more than one person, enter the number of people that use the item in the "use by more than one person" column.

Provide manufacturer, model number, and dimensions. List all components for multi-component units (e.g., personal computers).

Indicate any equipment that needs to be lockable or in a secured area.

Comments:

TK&A

TSOI / KOBUS & ASSOCIATES
ARCHITECTS

G. Equipment: continued

Equipment Schedule

Item no.	Description	Qty.	Manufacturer	Model no.	Dimensions depth,width,height	Indiv use	Share use	Dept use	Share w/other dept.	Remarks

TK&A ⋁ TSOI / KOBUS & ASSOCIATES
ARCHITECTS

H. Additional Information

If you think of any other important information about your workspace that we did not ask for in this questionnaire, please write it in the space below.

TK&A ⊻ TSOI / KOBUS & ASSOCIATES
ARCHITECTS

Example Small Projects _____ **Introduction**

The following questionnaire has been developed to determine your department and space planning needs. Please take the time to carefully answer all questions. At least one questionnaire should be complete for each Department. Please photocopy the blank form if more copies are required.

Department: _____ Your Name: _____
Current Location: _____ Title: _____
Phone: _____ Date: _____

This survey has been reviewed and approved by your department manager: _____

_____ **General Information**

Briefly describe the *function* of this Department. Please attach a current copy of your organization chart.

_____

_____

_____

Indicate the *hours of operation* for your Department. (Check all that apply)

☐ Normal Business Hours   ☐ Weeknight Overtime
☐ Evening/Night Shifts   ☐ Weekend Overtime
☐ Weekend Shifts   ☐ _____

Indicate the level of *security* required for your Department. (Check all that apply)

☐ Low – standard building security   ☐ Security is required for confidential
☐ Medium verification required before outside ☐ Security is required for confidential materials/documents
     Visitors are admitted
☐ High – area is restricted to company personnel ☐ Special security devices are required (i.e.: cameras,
☐ Maximum – area is restricted department   ☐   alarms, mantraps, etc.)
     personnel

Indicate the types and frequency of *visitors* your Department experiences. (Check all that apply)

☐ In-house visitors   ☐ Department receives visitors daily
☐ Outside vendors and/or consultants   ☐ Department receives visitors a few times per week
☐ Customers and clients   ☐ Department receives visitors a few times per month
☐ Messengers and delivery persons   ☐ Visitors stay within the department for days at a time

Indicate this departments *equipment and environmental systems* requirements. (Check all that apply)

☐ Mainframe computer system   ☐ Back-up power (UPS, emergency generator)
☐ Local Area Network (LAN) system ☐ Overtime/24 hour air conditioning
☐ Wide Area Network (WAN) system   ☐ _____

What general feeling do you have about our current environment (likes? Dislikes?)?

_____

_____

_____

Page 1

APPENDIX E.4 Tsoi/Kobus & Associates: Example Small Projects. An example of the questionnaire that Tsoi/Kobus & Associates use to collect pertinent information when working on smaller projects.

Staff Projections

Please list below descriptions for staff that make up your department (i.e.: Manager, Professional, Technician, Secretary). In the columns provided, indicate whether these staff are Full-time, Part-time, or Consultants and the quantity for each. You may need to list some positions more than once to accommodate different staff types. The *Remarks* column is provided for any unusual cases such as staff worksharing.

Staff Function/Position	Staff Type (Check one only)			Quantity			Remarks
	Full-time	Part-time	Consultant	Current	End of 1999	End of 2001	
Total							

Adjacency Requirements

In order to provide the most functionally efficient workplace, it is necessary to determine the *adjacency* needs for your group. Please list below other Departments and amenities within the corporation that your group needs to be near.

Critical: _____

Important: _____

Desirable: _____

Please describe the specific internal adjacencies, proximities or working relationships for your division. For example: "copier must be immediately adjacent to secretary".

_____

_____

_____

Support Space

Support Space is an area or room that is shared within a department such as copy areas and storage rooms. Below are some typical common areas that may be required by your department. Please add any additional spaces that may be needed by your group and indicate the quantity of rooms or spaces needed. For special spaces such as Work Rooms, please give a brief description of their function.

Meeting Rooms	Frequency of Use per Month	Description
Meeting Rooms (Small – cap. 4-6)		
Meeting Rooms (Medium – cap. 8 – 10)		
Meeting Room (Large – cap. 12 – 14)		
Meeting Rooms (Special – cap. over 16)		
Open Meeting Areas		

Common Area	Required Area	Seating Capacity	Frequency Of Use	Shared: Yes/No	Description
Work Room					
Special Equipment Area					
Storage					
Shared Computer Workstation					
Reference Library					
Small Copy Area					
Open File Areas					
File Rooms					
Mail Areas					
Labs					

If any of the above *Support Spaces* have special adjacency, equipment or security requirements, please make note of this in the space provided below.

_____

_____

_____

_____

_____

Open Area Files & Equipment

This page identifies filing, storage and equipment in the **Open Area** of your department. In the spaces provide please indicate the current quantity of each item and the projected amount for the future years. Under the *Notes* column, please highlight special requirements such as fire rated, lockable, etc. Do <u>NOT</u> list storage units, cabinets and equipment that is located within a staff members office or workstation unless it should be located in an open area in the future.

Files

Projected Quantity by Year End

Lateral Files		Current	2001	2003	2005	Notes
	2-drwr lateral file cabinet					
	3-drwr lateral file cabinet					
	4-drwr lateral file cabinet					
	5-drwr lateral file cabinet					

Vertical Files		Current	2001	2003	2005	Notes
	2-drwr vertical file cabinet					
	3-drwr vertical file cabinet					
	4-drwr vertical file cabinet					
	5-drwr vertical file cabinet					

Bookcases		Current	2001	2003	2005	Notes
	2-shelf bookcase					
	3-shelf bookcase					
	4-shelf bookcase					
	5-shelf bookcase					

Wall Mounted or Built-In Shelves		Current	2001	2003	2005	Notes
	Indicate the number of linear feet					

Equipment

Projected Quantity by Year End

Copiers		Current	2001	2003	2005	Notes
	Small					
	Large					

Computer Terminals		Current	2001	2003	2005	Notes
	Shared Personal Computer					
	Dedicated Terminal					

Printers & Fax		Current	2001	2003	2005	Notes
	Networked Laser Printer					
	Desktop Line Printer					
	Floor Standing Line Printer					
	Facsimile Machine					
	Combination Printer/Fax					

Miscellaneous Equipment		Current	2001	2003	2005	Notes
	Typewriter					
	Microfiche Reader/Printer					

Nicolette Gordon, Interior Architecture + Design Mount Ida College— Senior Thesis Presentation

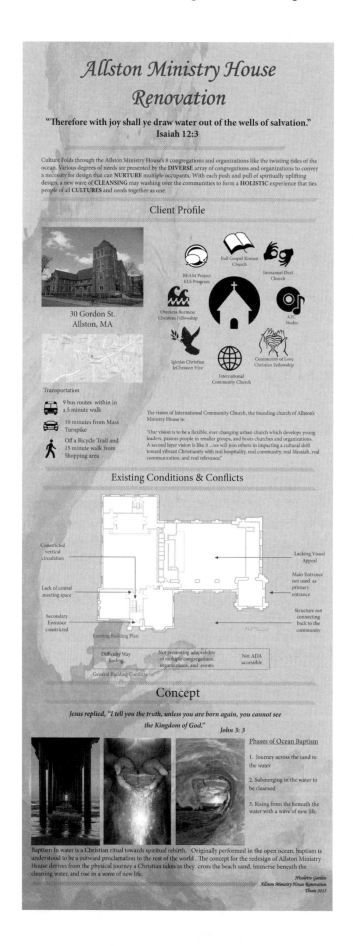

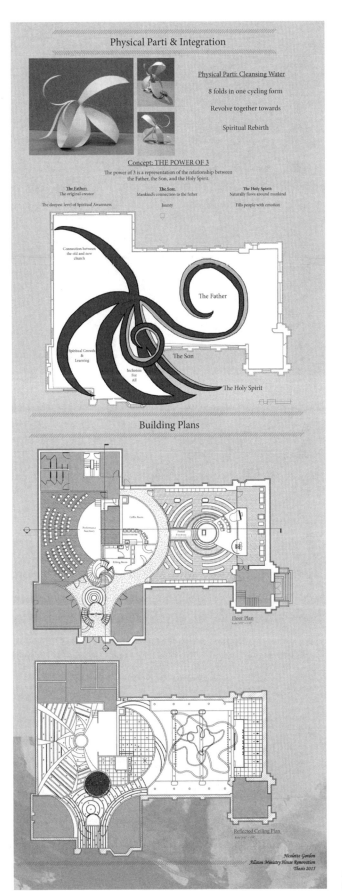

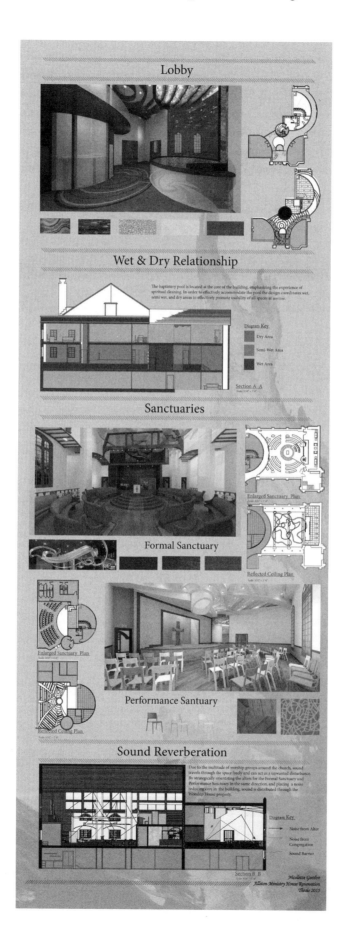

Margulies Perruzzi Architects Programming Forms

Dianne A. Dunnell, IIDA, NCIDQ certificate #015756, is an Associate Partner and Director of Interior Design at Margulies Perruzzi Architects, a multidisciplinary firm in Boston, Massachusetts.

Margulies Perruzzi Architects, implements numerous programming tools when gathering pertinent information from her clients. Appendix G.1, G.2 and G.3 are examples of the program forms that she uses to organize all the data collected from interviews, questionnaires and the like. The forms are created using excel for ease of use, change and accuracy of information.

CLIENT NAME	**DESIGN FIRM NAME**

Issued:
Revised:

MASTER PROGRAM SUMMARY

Department name:	B77 DE group
Representative:	Jane Smith
Adjacencies:	WF Group

Periods			Current	Year 1	Year 2	Year 3	Year 5
Most Likely growth		Office		1%	1%	0%	TBD
		Cube		4%	9%	4%	TBD

Comments:
Current B77 cube vs office counts from Jane Smith
Current flex staff counts from Jane Smith

Year 1 growth % from Jane Smith. (1% office/ 9% Flex growth.)
Client to confirm the Year 2 growth %
Year 3 growth not to exceed 500 as noted from Jane Smith
Year 5 growth counts are TBD.

Non office components qty/pp= industry standard.
Non office components SF= industry standard.

Average Current SF/PP: 138

Head count per office/workstation

Offices	SF	Current	Year 1	Year 2	Year 3	Year 5
Sizes varies	TBD	56	-	-	-	-
Office/Cube	TBD	-	-	-	-	-
Visitor	TBD	-	-	-	-	-
shared- 2p	150	-	-	-	-	-
shared- 3p	225	-	-	-	-	-
Total		56	57	57	57	TBD

Workstations	SF	Current	Year 1	Year 2	Year 3	Year 5
Sizes varies	TBD	330				-
Staff (6x7)	42	-				-
Contractors/interns (6x7)	42	-				-
Touchdowns (6x4.5)	27	-				-
Flex	TBD	46				-
Total		376	391	426	443	TBD
Subtotal		432	448	483	500	TBD

Total SF for staff	59,445	61,591	66,512	68,858	TBD

Non-office component

Ratio: (qty/pp)			SF	Qty				
1	500	Assembly 40+	1500	1	1	1	1	TBD
1	100	Large Conference (12-20 people)	300	4	4	5	5	TBD
1	50	Medium Conference (8-12 people)	150	9	9	10	10	TBD
1	25	Huddle room (4-6 people)	100	17	18	19	20	TBD
1	10	Enclosed Workspace (2 person)	49	43	45	48	50	TBD
1	40	Filing	150	11	11	12	13	TBD
1	40	Copy/print	150	11	11	12	13	TBD

Required area

Non-office component SF	10,973	11,369	12,277	12,710	TBD

Grand Total SF required	70,417	72,960	78,789	81,568	TBD
SF for staff + Non Office components					

APPENDIX G.1 Design Programming Form—By Department.

CLIENT NAME   **DESIGN FIRM NAME**

Issued:
Revised:

MASTER PROGRAM SUMMARY

			Proposed	Proposed	Required	Comments:
			OPTION 5	OPTION 6	IN 5 YRS	
	Ratio:	Office	5%	5%	TBD	Est. Carpetable SF
		Wrkstg	95%	95%	TBD	B77 areas 1-10

Head count per office/workstation

	Proposed OPTION 5	Proposed OPTION 6	Required IN 5 YRS		
Offices	0	0	TBD	B77 Floor 1 SF:	12,500 SF
10x10	3	0		B77 Floor 2 SF:	56,000 SF
10x11	0	3		Total	68,500 SF
Total in pilot plan	3	3			
Est total number of offices in B77 & B71 (based on repeat qty)	44	44	TBD	B71 Floor 1 SF:	2,000 SF
				B71 Floor 2 SF:	9,000 SF
				Total	11,000 SF
Worksettings					
5x6 ABW benching	60	0	TBD	B71 & B77 SF combined	79,500 SF
6x6 ABW benching	0	21			
6x6 Non ABW benching	0	30		No. of pilot layout repeats in B77 & B71 combined	14.5
Addl 6x6 ABW benching possible (in 13.5 repeat)	0	9			
Total in pilot plan	60	60			
Est total number of worksettings in B77 & B71 (based on repeat qty)	870	861	TBD		

	Proposed OPTION 5	Proposed OPTION 6	Required IN 5 YRS
Total seat counts (B77 & B71)	**914**	**905**	**869**
Seat count difference from 2020 req'd count	45	36	

Total Non Office components (to be provided in B77 & B71)

Ratio: (qty/pp)			SF	Req'd	Provided	Req'd	Provided	Req'd		
1	500	Assembly 40+	1500	2	0	2	0	2	Common Areas req'd in 5 years	
1	100	Large Conference (12-20 people)	300	9	0	9	0	9	Archive/storage	1	500
1	50	Medium Conference (8-12 people)	150	18	0	18	0	17	4 Network Closets	1	320
1	25	Project/ Huddle room (4-6 people)	100	37	44	36	18	35	Mechanical rm	1	700
1	10	Silence/ Quiet Rms (2 person)	49	91	44	90	73	87	Computer rm	1	900
1	40	Filing	150	23	0	23	0	22	Other		TBD
1	40	Copy/print	150	23	15	22.61	15	22	TOTAL SF		2,420

Additional Non Office components SF required

	OPTION 5	OPTION 6
Assembly 40+ (qty 1 addl reqd)	1,500	1,500
Large Conference rm (12-20 people)	2,700	2,700
Medium Conference (8-12 people)	2,700	2,700
Filing (Assumed not req'd in new ABW layouts)	0	0
Common areas (see listing on right column)	2,420	2,420
Total SF required	**9,320**	**9,320**

	OPTION 5	OPTION 6
SF of pilot plan	4,972	5,568
No. of pilot layout repeats in B77 & B71 combined	14.5	14.5
Total SF of office components in B77 & B71 combined	72,094	80,736
Total SF for additional program spaces	9,320	9,320
Grand total SF required:	81,414	90,056
(Note: This excludes SF for building common elements.)		
B71 & B77 est SF (carpetable SF) (Excludes SF for building common elements.)	79,500	79,500
Est SF/Person per option	87	88
SF Difference	-1,914	-10,556
Note: Add'l SF maybe desired for increased qty of non-office components		

APPENDIX G.2 Design Programming Form—Overall.

Programming Form - Staffing

Personnel, Equipment, Centralized Filing for Offices, Reference/Supply, Enclosed Areas

Office Name:		Division/Regional Management:	
Office Number: [number here]		Approved By:	
Dept Name: [name here]		Date:	
Dept Number: [number here]			

Form Completed By: [dept head name here]		Home Office Management:	
Date: [date completed here]		Approved By:	
		Date:	

	Standards		5 Year Staff Projections (year end)						Design	Comments
	Space size	Square Feet	Current Staff	2015 Staff	2016 Staff	2017 Staff	2018 Staff	2019 Staff	Year *2020	
PERSONNEL @ Vice President level										
[Name A]	12'-0" x 18.75'	180							0	
[Name B]	12'-0" x 18.75'	180							0	
[Name C]	12'-0" x 18.75'	180							0	
[Name D]	12'-0" x 18.75'	180							0	
		Total Staff	0	0	0	0	0	0	0	

	Standards		5 Year Staff Projections (year end)						Design	Comments
	Space size	Square Feet	Current Staff	2015 Staff	2016 Staff	2017 Staff	2018 Staff	2019 Staff	Year *2020	
PERSONNEL @ Director level										
[Name A]	10'x12'	120							0	
[Name B]	10'x12'	120							0	
[Name C]	10'x12'	120							0	
[Name D]	10'x12'	120							0	
	10'x12'	120							0	
		Total Staff	0	0	0	0	0	0	0	

	Standards		5 Year Staff Projections (year end)						Design	Comments
	Space size	Square Feet	Current Staff	2015 Staff	2016 Staff	2017 Staff	2018 Staff	2019 Staff	Year *2020	
PERSONNEL @ Manager with direct report & "I" individual contributors										
[Name A]	10'x12'	120							0	
[Name B]	10'x12'	120							0	
[Name C]	10'x12'	120							0	
[Name D]	10'x12'	120							0	
	10'x12'	120							0	
	10'x12'	120							0	
		Total Staff	0	0	0	0	0	0	0	

	Standards		5 Year Staff Projections (year end)						Design	Comments
	Space size	Square Feet	Current Staff	2015 Staff	2016 Staff	2017 Staff	2018 Staff	2019 Staff	Year *2010	
PERSONNEL @ Manager Cubicle- Manager, Team leaders, Project Manager, Senior Individual contributors										
[Name A]	7'x14'	98							0	
[Name B]	7'x14'	98							0	
[Name C]	7'x14'	98							0	
[Name D]	7'x14'	98							0	
	7'x14'	98							0	
		Total Staff	0	0	0	0	0	0	0	

	Standards		5 Year Staff Projections (year end)						Design	Comments
	Space size	Square Feet	Current Staff	2015 Staff	2016 Staff	2017 Staff	2018 Staff	2019 Staff	Year *2010	
PERSONNEL @ Administrative Cubicle- Secretary, Receptionist, Project leaders and Individual constributors										
[Name A]	7'x14'	98							0	
[Name B]	7'x14'	98							0	
[Name C]	7'x14'	98							0	
[Name D]	7'x14'	98							0	
	7'x14'	98							0	
		Total Staff	0	0	0	0	0	0	0	

	Standards		5 Year Staff Projections (year end)						Design	Comments
	Space size	Square Feet	Current Staff	2015 Staff	2016 Staff	2017 Staff	2018 Staff	2019 Staff	Year *2020	
PERSONNEL @ Associate Cubicle- Representatives, Processor part time and Contracted associates										
[Name A]	7'x7'	49							0	
[Name B]	7'x7'	49							0	
[Name C]	7'x7'	49							0	
[Name D]	7'x7'	49							0	
[Name E]	7'x7'	49							0	
[Name F]	7'x7'	49							0	
[Name G]	7'x7'	49							0	
[Name H]	7'x7'	49							0	
[Name I]	7'x7'	49							0	
[Name J]	7'x7'	49							0	
	7'x7'	49							0	
		Total Staff	0	0	0	0	0	0	0	

EQUIPMENT		Square Feet	Current	2015	2016	2017	2018	2019	Design Year *2020	Comments
Copier		15							0	
Printer		4							0	
Fax		4							0	
Shared Computers		8							0	
Pitney Bows machine		8							0	
Shredder		4							0	
Filtered water units- floor models		4							0	
Other (explain)									0	
Other (explain)									0	
							Total Equipment		0	

STORAGE (if many files req'd-see 'Storage & Filing' form.)		Square Feet	Current	2015	2016	2017	2018	2019	Design Year *2020	File/Shelf Dimensions
36" Lateral Files- 3 drawer		5							0	
36" Lateral Files- 4 drawer		5							0	
42" Lateral Files- 3 drawer		5							0	
42" Lateral Files- 4 drawer		5							0	
Vertical Files - 5 drawer		4							0	
Tab Files (include dimensions)		6							0	
Shelving units- 5 shelves (include dimensions)		5							0	
Shelving units- 4 shelves (include dimensions)		5							0	
Shelving units- 3 shelves (include dimensions)		5							0	
Bookcases- 2 shelf (include dimensions)		5							0	
Bookcases- 4 shelf (include dimensions)		5							0	
Tables (include dimensions)		15							0	
Storage Cabinets- 2 doors (include dimensions)		5							0	
Mail Sorter - (indicate size and type)		4							0	
Mail cart		8							0	
Lge recycle bins		9							0	
Lge trash bins		9							0	
Other (expalin)		9							0	
Other (explain)									0	
							Total Storage		0	

ENCLOSED ROOMS		Square Feet	Current	2015	2016	2017	2018	2019	Design Year *2020	Comments
Storage Room		120							0	
File Room		120							0	
Tel/data		100							0	
Lunch Room		225							0	
Reception		225							0	
Closet		30							0	
Conference Room - Large		150							0	
Conference Room - Small		300							0	
							Total Enclosed Rooms		0	

					Projected Assigned USF		0
					Circulation (45%)		0
TOTAL PROJECTED DEPARTMENTAL ASSIGNED USF							0

*Design Year is the year which the floorplan will be designed for. If another year should be used, please change the year shown and update the formula in the Design Year Column.

Additional Comments:

Production2:Bloomsbury:16145bbf_ProgrammingResearch:Working_Files:03_Art_Files:00_Source_Art_New:new:Appendices:Figures:G3 MPA_ Programming Form.xls
11/14/16

Margulies Associates
6/12/07 Version

APPENDIX G.3 Programming Form—Staff Count.

DCAMM Supplementary Information

APPENDIX I.1
DCAMM DESIGNERS
PROCEDURES MANUAL

The information for the Guidelines for the preparation of Studies for Building Projects for State Agencies can be accessed via the following web address: http://www.mass.gov/anf/docs/dcam/dlforms/stu-guide.pdf

The following items should be reviewed during progress workshops based on the approved work plan:

- "A" Conference
- "S" Conference
- Project Management to meet Milestones

8.4   **Typical Table of Contents**
(Actual contents will vary with type of study)
  (i)   Certification
  (ii)   Preface
  (iii)   Acknowledgments - project participants.
          - Agencies: Include names of relevant commissioners, directors, project manager, etc.
          - Design team: participants in consulting firms.
  (iv)   Table of Contents
  (v)   List of tables
  (vi)   List of illustrations

1.   **Executive summary** (major issues, findings and recommendations.)
2.   **Introduction**
      - Statement of objectives
      - Methodology
      - Project history and background
3.   **Existing conditions**
4.   **Proposed program needs**
5.   **Codes and standards**
6.   **Alternative solutions**
7.   **Evaluation of alternatives**
8.   **Preferred solution** - final program description, design criteria and schematic design.
9.   **Systems Narrative**
10.   **Cost estimate**
11.   **Implementation Schedule**

Taken from (http://www.mass.gov/anf/property-mgmt-and-construction/design-and-construction-of-public-bldgs/designer-selection-process/dsb-forms-instructions-and-manuals/manuals/designer-procedures-manual.html)

- ST-01 Problem Statement and Work Plan
- ST-02 Problem Analysis and Existing Conditions
- ST-01R Problem Re-Statement and Work Plan Revision
- ST-EV(P) Designer Mid-Performance Evaluation
- ST-03 Alternative Solutions
- ST-GW Global Workshop
- ST-04 Consensus Solution
- ST-05 Draft Study Submission
- ST-09 Final Study Submission, all components
- ST-EV(F) Final Performance Evaluation
- ST-CERT Study Certification Products/ Deliverables—A finalized checklist must be submitted with all materials.
- Volume 1—Description and Goals; Work Plan
- Volume 2—Problem Analysis: Existing Conditions, Space Needs, Schedule and Cost Constraints
- Volume 3—Potential Solutions
- Volume 4—Consensus Solution, Concept Design and Final Program
- Cost estimate
- Permitting
- Access issues
- Life cycle cost analysis
- Design and construction schedule
- Mechanical, Electrical, Etc.
- Mass LEED Plus compliance
- Volume 5—Records of Meetings and Communications, project related reference information Designers Procedures Manual Checklist – Study Phase 26 August 2008 Performance
- ST-EV (F): Final Performance Evaluation must now be complete.
- Designer evaluation
- Continuation of the Designer

There is a lot of information to review and the typical table of contents, seen to the left, contains a lot of requirements that are addressed in the textbook.

APPENDIX I.2
DCAMM GUIDELINES FOR THE PREPARATION OF STUDIES FOR BUILDING PROJECTS FOR STATE AGENCIES

Taken from http://www.mass.gov/anf/docs/dcam/dlforms/stu-guide.pdf 2000

There is a lot of information to review and the typical table of contents contains a lot of requirements that are addressed in the textbook

The following listing of activities should be considered minimum, generic requirements.

- Project Justification
- Statement of Problem
- Objectives, Process and Schedule of Study (work plan)
- Existing Conditions: Analyze existing conditions, including activities, buildings, site and environment.
- Program Needs: Information should be developed on the following types of needs of the proposed facility:

RELATIONSHIP OF NEEDS	PRIORITY OF NEEDS
direct needs (e.g., housing)	immediate needs
indirect needs (e.g., recreation)	short term needs
side effects (e.g., impact on utilities) (e.g., temporary relocation)	longer term needs

- Standards and Policies
- Preliminary Program: The suggested format includes: a. Functional description (e.g. functions, activities) b. Qualitative criteria (e.g. appearance, security) c. Organizational criteria (e.g. location arrangement) d. Quantitative criteria (e.g. number, size) e. Technical criteria (e.g. equipment) Criteria should be performance oriented rather than prescriptive, where possible. Conceptual diagrams are required to illustrate the design criteria

- Development of Alternatives: Emphasis should be placed on developing a few (up to three), reasonable, economical and practical solutions to evaluate. Each alternative should satisfy the standards, policies and goals.
- Evaluation of Alternatives: Evaluation will include an examination of the degree to which alternatives fulfill stated design criteria. Emphasis should be on major criteria which can be used to judge if alternatives meet basic requirements, including efficiency and cost effectiveness.
- Recommendation of Preferred Solution: A preferred solution shall be recommended in the final study report. Final Program for Preferred Solution: All program requirements for the preferred solution shall be documented in a detailed and explicit statement of design and operational criteria. The criteria should be written to be used in four ways: a) as confirmation of the user's needs; b) as precise instructions or "design directions" to the final designer; c) as a basis for cost estimating, and d) as a basis for post-occupancy evaluation.
- Compliance with Codes and Regulatory Standards: The designer shall identify in the report all codes and public regulations required for design and construction, and the preferred solution shall comply with these codes and regulations.
- Study Schematic Design: The purpose of the study schematic design is: a) to demonstrate the practical operation of the design criteria, codes and standards, to prove that a workable solution is possible; b) to develop accurate cost estimates; and c) to illustrate the preferred design solution

- Design Content: The content of the schematic design should include, where appropriate: a) An outline of major site and architectural features, including functional arrangements; b) An outline of major construction systems and materials; c) An outline of major mechanical and electrical systems; d) The source and method of obtaining all utilities; e) An outline of storm water and sanitary sewage disposal systems; f) The location and number of other significant cost items; and g) Delineation of any special features

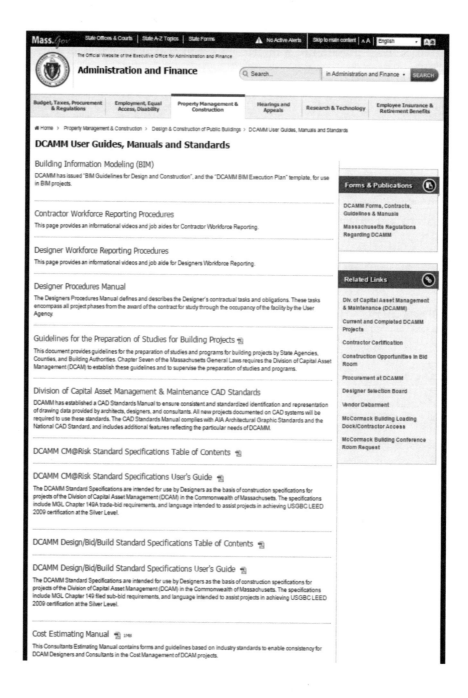

Salem Probate & Family Court Renovation

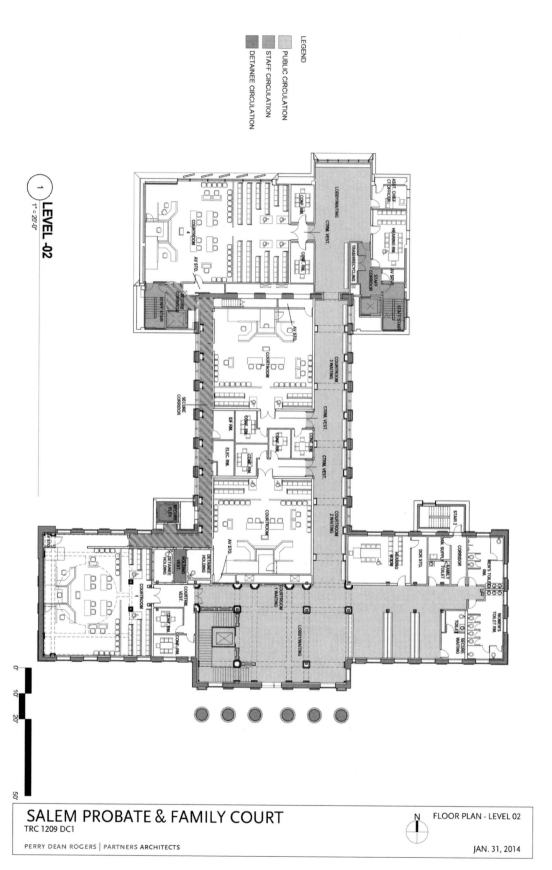

LEGEND

DETAINEE CIRCULATION
STAFF CIRCULATION
PUBLIC CIRCULATION

LEVEL -02
1" = 20'-0"

SALEM PROBATE & FAMILY COURT
TRC 1209 DC1
PERRY DEAN ROGERS | PARTNERS ARCHITECTS

FLOOR PLAN - LEVEL 02

JAN. 31, 2014

APPENDIX I.1 Perry Dean Rogers | Partners Architects Enlarged floorplan of level 2.

SCHEME A | No Envelope Change

LEVEL 2

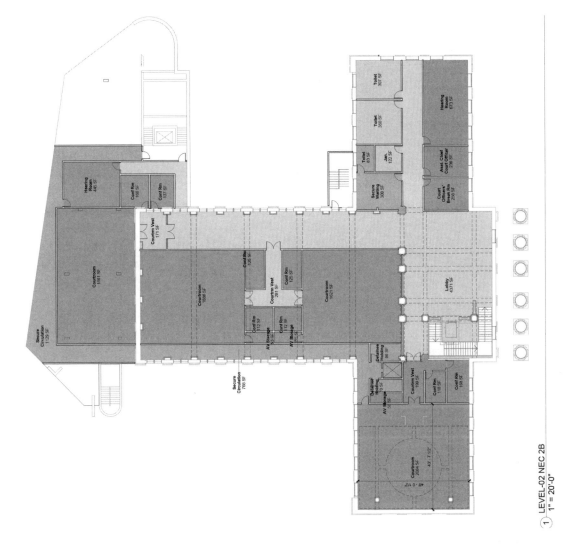

Secure
Circulation
1,129 SF

Hearing
Room
445 SF

Conf Rm
160 SF

Conf Rm
137 SF

Courtroom
1,081 SF

Courtm Vest
171 SF

Courtroom
1,096 SF

Conf Rm
125 SF

Courtm Vest
201 SF

Conf Rm
125 SF

Conf Rm
112 SF

Conf Rm
112 SF

AV Storage
63 SF

AV Storage
63 SF

Courtroom
1,021 SF

Secure
Circulation
798 SF

Detainee
Holding
75 SF

Detainee
Holding
66 SF

AV Storage
36 SF

Courtm Vest
109 SF

Conf Rm
118 SF

Conf Rm
168 SF

Courtroom
2,064 SF

48' 7 1/2"

45' 0"

Toilet
307 SF

Toilet
300 SF

Toilet
83 SF

Jan.
122 SF

Secure
Waiting
300 SF

Hearing
Room
673 SF

Asst. Chief
Court Officer
206 SF

Court
Officers'
Break Rm
206 SF

Lobby
4,011 SF

1 LEVEL-02 NEC 2B
   1" = 20'-0"

APPENDIX I.2 Perry Dean Rogers | Partners Architects Scheme A—with no envelope change.

SCHEME B | North Addition

LEVEL 2

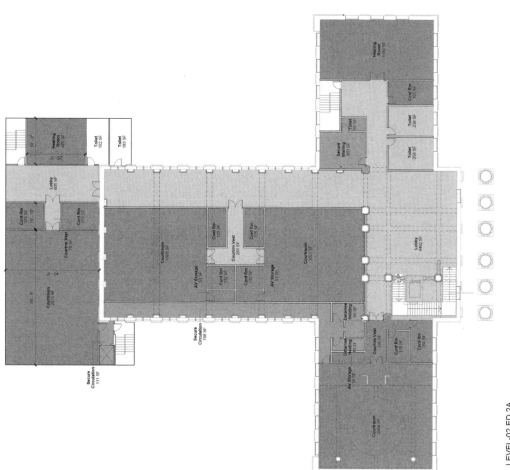

1 LEVEL-02 ED 2A
  1" = 20'-0"

APPENDIX I.3 Perry Dean Rogers | Partners Architects Scheme B – with envelope change & addition to the North of the building. This was the option that was selected.

Helpful Resources

A list of helpful websites for Interior Design, Research, Codes, Databases

- 100 Resilient Cities http://www.100resilientcities.org
- AARP http://www.aarp.org/families/home_design
- ADA (American Disabilities Act) http://www.ada.gov
- AIA (American Institute of Architects) http://www.aia.org/pia/health
- Allsteel Office http://www.allsteeloffice.com/AllsteelOffice
- AMD3 Foundation http://www.amd3.org
- American Academy of Healthcare Interior Designers http://www.aahid.org
- American Educational Research Association http://www.aera.net/
- ANSI (American National Standards Institute) http://www.ansi.org
- APA (American Psychological Association) http://www.apa.org
- APPA (The Association of Higher Education Facilities Officers)http://www.appa.org
- ArchNewsNow http://www.archnewsnow.com
- ASID (American Society of Interior Design) http://www.asid.org
- ASTM (American Society for Testing and Materials) http://www.astm.org
- Athena Sustainable Materials Institute www.athenasmi.org
- Bibme http://www.bibme.org/bibliography/help
- BOMA (Building Owners and Managers Association) http://www.boma.org
- Building Green http://www.buildinggreen.com
- Building Industry Exchange http://www.building.org
- Buildings Magazine http://www.buildings.com
- Building Operating Management Magazine http://www.facilitiesnet.com
- Carmun Connective Wisdom http://www.carmun.com/easy-bibliography-formatting-APA-MLA.php
- CEUD (Centre for Excellence in Universal Design) http://universaldesign.ie/About-Us/
- Center for Active Design www.centerforactivedesign.org
- Center for Health Design http://www.healthdesign.org

- Center for Disease Control and Prevention http://www.cdc.gov/
- Chain Store Age http://www.chainstoreage.com
- Council for Interior Design Accreditation, CIDA http://www.accredit-id.org
- Colorado State University's online learning environment, the Writing Studio http://writing.colostate.edu/index.cfm
- Community & Regional Resilience Institute (CARRI) http://www.resilientus.org
- Contemporary Long Term Care http://www.cltcmag.com
- Contract Magazine http://www.contractmagazine.com
- CorCoreNet http://www.corenetglobal.org
- Corporate Design Foundation http://www.cdf.org
- Display and Design Ideas Magazine http://www.ddimagazine.com
- Design Intelligence http://www.di.net
- Dezignaré Interior Design Collective, Inc. http://www.dezignare.com
- Dwell http://www.dwell.com
- Easy Bib http://www.easybib.com/
- Elle Décor http://www.elledecor.com
- Facility Care http://www.facilitycare.com
- FM Global Resilience Index http://www.fmglobal.com/research-and-resources/tools-and-resources/resilienceindex#!year=2016&idx=Index&handler=map
- Frame Magazine http://www.framemag.com
- Furniture Today http://www.furnituretoday.com
- Green Guide for Health Care™ http://www.gghc.org
- Health Facilities Management Magazine http://www.hfmmagazine.com
- Health Product Declaration Collaborative www.hpd-collaborative.org
- Hospitality Design (HD) http://www.hdmag.com/hospitalitydesign/index.jsp
- Hotel Online http://www.hotel-online.com
- HPD Library hpd.smithgroupjjr.org
- IBC (International Building Code) http://www.iccsafe.org/
- IFI (International Federation of Interior Architect/Designer) http://www.ifiworld.org/
- IFMA (International Facility Management Association) http://www.ifma.org
- IFDA (International Furnishings and Design Association) http://www.ifda.com
- IIDA (International Interior Design Association) http://www.iida.org
- InformeDesign http://www.informedesign.org/
- InfoTile.com http://www.infotile.com
- Institute for Family- Centered Care http://www.familycenteredcare.org
- Institute for Human Centered Design http://www.humancentereddesign.org/
- Insurance Institute for Business & Home Safety https://disastersafety.org/
- Interior Design Educators Council, IDEC http://www.idec.org
- Interior Design Magazine http://www.interiordesign.net
- Interiors & Sources Magazine http://www.isdesignet.com
- International Home Furniture Market http://www.highpointmarket.org
- International WELL Building Institute™ (IWBI) http://www.wellcertified.com/about
- The Journal of Interior Design http://www.journalofinteriordesign.org
- The Librarians' Internet Index http://lii.org

- Lean Construction Institute http://www.leanconstruction.org/
- Lighting Research Center http://www.lrc.rpi.edu
- MADCAD http://www.madcad.com/index.php
- Metropolitan Home http://www.methome.com
- Mindful Materials www.hksinc.com/mindful-materials/
- National Association of Store Fixture Manufacturers http://www.nasfm.com
- National Kitchen & Bath Association NKBA http://www.nkba.org
- National Safety Council http://www.nsc.org
- National Council for Interior Design Qualification (NCIDQ) http://www.ncidq.org
- NeoCon World's Trade Fair http://www.merchandisemart.com/neocon
- Perkins+Will Transparency www.transparency.perkinswill.com
- ONTHERAIL http://www.ontherail.com
- Pharos Project www.pharosproject.net
- ProQuest http://www.proquest.com/products_umi/dissertations
- Research Design Connections http://www.researchdesignconnections.com
- Restaurant Business http://www.restaurantbiz.com
- Resilient Design Institute http://www.resilientdesign.org/about/
- Retail Design is the industry's first retail design weblog http://retaildesignblog.net/tag/diva/
- Retail Traffic http://retailtrafficmag.com/
- Shopping Centers Today http://www.icsc.org
- Social Research Methods http://www.socialresearchmethods.net
- Society for the Advancement of Gerontological Environments (SAGE) http://www.sagefederation.org
- Society for the Arts in Healthcare (SAH) http://www.theSAH.org
- Steelcase http://www.steelcase.com/na/
- Step Inside Design http://www.stepinsidedesign.com
- The American Society for Healthcare Engineering http://www.ashe.org
- The Center for Inclusive Design and Environmental Access http://idea.ap.buffalo.edu/
- The Center for Universal Design www.design.ncsu.edu/cud)
- The Network on Building Resilient Regions (BRR) http://brr.berkeley.edu/
- The OWL at Purdue http://owl.english.purdue.edu/owl/resource/560/01
- United States Access Board https://www.access-board.gov
- U.S. Department if Housing and Urban Development. Fair Housing Accessibility Guidelines. http://portal.hud.gov/hudportal/HUD?src=/program_offices/fair_housing_equal_opp/disabilities/fhefhag
- U.S. Department of Health and Human Services http://www.hhs.gov/ohrp/
- U.S. Department of Labor Occupational Safety and Health Administration http://www.osha.gov/SLTC/
- U.S. Green Building Council, (USGBC): http://www.usgbc.org
- U.S. General Services Administration http://www.gsa.gov
- USACE Center of Expertise For Preservation of Historic Buildings & Structures http://www.nws.usace.army.mil
- VMSD (Visual Merchandising and Store Design) http://www.visualstore.com
- WELL Building Standard www.wellcertified.com

Glossary

action research A focused effort toward finding a solution to improve the quality of the performance of an organization, a group, or an individual in a particular setting. Educators or practitioners who analyze the data to improve the outcomes often perform action research.

activity map A diagram that shows what people are doing when performing a task.

ADA codes The Americans with Disabilities Act's accessibility guidelines for buildings and facilities.

adjacency matrix A visual tool created to illustrate, confirm, and clarify clients' needs and significant relationships between spaces. A helpful tool in the development and analysis of spatial relationships.

adjacency requirements Identification of the placement of programmatic requirements by categorizing what spaces needs to be located next to each other.

aging in place When older individuals choose not to move from their home after retirement.

American National Standards Institute The standards and conformity assessment system. "ANSI facilitates the development of American National Standards (ANS) by accrediting the procedures of standards developing organizations (SDOs). These groups work cooperatively to develop voluntary national consensus standards. Accreditation by ANSI signifies that the procedures used by the standards body in connection with the development of American National Standards meet the Institute's essential requirements for openness, balance, consensus and due process." (https:// ansi.org/about ansi/introduction)

American Society of Interior Design (ASID) An organization for professional interior designers. A network devoted to keep members updated on the latest products and styles in the industry. Also devoted to codes and applying them to designs (www. asid.org).

analyzing descriptive data Reviewing and analyzing what a researcher has observed and documented.

anthropometry/anthropometrics The scientific measurement and collection of data regarding a human's physical motion and range of movement.

asset management The use and overseeing of a person's or company's finances.

axial coding An approach to coding where categories are related to their subcategories to form more precise and complete explanations about phenomena.

barrier-free design Design that keeps all pathways free of objects or anything that may block and protrude into a means of passage; a design that keeps people safe from injury and harm.

Bauhaus School In 1919, the German architect Walter Gropius founded this school in Weimar, Germany. The school and philosophy promoted individual creative expression and collaboration among the art and design disciplines to create environments.

behavioral mapping The process of observing current conditions of an environment in order to gain insight into that environment. For example, you could observe how students enter a classroom and notice the seats they first select based on the layout of that room.

Building Information Modeling (BIM) The process used when all project team members (architects, engineers, interior designers and project managers) are working on a project and use intelligent 3D modeling software to design, construct, and manage a building.

Building Owners and Managers Association "The Building Owners and Managers Association (BOMA) International is a federation of 91 BOMA U.S. associations

and 18 international affiliates. Founded in 1907, BOMA represents the owners and managers of all commercial property types including nearly 10.5 billion square feet of U.S. office space that supports 1.7 million jobs and contributes $234.9 billion to the U.S. GDP. Its mission is to advance a vibrant commercial real estate industry through advocacy, influence and knowledge.?" http://www.boma.org/about/Pages/default. aspx

bubble diagram A visual diagram of spaces' functions depicted in bubble form to give the client an overall idea of where each space will be in relation to the others.

building code requirements Rules and regulations to be followed for safety in the built environment.

case study research In-depth studies of a particular instance, event, or situation (i.e., a case).

color theory The understand of color mixing, color combinations, and the visual impact of color.

comparative case studies Research that involves other facilities in the client's industry and other industries that may use innovative technologies or approaches that could be universalized or used in the client's situation.

concept A preliminary idea sought at the beginning of a project in order to obtain and create an idea for the design.

concept diagram How the designer begins to organize the physical space in relationship to a conceptual idea.

concept statement The anticipated or desired outcome of a design. When approaching a project, much is unknown because many of the ideas have not been explored yet; therefore, the statement is not definitive but is meant to be challenged by one's own research.

connoisseurship The process of observing the meaning, goals, and objectives of an educational program.

construction documents The final set of documents used for construction. Contract documents are considered a legal form of documentation of what will be built.

contract documents These include working drawings and specifications. Often these are the ones that are submitted to be bid on; once agreed upon are considered legal and binding documents between all parties involved.

Council for Interior Design Accreditation (CIDA) A nonprofit organization that promotes high academic standards in interior design schools. CIDA ensures that its guidelines for what should be taught are met by visiting its accredited institutions once every six years (www.accredit-id.org).

critical instance case studies An examination of one or more sites for either the purpose of examining a situation of unique interest with little to no interest in generalizationability or to call into question or challenge a highly generalized or universal assertion. This method is useful for answering cause-and-effect questions.

critique An act in which someone, usually an expert or a peer, shares his or her personal expertise and/or opinion regarding a presentation of student work.

cumulative case studies Combined information from more than one case study collected at different times.

demographics Human population statistics of a specific location.

department personnel population study A study to estimate growth or reduction in staff. It compares the personnel projections with the operating units to determine which units will grow and which units will remain stable or decrease.

design development The phase that usually follows schematic design and involves the development of the design.

diagrams Designers use diagrams to help explore or articulate an idea. A diagram can be executed as a drawing, model or graphic image.

diagrammatic information The transformation of written information into visual information.

École des Beaux Arts (School of Fine Arts) founded in 1648 by Cardinal Mazarin. Disciplines focused on architecture, drawing, painting, sculpture, engraving, modeling, and gem cutting. The school was originally created for the purpose of having artists available to decorate the palaces and paint the royal portraits in France. Now it is a destination for those studying studio arts.

energy efficiency The conservation of the amount of power and cost it may take to run something.

environmental behavior Conduct involving a concern for the environment and an acknowledgment of what may harm it. It also involves developing new ways to improve our surroundings in a healthy, not harmful manner.

ergonomics The study and design of how people interact efficiently and safely with objects in the built environment.

ethnography The study of making observations in the field with a group in its natural setting. It is important to record as much as possible in the setting in order to document the research.

evidence-based design (EBD) A system for analyzing data and then emphasizing credible evidence as the foundation of decision making.

exploratory case study Condensed, descriptive case studies. Also referred to as pilot studies.

facilities planning The ability to communicate design in terms of financial impact so that corporate leaders can understand and utilize space, design, and knowledge to make complex facilities decisions.

floor usable area The usable area available for the primary occupancy in an office, store, or building. It is the usable total area minus the common areas, also known as net space.

flow diagram An illustration of a path being used as well as alternatives that could be developed. Flow diagrams can illustrate volume of usage, multiplicity of uses, and conflicts associated with usage. It can also help the programmer understand the function at hand.

formal and numerical methods A test of a specific group using statistical methods to analyze the data.

global perspective Awareness of the world and its diverse cultures. It is important for design students to be aware of world views and design consideration that are relevant and can be embraced by all.

green/sustainable design A movement dedicated to create a cleaner, "greener" lifestyle in our environment through the use of renewable resources and energy. Often accompanied by a refusal to work with materials that harm the earth with harsh chemicals and other unsustainable materials and processes.

gross measured area The total area within the building minus the exterior wall.

hard-line documentation The term used when a design is finalized and ready to go to "hard-lines," which become the final set of construction documents. Can be done by hand or by using CAD software.

healthcare design Design specifically for facilities that help improve one's well-being, including places such as hospitals, clinics, cancer centers, dental offices, and hospices.

historic preservation and restoration The preservation of historic structures.

historical research As it applies to interior design programming, the collection of information from printed and otherwise documented material. Books, periodicals, newspapers, and journals are some options for collecting historical research.

human factors A physical or cognitive property of an individual or social behavior that is specific to humans and that influences functioning of technological systems as well as human-environment equilibriums.

illustrative case studies Descriptions intended to add in-depth examples.

InformeDesign The first searchable database of design and human behavior research on the internet. InformeDesign currently contains "practitioner friendly" research summaries of findings from research literature and scholarly journals related to design and human behavior (*www.informedesign. umn.edu*).

Integrated Project Delivery (IPD) In the IPD model, all key players come to the table at the beginning of the project.

interactive research Research that occurs when the researcher becomes not only just an observer but also a participant. Most often includes interviewing users of a specific space.

interior architecture A common term in Europe meaning the same as interior design. Recently becoming a common term in the United States, interior architecture implies that one has been trained in interior design and has knowledge of structural and load-bearing requirements.

internal consistency reliability Assessment of the consistency of results across items within a test.

Internal Review Board (IRB) The IRB reviews proposals related to human and animal subjects.

International Building Code (IBC) A book filled with safety guidelines for the building industry (www.iccsafe.org).

International Code Council (ICC) A membership association dedicated to building safety and fire prevention. The ICC develops the codes used to construct residential and commercial buildings, including homes and schools. Most U.S. cities, counties, and states that adopt codes choose the international codes developed by the International Code Council (www.iccsafe. org).

International Facility Managers Association IFMA is the world's largest and most widely recognized international association for facility management professionals. (www.ifma.org).

International Fire Code (IFC) Requirements relating to fire protection systems, including the most common types of automatic sprinkler systems, alternative automatic extinguishing systems, and stand-pipe systems. It also involves types of fire alarm and detection and smoke control systems, and addresses additional means to assist or enhance fixed fire protection systems, such as portable fire extinguishers (www.iccsafe.org).

International Fuel Gas Code (IFGC) Requirements that address the design and installation of fuel gas systems and gas-fired appliances through requirements that emphasize performance. This is a comprehensive, excellent reference for code officials, engineers, architects, inspectors, plans examiners, contractors, and anyone who needs a better understanding of these regulations. Prescriptive and performance-based approaches to design are emphasized (www.iccsafe.org).

International Interior Design Association (IIDA) One of the largest professional interior design organizations. (www.iida.org)

International Mechanical Code (IMC) Minimum regulations for mechanical systems using prescriptive and performance-related provisions (www.iccsafe.org).

International Plumbing Code (IPC) Requirement that emphasizes performance for the design and installation of plumbing systems. Provisions are provided for fixtures, piping, fittings, and devices, as well as design and installation methods for water supply and sanitary and storm drainage. The code provides comprehensive minimum regulations for plumbing facilities using prescriptive- and performance-related provisions. The objectives of the code provide for the acceptance of new and innovative products, materials, and systems (www.iccsafe.org).

International Residential Code (IRC) A code that establishes minimum regulations for one- and two-family dwellings of three stories or less. It brings together all building, plumbing, mechanical, fuel gas, energy, and electrical provisions for these residences (www.iccsafe.org).

inter-rater or inter-observer reliability Assessment of the degree to which different raters/observers give consistent estimates of the same phenomenon.

Journal of Interior Design A scholarly, referred publication dedicated to issues related to the design of the interior environment.

laboratory experiments Scientific research into a particular problem or question. Usually employing statistical techniques and sample groups whose selection can vary from specific to random.

lean design Lean engages all levels of the organization in the elimination of waste in all processes. Many have applied this to design as an overarching philosophy in order to improve efficiency and effectiveness.

LEED LEED stands for the Leadership in Energy and Environmental Design. LEED Professional Accreditation distinguishes building professionals with the knowledge and skills to successfully steward the LEED certification process. (*www.usgbc.org*).

LEED AP An individual may use LEED AP as part of their credentials, demonstrating that they have passed the exam and have

a thorough understanding of green building practices and principles and the LEED Rating System. There are LEED categories that one can focus on to designate their specialty areas.

life cycle cost The amount one pays for the length of useful life of an object.

lighting design The act of producing effective illumination through the use of daylight and artificial illumination.

Likert scale The method of scaling and evaluating responses developed by Rensis Likert, a sociologist at the University of Michigan from 1946 to 1970. It involves summary charts and records detailed adjacency requirements between specific areas within the various units.

literature review An evaluation of the information found in a literature search and the selection of sources relevant to the topic.

location overview An overall look at a site. It may consist of a study of maps, major forms of transportation, and environmental features. It does not have to be extensive, but it should cover the country and state of the site, and include maps that visually place the site in a larger context.

location productivity How well a residential or business site is efficient in its locality.

MacLeamy curve In 2004 Patrick MacLeamy, FAIA, drew the set of curves based on his observations that design projects become more complex and difficult to change the more developed they are. The MacLeamy Curve illustrated the advantages of making design decisions earlier in the project when opportunity to influence positive outcomes is maximized and the cost of changes minimized.

macro-to-micro A process that starts on a large scale by taking the big idea and obtaining as much information as needed and then moving to the smaller scale, where detailed and precise considerations can then be made.

mediator One who promotes collaboration between two parties.

mixed methods approach A combination of quantitative and qualitative research techniques applied to the same data.

museum and exhibit design Design intended for places that display either historical or artistic material. Objects on display may be captured through the use of special lighting and how they are aesthetically positioned.

National Architectural Accrediting Board (NAAB) The sole agency authorized to accredit professional degree programs in architecture in the United States (www. naab.org).

National Council for Interior Design Qualification (NCIDQ) A national exam that tests minimum competency in the field of interior designer (www.ncidq.org).

net-to-gross ratios A measurement of usable floor space compared to total floor space.

observational research Research where a designer photographs or videotapes a specific space over time. This form of analysis is extremely helpful, as it provides an outside snapshot peering into the day and life of users and how they interact with their space. It also allows for the documentation of long periods of time, which can show repeating themes.

parallel-forms reliability An assessment of the consistency of the results of two tests constructed in the same way from the same content domain.

parti Parti (also parti') [pahr-tee, pahr-tee] is the basic or most true/primary foundation of a design solution. It is a scheme or variation of schemes that strengthens the foundation of a design idea.

physiological human interaction The ways that an individual reacts in a given environment, showing what one's body and mind become accustomed to in any given situation.

pilot studies Small studies typically performed before implementing a large-scale study.

precedent studies Studies that focus on one specific type of design and compare a group of similar examples.

presentation boards A type of documentation that shows the phases of design, emphasizing the concept throughout. Professionals and students use presentation boards to display their work on a project. They can include floor plans, sketches, drawings, material, finishes, and furnishings.

problem statement A clear and concise statement contained within the first chapter of a programmatic research that describes the problem to be solved. Ideally, it should be one sentence, with accompanying sentences that identify a range of sub-problems.

professional design practitioner An individual who has the appropriate education, examinations, and experience to designate them as a professional.

professional practice An understanding of all aspects of being a successful design professional.

program effects Effects that use the case study to examine causality and usually involve multisite, multimethod assessments.

program implementation To put into practice a plan to accomplish the goal.

program summary Produced at the end of the interview process, a complete synopsis of all research made before moving on to other design phases. It includes space needs calculated as a sum of the parts, appropriate markups for circulation, rentable factors, and so on.

programming The first predesign step in the design process. Provides a time for designers to research, explore, and investigate numerous facets of a project type in order to gain greater insight into the scope of work.

programming document A comprehensive report that details the programmatic requirements for a project. Addresses an abundance of issues in an attempt to identify and outline the needs for the potential users of the space.

project schedule A specific agenda that includes deadlines of what needs to be done so that a task will be completed in a timely and proficient manner.

qualitative observational research Research in which the observer's role is to record group interactions and behaviors as objectively as possible using various qualitative inquiry tools (e.g., interviews, questionnaires, impressions, and reactions). It consists of many different approaches that often overlap and possess subtle distinctions. The type of approach used depends on the research question and area of discipline.

qualitative research A form of research that relies on discovery, observations of meanings, and interpretations by studying cases intensively in natural settings and by subjecting the resulting data to analytic induction.

quantitative research A form of research that is grounded in the assumption that features of the social environment constitute an objective reality that is relatively constant across time and settings. The dominant methodology is to describe and explain features of this reality by collecting numerical data on observational behaviors of samples and by subjecting these data to statistical analysis (Borg and Gall).

references or works cited A documentation of sources. Documenting sources saves time when returning to the sources. Also used to properly cite material and give credit where it is due.

Registered Architect A person trained in the field of architecture who has passed the National Council of Registration Boards (NCARB) exam demonstrating minimum competency (www.ncarb.org).

reliability When conducting research it is important that the instrument that is being used (test, survey/experiment) yields the same results when repeated.

request for proposal (RFP) A type of bidding announcement in which a company and/or design firm announces that they are seeking proposals for a particular project.

request for quote (RFQ) A request from designers that seeks out suppliers and or manufactures to bid on specific products and/or services.

research The systematic and careful process of collecting, analyzing, and interpreting information (data) in order to increase awareness and understanding of a particular subject.

resiliency The ability to prepare and recover quickly when faced with a natural, manmade, cyber, or physical disasters.

schedules A means of organization that helps achieve goals on meeting a deadline. Especially necessary to have during the construction documentation phase of design.

schematic design The second step in the design process after programming. It documents some schematic layout options of the design problem. It can also include preliminary ideas of materials, textiles, plumbing, furniture, window, and lighting selections. Everything is done in a schematic fashion, and often more than one design option will be explored at this time.

selective coding Data collected, analyzed, and categorized into main themes. This is a useful tool when analyzing thick or thin descriptions of space or interviews.

sketches Loose drawings used to document preliminary thoughts and ideas. Typically, sketches are hand-drawn or quick renderings using a computer.

space-planning adjacencies Approximations of what will be next to each other in the design of any given vicinity.

Space utilization studies A study conducted to provide companies with evidence not only as to how their current space is being used but also how they can improve their current space.

specifications Documentation of precise details and information of materials, finishes, and furnishings used in order to obtain specific supplies needed to complete a project. Generated for furnishings, equipment, materials, accessories, and lighting. These can be separate from the working drawings or be included within the packet.

square footage A means of calculating the buildings' over all floor area.

stacking diagrams Initial studies of vertical relationships between program elements.

stacking plan A tool that programmers implement for the study of space both horizontally and vertically. Helps to visually articulate to the client the number of floors and the adjacency relationship to each department.

stakeholders Investors or individuals that have an interest in the business.

statistics A set of tools used to organize and analyze data. Used to describe the characteristics of groups, statistics can help one analyze individual variables, relationships among variables, and differences between groups. They represent a collection of quantitative data.

strategic planning Planning where an organization looks at its entire structure to determine its goals and how to achieve them for a specific duration.

survey A study that uses questionnaires or interviews to collect data from participants in a sample concerning characteristics, experiences, and opinions in order to generalize the findings about that sample.

survey methods A common method used in business, educational, healthcare, and government settings. Surveys are implemented to retain an abundance of information based on the research topic.

test-retest reliability Used to assess the consistency of a measure from one time to another.

thesis statement A statement that summarizes the main point of a paper. The thesis statement contains a clear position of the research or the essay. Often it will be expressed in a sentence or two. It is sometimes limited and does not encompass solving the problem but merely addresses issues and ideas about the problem.

thick description A process used to give an in-depth written account of the study being evaluated.

thin description A process that outlines the facts with no elaboration. May sometimes be formatted in bullet form.

topic The subject, study, or theme that one is planning to research during the programming phase of design.

traffic map A diagram that shows the paths people take through a given space.

triangulation A system that involves using at least three strategies when conducting research.

United States Green Building Council (USGBC) An environmental agency, that is U.S. based. When seeking input to include and plan for energy concepts, the USGBC is an excellent place to start. Encompassing an abundance of information, its website lists local chapters, including professional and student chapters, where more relevant regional data can be obtained (www.usgbc.org).

universal design Universal design is the design and composition of an environment so that it can be accessed, understood, and used to the greatest extent possible by all people, regardless of their age, size, or disability. This includes public places in the built environment, such as buildings, streets, or spaces that the public have access to; products and services provided in those places; and systems that are available, including information and communications technology (ICT). (Disability Act, 2005)

validity The degree to which a study accurately reflects or assesses a specific concept that a researcher is attempting to measure. When research is valid, it accurately reflects and assesses the specific concept measured.

venture capital Funds that are invested into new start-up companies by professionals and outside investors.

way-finding methods A means of directing and informing people, such as signage, landmarks, color, lighting, and maps.

WELL Building Standard is an evidence-based system for measuring, certifying and monitoring the performance of building features that impact health and well-being (www.wellcertified.com)

working drawings A complete set of drawing involved in a project. Working drawings consist of a title sheet, an index of the drawings that are included, site plans, floor plans, electrical plans, reflected ceiling plans, elevations, details, cabinetwork, fixtures, moldings, and schedules.

World Green Building Council The World Green Building Council is a network of national green building councils in more than one hundred countries, making it the world's largest international organization influencing the green building marketplace.

zoning map A map that acts as a blueprint for a community's future development showing how land is divided to accommodate varied development interests.

Resources

AIA. (2007). *AIA, American Institute of Architects*, Retrieved July 6, 2007, from http://www.aia.org/media/Birse.

The American Instute of Archtects. (2007). *Integrated project delivery: A guide*. Published Report. Washington, D.C.: AIA, AIA California.

Alexander, W. C. (1974). *A pattern language: Towns, buildings, construction*. Oxford University Press, Incorporated.

Allen, P., Jones, L., & Stimpson, M. (2004). *Beginnings of interior environments* (9th ed.). Upper Saddle River, NJ: Pearson, Prentice Hall.

Alvermann, D., O'Brian, D., & Dillion, D. (1996). On writing qualitative research. *Reading Research Quarterly, 1*(13), 114–120.

American Society of Interior Designers. (2014*). Interior design 2014 outlook and state-of-the-industry research report*. Washington, D.C.: ASID.

American Society of Interior Designers. (2015*). Interior design 2015 outlook and state-of-the-industry research report*. Washington, D.C.: ASID.

Anderson, C. (2007). *Ladder 28 restaurant & grille*. Unpublished undergraduate thesis, Mount Ida College, Newton, MA.

Anderson, D. (2015). *The Divine Lorraine Hotel, a barrier free boutique museum hotel*. Location: Philadelphia, PA. Unpublished undergraduate thesis, Mount Ida College, Newton, MA.

Anthony, E. (2007). *Spa Rumford*. Unpublished undergraduate thesis, Mount Ida College, Newton, MA.

Anthony, K. (1991). Design juries on trial: The renaissance of the design studio. New York: Van Nostrand Reinhold.

Arca, A. (2015). Critical analysis of veteran inpatient facilities: Improving patient wellbeing through Interior Design Strategies. Unpublished master's thesis, Mount Ida College, Newton, MA.

Aronson, J. (1994). A pragmatic view of thematic analysis. *The Qualitative Report*. Retrieved August 19, 2003, from http://www.nova.edu/ssss/QR/BackIssues/QR2- 1/aronson.html.

ASID. (2016, April 12). *American Society of Interior Designers*. Retrieved from http://www.asid.org.

Benander, A. (2007). Residential lofts: Cincinnati, Ohio. Unpublished undergraduate thesis, Mount Ida College, Newton, MA.

Bonneville, L. (2016). Personal communication, March 7, 2016.

Bosworth, F. H., & Jones, R.C.(1932). *A study of architectural schools*. New York: Scribner.

Brise, T. (2011). *Charlesview Youth Hostel*. Location: Boston. Unpublished undergraduate thesis, Mount Ida College, Newton, MA.

Brockelman, A. (2016). Personal communication, July 13, 2016.

Cavataio, C. (2007). Personal communication, May 27, 2007.

CIDA. (2015, April 12). *Council for interior design accreditation*. Retrieved from http://www.accredit-id.org.

Cilano, J. (2006). *Dessert Works*. Unpublished undergraduate thesis, Mount Ida College, Newton, MA.

City-Data. (2015, September). *Boston, Massachusetts*. Retrieved from http://www.city-data.com/city/Boston-Massachusetts.html.

Clandinin, J., & Connelly, M. (1994). Personal experience methods. In N. Denzin & Y. S. Lincoln (Ed.), *Handbook of qualitative research* (pp. 413–427). Thousand Oaks, CA: Sage publications, Inc.

Clarke, G. (2016). Personal communication, March 2016.

Creswell, J. W. (1998). *Qualitative inquiry and research choosing among five traditions*. Thousand Oaks, CA: Sage Publications Inc.

DaForno, L. (2016). Personal communication, July, 2016.

Davis, C. (2013). *Healing through holistic design*. Unpublished master's thesis, Mount Ida College, Newton, MA.

Denzin, N. K., & Lincoln, Y. S. (1994). *Handbook of qualitative research*. Thousand Oaks, CA: Sage publications Inc.

Department of Housing and Community Development Massachusetts. (n.d.). *Wellesley: Norfolk County*, Retrieved August 29, 2006, from *www.mass.gov/dhcd/iprofile/324.pdf*.

Dessert Works. (2006, August 27). Retrieved from http://www.desserworks.net.

Disnmore, L. (2007). *RAW Sushi Bar*. Unpublished undergraduate thesis, Mount Ida College, Newton, MA.

Dohr, J., & Guerin, D. (2007). Part 1: Research-based practice. InformeDesign, Retrieved March 2007 from www.http://www.informedesign.org.

Dozois, P. (2001). *Construction through critique: The dialogic form of design studio teaching and learning*. Unpublished master's thesis, The University of Manitoba, Canada.

Drucker, P. (1992). *Managing for the future: The 1990s and beyond*. New York: Penguin.

Duderstadt, J., Atkins, D., & Van Houweling, D. (2002). *Higher education in the digital age: Technologies issues and strategies for American colleges and universities*. Westport, CT: Praeger Publishers.

Duerk, D. P. (1993). *Architectural programming: Information management for design*. New York, NY: John Wiley & Sons, Inc.

Dunnell, D. (2016). Personal communication, May 27, 2016.

Dutton, T. (1991). The hidden curriculum and the design studio; Toward a critical studio pedagogy. In T. A. Dutton (Ed.), *Voices in architectural education; Culture politics and pedagogy*. (pp. 165–194). New York, NY: Bergin &Garvey.

Eisner, E. (1985). *The art of educational evaluation*. New York, NY: Taylor & Francis, Inc.

Eisner, E. (1998). *The enlightened eye. Qualitative inquiry and the enhancement of educational practice.* Upper Saddle River, NJ: Merrill, Prentice Hall.

Eisner, E. (2002). *The arts and the creation of mind.* New Haven, CT: Yale University.

Ela Ebang, L. (2015). *Global sustainability and how to implement it in Equatorial Guinea.* Unpublished master's thesis, Mount Ida College, Newton, MA.

Fior, M. (2015). Personal communication, November 12, 2015.

Gall, M., Borg, W. J., & Gall, J. (1996). *Educational research, an introduction.* White Plains, NY: Longman.

Gedick, C. (2015). *Pallet house: An adequate living solution for Native American reservations.* Unpublished master's thesis, Mount Ida College, Newton, MA.

Gordon, N. (2015). *Ministry House renovation, an inclusive house of worship.* Location: Allston, MA. Unpublished undergraduate thesis, Mount Ida College, Newton, MA.

Gouveia, M. (2004). *The Fitness Mill: A community athletic and recreational center.* Unpublished undergraduate thesis, Mount Ida College, Newton, MA.

Gouveia, M. (2008). Personal communication, May 27, 2008.

Gregg, G. (2003). What are they teaching art students these days? Seventy years after the first degrees in art appeared, schools are wondering how to fit it all in: New technology, theory, marketing savvy, and a growing list of emerging forms. *Art News, April.*

Guba, N. K., & Lincoln, Y. S. (1985). *Naturalistic inquiry.* Beverly Hills, CA: Sage Publications Inc.

Harding, J. (2008). Personal communication, March 24, 2008.

Heerdt, N. (2007). *The Waterfront: A jazz bar and lounge.* Unpublished

undergraduate thesis, Mount Ida College, Newton, MA.

Huberman, A. M., & Miles, M. B. (1984). *Qualitative data analysis: A sourcebook of new methods,* Newbury Park, CA: Sage Publications.

Huberman, A. M., & Miles, M. B. (1994). Data management and analysis methods. In N. Denzin & Y. S. Lincoln (Ed.), *Handbook of qualitative research* (pp. 428–444). Thousand Oaks, CA: Sage Publications, Inc.

IDEC. (2015, October 10). *Interior Design Educational Council.* Retrieved from http://www.idec.org/.

IIDA. (2015, October 12). *International Interior Design Association.* Retrieved from http://www.iida.org/.

International WELL Building Institute. (2016, February 18). Retrieved from http://www.wellcertified.com/.

Jackson, B. (2015). Personal communication, November 20, 2015.

Janesick, V. J. (1994). The dance of qualitative research design; metaphor, methodology, and meaning. In N. Denzin & Y. S. Lincoln (Ed.), *Handbook of qualitative research* (pp. 209–219). Thousand Oaks, CA: Sage Publications Inc.

Johnson, A. (2007). *Catskill Hotel NY.* Unpublished undergraduate thesis, Mount Ida College, Newton, MA.

Johnson, M. (2014). *Planning for resiliency: Portable living structures.* Unpublished master's thesis, Mount Ida College, Newton, MA.

Karanfiloglu, S. (2015). Personal communication, July 29, 2015.

Kaye, C., & Blee, T. (Eds.). (1997). *The arts in health care: A palette of possibilities.* Great Britain: Biddles Ltd.

Koberg, D. & Bagnall, J. (1991). *The universal traveler: A soft-system guide to creativity, problem solving and the process of reaching goals.* Los Altos, CA: Crisp Publications, Inc.

Kopacz, J. (2016). Personal communication, February 26, 2016.

Labuschagne, A. (2003). Qualitative research—Airy fairy or fundamental? *The Qualitative Report, 8*(1).

Leedy, P. (2005). Practical research, planning and design, 8th edition. Upper Saddle River, NJ: Pearson Merrill Prentice Hall.

Lowe, C. (2016). Personal communication, July 15, 2016.

Mattingly, M. (2007). *Center for Sustainable Design Education; Boston MA.* Unpublished undergraduate thesis, Mount Ida College, Newton, MA.

McGoldrick, C. (2016). Personal communication, April 16, 2016.

NAAB (2015, June, 16). The *National Architectural Accrediting Board*, Retrieved from http://www.naab.org.

National Council for Interior Design Qualification (NCIDQ). (2016). *Certification & licensure, regulatory agencies, definition of interior design, exam eligibility requirements.* Retrieved, April 2016, from http://www.ncidq.org.

Neilson, K., & Taylor, D. (2002). *Interiors an introduction* (3rd ed.). New York: McGraw-Hill.

Patten, K., (2007). *Wagon Wheel-Market.* Unpublished undergraduate thesis, Mount Ida College, Newton, MA.

Pena, W. (1987). *Problem seeking: An architectural programming primer* (3rd ed.). Washington D.C.: AIA Press.

Pile, J. (1995). *Interior design.* Englewood Cliff, NJ: Prentice Hall, Inc.

Piotrowski, C. (2004). *Becoming an interior designer.* Hoboken, NJ: John Wiley & Sons, Inc.

Ransdell, M. (2015). Personal communication, October 8, 2015.

Richard, J. (2006). *College residence hall.* Unpublished thesis, Mount Ida College, Newton, MA.

Riggs, J. (2016). Personal communication, January 12, 2016.

Roblee, S. (2007). *There's not enough art in our schools: Art department renovation, Schroon Lake Central School.* Unpublished thesis, Mount Ida College, Newton, MA.

Rutledge, K. (2015). *Restrictions and resident empowerment in domestic violence shelter design: An exploration and response.* Unpublished master's thesis, Florida State University.

Schön, D. A. (1985). *The design studio: An exploration of its traditions and potentials.* London: RIBA Publications Limited.

Scott-Webber, L. (1998). *Programming; A problem solving approach for users of interior spaces.* DAME publications, Inc.

Shanahan, C. (2015). Personal communication, April 12, 2015.

Shibles, C. (2008). *Neonatal intensive care unit.* Unpublished thesis, Mount Ida College, Newton, MA.

Social Research Methods. (2008, May 14,). *Online social research methods,* retrieved from *http://www.socialresearchmethods.net/tutorial/Brown/lauratp.htm.*

Stake, R. E. (1994). Case studies. In N. Denzin & Y. S. Lincoln (Ed.), *Handbook of qualitative research* (pp. 236–247). Thousand Oaks, CA: Sage Publications Inc.

Stewart, N. (2006). *Healing with art.* Unpublished undergraduate thesis, Mount Ida College, Newton, MA.

Stone, D. (2016). Personal communication, May 27, 2016.

Strauss, A., & Corbin, J. (1998). *Basics of qualitative, research: Techniques and procedures for developing grounded theory.* (2nd ed.). Thousand Oaks, CA: Sage Publications, Inc.

TAC. (1981). *The Architects Collaborative: Examples of programming documentation.* Unpublished Report, Cambridge, Massachusetts.

Tate, A. (1987). *The making of interiors: An introduction.* New York, NY: Harper & Row.

Timmerman, K. (2015). *Millennials + Home: Design understanding the needs of the millennial generation in their housing environment.* Location: Los Angeles, CA. Unpublished master's thesis, Florida State University.

Trochim, William M. (n.d.)*The research methods knowledge base*, 2nd Edition. Retrieved June 16, 2008, from http://www.socialresearchmethods.net/kb/reltypes.php.

USGBC. (2016, May 5). *United States Green Building Council.* Retrieved from http://www.usgbc.org.

United States General Service Administration. (2016). *2003 facilities standards (P100) architectural and interior design.* Retrieved 2016, from http://www.gsa.gov/portal/category/21052.

University, C. S. (2002, July 31). *An online resources for teachers and writers,* retrieved from http://writing.colostate.edu.

U.S. Office of Personnel Management (OPM). (1991). Position classification flysheet for interior design series, GS-1008. Retrieved June 4, 2006, from http://www.opm.gov/fedclass/gs1008.pdf.

Verbridge, J. (2007). Personal communication, January 14, 2007.

Wallace, C. (2015). Personal communication, September 3, 2015.

Waxman, L., & Clemons, S. (2007). Student perceptions: Debunking televisions' portrayal of interior design. *Journal of Interior Design, 32*(2), v–xi.

Wendt, K. (2015). Personal communication, June 27, 2015.

Westgate, K. (2014). Providing a refuge to youth exiting the foster care system: Promoting their indomitable strength while developing a sense of independence and sovereignty within the community. Unpublished undergraduate thesis, Mount Ida College, Newton, MA.

White, E. (1982). Project programming: A growing architectural service. Florida A&M University, Tallahassee.

Wikimedia Foundation, Inc. (2006). *New York State.* Retrieved October 30, 2006, from http://en.wikipedia.org/wiki/New_York.

Credits

Box 4.2c Caitlin Davis, Mount Ida College Graduate Student

Box 4.2d Caitlin Davis, Mount Ida College Graduate Student

Box 4.2e Caitlin Davis, Mount Ida College Graduate Student

Box 4.2f Caitlin Davis, Mount Ida College Graduate Student

Box 4.2g Caitlin Davis, Mount Ida College Graduate Student

CHAPTER 5

5.1 SuperStock

5.2 Screen shot of CREDO Mind Mapping tool

5.3 Screen shot of CREDO Mind Mapping tool

5.4 Screen shot of CREDO Mind Mapping tool

5.5 Liz Carter, Mount Ida College

5.6 Liz Carter, Mount Ida College

5.7 Stephanie Scheivert, Corcoran College of Art + Design

5.8 Taylor Brise, Mount Ida College

5.9 Taylor Brise, Mount Ida College

5.10 Taylor Brise, Mount Ida College

5.11 Taylor Brise, Mount Ida College

5.12 Taylor Brise, Mount Ida College

5.13 Taylor Brise, Mount Ida College

5.14 Erin Anthony, Mount Ida College

5.15 Erin Anthony, Mount Ida College

5.16 Erin Anthony, Mount Ida College

5.17 Kate Wendt, Tsoi/Kobus & Associates

5.18a Tsoi/Kobus & Associates

5.18b Tsoi/Kobus & Associates

5.18c Tsoi/Kobus & Associates

5.18d Tsoi/Kobus & Associates

Box 5.1a Kassandra Westgate information adapted from Children's Bureau

Box 5.1b Kassandra Westgate, information adapted from Children's Bureau

Box 5.1c Kassandra Westgate, information adapted from Children's Bureau

Box 5.1d Kassandra Westgate, information adapted from Children's Bureau

Box 5.1e Kassandra Westgate, information adapted from Children's Bureau

Box 5.1f Kassandra Westgate, information adapted from Children's Bureau

Box 5.1g Kassandra Westgate, information adapted from Children's Bureau

Box 5.1h Kassandra Westgate, information adapted from Children's Bureau

Box 5.2a Catherine Shibles, Mount Ida College

Box 5.2b Catherine Shibles, Mount Ida College

Box 5.2c Catherine Shibles, Mount Ida College

Box 5.2d Catherine Shibles, Mount Ida College

Box 5.2e Catherine Shibles, Mount Ida College

Box 5.2f Catherine Shibles, Mount Ida College

Box 5.2g Catherine Shibles, Mount Ida College

Box 5.3 Erin Anthony, Mount Ida College

Box 5.4 Lucrecia Ela Ebang, Mount Ida College, Graduate Student

Box 5.4b Lucrecia Ela Ebang, Mount Ida College, Graduate Student

Box 5.4c Lucrecia Ela Ebang, Mount Ida College, Graduate Student

Box 5.4d Lucrecia Ela Ebang, Mount Ida College, Graduate Student

Box 5.4e Lucrecia Ela Ebang, Mount Ida College, Graduate Student

Box 5.4f Lucrecia Ela Ebang, Mount Ida College, Graduate Student

CHAPTER 6

6.1 Christine Shanahan, HVS Design Group

6.2 Monica Mattingly Mount Ida College

6.3 Monica Mattingly Mount Ida College

6.4a Monica Mattingly Mount Ida College

6.4b Monica Mattingly Mount Ida College

6.5 Nicole Stewart, retrieved Oct. 30, 2006, from *http://geology. com/state-map/new-york.shtml*

6.6 Nicole Stewart, retrieved Nov. 1, 2006, from http://green-wichny.org/tourist/v-tour.cfm

6.7 Nicole Stewart, retrieved Oct. 30, 2006, from http://geology. com/state-map/new-york.shtml

6.8 Nicole Stewart, retrieved Oct. 30, 2006, from *http://www. trailwaysny.com/*

6.9 Kristen Repa, Dessert Works

6.10a Monica Mattingly, Mount Ida College

6.10b Monica Mattingly, Mount Ida College

6.11a Erin Anthony,. Google Maps and Google Earth

6.11b Erin Anthony,. Google Maps and Google Earth

6.12 Erin Anthony,. Google Maps and Google Earth

6.13a Erin Anthony, Mount Ida College

6.13b Erin Anthony, Mount Ida College

6.13c Erin Anthony, Mount Ida College

6.13d Erin Anthony, Mount Ida College

6.13e Erin Anthony,. Google Earth

6.14 Rose Mary Botti-Salitsky Ph.D.

5.15a Nicolette Gordon, Mount Ida College

5.15b Nicolette Gordon, Mount Ida College

6.16a Nicolette Gordon, Mount Ida College

6.16b Nicolette Gordon, Mount Ida College

6.16c Nicolette Gordon, Mount Ida College

6.16d Nicolette Gordon, Mount Ida College

6.17 Nicolette Gordon, Mount Ida College

6.18a Nicolette Gordon Mount Ida College

6.18b Nicolette Gordon, Mount Ida College

6.18c Nicolette Gordon, Mount Ida College

6.18d Nicolette Gordon, Mount Ida College

6.18e Nicolette Gordon, Mount Ida College

6.18f Nicolette Gordon, Mount Ida College

6.18g Nicolette Gordon, Mount Ida College

6.18h Nicolette Gordon, Mount Ida College

6.18i Nicolette Gordon, Mount Ida College

Box 6.1a Domeny Anderson, Mount Ida College

Box 6.1b Domeny Anderson, Mount Ida College

Box 6.1c Domeny Anderson Mount Ida College

CHAPTER 7

7.1	Rose Mary Botti-Salitsky Ph.D.
7.2	Photo © B.O'Kane/Alamy
7.3	Bill Lebovich/Library of Congress
7.4	Katie Timmerman, Florida State University Graduate Student
7.5	Katie Timmerman, Florida State University Graduate Student
7.6	Katie Timmerman, Florida State University Graduate Student
7.7	Katie Timmerman, Florida State University Graduate Student
7.8	Katie Timmerman, Florida State University Graduate Student
7.9	Liz Carter, Mount Ida College
7.10	Ashley Benander, Mount Ida College
Box 7.1a	Marlo Ransdell PhD, Florida State University Faculty

CHAPTER 8

8.1	Katrina Rutledge, Florida State University Graduate Student
8.2	Katrina Rutledge, Florida State University Graduate Student
8.3	Katrina Rutledge, Florida State University Graduate Student
8.4	Katrina Rutledge, Florida State University Graduate Student
8.5a	Katrina Rutledge, Florida State University Graduate Student
8.5b	Katrina Rutledge, Florida State University Graduate Student
8.6	Katrina Rutledge, Florida State University Graduate Student
8.7	Katrina Rutledge, Florida State University Graduate Student
8.8	Katrina Rutledge, Florida State University Graduate Student
8.9	Katrina Rutledge, Florida State University Graduate Student
8.10	Katrina Rutledge, Florida State University Graduate Student
8.11	Ashley Johnson, Mount Ida College
8.12	Ashley Johnson, Mount Ida College
8.13	Spagnolo Gisness & Associates |SGA
8.14	Jeanna Richard, Mount Ida College
8.15	Jeanna Richard, Mount Ida College
8.16	Jeanna Richard, Mount Ida College
8.17	Jeanna Richard, Mount Ida College
8.18	Jeanna Richard, Mount Ida College
8.19	Lisa C. Bonneville, Bonneville Design
8.20	Lisa C. Bonneville, Bonneville Design
8.21	Lisa C. Bonneville, Bonneville Design
8.22	Lisa C. Bonneville, Bonneville Design
8.23	Lisa C. Bonneville, Bonneville Design
Box 8.1a	Rose Mary Botti-Salitsky Ph.D.

CHAPTER 9

9.1	Florida State University Graduate Student Katrina Rutledge
9.2	Florida State University Graduate Student Katrina Rutledge
9.3	Florida State University Graduate Student Katrina Rutledge
9.4	Florida State University Graduate Student Katie Timmerman
9.5	The Architects Collaborative TAC
9.6a	Edward Tufte
9.6b	Cassidy Dickeson, Mount Ida College
9.7a	Marcia Gouveia, Mount Ida College

9.7b   Marcia Gouveia, Mount Ida College

9.8   The Architects Collaborative TAC

9.9   S. Christine Cavataio, Newbury College

9.10   S. Christine Cavataio, Newbury College

9.11   Michael Fior Visiting Professor Endicott College

9.12   Endicott College

9.13   Endicott College

9.14   Kelsey Creamer, Endicott College

9.15   Kelsey Creamer, Endicott College

9.16   Dianne A. Dunnell, Interior Design Director & Associate Partner MPA | Margulies Perruzzi Architects

9.17a   MPA | Margulies Perruzzi Architects

9.17b   MPA | Margulies Perruzzi Architects

9.18   MPA | Margulies Perruzzi Architects

9.19   MPA | Margulies Perruzzi Architects

9.20   MPA | Margulies Perruzzi Architects

9.21   MPA | Margulies Perruzzi Architects

9.22   MPA | Margulies Perruzzi Architects

9.23   MPA | Margulies Perruzzi Architects

9.24   MPA | Margulies Perruzzi Architects

9.25   MPA | Margulies Perruzzi Architects

9.26   MPA | Margulies Perruzzi Architects

Box 9.1a Stephanie McGoldrick, Assistant Professor | Interior Architecture + Design Mount Ida College

Box 9.1b Nicole Handzel, Interior Architecture + Design, Mount Ida College

Box 9.1c Mary Kate Reidy, Interior Architecture + Design, Mount Ida College

Box 9.1d Kerri LaBerge, Interior Architecture + Design, Mount Ida College

Box 9.2a Laurie DaForno, AIA, LEED AP BD+C, Architect Tsoi/Kobus & Associates

Box 9.2b Laurie DaForno, AIA, LEED AP BD+C, Architect

Box 9.2c Laurie DaForno, AIA, LEED AP BD+C, Architect

Box 9.3a Monica Mattingly, Mount Ida College

Box 9.3b Monica Mattingly, Mount Ida College

Box 9.3c Monica Mattingly, Mount Ida College

CHAPTER 10

10.1   Massachusetts state agency Division of Capital Asset Management and Maintenance

10.2   Massachusetts state agency Division of Capital Asset Management and Maintenance

10.3   Anne Brockelman, AIA, LEED AP BD+C, Perry Dean Rogers | Partners Architects

10.4   Massachusetts state agency Division of Capital Asset Management and Maintenance

10.5   Perry Dean Rogers | Partners Architects

10.6   Perry Dean Rogers | Partners Architects

10.7   Perry Dean Rogers | Partners Architects

10.8   Perry Dean Rogers | Partners Architects

10.9a   Building Conservation Associates

10.9b	Building Conservation Associates	Box 10.1b	NELSON - Phtography © Halkin Mason Photography LLC
10.10a	Massachusetts state agency Division of Capital Asset Management and Maintenance	DCAMM	Box 10.1c	NELSON - Phtography © Halkin Mason Photography LLC
10.10b	Perry Dean Rogers	Partners Architects	Box 10.1d	NELSON - Phtography © Halkin Mason Photography LLC
10.11	Perry Dean Rogers	Partners Architects	Box 10.1e	NELSON - Phtography © Halkin Mason Photography LLC
10.12	Perry Dean Rogers	Partners Architects	Box 10.1f	NELSON - Phtography © Halkin Mason Photography LLC
10.13a	Perry Dean Rogers	Partners Architects	Box 10.1g	NELSON - Phtography © Halkin Mason Photography LLC
10.13b	Perry Dean Rogers	Partners Architects	Box 10.1h	NELSON - Phtography © Halkin Mason Photography LLC
10.14a	Perry Dean Rogers	Partners Architects	Box 10.1i	NELSON - Phtography © Halkin Mason Photography LLC
10.14b	Perry Dean Rogers	Partners Architects		
10.15	Perry Dean Rogers	Partners Architects		
10.16	Perry Dean Rogers	Partners Architects		
Box 10.1a	David D. Stone, IIDA, LEED AP ID+C, NCIDQ – Design Director NELSON Boston	Box 10.2	Colleen Lowe, U.S. Department of Veterans Affairs (VA)

Index